PROBLEM SOLVING with Structured FORTRAN 77

PROBLEM SOLVING

WITH STRUCTURED FORTRAN 77

D.M. Etter

University of New Mexico, Albuquerque

he Benjamin/Cummings Publishing Company, Inc.
Ienlo Park, California · Reading, Massachusetts · London ·
msterdam · Don Mills, Ontario · Sydney

To Ruth, a special friend

Sponsoring Editor: Alan Apt
Production Coordinator: Charles Hibbard
Book Designer: Marilyn Langfeld
Cover Designer: John Edeen

Library of Congress Cataloging in Publication Data

Etter, D. M.

Problem solving with structured FORTRAN 77.

Includes index.
1. FORTRAN (Computer program language) 2. Structured programming. 3. Problem solving—Data processing.
I. Title. II. Title: Problem solving with structured F.O.R.T.R.A.N. 77.
QA76.73.F25E848 1984 001.64'24 83-26653
ISBN 0-8053-2522-0

ABCDEFGHIJ-HA-8987654

The Benjamin/Cummings Publishing Company, Inc.
2727 Sand Hill Road
Menlo Park, California 94025

The Benjamin/Cummings Series in Structured Programming

R. Billstein, S. Libeskind, and J. Lott
Problem Solving with Logo (1985)

G. Booch
Software Engineering with Ada (1983)

D. M. Etter
Structured FORTRAN 77 for Engineers and Scientists (1983)

D. M. Etter
Problem Solving with Structured FORTRAN 77 (1984)

D. M. Etter
Structured WATFIV for Engineers and Scientists (1985)

D. M. Etter
Problem Solving with Structured WATFIV (1985)

P. Linz
Programming Concepts and Problem Solving: An Introduction to Computer Science Using Pascal (1983)

A. Kelley and I. Pohl
A Book on C (1984)

W. J. Savitch
Pascal: An Introduction to the Art and Science of Programming (1984)

R. W. Sebesta
VAX 11: Structured Assembly Language Programming (1983)

R. W. Sebesta
PDP-11: Structured Assembly Language Programming (1985)

BRIEF CONTENTS

DETAILED CONTENTS

Each chapter ends with a Summary, Key Words, Debugging Aids, Style/Technique Guides, and Problems.

PREFACE TO THE INSTRUCTOR

PROBLEM SOLVING

This text begins with a chapter devoted entirely to problem solving. We present a number of complete solutions to a variety of problems. The solutions are developed using a five-phase design process:

1. State the problem clearly.
2. Describe the input and output.
3. Work the problem by hand for a specific set of data.
4. Develop an algorithm that is general in nature.
5. Test the algorithm with a variety of data sets.

The solution to the problem presented in each problem solving section is developed using this five-phase process. There are 18 of these problem solving sections, or small case studies, in the text.

TOP-DOWN DESIGN

Top-down design is used in the algorithm development as we decompose the problem solution into a series of general steps and then refine the solution in a detailed form using pseudocode. The SEQUENCE, WHILE loop, and IF THEN ELSE structures are used in the pseudocode. Since pseudocode does not have standard forms, forms were chosen that are in general agreement with most pseudocode notation. The pseudocode for the IF THEN ELSE structure is expanded to include the CASE structure, and thus provide an easier conversion to FORTRAN later.

STEPWISE REFINEMENT

The steps in top-down design are so critical to understanding an algorithm and being able to develop new algorithms that we emphasize these steps throughout the text, in all complete programs and in all problem solving sections. The initial decomposition is shown in a block diagram and the *refined pseudocode* is shown in a second color for easy reference. Although pseudocode is used throughout the text, flowcharts are covered in Appendix A and thus can be used as the instructor desires.

EARLY PROGRAMMING

Chapter 2 introduces the student to computers, languages, and the compilation-linkage-execution process of running computer programs. Timesharing and interactive processing are emphasized, but batch processing is also included. This chapter introduces FORTRAN statements to read information, compute new information, and then print this new information. Thus, we begin writing complete programs in the same chapter in which we introduce the computer. Top-down design, although very simple at this point, is used in developing complete programs.

FORMAT-FREE I/O

We have presented list-directed I/O, and use it exclusively until we get to Chapter 7 (File Handling), where formatted I/O is necessary for sequential and direct access files. It is always difficult to decide how to present I/O, primarily because every instructor has strong preferences on this subject. We feel that trying to present both list-directed and formatted I/O all the way through the text is cumbersome, if we provide adequate coverage to both techniques. If we start with list-directed I/O and bring formatted I/O in later, where do we introduce it? Different instructors will want it introduced at different places, and we cannot adequately support each instructor's needs if we bring it in too early or too late.

In our previous text, *Structured FORTRAN 77 for Engineers and Scientists,* we discussed list-directed I/O and formatted I/O, but used formatted I/O almost exclusively. For a general audience, however, we felt that this added detail was not necessarily an advantage. Our solution was to use list-directed I/O exclusively in this text. We were pleasantly surprised to find very few places where we really would have preferred formatted I/O. With careful use of literals, we were able to generate very readable output with list-directed output.

FORMATTED I/O

Now, how do we meet the needs of the instructor who wants to use formatted I/O either from the beginning, or at some later point in the course? We have included formatted I/O in Appendix B, but the material is written as if it were a chapter. It includes examples, complete programs, and many problems for students to work. By including it as an appendix instead of a chapter, we give the instructor the choice of when to use it. It is written with enough explanation that a student can cover the material as needed if it is not mentioned in the course.

CONTROL STRUCTURES AND LOOPS

With control structures, the topic of Chapter 3, a wide range of new problems can be solved with a computer. The statements for selection (IF statements) and the statements for repetition (WHILE loops and DO loops) are covered in this chapter. We decided to combine these topics so that we could present problems with simple loops very quickly. Most realistic problems that use selection processes also use loops, so we feel that this combination works well. As a result, this chapter is long, and should not be covered as fast as some of the other chapters because of the number of new statements introduced. The level of difficulty of the problems at the end of the chapter is graduated to match the order of the material presented; problems can therefore be assigned as soon as the chapter is begun. Character data is introduced in this chapter to give the student time to become comfortable using it for input and output before we get to Chapter 6, which presents special techniques and operators for character string manipulations.

ARRAYS

In Chapter 4 we present arrays, with emphasis on one- and two-dimensional arrays. Through examples and discussions we help students learn how to determine whether they really need to use an array—and if so, whether a one-dimensional array fits the problem better than a two-dimensional array. A brief discussion is included on higher-dimensional arrays. Simple data files are presented in this chapter because more data can be processed with arrays than is easily entered by hand. Both input and output data files are used frequently in the rest of the text. Trailer signals and end-of-file detection are also covered. Finally, sorting, insertion, and deletion algorithms are also presented in the problem solving sections of this chapter.

SUBPROGRAMS

Subprograms are presented in Chapter 5. This topic is an important one in top-down design because many of the steps in the initial decomposition of a problem solution can be implemented as functions and subroutines. Portions of a main program are included in each example to show the reference to the subprogram. The algorithms developed in the problem solving sections include those for inserting and deleting items in a list. The concept of testing subprograms with a driver program is presented, and driver programs are included in the solutions in problem solving sections.

CHARACTER STRINGS

Character string processing is developed in Chapter 6 with a large number of examples that emphasize the use of substring references, the concatenation operator, and intrinsic functions such as INDEX. An alphabetical sort subroutine that removes leading blanks is developed. A subroutine to print a bar graph from an array of numerical data is developed, with an argument to specify the maximum line size in the bar graph. Numerous text processing examples are also illustrated. The final problem solving example computes the average word length in a given piece of text material.

FILE PROCESSING

Sequential file processing and direct file processing are presented in Chapter 7. Simple format specifications are included so that formatted I/O can be used with external files. A number of new statements that relate to file usage are presented and illustrated with examples. One problem solving section develops a merge of three sequential data files, and another develops a program to update a warehouse inventory which is stored in a direct access file. The concept of an internal file is also discussed with examples.

Chapter 8 summarizes a number of features not included earlier. These topics fall into two categories. One category contains features that are not frequently used but that are necessary for certain applications, such as double precision and complex numbers. The other category contains features that are seldom used because new features of FORTRAN 77 (which have already been presented) provide better ways of solving the same problems. These latter topics are presented in order to provide complete coverage of FORTRAN 77. Such topics are still included in the language primarily so that programs written in earlier versions can still be used without modification.

ORGANIZATION

We recommend that the material in this text be covered sequentially. The first seven chapters are critical to a complete coverage of the powerful statements and techniques in FORTRAN. The material is intended for a general audience with no prior computer background. The examples cover a wide range of applications to show the variety and breadth of problems that can be solved with FORTRAN.

SECOND COLOR

A second color is used to identify pseudocode solutions throughout the text. Key statements in FORTRAN programs are also highlighted in color. All FORTRAN statements, output from programs, and data file contents are printed in a special typeface to distinguish them clearly from the other material.

STYLE/TECHNIQUES

Two special sections are included at the end of each chapter. A Style/Technique Guide promotes good programming habits that stress readability and simplicity. Although there are entire books devoted to programming style and technique, this topic is included in each chapter with the premise that developing such habits is an integral part of learning the language.

DEBUGGING AIDS

A Debugging Aids section outlines efficient methods of locating and correcting program errors associated with the programming techniques described in the chapter. With guidance from this section, the student learns consistent methods for spotting and avoiding the common errors associated with each new FORTRAN statement.

INSTRUCTOR'S GUIDE

An Instructor's Guide is available. It contains viewgraphs that use new examples, quizzes and solutions, new computer projects, and complete solutions to the end-of-chapter problems.

SOFTWARE

Since learning is an active process, not a passive one, we have also designed a software supplement to work in conjunction with this text. This supplement consists of a set of files on a tape that contain solutions to the problem solving problems presented in the text so that the student can immediately begin running and "playing with" the programs being studied in the text. Once the student understands a particular program, a modifications file suggests simple changes that will either improve the program or give it an additional operation to perform. Since the original program file already exists, making changes requires only minor editing steps before the student is ready to test the modifications. This procedure emphasizes hands-on experience with the programs as they are being studied.

The tape that contains the files discussed is available to all instructors using this text. Ideally, the instructor will request this software supplement from the publisher and then load the files into a computer library that can be directly accessed from the student's terminal. Further inquiries about these files or the supplement should be addressed to your local Benjamin/Cummings representative or the Benjamin/Cummings Publishing Company, 2727 Sand Hill Road, Menlo Park, California 94025.

PREFACE TO THE STUDENT

HOW TO USE THIS BOOK

The influence of computers on our lives grows with each new technological advance. Whether or not we use this influence to our advantage depends a great deal on our understanding of the computer's abilities and limitations. This text is designed to begin your computer education by introducing you to the process of problem solving with the computer language FORTRAN 77. The text does not assume any previous computer experience.

Chapter 1 is an introduction to the problem solving procedure that we use throughout the text. This chapter is very important, and should be read carefully before continuing to Chapter 2. Chapter 2 is an introduction to computers, and presents a few FORTRAN statements so that you can immediately begin writing programs. If you have some prior computer experience, you will find that you can cover this chapter quickly.

Beginning with Chapter 3, we present the features of FORTRAN that make it such a versatile and powerful language. Our presentation includes many examples, with a continued emphasis on the problem solving procedure from Chapter 1. Chapters 3 through 7 should be covered sequentially. Chapter 8 contains a number of miscellaneous topics that may be useful in special applications but are not routinely used.

SECOND COLOR

A second color is used to identify pseudocode solutions throughout the text. In addition, key statements in FORTRAN programs are highlighted in color. All FORTRAN statements, output from programs, and data file contents are printed in a special typeface to distinguish them clearly from the other material.

DEBUGGING AND STYLE

Each chapter contains two special sections. A Debugging section points out errors commonly made with the FORTRAN statements presented in the chapter, and makes suggestions for avoiding them. A Style/Technique section includes guidelines for developing a programming style that stresses readability and simplicity. It is a good idea to review these sections periodically as you progress through the text.

PROBLEM SOLVING

Programming, like most skills, becomes easier with practice. A large number of problems are included at the end of each chapter. Solutions to selected problems are given at the end of the text.

ACKNOWLEDGMENTS

I feel fortunate to have had a group of conscientious, diligent, and often critical reviewers during the development of this text. This group of special reviewers included Prof. H. Etlinger, Prof. G. Eerkes, Prof. A. Prengel, Prof. R. Lievano, Prof. D. Stevenson, Prof. D. Doud, Prof. T. Seidman, and Prof. R. Bisland. The encouragement of Alan Apt, Computer Science Editor, and the support of his Associate Editor Mary Koto and Production Coordinator Charles Hibbard are also appreciated. Finally, I wish to thank Laura White, Barbara Johnston, and Nancy Koschmann-Seemanns for their advice and suggestions.

PROBLEM SOLVING APPLICATIONS

Chapter 3

Chapter 4

Chapter 5

Chapter 6

Chapter 7

Chapter 8

© Jeff Albertson/Stock, Boston

PROBLEM SOLVING—A Game of Chess

Many similarities exist between the process of learning to play chess and that of learning to use a computer. In chess you must first learn the moves that each chess piece can make; in programming, you must learn the small set of instructions in a computer language. The next step in chess is to learn techniques and game plans for winning. In programming, you learn techniques and methods for solving commonly encountered problems. To improve in either chess or programming, you must then practice, and learn from your mistakes. Fortunately the analogy ends here, because problem solving with the computer does not pit programmer against computer, with only one winner. In programming, the computer is simply a tool to solve problems using the methods and techniques that you describe in your programs.

1

STRUCTURED PROBLEM SOLVING

INTRODUCTION

Problem solving is an activity in which we participate every day. The problems range from balancing our checkbooks to finding the quickest route to work. Many of the problems we face can be solved by computers if we learn how to communicate with them, using computer languages such as FORTRAN. Some people believe that if we describe a problem to a computer, it will solve it for us. Programming would be simpler if this were the way computers worked, but unfortunately it is not. Computers only perform the steps that we describe. You may wonder, then, why we go to the effort of writing computer programs to solve problems, if we have to describe every step. Good question! The answer is that while computers can perform only simple tasks, they perform them extremely accurately and at fantastic speeds. In addition, they never get bored. Imagine sitting at a desk balancing checkbooks eight hours a day, five days a week, year after year. This is a pretty dismal thought, and yet thousands of accounts must be balanced every month in each bank in the country. Once the steps involved in balancing a checking account have been carefully described to a computer, however, it can balance accounts 24 hours a day, with more speed and accuracy than a group of bookkeepers.

While we have been stressing the advantages of using computers to solve problems, we should not forget that someone must first describe the steps to the computer in the proper language. We will spend much of this text teaching you the FORTRAN language, but the language is useless unless you can break a problem solution into steps that a computer can perform. Therefore, this first chapter is devoted to describing the steps of problem solving. We will structure our problem solving techniques so that we can easily translate the steps into the limited number of FORTRAN instructions.

1-1 DESIGN PROCESS

The procedure we will use to design solutions to problems has five phases, which will be used each time we present a complete problem solution. Understanding the phases is easier if we go through them with a familiar problem. The memory of the first time you balanced your checkbook is probably not a fond one. In fact, balancing a checkbook can be a very frustrating job—not just the first time, but every time you do it. It is also one of those tasks that do not go away; it reappears monthly. Relief is in sight, though, because we are going to use this example to illustrate our problem solving steps. After you finish Chapter 3, you can convert these steps into a computer program to balance your checkbook.

The **first phase** of our design process is to state the problem clearly. It is very important to give a clear concise statement of the problem to avoid any misunderstandings. For our example, the *problem statement* is:

Compute the balance of your checking account.

The **second phase** is to describe carefully any information or *data* needed to solve the problem and then describe the way the final answer is to be presented. These items represent the *input* and the *output* for the problem. Collectively, they are referred to as *input/output,* or *I/O.* In our example the input information comes from two sources: the list of checks you have written, and any deposit receipts. It also includes the final balance from the last time you balanced your checking account. The output is the new final balance. This input and output information is shown on the facing page.

The **third phase** is to work the problem by hand, using a simple set of data. Have you balanced your checking account lately? If you have been putting this off, now is a great time to do it, because we need to do a problem by hand. (Did you know that a recent study revealed that only one out of six people balance their checking account every month?) Your checks should be listed in the checkbook register in the order in which you wrote them. Are your deposits also entered in the order in which they were made? Check your deposit receipts. If you have any deposits automatically made to your

INPUT: CHECKS WRITTEN AND PREVIOUS BALANCE

RECORD ALL CHARGES OR CREDITS THAT AFFECT YOUR ACCOUNT

NUMBER	DATE	DESCRIPTION OF TRANSACTION	PAYMENT/DEBIT (−) $		√ T	FEE (IF ANY) (−) $	DEPOSIT/CREDIT (+) $		BALANCE $	
									294	86
152	3/1	Garden Apartments	425	00						
153	3/5	First Rate Auto Sales	200	00						
154	3/8	Cash	75	00						
155	3/15	Bell Telephone	32	46						
156	3/20	Cash	50	00						
157	3/20	PG+E	86	91						
158	3/24	Mastercharge	56	82						

REMEMBER TO RECORD AUTOMATIC PAYMENTS / DEPOSITS ON DATE AUTHORIZED.

INPUT: DEPOSITS MADE

FOR DEPOSIT TO THE ACCOUNT OF

John D. Smith
Mary A. Smith
100 Center Street
Alma, NJ

DATE 3/1 1983

John D. Smith
SIGN HERE FOR LESS CASH IN TELLERS PRESENCE

CASH	CURRENCY		
	COIN		
LIST CHECKS SINGLY		550	00
TOTAL FROM OTHER SIDE			
TOTAL		550	00
LESS CASH RECEIVED		100	00
NET DEPOSIT		450	00

USE OTHER SIDE FOR ADDITIONAL LISTING

BE SURE EACH ITEM IS PROPERLY ENDORSED

FOR DEPOSIT TO THE ACCOUNT OF

John D. Smith
Mary A. Smith
100 Center Street
Alma, NJ

DATE 3/15 1983

John D. Smith
SIGN HERE FOR LESS CASH IN TELLERS PRESENCE

CASH	CURRENCY		
	COIN		
LIST CHECKS SINGLY		550	00
TOTAL FROM OTHER SIDE			
TOTAL		550	00
LESS CASH RECEIVED		100	00
NET DEPOSIT		450	00

USE OTHER SIDE FOR ADDITIONAL LISTING

BE SURE EACH ITEM IS PROPERLY ENDORSED

FCB FIRST CITY BANK
3620 Main St.
Alma, NJ

OUTPUT: FINAL BALANCE

account, be sure to include them. We now have all the data together. Go through the register, line by line, adding any deposits and subtracting checks. We said to do it by hand, but use a calculator if you have one!

Output: Updated Check Register with Final Balance

RECORD ALL CHARGES OR CREDITS THAT AFFECT YOUR ACCOUNT

NUMBER	DATE	DESCRIPTION OF TRANSACTION	PAYMENT/DEBIT (−)	√ T	FEE (IF ANY) (−)	DEPOSIT/CREDIT (+)	BALANCE $ 294 86
152	3/1	Garden Apartments	$ 425 00		$	$ 450 00	425 00 319 86
153	3/5	First Rate Auto Sales	200 00				200 00 119 86
154	3/8	Cash	75 00				75 00 44 86
155	3/15	Bell Telephone	32 46			450 00	32 46 462 40
156	3/20	Cash	50 00				50 00 412 40
157	3/20	PG + E	86 91				86 91 325 49
158	3/24	Mastercharge	56 82				56 82 268 67

REMEMBER TO RECORD AUTOMATIC PAYMENTS / DEPOSITS ON DATE AUTHORIZED.

The **fourth phase** is to describe, in general terms, the steps that you performed by hand. This sequence of steps that solve the problem is called an *algorithm*. In later sections we discuss some useful techniques for developing and describing algorithms, but for now we will write them in a longhand form. As you read the algorithm, remember the steps you just performed with your calculator. They should be similar to these steps.

Checking Account Algorithm

Step 1 Start with the final balance from the last time that the account was balanced.

Step 2 As long as there are more transactions (checks or deposits), continue to step 3. When there are no more new transactions, skip to step 5.

Step 3 If the next transaction is a deposit, add the amount to the balance. If the next transaction is a check, subtract the amount from the balance.

Step 4 Return to step 2.

Step 5 Circle the final balance.

Step 6 Stop.

The **fifth phase** of problem solving is to test the solution steps (or algorithm) that you have just described. *Testing* an algorithm is not an easy task. We can usually find data for which our algorithm works correctly, but it's just as important to search for sequences of data that cause our algorithm to fail. Remember that these algorithms are eventually going to be translated into FORTRAN; we want them to work for any valid set of data. Thus, a correct algorithm for balancing a checking account should work properly for anyone who has a checking account. A good way to test this algorithm would be to use an old bank statement which has a starting balance, current checks and deposits, and a new final balance. Use the input transactions as data for stepping through the algorithm and compare your final balance to the one on the bank statement. Here is an example to use if you do not have one of your own.

FCB **FIRST CITY BANK** 3620 Main St.
Alma, NJ

JOHN D. SMITH
MARY A. SMITH
100 CENTER STREET
ALMA, NJ

CHECKING ACCOUNT TRANSACTIONS

AMOUNT	DATA	DESCRIPTION	BALANCE
		BEGINNING BALANCE	294.86
450.00+	3/2	DEPOSIT	744.86
425.00-	3/7	CHECK	319.86
75.00-	3/8	CHECK	244.86
450.00+	3/15	DEPOSIT	694.86
50.00-	3/20	CHECK	644.86
32.46-	3/25	CHECK	612.40
86.91-	3/25	CHECK	525.49
200.00-	3/28	CHECK	325.49
56.82-	3/31	CHECK	268.67
5.00-	3/31	SERVICE CHARGE	263.67

Using the initial balance along with the check and deposit transactions in the previous bank statement, we find that the final balance from using our algorithm does not match the final balance on the bank statement. (You were afraid that would happen, weren't you? Is this why you quit balancing your checking account?)

The computer program that printed the bank statement came from an algorithm that initially probably looked similar to ours. However, as we look at the bank statement more closely, we see that a service charge was subtracted. We neglected to include this in our original algorithm. Service charges are computed differently for different types of accounts; in order to modify our algorithm, we have to be specific about the service charge. Assume, for simplicity, that our account is charged $5.00 per month with no limitations on the balance or number of transactions. Now we can modify our previous algorithm, based on the information we gained from testing it with new data. More about testing algorithms will be said in a later section.

MODIFIED CHECKING ACCOUNT ALGORITHM

Step 1 Start with the final balance from the last time that the account was balanced.

Step 2 As long as there are more transactions (checks or deposits), continue to step 3. When there are no more new transactions, skip to step 5.

Step 3 If the next transaction is a deposit, add the amount to the balance. If the next transaction is a check, subtract the amount from the balance.

Step 4 Return to step 2.

Step 5 Subtract a $5.00 service charge.

Step 6 Circle the final balance.

Step 7 Stop.

Before we go to the next section, which discusses the structure of algorithms and how to describe them, we list the five *design phases* for solving problems:

1. State the problem clearly.
2. Describe the input and output.
3. Work the problem by hand for a specific set of data.
4. Develop an algorithm that is general in nature.
5. Test the algorithm with a variety of data sets.

These five phases are used as we develop algorithms in the problem solving sections throughout the rest of the text.

1-2 ALGORITHM STRUCTURE AND PSEUDOCODE

In order to be consistent in the way we describe algorithms, we will use a set of standard forms or structures. When an algorithm is described in these standard structures, it is a *structured algorithm*. When the algorithm is converted into computer instructions, the corresponding program is a *structured program*. Each structure is described in a notation called *pseudocode*. Since pseudocode is not really computer code, it is language independent. That is, the pseudocode depends only on the steps needed to solve a problem, not on the particular computer language that will be used. (*Flowcharts* are another way of describing the steps in algorithms. Since flowcharts are not used as much as pseudocode, these chapters do not include them. However, Appendix A contains a complete discussion of flowcharts with examples. Each algorithm that is developed in a problem solving section is included in flowchart form in this appendix.)

The steps to solving problems can be divided into three major structures:

1 SEQUENCE—This structure contains steps that are performed one after another, or sequentially. This is the type of structure we use when we give directions. "First, go to the stop sign. Second, turn left. Then, go to the third traffic light. . . ."

2 IF THEN ELSE—This structure asks a question or tests a condition to determine which steps are to be performed. For example, in the checking account algorithm we need to know whether a transaction is a deposit or a check. "If" it is a deposit, "then" we add the corresponding amount; otherwise (or "else"), we subtract the amount.

3 WHILE loop—This structure allows us to build *loops,* which are steps in an algorithm that are repeated. The steps in a WHILE loop are repeated while a certain condition occurs. Look back at the checking account algorithm on page 6. Steps 2, 3, and 4 are repeated "while there are more transactions."

Other special structures are sometimes also included in a list of algorithm structures. Generally, these other structures are special forms of the three structures presented here, so we do not include them as separate structures. In the detailed discussion of these three structures, we include a description of the REPEAT UNTIL loop and the CASE structure.

SEQUENCE

The SEQUENCE structure does not need a special pseudocode notation. If we list a series of steps one after another, it is clear that they are to be performed sequentially. However, the individual steps are described with pseudocode. The best way to present pseudocode is through a series of examples.

We begin with input to an algorithm. This step is performed with a READ statement, because we are reading new information. Following the word READ we list the information that is being read. For example, to read the transaction type (deposit or check) and the corresponding amount, we use the following pseudocode:

```
READ type, amount
```

Note that the word that defines this as an input statement is in capital letters while the rest are in lower case letters. The words *type* and *amount* are chosen as you develop the pseudocode. We could also have used the statement:

READ transaction type, transaction amount

Output statements are very similar. For instance, we indicate that the final balance is to be printed with the statement:

PRINT balance

When describing the output we may also want to cause some descriptive words to be printed, in addition to any values that we have computed. That is, instead of seeing this output:

$123.87

we might prefer this form:

FINAL BALANCE $123.87

Special words are indicated in pseudocode by enclosing them in apostrophes. The pseudocode statement to produce the above output is then:

PRINT 'FINAL BALANCE', balance

Computations are indicated in pseudocode with an arrow, as in:

balance ← balance + amount

We read this statement as "amount is added to balance, giving the new balance" or "balance is replaced by the sum of the old balance plus amount." Another example of a computation statement is:

average ← total/12

This statement can be read as "total is divided by 12, giving average" or "average is replaced by total divided by 12."

IF THEN ELSE

The IF THEN ELSE structure has a number of forms. For instance, the ELSE clause may be omitted, as in the statement "If the transaction is a deposit, then add the transaction amount to the balance." The pseudocode that we will use for this form is illustrated below:

```
IF type = 'DEPOSIT'                          (IF form)
   balance ← balance + amount
END IF
```

If the condition "type = 'DEPOSIT'" is true, then amount is added to balance. If the type is not 'DEPOSIT', then the addition step is skipped. Since we are looking for a specific word in the transaction type, we indicate that by putting it in capital letters and inserting apostrophes around it, just as we did for specific words that we wanted to print in the PRINT statement. Note that a special indicator (END IF) is used to clearly identify the end of the structure since more than one statement could also be performed if the condition is true, as shown below:

```
IF type = 'DEPOSIT'                                    (IF form)
   balance ← balance + amount
   PRINT 'UPDATED BALANCE =', balance
END IF
```

When the ELSE clause is included in the IF THEN ELSE structure, the pseudocode is expanded as illustrated below:

```
IF type = 'DEPOSIT'                               (IF ELSE form)
   balance ← balance + amount
ELSE
   balance ← balance − amount
END IF
```

If the type is 'DEPOSIT', then amount is added to balance. However, if the type is not 'DEPOSIT', then amount is subtracted from balance. Again, multiple statements can be included in the portion executed if the condition is true or in the portion executed if the condition is false.

The last form of the IF THEN ELSE structure that we will use allows us to test multiple conditions. This form is sometimes called a CASE structure because it examines multiple cases or conditions. An example of this structure is:

```
IF type = 'DEPOSIT'                            (IF ELSE IF form)
   balance ← balance + amount
ELSE IF type = 'CHECK'
   balance ← balance − amount
END IF
```

With this structure, the balance is correctly updated when the type is either 'DEPOSIT' or 'CHECK'. If the type is neither of these, then the balance is not changed. Note the rather subtle differences between this example and the one with the IF ELSE form. If the transaction type is not a deposit, the IF ELSE form always subtracts the corresponding amount from the balance. The IF ELSE IF form subtracts only checks, and ignores any transactions that are not deposits or checks.

To illustrate this with an example, suppose your account is one that earns interest on money left in the account for the entire month. A possible transaction is one whose type is 'INTEREST EARNED', with a corresponding amount that should be added to the balance. If this transaction is processed with the previous IF ELSE form, the interest amount is subtracted because the type is not 'DEPOSIT'. If this transaction is processed with the IF ELSE IF form, the balance does not change because neither condition is true. Look back at the two forms and be sure you understand the distinction. It is also important to recognize that neither form handles this transaction properly. If 'INTEREST EARNED' is a valid transaction type, then our algorithm should be modified to handle it correctly; if it is not a valid transaction type, then the algorithm should print an error message when it occurs. A final ELSE clause in the IF ELSE IF form will allow us to correctly handle deposits, checks, and interest earned, and still test for errors. The modified form is:

```
IF type = 'DEPOSIT' or 'INTEREST EARNED'        (IF ELSE IF form)
   balance ← balance + amount
ELSE IF type = 'CHECK'
   balance ← balance − amount
ELSE
   PRINT 'ERROR IN TRANSACTION TYPE'
END IF
```

When this form is executed, it correctly handles deposits, checks, and interest earned amounts. For any other type of transaction, an error message is printed.

WHILE LOOP

An example of the pseudocode for a WHILE loop is:

```
WHILE more transactions DO
   (steps in the loop)
END WHILE
```

The steps in the loop are executed as long as there are more transactions. The words WHILE, DO, and END WHILE are capitalized because they define the WHILE loop structure in pseudocode.

An *iterative loop* or *counting loop* is a loop that is repeated a specific number of times. For example, suppose we wanted to know our average checking account balance from the last 12 bank statements. This would involve looking up final balances on the 12 previous statements so that we could add them together. This then represents an iterative loop that is repeated 12 times. Iterative loops can be considered to be a special form of a WHILE loop in which a *counter* has been introduced. The counter represents the number of times that the loop has been executed. The counter is initialized to a value (usually 0) before the loop is executed. Inside the loop, the counter is incremented (usually by 1). The loop is executed while the value of the counter is less than the specified value. Thus, the pseudocode for a loop that is to be executed 12 times is:

```
count ← 0
WHILE count < 12 DO
   (steps in the loop)
   count ← count + 1
END WHILE
```

Another special form of the WHILE loop structure that is sometimes presented separately is the REPEAT UNTIL loop. In this loop, a set of statements is executed until a condition is true. An example of this loop is:

```
REPEAT
    (set of steps)
UNTIL A < B
```

Using the WHILE loop structure, we can rewrite this as:

```
WHILE A ≥ B DO
    (set of steps)
END WHILE
```

These two forms seem equivalent, but there is one difference. In the REPEAT structure, the set of steps is executed before the test is made; the test is made first in the WHILE loop. Thus, if A = 3 and B = 5, the set of steps will be executed once in the repeat loop but not at all in the WHILE loop. Thus, you must be careful when converting one form to the other to add steps necessary to make them exactly equivalent.

Now that we have presented the pseudocode for the three main structures and for the steps included in them, we can write pseudocode for complete algorithms. For a consistent style, we will begin the pseudocode for a complete algorithm with an arbitrary name (but one that applies to the problem) followed by the word BEGIN. The algorithm will terminate with a final END. Indenting is also a matter of style, but we will indent steps inside a structure to improve the readability of the pseudocode. An example of this outer structure is then:

```
CHECKING:  BEGIN
              (pseudocode for the algorithm)
           END
```

Now we can write the pseudocode for the checking account algorithm that we developed in the previous section. We will assume that there are three valid forms of transactions: deposits, checks, and interest earned.

PSEUDOCODE FOR CHECKING ACCOUNT ALGORITHM

```
CHECKING1:  BEGIN
               balance ← old balance
               WHILE more transactions DO
                  READ type, amount
                  IF type = 'DEPOSIT' or 'INTEREST EARNED'
                     balance ← balance + amount
                  ELSE IF type = 'CHECK'
                     balance ← balance − amount
                  ELSE
                     PRINT 'ERROR IN TRANSACTION TYPE'
                  END IF
               END WHILE
               balance ← balance − $5.00
               PRINT 'FINAL BALANCE', balance
            END
```

As you compare the pseudocode with the longhand form, you should see several advantages to the pseudocode. Most importantly, it shows the structure of the algorithm immediately. The indenting and the words such as WHILE and IF indicate that the overall structure is a WHILE loop with an IF THEN ELSE structure inside. To determine this from the earlier version of the algorithm, we have to read the entire algorithm.

Another advantage of using standard notation is that it becomes easier to read algorithms written by other people. Because the pseudocode can be read by non-programmers, it is often included in the documentation that accompanies a program to describe how it is to be used. Finally, as we will see in the next chapter, it is easier to convert our pseudocode into FORTRAN 77 than it is to convert the longhand English.

1-3 TECHNIQUES FOR ALGORITHM DEVELOPMENT

The previous section presented the structures that represent the building blocks that we use to develop an algorithm. But, where do we start? First, we must thoroughly understand the problem statement and must have done an example by hand. This preparation sometimes makes the solution so obvious that we can define the necessary steps right away. Unfortunately, developing most solutions requires more effort. The procedure that we will use in our algorithm development in this text is based on *top-down design.* Top-down design is composed of two techniques, decomposition and stepwise refinement.

The first technique, *decomposition,* is a form of "divide and conquer." We break the problem into a series of smaller problems, and then address each one separately. Each part of the overall problem is described in general terms.

Stepwise refinement, the other technique, starts with this general description of the steps to the problem solution, and successively refines and describes each step in greater detail. The refining continues until the solution is specific enough for the application, or specific enough to convert into computer instructions.

The advantage of decomposition is that we can initially think of the overall steps required without getting lost in the details. The details of the solution are introduced only as we begin the refinement of our algorithm. We will show the decomposition in a block diagram to emphasize that we are breaking the solution into a series of sequentially executed steps. As we begin refining these general steps, we will switch to pseudocode in order to begin including the necessary structure in our solution.

To illustrate top-down design, we return to the checking account illustration. A problem that we mentioned earlier was computing the average balance over the last 12 bank statements. Even when a problem seems very simple, such as this one, we recommend using the five-phase process for solving it.

1 State the problem clearly.

Compute the average balance from your last 12 bank statements.

2 Describe the input and output.

INPUT: final balance from the last 12 bank statements
OUTPUT: average balance

3 Work the problem by hand for a specific set of data.

Here is a chance to use some of your own data again. Somewhere near the top of your last bank statement should be a summary of information for that month. Locate the old or previous balance and circle it.

FCB **FIRST CITY BANK** 3620 Main St.
Alma, NJ

```
JOHN D. SMITH
MARY A. SMITH
100 CENTER STREET
ALMA, NJ

*****************CHECKING ACCOUNT INFORMATION*****************

PREVIOUS BALANCE ON THE STATEMENT OF MARCH 1, 1983           $294.86
PLUS 2 DEPOSITS TOTALLING                                     900.00
MINUS 7 CHECKS AND OTHER DEDUCTIONS TOTALLING                 931.19
NEW BALANCE ON THIS STATEMENT OF APRIL 1, 1983                263.67
```

Now locate the statements for the previous 11 months. (Even if you do not balance your account regularly, surely you keep all the statements together in a drawer.) Make a list of balances like the following list that we will be using for our example.

MONTH	BALANCE
April	$476.32
May	322.05
June	146.98
July	236.86
August	352.04
September	401.86
October	302.65
November	22.03
December	15.80
January	186.20
February	297.55
March	294.86

Now get out your calculator. Going through the steps is important. Remember to clear your calculator before you start adding balances. For the data above, our total is $3055.20. Dividing this by 12 gives an average balance of $254.60.

4 Develop an algorithm that is general in nature.
To begin developing an algorithm, we start with the decomposition of the problem into a series of smaller problems. Remember, this is a form of "divide and conquer."

DECOMPOSITION

Read and total the balances from the last 12 bank statements
Divide the total by 12 to get the average
Print the total

REFINEMENT IN PSEUDOCODE

```
MONTHLY:  BEGIN
            total ← 0
            count ← 0
            WHILE count < 12 DO
              READ balance
              total ← total + balance
              count ← count + 1
            END WHILE
            average ← total/12
            PRINT 'MONTHLY AVERAGE', average
          END
```

Since this was a simple algorithm, only one refinement was needed. Several refinements are often necessary for more complex problems.

5 Test the algorithm with a variety of data sets.
If we use our example data in the refined algorithm, the output is:

MONTHLY AVERAGE $254.60

Similar results are obtained with different sets of data.

Because these techniques are so important in developing correct yet simple algorithms, we illustrate them again in the two problem solving sections at the end of this chapter and also frequently throughout the text. The best way to become proficient with these techniques is to study example pseudocode solutions and then apply the ideas to similar problems. Color is used for pseudocode throughout the text so that it can be referred to easily.

1-4 EVALUATION OF ALTERNATE SOLUTIONS

There are always many ways to solve the same problem. We emphasize this early because you may be dismayed when you find that your algorithms contain steps different from those of other students. In most cases, there is not a best solution to a problem. However, some solutions are definitely better than others. Don't assume that the best solution is also the shortest solution; experience has shown that this is not always the case. A good solution is one that is simple to understand and clearly written. Subtle or clever steps may shorten the algorithm, but should be used only if the overall clarity of the algorithm is improved.

Try to think of several ways to solve a problem when you begin developing the general solution. As you refine the solution, choose the one that is the most simple and straightforward. Sometimes you will need to write the refined pseudocode for a couple of ways of solving the problem before you can choose the simplest approach.

Another way to solve the checking account balance problem is to keep totals of all deposits, all interest earned, and all checks. Then, at the end of the algorithm, add the deposit total and interest total and subtract the check total from the old balance. This is a reasonable solution, but not as simple as the solution presented earlier. Compare the pseudocode CHECKING2 to CHECKING1 presented on page 11.

ALTERNATIVE PSEUDOCODE FOR CHECKING ACCOUNT ALGORITHM

```
CHECKING2:  BEGIN
               balance ← old balance
               deposit ← 0
               interest ← 0
               checks ← 0
               WHILE more transactions DO
                  READ type, amount
                  IF type = 'DEPOSIT'
                     deposit ← deposit + amount
                  ELSE IF type = 'INTEREST EARNED'
                     interest ← interest + amount
                  ELSE IF type = 'CHECK'
                     checks ← checks + amount
                  ELSE
                     PRINT 'ERROR IN TRANSACTION TYPE'
                  END IF
               END WHILE
               balance ← balance + deposit + interest
                          − checks − $5.00
               PRINT 'FINAL BALANCE', balance
            END
```

Can you think of a problem for which CHECKING2 is a good solution? If you look at the section of bank statement on page 13 that we used previously, you will see that the balance summary included the deposit total and the total of checks and other deductions. The computer program that prints this statement came from an algorithm that was more like CHECKING2 than CHECKING1 because CHECKING1 did not keep these extra totals. Thus, while CHECKING1 is a better solution if we want only a final balance, CHECKING2 is a good solution if we also want transaction summaries.

1-5 ERROR CONDITIONS

When we write an algorithm to solve a problem, we begin with the assumption that the input data will be correct. As we refine the algorithm, there are usually logical places to test the data for *error conditions.* It is important to distinguish between an error in the algorithm and an error condition in the data. Any error discovered in the algorithm must be corrected so that the modified algorithm correctly performs the steps specified in the problem statement. Error conditions in the data are data values which are not valid or desirable, but may still occur. Thus, a correct algorithm must include steps to handle certain error conditions in the data. For example, the algorithm described on page 11 is a correct algorithm for balancing a checking account with transactions that are deposits, interest, or checks. If a transaction is read that is not 'DEPOSIT', 'INTEREST EARNED', or 'CHECK', then this is an error condition in the data, and an appropriate error message is printed. If the problem statement is changed to include transactions for overdraft charges, then the algorithm is incorrect and must be modified to include this new valid transaction.

When you are developing an algorithm, how do you know which error conditions in the data could occur? Sometimes the problem statement will include a list of error conditions that might occur and indications of how to handle them. It is more likely that the problem statement will not mention error conditions at all. When you have no information on error conditions, our advice is to include error checks that fit easily into the structure of your algorithm. For example, in the checking account algorithm, since we tested for transactions that were deposits, interest, or checks, it was very easy to add an ELSE clause to test for invalid transaction types. As we develop algorithms throughout this text, you will learn more about typical error conditions that can occur. Unless judgements are made concerning which error conditions to include, a program becomes primarily statements that perform error checks.

Once you have decided that an error condition will be handled in your algorithm, you still have to decide what to do if it occurs. Usually, you have two choices. Either print an error message and exit the algorithm, or print an error message but continue executing the steps in the algorithm. Note that in either case an error message is printed. Be sure that the error message is specific. Do not use messages such as 'ERROR', 'ERROR CODE 3', 'YOU

BLEW IT!', or 'SOMETHING IS WRONG'. Since you made a specific test to determine that the error occurred, use that information in your error message.

Examples of more descriptive messages are 'ERROR IN TRANSACTION TYPE' and 'PRESSURE VALUE EXCEEDS SAFETY LIMIT'. If the error condition occurred in the input data, we recommend that you continue performing steps in the algorithm so that you can check the rest of the data for errors. The final result will be wrong, but hopefully you will locate all the errors in the data and can get valid results after the input data is corrected. If the error is not in the input data, then it is probably advisable to exit the algorithm immediately after printing an appropriate error message.

Finally, check all loops to see if they could become infinite loops under certain conditions. An *infinite loop* is one in which the WHILE condition is always true. Consider the following WHILE loop:

```
count ← 0
WHILE count < 12 DO
   (steps in the loop)
END WHILE
```

Suppose that the steps in the loop do not modify count. Then count is always 0, which is always less than 12, and thus we have an infinite loop. This example is a case of an algorithm error and requires a modification in the algorithm itself. Infinite loops cannot always be detected before the steps of an algorithm are performed because the loop may depend on values related to the input data. For example, consider the following steps:

```
READ n
count ← 0
WHILE count < n DO
   (steps in the loop)
   count ← count + 1
END WHILE
```

If n is less than 0, this becomes an infinite loop because count increases in value and thus will always be greater than n. Since it is not always possible to avoid an infinite loop, you may be worried about the effect that this will have on the computer. In Chapter 2, we will explain more about the program execution process, but be assured that the computer can figure out when it is in an infinite loop, and will exit on its own. It will then terminate your program, and usually will print an error message to the effect that you have exceeded a time limit that is set by your computer system.

1-6 GENERATION OF TEST DATA

Generating test data is an important part of testing an algorithm. As we have already mentioned, it is usually not difficult to create test data that works correctly with an algorithm. It is more difficult, though, to generate data that will test each step in an algorithm. For each condition tested in the algorithm (in WHILE loops and IF THEN ELSE structures), data should be included that yields true conditions and other data included that yields false conditions. By using test data that represents both values, we are testing different *paths* or sets of steps that are executed together. As you begin putting test data together and trying it in the algorithm, you will find that it is usually easier to test an algorithm with a number of small sets of data than to test it with one large set of data. To test the checking account balance algorithm, here are some of the test sets that we would use:

Set 1 Use the data from the hand problem. (If this doesn't work in the algorithm, we aren't off to a good start!)

Set 2 Include all three valid transaction types, but choose amounts so that the final balance is negative.

Set 3 Use set 2 data but also add a couple of invalid transaction types, such as:

OVERDRAFT CHARGE	$10.00
NEW CHECKS PRINTED	$15.50

The algorithm should indicate that there were two errors in transaction type, but give the same balance as in set 2.

Since this algorithm is not complicated, neither is generating test data for it. As we develop more complicated algorithms throughout the text, we will suggest types of data that should be used in testing them.

What do you do if you find an error in the algorithm while testing it? If the error is a major one, go back to the algorithm development phase and begin again. For smaller errors, you will find that you have a natural tendency to patch the old algorithm and retest it on the data set that did not work correctly on the initial algorithm. If the algorithm now works, you assume that it is correct. Unfortunately, this approach has some flaws in it. How do we know that the new algorithm will still work for the data that has already been tested on the initial algorithm? Clearly we do not know that, and thus we must start the test procedure over whenever we modify an algorithm.

An algorithm should correctly handle all the test data sets before we assume it is correct. If the algorithm correctly handles all the test data, should we really assume it is correct? We generally do, but actually all that we know for sure is that it works on our test data. If we did a careful job developing the algorithm and generating test data, then we can have confidence in our algorithm. Computer science curricula usually include a course in proving the correctness of algorithms. Since this subject is beyond the scope of this book, we again stress the importance of careful algorithm development and thorough generation of test data so that we can be confident of the correctness of our algorithms.

As a final note on the generation of test data, we want to mention a technique that is commonly used in industry and business. In projects that include the development of long or complex algorithms, it is very common for one group of people to develop an algorithm and for another group of people to generate test data and do the actual testing. You could use this technique with long or complex algorithms that you develop. Ask a friend (preferably someone else in your class) to help you generate test data—but do your own testing.

1-7 PROBLEM SOLVING— GRADE POINT AVERAGE

In this section we develop an algorithm to compute a grade point average. Since the problem is more complicated than the checking account problem, we will use two refinements to derive our final algorithm. The five design phases presented earlier in the chapter will again be used as the framework for solving this problem.

PROBLEM STATEMENT

You have just received grades for your college courses. Compute your grade point average, using a 4.0 system.

INPUT/OUTPUT DESCRIPTION

The input information is contained on the final grade form which gives each course number, the number of credit hours for the course, and its letter grade. The output should be the words 'GRADE POINT AVERAGE' followed by the computed grade point average.

HAND EXAMPLE

We use the grades from the following form for our hand example:

Gold Trail University
Alma, NJ

JANE DOE FRESHMAN SPRING SEMESTER 1984

Course	*Credit hours*	*Final Grade*
INTRO. TO COMPUTING	3	A
ENGLISH I	3	B
BIOLOGY	4	C
AMERICAN HISTORY	3	B
COLLEGE ALGEBRA	3	B

Each letter grade needs to be converted to a number grade using the following table:

LETTER GRADE	NUMBER GRADE
A	4.0
B	3.0
C	2.0
D	1.0
F	0.0

The number grade is multiplied by the number of credit hours to get the number of points for a specific class. Since the grade point average is the total number of points divided by the total number of credit hours, we need to compute the number of points for each class and then total the hours and the points.

COURSE	CREDIT HOURS	LETTER GRADE	NUMBER GRADE	POINTS
Intro to Computing	3	A	4.0	12.0
English I	3	B	3.0	9.0
Biology	4	C	2.0	8.0
American History	3	B	3.0	9.0
College Algebra	3	B	3.0	9.0
Totals	16			47.0

The grade point average is then 47.0 divided by 16, or 2.94.

ALGORITHM DEVELOPMENT

After working the hand example, we are ready to develop the algorithm. The top-down design with its decomposition into general steps and the first refinement into pseudocode are given below:

DECOMPOSITION

Read grades
Compute total number of hours
Compute total number of points
grade point average ← total points/total hours
Print grade point average

Initial Refinement in Pseudocode

```
GPA:  BEGIN
         total points ← 0
         total hours ← 0
      WHILE more courses DO
         READ new hours, letter grade
         total hours ← total hours + new hours
         convert letter grade to number grade
         new points ← number grade × new hours
         total points ← total points + new points
      END WHILE
      grade point average ← total points/total hours
      PRINT 'GRADE POINT AVERAGE', grade point average
    END
```

We now need to refine the steps that are still not specific. In particular, we need to be more specific about the conversion of a letter grade to a number grade. The conversion is done with a sequence of tests. If the letter grade is A, then the number grade is 4.0. If the letter grade is B, then the number grade is 3.0, and so on. These tests translate easily to an IF THEN ELSE structure. In the final ELSE clause we can print an error message if the letter grade is invalid. We will also set the number grade to 0 and subtract new hours from total hours if an invalid grade is detected. Look at the following algorithm before reading the next paragraph to see if you can determine the reason for these last two steps in the ELSE clause.

If an error in the letter grade occurs, we want to skip the course. That is, we do not want the total hours and total points to reflect any changes. Therefore, we set the number grade to 0 so that the total points will not change. At the beginning of the WHILE loop we added new hours to total hours, so if an error occurs we must also subtract that value from total hours. These two steps ensure that the total hours and total points contain only valid information.

Final Refinement in Pseudocode

```
GPA:   BEGIN
          total points ← 0
          total hours ← 0
          WHILE more courses DO
             READ new hours, letter grade
             total hours ← total hours + new hours
             IF letter grade = A
                number grade ← 4.0
             ELSE IF letter grade = B
                number grade ← 3.0
             ELSE IF letter grade = C
                number grade ← 2.0
             ELSE IF letter grade = D
                number grade ← 1.0
             ELSE IF letter grade = F
                number grade ← 0.0
             ELSE
                PRINT 'ERROR IN LETTER GRADE'
                number grade ← 0.0
                total hours ← total hours − new hours
             END IF
             new points ← number grade × new hours
             total points ← total points + new points
          END WHILE
          grade point average ← total points/total hours
          PRINT 'GRADE POINT AVERAGE', grade point average
       END
```

TESTING

Test the algorithm first with the hand example. Then try a couple of your previous grade forms or some from your friends. As we look for limitations in our algorithm, we find that it will not work correctly if the total hours are zero because dividing by zero is undefined. If this algorithm is going to be the basis of a computer program, a check for this error condition should be made since the condition could happen. For example, if a student took an incomplete (I) as the grade in all courses because of illness, the grades would be skipped as invalid and the final grade point would be computed as zero divided by zero. A test just before the final computation could be used to avoid this division if the total hours were zero. Is there a problem if the total points are zero but the total hours are greater than zero? No, that is not a problem. The grade point average in this case is computed to be 0.00, and could occur if a student received an F in all courses.

1-8 PROBLEM SOLVING—STATE TAX TABLE

In this section we develop an algorithm to generate a tax table similar to that used by clerks in retail stores to look up the sales tax that is to be added to a sales amount. The algorithm development is again presented in five phases.

PROBLEM STATEMENT

Generate a state tax table that will compute the tax on amounts from $0.00 to $100.00 in steps of $0.10.

INPUT/OUTPUT DESCRIPTION

The only information necessary to begin computing the table is the state tax percentage rate. In order to make our algorithm flexible, we will read that value at the beginning so that the rate can be changed without requiring a change in the algorithm itself. The output is a table with columns for sales amount and tax amount.

HAND EXAMPLE

Using the information from the first two phases, we can begin computing entries to the table. For the hand example we will use a tax rate of 6.5%.

SALES	TAX
$0.00	$0.00
0.10	?

As we compute the tax for $0.10, we find that a question arises. The tax due is 0.10×0.065 which is equal to 0.0065. If we round this to two decimal digits, the tax is 0.01, but if we use the first two digits, the tax is 0.00. Judging from the way most taxes work, we will assume that we should round. It will be important to indicate in our algorithm that the tax values are being rounded. We can now compute a few more entries in the table to see if any other questions arise.

SALES	TAX
$0.00	$0.00
0.10	0.01
0.20	0.01
0.30	0.02
0.40	0.03
0.50	0.03
0.60	0.04

The rest of the computations seem to be straightforward, so we now go to the next phase.

ALGORITHM DEVELOPMENT

The algorithm for this problem solution contains a loop that prints a line in the table each time the loop is executed. This loop could be described as a WHILE loop that is executed while the sales amount is less than or equal to $100.00. It could also be described as an iterative loop since it is executed a specific number of times. (How many times is it executed? The answer is 1001 times. If you did not get 1001, go back to the problem description and read it again. Are you counting the first line?) We will choose an iterative loop for this algorithm. The top-down design is shown with the decomposition into general steps and the refinement into detailed steps in pseudocode.

Decomposition

Read tax rate
Print tax table

Refinement in Pseudocode

```
TAXTBL:  BEGIN
            READ rate
            sales ← 0.00
            PRINT 'TAX TABLE'
            PRINT 'SALES      TAX'
            count ← 0
            WHILE count < 1001 DO
               tax ← rate × sales (rounded)
               PRINT sales, tax
               sales ← sales + 0.10
               count ← count + 1
            END WHILE
         END
```

Can you think of some alternate ways of computing the tax table? Instead of computing the tax on the entire sales for each line of the table, we could add the tax on $0.10 to the previous tax to get the new tax.

TESTING

To test this algorithm, we should go through the loop a few times from the beginning to see if it computes the first few lines correctly.

TAX TABLE

Sales	Tax
0.00	0.00
0.10	0.01
0.20	0.01
0.30	0.02

We can then skip a number of lines in the table, set sales to a number such as $99.60, and pick up there to see if the table is completed correctly.

99.60	6.47
99.70	6.48
99.80	6.49
99.90	6.49
100.00	6.50

The table is computed correctly. One last thing that we should check is the number of times that the loop is executed. Many people make the mistake of writing an algorithm that executes an iterative loop one time more than intended or one time less than intended. Since we print a line in the table for $0.00, in addition to 10 lines for each dollar, 1001 lines are printed and thus the loop should be executed 1001 times, not 1000 times.

SUMMARY

We have presented a five-phase procedure for developing problem solutions (algorithms). The procedure begins with a clear statement of the problem and continues with a description of the input or information available. The form of the output is also described; for instance, the output might be an average of recent bank statements or a table of sales tax amounts.

The algorithm to solve the specified problem is developed using top-down design. Decomposition assists in describing the general steps that have to be performed to solve the problem, and then stepwise refinement guides us in refining the steps and adding the detail necessary to perform them. Pseudocode is a way of describing these steps using structures that will be easy to convert into computer languages. There are usually many ways to solve a problem, and we want to choose simple, easy-to-understand solutions. These solutions will then be easier to test for correctness and easier to modify if we should need to modify them to fit new problem statements.

KEY WORDS

algorithm
CASE structure
counter
counting loop
data
decomposition
design phases
ELSE clause
error condition
flowchart
IF THEN ELSE structure
infinite loop
input/output (I/O)
iterative loop
loop
path
problem statement
pseudocode
REPEAT UNTIL loop
SEQUENCE structure
stepwise refinement
structured algorithm
structured program
testing
top-down design
WHILE loop

DEBUGGING AIDS

An error in an algorithm or a computer program is called a *bug*. Therefore, finding and eliminating such errors is called *debugging*. A section on debugging at the end of each chapter summarizes and repeats the advice and techniques just presented.

1 Spend the time necessary to generate test data that adequately tests all paths through your algorithm.
2 Use several small sets of test data instead of one large set.
3 Be sure that you perform each step in the algorithm as specified. You know what you want the steps to do, but do they really specify what you want?
4 If you find a major error, go back to the algorithm development phase and begin again.
5 If you find a small error, modify the algorithm and begin the testing phase at the beginning.
6 If the algorithm is long or complex, ask someone else to help you generate test data.
7 Perform error checks on input data to verify that the data is valid. (Note that there is a difference between an algorithm error and a data error.)

STYLE/TECHNIQUE GUIDES

The guides presented in this section of each chapter will reinforce good habits in the construction and presentation of algorithms and computer programs. It is much easier to learn good habits from the beginning than to change bad habits later. Using poor style in algorithms and programs is much like using poor grammar when you talk. It makes a bad impression initially and will make it harder for you to get your point across and to develop credibility. The style that we recommend for describing algorithms has been used in the examples already developed.

1 Use pseudocode to describe your algorithm. This gives a uniform appearance to all your algorithms and allows other people to read them more easily.
2 Use only a small number of structures in constructing the algorithm. We prefer using the SEQUENCE structure, the IF THEN ELSE structure and its three forms, and the WHILE loop structure.
3 Indent the internal steps of loops and IF THEN ELSE structures.
4 Do the decomposition step for every algorithm. Even very simple problem solutions break into a series of general steps.

5 Do not try to develop every algorithm with one refinement. Use as many refinements as are needed to get to the level of detail that you want.

6 Model your algorithms in structure and appearance after those presented in the text.

7 Pseudocode is a flexible tool for describing algorithms. Do not be afraid to modify it to fit your own style, as long as the overall structures remain constant.

PROBLEMS

A good way to learn new techniques is to practice making small changes in an algorithm that is already written. This first set of problems requires modifications to the checking account algorithm, CHECKING1, which is on page 11. Start with the original algorithm each time you begin a new problem. Color is used on problem numbers to indicate that solutions to these problems are included at the end of the text.

1 Modify the check balancing algorithm to include a new transaction, 'NEW CHECKS PRINTED'. The corresponding amount should be subtracted from the balance.

2 Modify the check balancing algorithm to deduct a $7.50 overdraft charge any time that the balance goes below zero. Print an appropriate message each time this occurs.

3 Modify the check balancing algorithm to print the transaction type and amount if an error occurs.

4 Modify the check balancing algorithm to compute the service charge as follows: If the balance does not fall below $200, there is no service charge. If the balance falls below $200, then there is a $5 service charge.

5 Modify the check balancing algorithm to include a count of the number of checks processed. Print this count along with the final balance.

6 Modify the check balancing algorithm to compute the service charge in the following way: If 5 or fewer checks are processed, there is no service charge. If the number of checks is between 6 and 20, then the service charge is $5. If the number of checks is greater than 20, the service charge is $0.25 per check.

7 Modify the check balancing algorithm to compute an interest earned amount instead of expecting an interest earned transaction. The interest earned is $\frac{1}{2}$% of the minimum balance during the month. (Hint: To find the minimum balance, move the old balance into another total and call it "minimum balance." After computing each new balance, compare it to "minimum balance." If the new balance is smaller, put that value in "minimum balance.")

This set of problems requires modifications to the bank statement average algorithm, MONTHLY, which is on page 14. Start with the original algorithm each time you begin a new problem.

8 Modify the statement average algorithm to print each month's balance in addition to the final average.

9 Modify the statement average algorithm to compute a monthly average over the last 2 years.

10 Modify the statement average algorithm to read a number which will tell you how many months are to be used in the average. Print this in addition to the average.

11 Modify the statement average algorithm to include determining the maximum balance. Print this in addition to the average. (Hint: See problem 7.)

12 Modify the statement average algorithm to include determining the minimum balance. Print this in addition to the average. (Hint: See problem 7.)

13 Modify the statement average algorithm to determine the largest increase in balances from one month to another. Print this in addition to the average. (Hint: see problem 7.)

14 Modify the statement average algorithm to determine the smallest increase in balances from one month to another. Print this in addition to the average. (Hint: See problem 7.)

This set of problems requires modifications to the grade point average algorithm, GPA, which is on page 22. Start with the original algorithm each time you begin a new problem.

15 Modify the grade point average algorithm to print the hours and letter grade for an invalid grade.

16 Modify the grade point average algorithm to print 'HONOR ROLL' after the grade point average if it is 3.0 or above.

17 Modify the grade point average algorithm so that a grade of incomplete (I) is not used in the grade calculation and also is not printed as an error.

18 Modify the grade point average algorithm so that a grade of credit (CR) or no credit (NC) does not affect the calculation of the grade point average, but is printed when it is encountered.

19 Modify the grade point average algorithm so that a count of the number of classes is also printed in addition to the grade point average.

This set of problems requires modifications to the state tax table algorithm, TAXTBL, which is on page 24. Start with the original algorithm each time you begin a new problem.

20 Modify the state tax table algorithm so that the increment between lines in the table is $0.05.

21 Modify the state tax table algorithm so that the increment between lines is read, along with the tax rate.

22 Modify the state tax table algorithm so that the number of lines in the table is read, along with the tax rate.

23 Modify the state tax table algorithm so that an additional column is added which contains the sales amount plus the tax due.

24 Modify the state tax table algorithm so that it reads the starting and ending sales amounts for the table in addition to the rate.

Now that you are comfortable making changes to an existing algorithm, here are some new algorithms to develop. Remember to use the five-phase design process.

25 Given three packages of graph paper, each with a different number of sheets, develop an algorithm to determine the best buy for your money.

26 Develop an algorithm to compute your average grade point for the semesters of college that you have completed. If this is your first semester, compute your average grade point for your high school grades.

27 Develop an algorithm to compute the tuition at your school.

28 Develop an algorithm to compute the amount of interest that you will earn at the end of each month over a 2-year period on an initial deposit of $1000. Use a compound interest calculation.

29 Assume that you have just bought a car. Develop an algorithm to print a table giving the amount that you still owe at the end of each month, over the period of the payments.

30 Assume that you have just bought a car. Develop an algorithm to compute the number of months necessary to pay for the car if you pay $250 per month. Print the number of months necessary and the amount of the last payment.

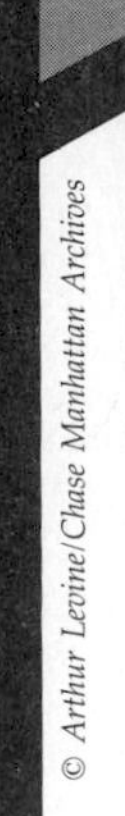

PROBLEM SOLVING—Foreign Currency Exchange

You are planning a trip to Europe between semesters. There are a number of items that you would like to purchase while you are there, but you need to convert the prices (in francs, lire, deutsche marks, pounds sterling, etc.) to dollars to see if you can afford the purchases. Write a computer program to perform these currency conversions. (See Section 2-6, page 59, for the solution.)

2

COMPUTER PROGRAMS

INTRODUCTION

In the first chapter we discussed techniques for solving problems. The problem-solving steps could be applied to any problem, independently of whether or not a computer was to be used. In this chapter we bring the computer into the picture. We discuss the different types of computers, from the super computers to the personal computers. We compare different computer languages, and point out some of the reasons for the existence of so many languages. Then we present a set of FORTRAN statements and begin translating our algorithms into complete FORTRAN programs.

2-1 COMPUTER ORGANIZATION

Computer components come in all sizes, shapes, and forms, from the super computers such as the CRAY-1 in Figure 2-1, to the minicomputers in Figure 2-2, to the microprocessor chip in Figure 2-3. All these computers have a common internal organization, which is shown in the block diagram in Figure 2-4. In large computer systems, each part is physically distinguishable from the others. In a microcomputer or minicomputer, all the parts within the dotted line may be combined in a single integrated circuit chip.

FIGURE 2-1 Large computer system. (Courtesy of Cray Research, Inc.)

The *processing unit* or *processor* is the part of the computer that controls all the other parts. The processor accepts *input* values and stores them in the *memory.* It also interprets the instructions in a computer program. If we want to add two values, the processor will retrieve them from the memory and send them to the *arithmetic logic unit* or *ALU.* The ALU performs the desired addition, and the processor will then store the result in the memory. If we desire, we may also direct the processor to *output* the result on printed paper. A small amount of memory, the *internal memory,* is used by the processing unit and the ALU in their processing, while most data is stored in *external memory.* The processor, internal memory, and ALU are collectively referred to as the *central processing unit* or *CPU.* Thus, a *microprocessor* is a CPU, but a *microcomputer* is a CPU with input and output capabilities.

The size of the computer system needed to solve a particular problem depends on the type of steps and the number of steps needed to solve the

FIGURE 2-2 Minicomputer system with terminals. (Courtesy of Digital Equipment Corporation.)

FIGURE 2-3 Microprocessor and integrated circuit chips. (Courtesy of Digital Equipment Corporation.)

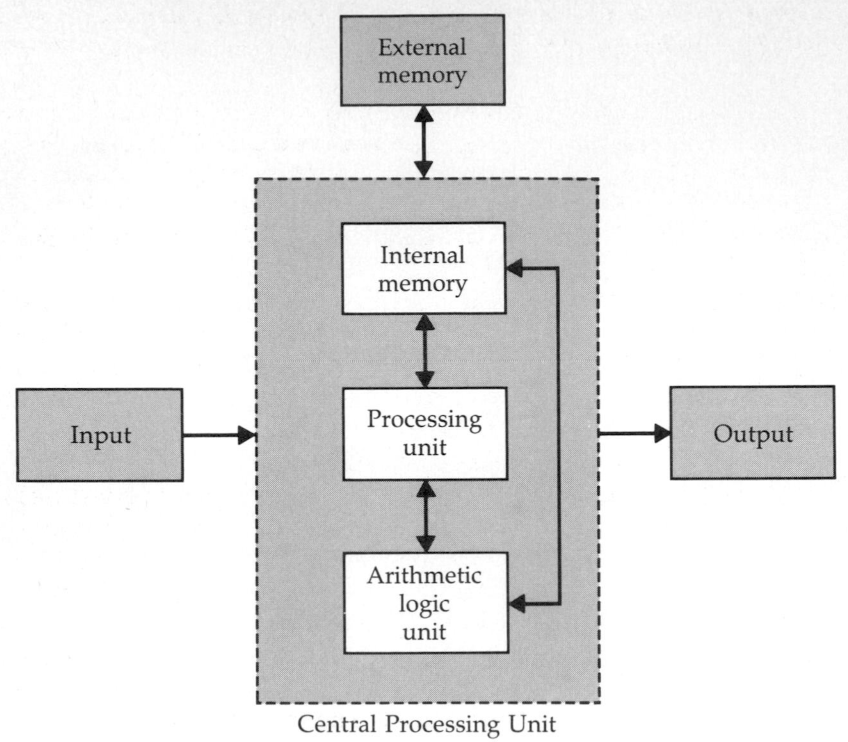

FIGURE 2-4 Block diagram of a computer.

problem. If the computer is to be part of a home security system, a microcomputer is sufficient; if the computer is to simulate a complex process, then a large computer system is necessary. The FORTRAN language is available on most computers, and thus we will be able to use a variety of computers for our programs.

When working with computers, you will often hear the terms *software* and *hardware*. Software refers to the programs that direct computers to perform operations, compute new values, and manipulate data. Hardware refers to the actual components of the computer, such as the memory unit, the processor, and the ALU. Thus, a person who works with software might write computer programs, while a person who works with hardware might design new components or connect devices together. For example, a hardware engineer might design the *interface* equipment necessary to connect a microprocessor to an input terminal.

2-2 COMPUTER LANGUAGES

Computer hardware is based on two-state (*binary*) technology; that is, computers are built from components that have two values, such as open or closed, on or off, plus or minus, high or low. These two values can represent the numbers 0 and 1, and hence computers are often defined to be machines capable of interpreting and understanding sequences of 0's and 1's called *binary strings*.

Since the human mind has been trained to think in terms of English-like phrases and formulas, we use languages such as FORTRAN to tell the computer the steps we want to perform. Then a special program called a *compiler* will translate the FORTRAN program into binary strings that the computer can understand. This compilation procedure will be discussed in the next section.

FORTRAN (*FOR*mula *TRAN*slation) is a language commonly used by engineers and scientists because of its orientation toward technical applications. FORTRAN 77 is a specific version of FORTRAN based on a set of standards established in 1977. It contains essentially all the statements of older versions, along with new features that enhance the language—particularly in the areas of character string processing and file handling. These enhancements expand the range of applications beyond technical applications. Because FORTRAN is based on standards, it becomes a very *portable* language; the same program will run on any system that adheres to the standards. Besides FORTRAN, there are many other *high-level* languages, such as BASIC, COBOL, Pascal, PL/I, ALGOL, and Ada. These languages are called high-level languages because they are English-like and reasonably easy for us to understand, as opposed to a low-level language such as the binary strings that computers understand. The solution to a specific problem could generally be programmed into any computer language. However, some languages were designed with specific types of problems in mind. COBOL was designed to handle business-related problems and file manipulations. BASIC, a language similar to FORTRAN, is commonly used with minicomputers and microcomputers (personal computers). ALGOL and Pascal are designed to reflect the theory of structured programming. PL/I is a language that combines many features of FORTRAN, COBOL, and ALGOL. Ada is a structured language designed for the government to be used in technical applications.

Learning a computer language has many similarities to learning a foreign language. Each step that you want the computer to perform must be translated into the computer language you are using. Fortunately, computer languages have a small vocabulary and no verb conjugations. However, computers are unforgiving in punctuation and spelling. A comma or letter in the wrong place will cause errors that keep your program from working. You will discover that you must pay close attention to many such details.

We have discussed high-level languages (such as FORTRAN) and low-level languages (binary or *machine language*). At another level are *assembly languages*. Assembly languages are between high-level and low-level languages and do not require a compiler to translate them into binary. A smaller program, called an *assembler*, translates the assembly language into machine language.

Most assembly languages do not have many statements, making them inconvenient to use. For example, you might have to do a series of additions to perform a single multiplication. Also, you have to understand certain elements of the design of the computer in order to use an assembly language. For these reasons, when given a choice, most people prefer to write programs in a high-level language. Assembly language is used primarily when the problem requires working with the internal binary storage of data.

Some of the statements in various high-level languages are illustrated in Table 2-1. Each section of code represents the calculation of an employee's salary based on the hours worked and the hourly pay rate. If the number of hours worked is less than or equal to 40, the salary to be paid is computed by multiplying the number of hours worked by the hourly pay rate. If the number of hours worked is greater than 40, then time-and-a-half is paid for the hours over 40. The different names used to represent hours worked, pay rate, and salary reflect the various rules within the individual languages. Also note the differences in punctuation among the various languages.

2-3 RUNNING A COMPUTER PROGRAM

In the previous section we defined a compiler as a program that translates a high-level language to machine language. This compilation step is the first step in running a program on the computer. As the compiler translates statements, it also checks for *syntax* errors. Syntax errors, also called *compiler* errors, are errors in the statements themselves, such as misspellings and punctuation errors. If syntax errors are found, the compiler will print error messages or *diagnostics* for you. After debugging your program, you can rerun it, again starting with the compilation step. Once your program has been compiled without errors, a *linkage editor* program performs the final preparations so that it can be submitted to the execution step. It is in the execution step that the statements are actually performed. Errors can also arise in the execution step; they are called *logic* errors, *run-time* errors, or *execution* errors. These errors are not in the syntax of the statement, but are errors in the logic of the statement that are detected only when the computer attempts to execute the statement. For example, the statement

```
X = A/B
```

is a valid FORTRAN statement that directs the computer to divide A by B and call the result X. The statement contains no syntax errors. Suppose, though, that the value of B is zero. Then, as we try to divide A by B, we are attempting to divide by zero, which is an invalid operation. Hence, we will get an execution error message. Logic errors do not always generate an error message. For instance, if we were supposed to use an interest rate of 10% in a calculation and we used 12% instead, no error would be detected by the computer although our answers would be wrong.

The FORTRAN program is often referred to as the *source program*. After it is converted into machine language by the compiler and prepared for execution by the linkage editor, it is in machine language and is now referred to as

TABLE 2-1 Examples of High-Level Languages

Language	Example Statements

FORTRAN

```
IF(HOURS.LE.40.0)THEN
   SALARY = HOURS*PAYRTE
ELSE
   SALARY = 40.0*PAYRTE +
               (HOURS - 40.0)*PAYRTE*1.5
ENDIF
```

COBOL

```
IF HOURS IS LESS THAN 40.0 OR
   HOURS IS EQUAL TO 40.0,
      COMPUTE SALARY = HOURS*PAYRATE
ELSE
      COMPUTE SALARY = 40.0*PAYRATE +
                 (HOURS - 40.0)*PAYRATE*1.5.
```

BASIC

```
    IF H > 40.0 THEN 200
    LET S = H*P
    GO TO 250
200 LET S = 40.0*P + (H - 40.0)*P*1.5
250   .
      .
      .
```

PL/I

```
IF HOURS <= 40.0 THEN
   SALARY = HOURS*PAYRATE;
ELSE
   SALARY = 40.0*PAYRATE +
               (HOURS - 40.0)*PAYRATE*1.5;
```

ALGOL

```
IF HOURS ≦ 40.0 THEN
   SALARY := HOURS X PAYRATE
ELSE
   SALARY := 40.0 X PAYRATE +
               (HOURS - 40.0) X PAYRATE X 1.5;
```

Pascal

```
IF HOURS <= 40.0 THEN
   SALARY := HOURS*PAYRATE
ELSE
   SALARY := 40.0*PAYRATE +
               (HOURS - 40.0)*PAYRATE*1.5;
```

Ada

```
IF HOURS <= 40.0 THEN
   SALARY := HOURS*PAYRATE;
ELSE
   SALARY := 40.0*PAYRATE +
               (HOURS - 40.0)*PAYRATE*1.5;
```

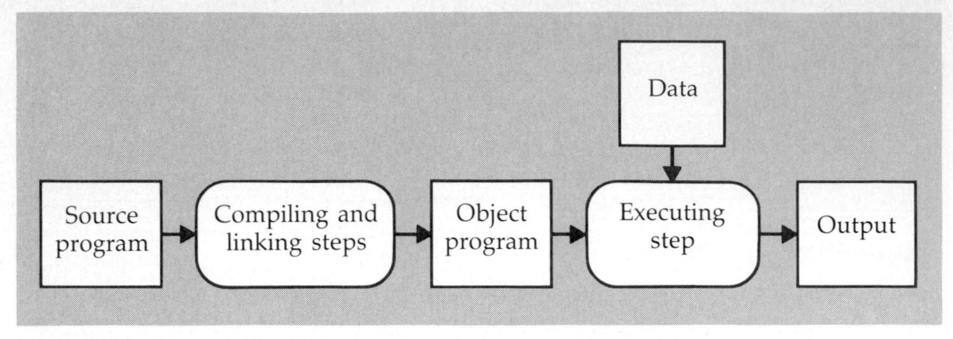

FIGURE 2-5 Compilation-linkage-execution process for running a computer program.

the *object program*. A diagram of this *compilation-linkage-execution* process is shown in Figure 2-5.

It is uncommon for a program to correctly compile, link, and execute on the first run. Therefore, do not become discouraged if it takes several runs to finally get answers. When you do get answers from your program, do not assume that they are correct. If possible, check your answer with a calculator or check to see if the answer makes sense. For example, if the answer represents the weight of a boxcar, then 5 pounds is not reasonable and suggests that you have given the computer incorrect data or an incorrect program to execute.

Two methods are used for running computer programs—*batch processing* and *time-sharing*. In most batch processing systems, your program is entered on cards using a card reader. The computer stores the program in its memory and will compile and execute it when it is next in line. The output of a batch processing system is usually printed on a line printer. Time-sharing systems, however, usually use terminals for entering programs. *Hard-copy terminals* use paper to record the input and output from the computer, while *CRT* (*cathode ray tube*) *terminals* use a video screen to display the input and output. In either case, the program is typed into the terminal, followed by a command such as RUN, which immediately begins the processing. This technique is called time-sharing because the computer does one step of a program from one terminal, one step of a program from another terminal, and so on until it is back to the first terminal. The computer then performs the next step in each program. We usually do not notice the time between steps because the computer executes a statement so fast. We seem to have the undivided attention of the computer, although we are actually sharing it with many other terminal users.

Most time-sharing systems allot each user a specified amount of memory to be used as a *workspace* in the computer. This workspace is usually divided into a *temporary workspace* and a *permanent workspace*. As you enter programs or data into the temporary workspace, you can *edit* the information, which means you can add to it, delete portions of it, or modify it with the use of a program called an *editor*. When you have the program or data in the form

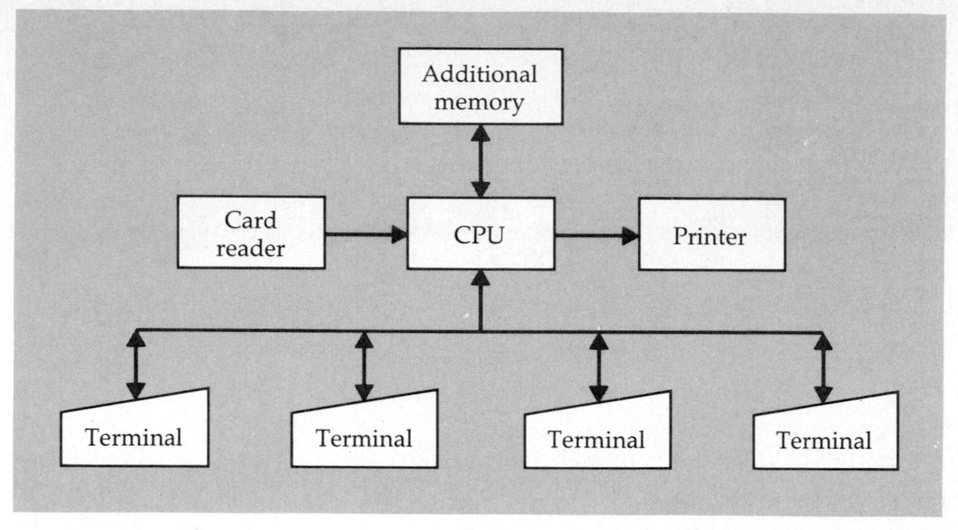

FIGURE 2-6 Computer system with batch processing and time-sharing.

that you want, you can then *save* it in the permanent workspace. You can then *clear* the temporary workspace and begin entering new information, or *log off* the terminal. The next time you *log on* the terminal, you can *load* any information that was previously saved in your permanent workspace into your temporary workspace.

A diagram of a computer system that supports both time-sharing and batch processing is shown in Figure 2-6. The additional memory is used by the time-sharing system.

Time-sharing or using a personal computer such as the one shown in Figure 2-7 is called *interactive computing* because we are interacting with the computer more than in a batch processing system. This increased interaction results in more efficient use of your time, because you have fewer delays. For instance, you do not have to wait for the line printer to finish printing someone else's output before yours can be printed; you have your own dedicated output device in front of you.

2-4 INPUT AND OUTPUT

In this section we present FORTRAN statements to print information and to read information. With these basic operations, we can construct simple but complete FORTRAN programs. Each time a new FORTRAN statement is introduced, it will be enclosed in a box with the general form of the statement inside for quick reference.

Before we discuss the types of numbers that can be stored in computers and some specific statements, we need to indicate the form to use for entering FORTRAN statements into your terminal or for keypunching them into com-

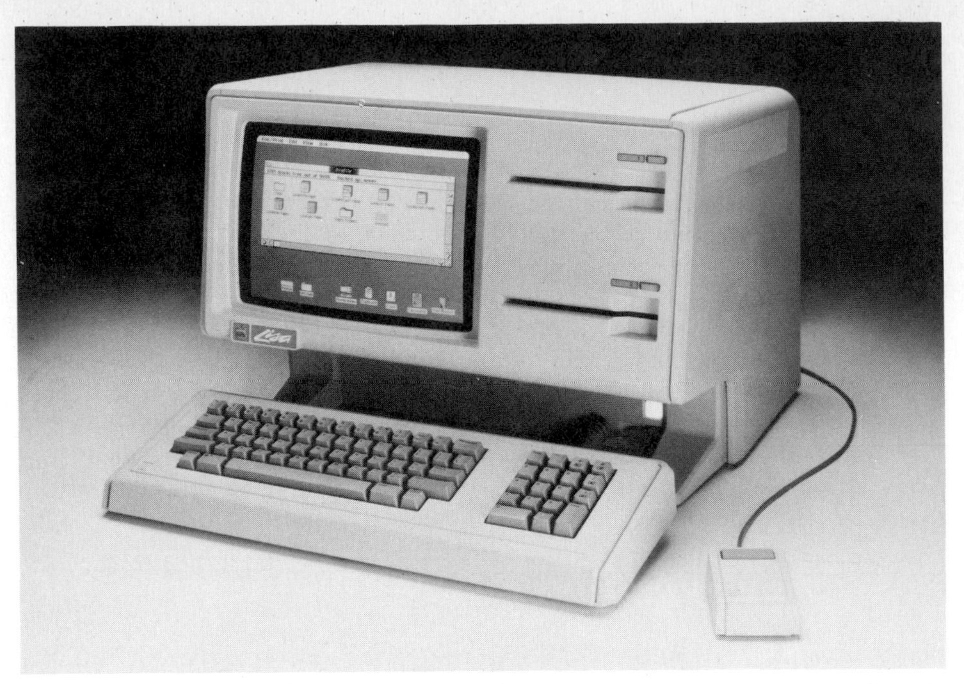

FIGURE 2-7 Personal computer system for interactive computing. (Courtesy of Apple Computer, Inc.)

puter cards. The same rules generally apply to either form; they specify where to put information on a terminal line or a computer card.

1 Columns 1 through 5 are reserved for statement numbers (also called labels), which must be nonzero positive integers. You do not have to number every statement, but, as you will see in later chapters, some statements do need numbers so they can be referenced. If column 1 contains an asterisk or the letter C, the line is a comment line. The information on comment lines is printed in your program listings but is not converted into machine language.

2 Column 6 is used to indicate that a statement has been continued from the previous line. Any nonblank character except a zero can be punched in column 6 of the second line to indicate continuation. A FORTRAN statement may have several continuation lines if it is too long to fit on one line or card.

3 FORTRAN statements start in column 7. The statement can extend to the end of the terminal line or through column 72 of a computer card.

Some terminal editors require that you number each line. These line numbers are used in editing, but cannot be referenced by a FORTRAN statement. Therefore, if you are using one of these editors, all statements will have a line number and statements that are referenced in your program will also have a FORTRAN reference number.

CONSTANTS AND VARIABLES

Numbers are introduced into a computer program either directly with the use of *constants* or indirectly with the use of *variables.* Constants are numbers used directly in computations, such as −7, 3.141593, and 32.0. Constants may contain plus or minus signs and decimal points, but they may not contain commas. Thus 3147.6 is a valid FORTRAN constant but 3,147.6 is not. Variables are named memory locations that store values. The value of a constant does not change, but operations performed on a variable can change its value.

When working with a high-level language such as FORTRAN, we can visualize the storage of variables in the computer memory as shown below:

AMOUNT	36.84	VOLUME	183.0
RATE	.065	TOTAL	486.5
TEMP	−17.5	INFO	72

A name is first given to each storage location to identify it uniquely; then each storage location may be assigned a value. Hence, in the examples shown, the storage location named TOTAL contains the value 486.5.

Each variable must have a different name, which you provide as you write your program. The names may contain one to six characters consisting of both alphabetic characters and digits; however, the first character of a name must be an alphabetic character. The following are examples of both valid and invalid variable names:

PRINCIPAL	Invalid name—too long
π	Invalid name—illegal character (π)
TEMP	Valid name
X2	Valid name
2X	Invalid name—first character must be alphabetic character
MONEY	Valid name
PI	Valid name
TAX-RT	Invalid name—illegal character (−)

Numerical values in FORTRAN can be one of four types: integer, real, double precision, or complex. *Integer*-type values are those with no fractional portion and no decimal point, such as 16, −7, 186, and 0. Since these values have no fractional portion or decimal point, they are also called *fixed-point* values. *Real*-type values, on the other hand, contain a decimal point and may or may not have digits past the decimal point, such as 13.86, 13., .0076, −14.1, 36.0, and −3.1. These real values are also called *floating-point* values. Double-precision values and complex values will be discussed in Chapter 8.

A storage location can contain only one type of value. The type of value stored in a variable can be specified by one of two methods: *implicit* typing or *explicit* typing. With implicit typing, the first letter of a variable name determines the type of value that can be stored in it. Variable names beginning with letters I, J, K, L, M, or N are used to store integers. Variable names beginning with one of the other letters, A → H and O → Z, are used to store real values. Thus, AMOUNT represents a real value and MONEY represents an integer value. An easy way to remember which letters are used for integers is to observe that the range of letters is I → N, the first two letters of the word *in*teger itself.

With explicit typing, a special FORTRAN statement is used to specify the type of a variable. For example, the statements

```
INTEGER WIDTH
REAL NUM, K
```

specify that WIDTH is a variable that will contain an integer value and that NUM and K are variables that will contain real values. These *specification* statements have the following general forms:

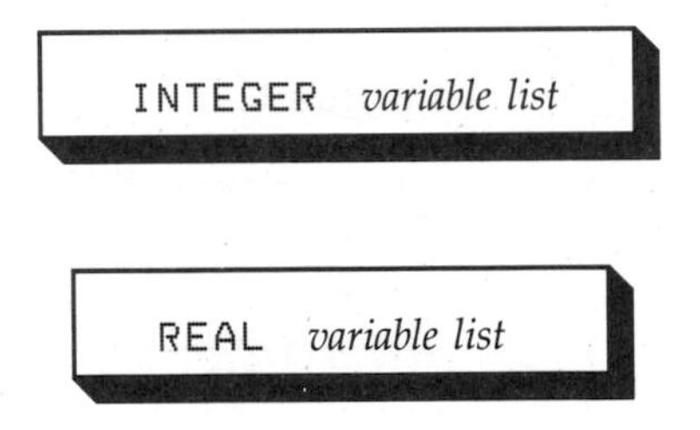

The variable list is the list of variable names which are being designated as integer names or real names. Specification statements are nonexecutable because they are used by the compiler to specify the nature of variables, but are not translated into machine language. Specification statements must be placed at the beginning of the program, before any executable statements.

It is very helpful to select a variable name that is descriptive of the value being stored. For example, if a value represents a tax rate, call it RATE or TAX. If the implicit typing of the variable name does not match the type of value to be stored in it, then use a REAL or INTEGER statement at the beginning of your program to specify the desired type of value. Some programmers prefer to list all variables on specification statements, including those correctly typed by the implicit rules.

LIST-DIRECTED OUTPUT

If we wish to print the value stored in a variable, it is necessary to tell the computer the variable's name. The computer can then access the storage location and print the contents, usually on computer paper or a terminal screen. Sometimes we are only interested in printing the value; other times we may also want to print the value on a new page of computer paper or center it on the output line. If we are interested in only the value of a variable, we use *list-directed* output; if we are interested in controlling where the value is printed, as we would for formal reports, we use *formatted* output. List-directed output will be used in the text, but Appendix B contains a complete description (with examples) of formatted output.

The general form of the PRINT statement is:

```
PRINT*, variable list
```

The asterisk specifies list-directed output. Generally, list-directed time-sharing output will be displayed on the terminal screen and list-directed batch output will be printed by the line printer. The variable names in the list must be separated by commas, and the values stored in those memory locations are printed in the order in which they are listed in the PRINT statement.

In our examples, computer output will usually be shown inside a symbol that represents a terminal screen, as illustrated in Example 2-1. Data values on the same line will be separated by blanks.

EXAMPLE 2-1 INCOME and GPA

Print the stored values of the variables INCOME and GPA.

Solution

COMPUTER MEMORY

INCOME	35000
GPA	3.15

FORTRAN STATEMENT

```
PRINT*, INCOME, GPA
```

COMPUTER OUTPUT

```
35000  3.1500
```

◇

In our examples, integer values are printed without any decimal positions and real values are printed with four decimal positions. The number of decimal positions printed for real values and the spacing between items will vary depending on the compiler used. When you run your first program (before the end of this section!), be sure to notice the number of decimal positions that your compiler uses. If a value to be printed is very large or very small, many compilers will automatically print the value in *scientific notation* or *exponential notation* instead of decimal form. Exponential notation expresses a value as a number between 0 and 1 multiplied by a power of 10. For example, 186,000,000,000 is equal to 0.186×10^{12} and would be printed by a PRINT statement as 0.1860E12. The letter E separates the number (0.1860) from the exponent or power of 10 (12).

EXAMPLE 2-2 Density, DENS

Print the stored value of the variable DENS.

Solution

COMPUTER MEMORY

DENS | 0.0000156 |

FORTRAN STATEMENT

```
PRINT*, DENS
```

COMPUTER OUTPUT

```
0.1560E-04
```

◇

Descriptive information (sometimes called *literal information* or *literals*) may also be included in the variable list by enclosing the information in single quote marks or apostrophes. This descriptive information is then printed on the output line along with the values of any variables also on the PRINT statement.

EXAMPLE 2-3 Literal and Variable Information

Print the variable RATE with a literal that identifies the value as representing a sales tax rate.

Solution

COMPUTER MEMORY

RATE | 0.065 |

FORTRAN STATEMENT

```
PRINT*, 'SALES TAX RATE IS', RATE, 'IN CALIFORNIA'
```

COMPUTER OUTPUT

```
SALES TAX RATE IS 0.0650 IN CALIFORNIA
```

◇

A new output line will be used each time a PRINT statement is executed.

EXAMPLE 2-4 Salary Information

Print the variables HOURS and PAYRT using descriptive headings.

Solution

COMPUTER MEMORY

HOURS	37.5
PAYRT	6.75

FORTRAN STATEMENTS

```
PRINT*, 'HOURS WORKED AND PAY RATE'
PRINT*, HOURS, PAYRT
```

COMPUTER OUTPUT

```
HOURS WORKED AND PAY RATE
37.5000 6.7500
```

◇

COMPLETE PROGRAMS

Only one additional statement is needed in order to be able to write complete FORTRAN programs. This statement, the END statement, identifies the physical end of our FORTRAN program for the compiler. The compiler stops translating statements when it reaches the END statement. Every FORTRAN program must end with the END statement, whose general form is:

```
END
```

Two other very simple statements that usually appear in FORTRAN programs should also be covered at this time. They are both optional, but they are useful in documenting a program. The PROGRAM statement clearly identifies the beginning of a program and assigns it a name. The general form of this statement is:

```
PROGRAM program name
```

Like a variable name, the program name can be one to six characters in length, begins with a letter, and contains only letters and digits. Some sample PROGRAM statements are:

```
PROGRAM TEST
PROGRAM COMPUT
PROGRAM SORT2
```

You should not use a variable in your program which has the same name as the program name.

The last statement presented in this section is the STOP statement which is a signal to the computer to terminate execution of the program. The END statement also serves this purpose, but the END statement can only appear once, at the physical end of the program. The STOP statement can appear anywhere in the program that makes sense, and it can appear as often as necessary. For example, some error conditions may be so severe that we want to stop executing the program as soon as they occur. Examples of this form will be included in Chapter 3. The general form of this statement is:

```
STOP
```

Many programs use both a STOP and an END at the end of the program, although the STOP is not necessary if it is followed immediately by the END statement.

We can now write a very simple but complete program. Try running it on your computer system. Check with your instructor for details concerning the computer that you will use.

EXAMPLE 2-5 Complete Program to Print a Name

Write a complete program to print your name.

Solution

The solution is so simple that we have only one step in the decomposition and pseudocode.

Decomposition

Print name

Refinement in Pseudocode

```
FIRST:  BEGIN
           PRINT 'MY NAME IS BILL R. ADAIR'
        END
```

FORTRAN Program

```
      PROGRAM FIRST
*
*   THIS IS MY FIRST COMPLETE PROGRAM
*
      PRINT*, 'MY NAME IS BILL R. ADAIR'
      END
```

Recall that an asterisk in column 1 indicates that the line is a comment; therefore it is not translated into machine language by the compiler. ◇

LIST-DIRECTED INPUT

We will frequently want to read information with our programs. The general form of a list-directed READ statement is:

READ*, *variable list*

The asterisk specifies list-directed input. Generally, list-directed batch input will read the data from computer cards, and list-directed time-sharing input will read the data from the terminal. Again, the variable names in the list must be separated by commas. The variables receive new values in the order in which they are listed in the READ statement. These values must agree in type (integer or real) with the variables in the list. When the program is run on a terminal, a special character called a *prompt*, such as a question mark, will be printed when the READ statement is being executed. At that time, you enter the new values for the variables, separated by commas or blanks. For card systems, the data card contains the new values, separated by commas or blanks. The location of the data card is very important. It does not go after the READ statement, but rather after the complete program.

Batch processing requires extra information, called *job control information*, in programs. Typically, this special information will be required before your program, between your program and its data, and after your program.

A READ statement will read as many data lines or data cards as needed to find new values for the variables in its list. Also, each READ statement will begin with a new line or data card.

EXAMPLE 2-6 Account Balances

Read the beginning and ending balances for a checking account.

Solution 1

FORTRAN STATEMENT

```
READ*, BEGIN, ENDING
```

DATA LINE

```
186.93, 386.21
```

COMPUTER MEMORY

BEGIN	186.93
ENDING	386.21

Solution 2

FORTRAN STATEMENTS

```
READ*, BEGIN
READ*, ENDING
```

DATA LINES

```
186.93
386.21
```

COMPUTER MEMORY

BEGIN	186.93
ENDING	386.21

Before these statements are executed, the contents of BEGIN and ENDING are unknown. ◇

Since the input device and output device are the same in time-sharing systems, *conversational computing* can be used in our programs that are run on terminals. Before data is to be entered, we can print a message that describes the data and the order of data values to be entered. After reading the data, we can print it for a validity check. This interaction between the program and the user who is entering the data resembles a conversation. In the next example, we illustrate this interaction in a complete program.

EXAMPLE 2-7 Read and Print Birthday

Write a complete program to read the month, day, and last two digits of the year of your birthday. Print them in the form month-day-year. Use a number for the month. We will discuss how to use alphabetical character strings, such as 'MARCH', in Chapter 3.

Solution

The solution to this problem is again very simple.

Decomposition

Read birthdate
Print birthdate

Refinement in Pseudocode

```
BIRTH:  BEGIN
           READ month
           READ day
           READ year
           PRINT month, day, year
        END
```

As we convert this to FORTRAN, we will print messages to explain the information that needs to be entered.

FORTRAN Program

```
      PROGRAM BIRTH
*
*  THIS PROGRAM PRINTS A BIRTHDATE
*  ENTERED FROM THE TERMINAL
*
      INTEGER DAY, YEAR
      PRINT*, 'ENTER BIRTH MONTH'
      READ*, MONTH
      PRINT*, 'ENTER BIRTH DAY'
      READ*, DAY
      PRINT*, 'ENTER LAST TWO DIGITS OF BIRTH YEAR'
      READ*, YEAR
      PRINT*, 'YOUR BIRTHDATE IS', MONTH, '-',
     +        DAY, '-', YEAR
      END
```

The information on the last PRINT statement required two lines, so a continuation character (+) was used in column 6 of the continued line.

```
ENTER BIRTH MONTH
?11
ENTER BIRTH DAY
?24
ENTER LAST TWO DIGITS OF BIRTH YEAR
?65
YOUR BIRTHDATE IS 11 - 24 - 65
```

2-5 ARITHMETIC COMPUTATIONS

Computations in FORTRAN may be specified with the assignment statement, whose general form is:

variable name = expression

The simplest form of an arithmetic expression is a constant. For example, if an interest rate of $10\frac{1}{2}\%$ is needed several places in a program, we can define a variable RATE with the value 0.105. Then each time we need this value, we can refer to RATE. The assignment statement that assigns a value to RATE, and thus *initializes* RATE, is:

```
RATE = 0.105
```

The name of the variable receiving a new value must always be on the left side of the equal sign. In FORTRAN, the equal sign can be read as "is assigned the value of." Thus, the statement above could be read "RATE is assigned the value 0.105."

It is important to recognize that a variable can store only one value at a time. For example, suppose the following two statements were executed one after another.

```
WIDTH = 36.7
WIDTH = 105.2
```

The value 36.7 is stored in the variable WIDTH after the first statement is executed. The second statement, however, replaces that value with the new value 105.2, and the first value is lost.

Consider these two statements:

```
TEMP1 = -52.6
TEMP2 = TEMP1
```

The first statement stores the value −52.6 in TEMP1. The second statement stores in TEMP2 the same value that is stored in TEMP1. Note that the value in TEMP1 is not lost; both TEMP1 and TEMP2 now contain the value −52.6.

Often we will want to calculate a new value using arithmetic operations with other variables and constants. For instance, assume that the variable RADIUS has been assigned a value, and we now want to calculate the area of a circle having that radius. To do so, we need to square the radius and then multiply by the value of π. Table 2-2 shows the FORTRAN expressions for the basic arithmetic operations. Note that an asterisk instead of an X is used to represent multiplication to avoid confusion since AXB (commonly used in algebra to indicate the product of A and B) represents a single variable name in FORTRAN. Division and exponentiation also have new symbols since we do not have a method for raising or lowering characters on a keypunch or terminal line.

TABLE 2-2 Arithmetic Operations in Algebraic Form and FORTRAN

OPERATION	ALGEBRAIC FORM	FORTRAN
Addition	$A + B$	A + B
Subtraction	$A - B$	A − B
Multiplication	$A \times B$	A*B
Division	$\frac{A}{B}$	A/B
Exponentiation	A^3	A**3

Since several operations can be combined in one arithmetic expression, it is important to determine the priorities of the operations (the order in which the operations are performed). For instance, consider the following assignment statement that calculates the area of a circle:

```
AREA = PI*RADIUS**2
```

If the exponentiation is done first, we compute $\pi \cdot (\text{RADIUS})^2$, but if multiplication is done first, we compute $(\pi \cdot \text{RADIUS})^2$. Note that the two computations yield different results. The order of priorities for computations in FORTRAN is given in Table 2-3 and follows the standard algebraic priorities.

TABLE 2-3 Priorities of Arithmetic Operations

PRIORITY	OPERATION
First	Parentheses
Second	Exponentiation
Third	Multiplication and division
Fourth	Addition and subtraction

Note that operations in parentheses are performed first. When executing the previous FORTRAN statement, the radius would be squared first and the result then multiplied by PI, thus correctly determining the area of the circle. Remember that we are assuming that PI and RADIUS have been initialized. The following statements also correctly compute the area of the circle:

```
AREA = PI*RADIUS*RADIUS
```

or

```
AREA = 3.141593*RADIUS*RADIUS
```

When there are two operations on the same priority level, as in addition and subtraction, all operations except exponentiation are performed from left to right as they are encountered in an expression. Thus, B − C + D would be evaluated as (B − C) + D. If two exponentiations occur sequentially in FORTRAN, as in A**B**C, they will be evaluated right to left, as in A**(B**C). Thus, 2**3**2 is 2^9 or 512 as opposed to (2**3)**2, which is 8^2 or 64.

A more complex arrangement is represented by the following expression for one of the real roots of a quadratic equation:

$$X1 = \frac{-B + \sqrt{B^2 - 4AC}}{2A}$$

where A, B, and C are coefficients of the quadratic equation. Since division by zero is not possible on a computer, we will assume $A \neq 0$. The value of X1 can then be computed in FORTRAN with the following statement, assuming that the variables A, B, and C have been previously initialized:

```
X1 = (-B + (B**2 - 4.0*A*C)**0.5)/(2.0*A)
```

To check the order of operations in a long expression, it is best to start with the operations inside parentheses. That is, find the operation done first, then second, and so on. The following diagram outlines this procedure, using underline braces to show the steps of operations. Beneath each brace is the value that has been calculated in that step.

```
X1 = (-B + (B**2 - 4.0*A*C)**0.5)/(2.0*A)
```

$$-B \qquad B^2 - 4AC \qquad 2A$$

$$-B + \sqrt{B^2 - 4AC}$$

$$\frac{-B + \sqrt{B^2 - 4AC}}{2A}$$

As shown in the final brace, the desired value is computed by this expression. The placement of the parentheses is very important in this statement. If the outside set of parentheses on the numerator were omitted, our assignment statement becomes:

```
X1 = -B + (B**2 - 4.0*A*C)**0.5/(2.0*A)
```

$$\underbrace{-B}\quad \underbrace{B^2 - 4AC}\quad \underbrace{2A}$$

$$\sqrt{B^2 - 4AC}$$

$$\frac{\sqrt{B^2 - 4AC}}{2A}$$

$$-B + \frac{\sqrt{B^2 - 4AC}}{2A}$$

As you can see, omission of the outside set of parentheses would cause the wrong value to be calculated as a root of the original quadratic equation. Omission of a different set of parentheses would result in the following expression:

```
X1 = (-B + B**2 - 4.0*A*C**0.5)/(2.0*A)
```

$$-B + B^2 - 4A\sqrt{C} \qquad 2A$$

$$\frac{-B + B^2 - 4A\sqrt{C}}{2A}$$

Again, the wrong value has been calculated. If all parentheses were omitted, the expression becomes:

```
X1 = -B + B**2 - 4.0*A*C**0.5/2.0*A
```

$$-B \qquad B^2 \qquad \sqrt{C}$$

$$\frac{4A\sqrt{C}A}{2}$$

$$-B + B^2 - \frac{4A^2\sqrt{C}}{2}$$

Still another incorrect value has been computed.

As shown in the previous examples, omitting necessary parentheses results in incorrect calculations. Using extra parentheses to emphasize the order of calculations is permissible. In fact, it is advisable to insert extra parentheses in a statement if it makes the statement more readable.

You may also want to break a long statement into several smaller statements. Recall that the expression $B^2 - 4AC$ in the quadratic equation is also called a discriminant. The solution could then be calculated with the following equations after initialization of A, B, and C:

```
DISCR = B**2 - 4.0*A*C
X1 = (-B + DISCR**0.5)/(2.0*A)
X2 = (-B - DISCR**0.5)/(2.0*A)
```

In the above statements, we assume that the discriminant, DISCR, is positive, thus enabling us to obtain the two real roots to the equation, X1 and X2. If the discriminant were negative, an execution error would occur if we attempted to take the square root of the negative value. Also, if the value of A were zero, we would get an execution error for attempting to divide by zero. In later chapters we will learn techniques for handling both these situations.

We often use variables as *counters* in our FORTRAN programs. We first initialize the counter to a certain value and then later, under certain conditions, change it to another value. An example of a statement to increment by 1 the counter COUNTR, which we will assume was explicitly declared with an INTEGER statement, is given below:

```
COUNTR = COUNTR + 1
```

At first, this statement may look invalid because, algebraically, COUNTR cannot be equal to COUNTR + 1. But remember, in FORTRAN, this statement means "COUNTR is assigned the value of COUNTR plus 1." Hence, if the old value of COUNTR is 0, the new value of COUNTR after executing this statement will be 1.

TRUNCATION AND MIXED MODE

When an arithmetic operation is performed using two real numbers, the *intermediate result* of the operation is a real value. For example, the circumference of a circle can be calculated as

```
CIRCUM = PI*DIAM
```

or

```
CIRCUM = 3.141593*DIAM
```

In both statements, we have multiplied two real values, giving a real intermediate result, which is then stored in the real variable CIRCUM.

Similarly, arithmetic operations between two integers yield an intermediate integer. For instance, if I and J represent two integers such that I ≤ J, then the number of integers in the interval I through J can be calculated with the following statement:

```
INTERV = J - I + 1
```

Thus, if I = 6 and J = 11, then INTERV will contain 6, the number of integers in the set {6, 7, 8, 9, 10, 11}.

Now consider the statement:

```
LENGTH = SIDE*3.5
```

Assuming implicit typing of the variables, we know that the multiplication between the two real values yields a real intermediate result. In this case, however, the real intermediate result is stored in an integer variable. When the computer stores a real number as an integer variable, it ignores the fractional portion and stores only the whole number portion of the real number. The loss of the fractional portion of a real value when it is stored in an integer variable is called *truncation*.

There are also computations with integers that give unexpected results. Consider the following statement that computes the average or mean of two integers, N1 and N2.

```
MEAN = (N1 + N2)/2
```

Since all the variables involved in the arithmetic operations are integers, the result of evaluating the expression will be an integer. Thus, if N1 = 2 and N2 = 4, the mean value is the expected value, 3. But if N1 = 2 and N2 = 1, the result of the division of 3 by 2 will be 1 instead of 1.5, because the division involves two integers and, hence, the intermediate result must be an integer. At first glance it might seem that we can solve this problem if we call the average by the real variable name AVE, instead of MEAN, and use this statement:

```
AVE = (N1 + N2)/2
```

Unfortunately, this does not correct our answer. The result of integer arithmetic is still an integer, and all we have done is move the integer result into a real variable. Thus, if N1 = 2 and N2 = 1, then (N1+N2)/2 = 1, and AVE = 1.0, not 1.5. One way of correcting this problem is to explicitly declare N1 and N2 to be real values and use the following statement to calculate the average:

```
AVE = (N1 + N2)/2.0
```

Note that there is a difference between rounding and truncation. With rounding, the result is the integer closest to the real number. Truncation, however, causes any decimal portion to be dropped. Thus, if we divide the integer 15 by the integer 8, the truncated result is 1, the integer portion of 1.875.

The effects of truncation can also be seen in the next statement, which appears to be calculating the square root of NUM.

```
ROOT = NUM**(1/2)
```

However, since 1/2 is truncated to 0, we are really raising NUM to the zero power. Hence, ROOT will always contain the value 1.0, no matter what value is in NUM.

We have seen that an operation involving only real values yields a real intermediate result, and an operation involving only integer values yields an integer intermediate result. FORTRAN also accepts a *mixed-mode operation*, which is an operation involving an integer value and a real value. The intermediate result of a mixed operation is always a real value. The final result depends on the type of the variable that is used to store the result of the mixed-mode operation. Consider the following arithmetic statement for computing the perimeter of a square whose sides are real values.

```
PERI = 4*SIDE
```

The above multiplication is a mixed operation between the integer constant 4 and the real variable SIDE. The intermediate result is real and is correctly stored in the real result PERI.

Using mixed mode, we can now calculate correctly the square root of NUM, using this statement:

```
ROOT = NUM**0.5
```

The mixed-mode exponentiation yields a real result, which is stored in ROOT.

To compute the area of a square with real sides, we could use the mixed-mode expression

```
AREA = SIDE**2
```

or the real-mode expression

```
AREA = SIDE**2.0
```

The result in both cases is real, but the mixed-mode form is preferable in this case. Exponentiation to an integer power is done internally in the computer with a series of multiplications such as SIDE times SIDE. If an exponent is real, however, the operation is performed by the arithmetic logic unit using logarithms. Thus, SIDE**2.0 is actually computed as antilog(2.0 × log(SIDE)). Using logarithms can introduce a small error into the calculations. While 5.0**2 is always 25.0, 5.0**2.0 is often computed to be

24.99999. Also, note that(−2.0)**2 is a valid operation while (−2.0)**2.0 is an invalid operation because the logarithm of a negative value does not exist and, hence, an execution error occurs. As a general guide when raising numbers to an integer power, use an integer exponent, even though the base number is real.

Mixed-mode expressions may still lose accuracy through truncation if there are operations between integers embedded in the expression. For instance, assume that we want to calculate the volume of a sphere with radius R. The volume is computed by multiplying 4/3 times π times the radius cubed. Hence, the following mixed-mode statement at first appears correct.

```
VOL = (4/3)*3.141593*R**3
```

The expression contains integer and real values, so the result will be a real value. However, the division of 4 by 3 will yield the intermediate value of 1, not 1.333333; therefore the final answer will be incorrect.

INTRINSIC FUNCTIONS

There are many simple operations commonly needed in algorithms, such as computing the square root of a value, computing the absolute value of a number, or computing the sine of an angle. Because these operations are so common, built-in functions called *intrinsic functions* are available to handle all these computations for us. Thus, instead of using the arithmetic expression X**0.5, we can use the intrinsic function SQRT(X). Similarly, we can refer to the absolute value of B by ABS(B). A list of some common intrinsic functions appears in Table 2-4, and a complete list of the intrinsic functions in the FORTRAN 77 language is contained in Appendix C, along with a brief description of each function.

Note that the name of the function determines the type (real or integer) of value that is being computed. Thus, the SQRT and ABS functions compute a real value, while the IABS function computes an integer value. The *argument*, or input to the function, is enclosed in parentheses and follows the name of the function. This argument can be any arithmetic expression, but must be the proper type. The input to the functions SQRT and ABS must be real (see Table 2-4), and the input to the function IABS must be integer. There are a few exceptions, but generally a function with real input has real output while a function with integer input has an integer output. Intrinsic functions will be discussed in more detail in Chapter 5.

Suppose the variable ANGLE contains the value of an angle in degrees, and we want to store the cosine of ANGLE in the variable COSA. From Table 2-4, we see that the cosine function COS assumes that its argument is in radians. We can change the degrees to radians (1 degree = $\pi/180$ radians) and compute the cosine of the angle in the following statement:

```
COSA = COS(A*(3.141593/180.0))
```

TABLE 2-4 Common Intrinsic Functions

Function Name and Argument	Function Value	Comment
SQRT(X)	$\sqrt{X}$	Square root of X
ABS(X)	$\|X\|$	Absolute value of a real number
IABS(I)	$\|I\|$	Absolute value of an integer number
SIN(X)	Sine of angle X	X must be in radians
COS(X)	Cosine of angle X	X must be in radians
TAN(X)	Tangent of angle X	X must be in radians
EXP(X)	e^X	e raised to the X power
ALOG(X)	$\log_e X$	Natural log of X, $X > 0$
ALOG10(X)	$\log_{10} X$	Common log of X, $X > 0$
INT(X)	Integer portion of X	Converts a real value to an integer value by truncation
REAL(I)	Real value of I	Converts an integer value to a real value
MOD(I,J)	Integer remainder of I/J	Remainder function, $J \neq 0$

The inside set of parentheses is not required, but serves to emphasize the conversion factor.

It is also acceptable to use one intrinsic function as the argument of another one. For example, we can compute $e^{|A|}$ with the expression EXP (ABS(A)). When *nesting* functions, as done here, be sure to enclose the argument of each function in its own set of parentheses. Using one function as the argument of another function is also called *composition* of functions.

It is important to observe that an intrinsic function and its argument represent a value. This value can be used in other computations or stored in other memory locations. It does not in itself, however, represent a storage location and thus a function can never appear on the left of an equal sign; it must always be on the right side of an equal sign. For example, to compute the square root of X, we can use the statement

```
ROOT = SQRT(X)
```

but we cannot reverse the order and begin the statement with SQRT(X) because SQRT(X) is not a variable name. The intrinsic square root function could be used in the computation of a root of the quadratic equation which was used in a previous example as shown below:

```
X1 = (-B + SQRT(B**2 - 4.0*A*C))/(2.0*A)
```

The next two sections solve two problems involving arithmetic computations. Hopefully, you will try running these simple programs on your computer, and a caution is thus necessary. Do not expect a program run on two different computers (or compilers) to yield exactly the same answers. Because of differences in the computer architectures (or the compiler programs), slight variations in the answers are to be expected. Therefore, if you run a sample program for which we got an answer of 13.7100, don't be surprised if your computer gives an answer of 13.7099.

2-6 PROBLEM SOLVING—FOREIGN CURRENCY EXCHANGE

The problem of converting currency of one country to another requires only a simple computation. Since we have not introduced the FORTRAN statements for loops (you do not have to wait long; they are in the next chapter), the algorithm will only convert one amount each time that it is performed. The fourth phase of our problem-solving process is algorithm development. Since we now know some FORTRAN, this phase will include decomposition, refinement, and translation of the refined algorithm into FORTRAN.

You are taking a trip to France soon. There are a number of items you would like to purchase, but you need to convert the prices in francs to dollars to see if you can afford them. Write a program to read a price in francs, convert it to dollars, and print it. Use the exchange rate of 6.2 francs to the dollar.

PROBLEM STATEMENT

Write a program to convert an amount in francs to dollars.

INPUT/OUTPUT DESCRIPTION

The input is a number that represents francs. The output will be the number read in francs and the computed value in dollars.

HAND EXAMPLE

After visiting Versailles, you plan to get an unframed print of a painting of the famous hall of mirrors. A friend has told you that the cost is 85 francs. To convert this to dollars, we divide 85 by 6.2. The print will cost $13.71.

ALGORITHM DEVELOPMENT

Decomposition

Read amount in francs
Convert amount to dollars
Print both amounts

Refinement in Pseudocode

```
CONVRT:  BEGIN
            READ francs
            dollars ← francs/6.2
            PRINT francs, dollars
         END
```

FORTRAN Program

```
      PROGRAM CONVRT
*
*   THIS PROGRAM CONVERTS FRANCS TO DOLLARS
*
      PRINT*, 'ENTER AMOUNT IN FRANCS'
      READ*, FRANCS
      DOLLAR = FRANCS/6.2
      PRINT*, FRANCS, 'FRANCS =', DOLLAR, 'DOLLARS'
      END
```

TESTING

Enter the program in your computer system and test it with the hand example. The output conversation will be:

```
ENTER AMOUNT IN FRANCS
?85.0
85.0000 FRANCS = 13.7100 DOLLARS
```

Why did we call the amount in dollars DOLLAR instead of DOLLARS? Change it and try DOLLARS in your program. It should give a compiler error because DOLLARS is too long for a variable name.

2-7 PROBLEM SOLVING—BACTERIA GROWTH

You are working part time in a laboratory as an assistant to a biologist who is doing research on a new strain of bacteria. Since the growth of bacteria in a colony can be modelled with an exponential equation (you know this from your college algebra class), you have offered to write a computer program that will predict how many bacteria will be in the colony after a specified amount of time. (You are also trying to get a raise, aren't you!) Suppose that, for this type of bacteria, the equation to predict growth is:

$$y_{new} = y_{old}\, e^{1.386t}$$

where y_{new} is the new number of bacteria in the colony, y_{old} is the initial number of bacteria in the colony, and t is the elapsed time in hours. Thus, when $t = 0$, we have:

$$y_{new} = y_{old}\, e^{1.386 \cdot 0} = y_{old}$$

PROBLEM STATEMENT

Using the equation

$$y_{new} = y_{old}\, e^{1.386t}$$

predict the number of bacteria (y_{new}) in a bacteria colony given the initial number in the colony (y_{old}) and the time that has elapsed (t) in hours.

INPUT/OUTPUT DESCRIPTION

The input will be two values, the initial number of bacteria and the time elapsed. The output will be the number of bacteria in the colony after the elapsed time.

HAND EXAMPLE

You will need your calculator or a logarithm table for these calculations. For $t = 1$ hour and $y_{old} = 1$ bacterium, the new colony contains:

$$y_{new} = 1 \cdot e^{1.386 \cdot 1} = 4.00$$

After 6 hours, the size of the colony is:

$$y_{new} = 1 \cdot e^{1.386 \cdot 6} = 4088.77$$

If we had started with 2 bacteria, after 6 hours the size of the colony is

$$y_{new} = 2 \cdot e^{1.386 \cdot 6} = 8177.54$$

(These numbers really make you appreciate penicillin!)

ALGORITHM DEVELOPMENT

Decomposition

Read y_{old}, t
Compute y_{new}
Print y_{old}, t, y_{new}

Refinement in Pseudocode

GROWTH: BEGIN
READ y_{old}, t
$y_{new} \leftarrow y_{old}\, e^{1.386t}$
PRINT y_{old}, t, y_{new}
END

FORTRAN **Program**

```
      PROGRAM GROWTH
*
*   THIS PROGRAM PREDICTS BACTERIA GROWTH
*
      PRINT*, 'ENTER INITIAL POPULATION'
      READ*, YOLD
      PRINT*, 'ENTER TIME ELAPSED IN HOURS'
      READ*, TIME
      YNEW = YOLD*EXP(1.386*TIME)
      PRINT*, 'INITIAL POPULATION =', YOLD
      PRINT*, 'TIME ELAPSED (HOURS) =', TIME
      PRINT*, 'PREDICTED POPULATION =', YNEW
      END
```

TESTING

The output from one of our hand examples is:

```
ENTER INITIAL POPULATION
?1.0
ENTER TIME ELAPSED IN HOURS
?6.0
INITIAL POPULATION = 1.0000
TIME ELAPSED (HOURS) = 6.0000
PREDICTED POPULATION = 4088.7722
```

Try some other values in the program. (Not by hand. Actually enter the program and use different data in it.) Can you make the numbers so large that you get an execution error? Computers do have upper limits, don't they? What if you enter a negative time? The population decreases instead of increasing. Once the population goes below 1, the model is not usable.

SUMMARY

In this chapter we have discussed the fundamental concepts of computers. The process of converting a computer program into a form that the computer can understand and execute was described. Most importantly, we introduced the basic FORTRAN statements for input, output, and computations. We have already written a number of complete programs. Hopefully, this has been so much fun that you are eager to begin Chapter 3 and learn how to use more new FORTRAN statements!

KEY WORDS

argument
arithmetic expression
arithmetic logic unit (ALU)
assembler
assembly language
batch processing
binary
bug
central processing unit (CPU)
compilation
compiler
constant
conversational computing
debugging
diagnostic
editor
execution
exponential notation
explicit typing
formatted I/O
FORTRAN 77
hardware
high-level language
implicit typing
initialize
integer value
interactive computing
intrinsic function
linkage
list-directed I/O
literal
logic error
machine language
memory
microcomputer
microprocessor
mixed-mode operation
permanent workspace
processor
real value
rounding
software
specification statement
syntax error
temporary workspace
time-sharing
truncation
variable

DEBUGGING AIDS

If a program is not working correctly, the first thing you should do is *echo* the values that you read in the program. That is, immediately after reading them, print them out to be sure that the values you want to give the variables are being used. A common mistake is to enter the data values in the wrong order. Instead of entering the initial number of bacteria followed by the elapsed time, you enter them in the reverse order.

If the input portion of your program is working correctly, check your assignment statements.

1 If the assignment statement is long, break it up into several smaller statements.

2 Double-check your placement of parentheses. Add parentheses if you are not sure what order the computer will use to compute the operations involved. Be sure that you always have the same number of left parentheses as right parentheses.

3 Review each variable name on the right side of the equal sign to be sure you have spelled it exactly as previously used. (Did you use V when you should have used VEL?)

4 Make sure all variables on the right side of the assignment statement have been previously initialized.

5 Be sure that arguments to intrinsic functions are in the correct units (e.g., trigonometric functions use angles in radians instead of degrees).

6 If you have mixed-mode operations for operations other than exponentiation, use the functions INT and REAL so that operations use all integer or all real values.

7 Finally, remember that explicit typing always overrides the implicit typing rules.

If you still are not getting correct answers, check the variable names on the PRINT statements. Do you have the correct names listed?

If these steps do not help you isolate your error, ask your instructor or a classmate to check the statement. If no one is available to check your statement and you cannot find the error, start over on a clean sheet of paper. Sometimes it is very hard to spot your own errors because you know what you want the statement to do, and you read that into the statement when searching for errors.

STYLE/TECHNIQUE GUIDES

A program should be written so that another person competent in FORTRAN could readily understand the statements and interpret the procedures. This is especially important since the person updating a program is not always the person who originally wrote it. These are challenging requirements to meet, and necessitate building good habits from the beginning when learning a language. The following guides will help you develop a style and technique that will enable you to meet these requirements.

1 Use variable names that indicate something about the values being stored in the variable. For instance, represent velocity by VEL instead of A, or X1, or something obscure. Use the specification statements if needed to specify the correct type for your variable names.

2 Use a consistent number of significant digits in constants. Do not use 3.14 as a value for PI in the beginning of your program and later use 3.141593 as the value at the end. Accomplish this con-

sistency by initializing variables that will be used frequently in the program such as

```
PI = 3.141593
```

and subsequently using PI instead of a constant as you need the value.

3 Break long expressions into smaller expressions and recombine them in another statement. A complicated fraction can be computed by first calculating a numerator, then calculating a denominator, and finally dividing in a separate statement.

4 Insert extra parentheses for readability. It is never wrong to insert extra pairs of parentheses, as long as they are properly located. Extra parentheses often make arithmetic expressions much more readable.

5 Do not mix modes except when beneficial, as in the case of exponents. For example, use B*3.0 instead of B*3, but use B**2 instead of B**2.0.

6 Use intrinsic functions where possible.

7 Explicit typing is an aid in program clarity as well as in error detection. Some programmers prefer to list all variables on specification statements, including those correctly typed by the implicit rules.

8 Develop the habit of echo printing values that you have read.

9 Print the physical units that correspond to numerical values that are being printed. This information is vital for proper interpretation of results.

PROBLEMS

Problems 1 through 10 contain both valid and invalid names. Explain why the invalid names are unacceptable. Identify the valid names as either real or integer type.

1 AREA

2 PERIMETER

3 SALARY

4 INTEREST

5 TAX-RT

6 NET

7 F(X)

8 2TIME

9 TIME2

10 $AMT

For problems 11 through 14, convert the equations into FORTRAN assignment statements. Choose valid variable names and show any explicit specifications that are necessary. Assume that all variables represent real values.

11 amount due = original amount − number of payments × payment amount

12 $\text{monthly payment} = \dfrac{\text{total cost} + \text{insurance}}{24}$

13 total = sales + 0.065 × sales

14 $\text{side} = \sqrt{\text{area}}$

For problems 15 through 18, convert the FORTRAN statements into algebraic form.

15 `GROSS = COMM*SALES + BONUS`

16 `SALARY = RATE*40.0 + RATE*1.5*OVER`

17 `CHECK = SALARY - STATE - FEDRL`

18 `PAYMON = YEARLY/12.0 - TAXES - BONDS`

For problems 19 through 27, compute the value that will be stored in the variable on the left side of the equation if the following values have been initialized.

```
R = 1.1     J = 2
I = 5       X = 6.1
```

(Show your answers in the correct form—real or integer type.)

19 `K = R`

20 `N1 = X`

21 `T = I`

22 `RJ = J`

23 `NUM = (I + 7)/5`

24 `TIME = X + 2.2/R`

25 `TOT = R + I/J + 13.5`

26 `TEMP = (X - R)**2/J`

27 `IBASE = R*J + J*X`

For problems 28 through 30, tell what the segment of code accomplishes.

28
```
A = B
B = A
```

29
```
C = A
A = B
B = C
```

30
```
I = R
R = I
```

We again practice some modifications to the programs given in this chapter before we develop new programs. Give the decomposition, refined pseudocode, and FORTRAN program for each problem. The first set of problems are modifications to the foreign currency program, CONVRT, given on page 60.

31 Modify the foreign currency program so that it converts dollars to francs.

32 Modify the foreign currency program so that it converts pounds sterling to dollars. (Use the exchange rate of 1 pound sterling to $1.95.)

33 Modify the foreign currency program so that it converts deutsche marks to dollars. (Use the exchange rate of 2.4 deutsche marks to $1.00.)

34 Modify the foreign currency program so that it converts dollars to pounds sterling and deutsche marks.

35 Modify the foreign currency program so that it converts francs to deutsche marks.

This set of problems involves modifications to the bacteria growth program, GROWTH, given on page 62.

36 Modify the bacteria growth program so that the time elapsed is entered in minutes even though the equation still requires a time in hours.

37 Modify the bacteria growth program so that the time elapsed is entered in days even though the equation still requires a time in hours.

38 Modify the bacteria growth program so that an initial population is read from the terminal. The program should then compute and print the percent increase in population as time increases from 2 hours to 3 hours.

39 Modify the bacteria growth program so that the program reads two time values from the terminal, where the first time is less than the second time. Compute and print the amount of growth between the two times, assuming an initial population value of 1.

40 Modify the bacteria growth program so that the program reads two time values from the terminal, with no restrictions on which time is larger. Compute and print the amount of growth between the two times, assuming an initial population value of 1. (*Hint:* Review the absolute value function and its intrinsic function description.)

41 Modify the bacteria growth program so that the program reads two initial population values and one time value from the terminal. Compute and print the predicted populations using the two different initial population values.

Here are some new programs to develop. Use the five-phase design process.

42 Write a program to convert pounds to tons.

43 Write a program to read the number of hours worked and the hourly pay rate for a student laboratory assistant. Compute and print the amount of money earned. Do not assume special rates for hours over 40.

44 Write a program to compute the perimeter of a rectangle.

45 Write a program to read the coordinates of two points, x_1, y_1, x_2, y_2. Compute the slope of the straight line between these two points where:

$$\text{slope} = \frac{y_2 - y_1}{x_2 - x_1}$$

Print the points and the slope of the line between them.

46 Write a program to read the diameter of a circle. Compute the radius, circumference, and area of the circle. Print these new values in the following form:

```
PROPERTIES OF A CIRCLE WITH DIAMETER XXXXXXX
(1) RADIUS = XXXXXXX
(2) CIRCUMFERENCE = XXXXXXX
(3) AREA = XXXXXXX
```

(Recall that $C = \pi d$ and $A = \pi r^2$, and $\pi = 3.141593$.)

47 Write a program to read a measurement in meters. Print the value read followed by the units, 'METERS'. Convert the measurement to kilometers, and print on the next line, again with the correct units. Convert the measurement to miles, and print on the third line, with correct units. (Recall that 1 mile equals 1.6 kilometers.)

48 A research scientist performed nutrition tests using three animals. Data on each animal includes an identification number, the weight of the animal at the beginning of the experiment, and the weight of the animal at the end of the experiment. Write a program to read this data and print a report. The report is to include the original information plus the percentage increase in weight for each test animal.

49 Write a program to read three resistance values (R_1, R_2, R_3) and compute their combined resistance R_c for the parallel arrangement shown below. Print the values of R_1, R_2, R_3, and R_c.

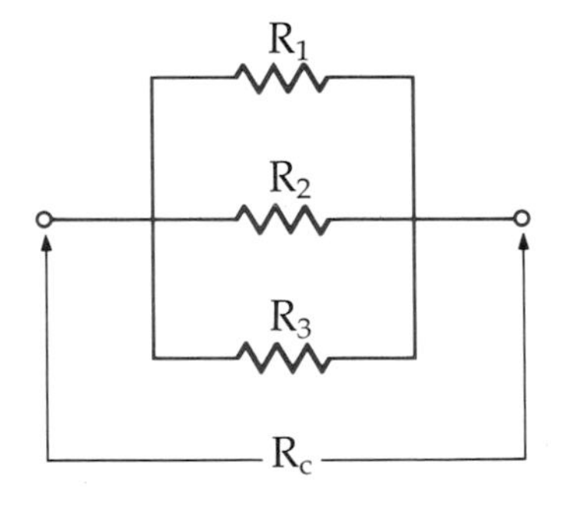

$$R_c = \frac{1}{\frac{1}{R_1} + \frac{1}{R_2} + \frac{1}{R_3}}$$

50 The distance between points (X_a, Y_a) and (X_b, Y_b) is given by

$$DIST = \sqrt{(X_a - X_b)^2 + (Y_a - Y_b)^2}$$

You are given the coordinates of three points

point 1: (X1,Y1)
point 2: (X2,Y2)
point 3: (X3,Y3)

Write a program to read the coordinates. Then calculate and print the distance DIST12 between points 1 and 2, the distance DIST13 between points 1 and 3, and the distance DIST23 between points 2 and 3.

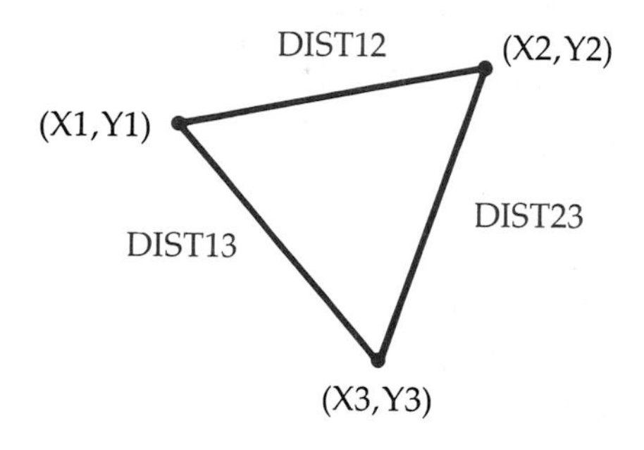

51 Write a program to read the following information from the terminal:

Year

Number of people in civilian labor force

Number of people in military labor force

Compute the percentage of the labor force that is civilian and the percentage that is military. Print the following information:

```
LABOR FORCE  -  YEAR XXXX

NUMBER OF WORKERS (THOUSANDS) AND PERCENTAGE OF WORKERS

CIVILIAN                XXXXXXX                 XXXXXXX
MILITARY                XXXXXXX                 XXXXXXX
TOTAL                   XXXXXXX                 XXXXXXX
```

© Frank Balthis/Jeroboam

PROBLEM SOLVING—Population Study

For a history report, you have been studying the ghost towns that once thrived during gold and silver mining. The population of one of these towns, Shakespeare, New Mexico, has been entered in a data file in your computer system. The period covered is 1880–1980. Write a computer program to determine the two consecutive years in which the population increase was the largest. (See Section 3-8, page 118, for the solution.)

3

CONTROL STRUCTURES

INTRODUCTION

In the last chapter we wrote complete FORTRAN programs, but the steps were executed sequentially, one after the other. The programs typically were composed of reading data, computing new data, and printing the new data. We now want to introduce FORTRAN statements which will allow us to control the sequence of the steps that are executed. This control is achieved through IF THEN ELSE structures and WHILE loops. In addition to presenting the FORTRAN statements for these *control structures,* we also introduce two new data types, character data and logical data. Character data is necessary if we want to work with data that is not numeric. For instance, we will want to use data that represents names, addresses, cities, states, text from a book, and quotations. We will begin using character data now to become more familiar with it. Then, in Chapter 6 (Character Strings) and in Chapter 7 (File Handling), we will specifically study methods and techniques unique to character data. Logical data is presented now because it is used in writing conditions which can be evaluated to be true or false. These conditions are then used in the IF THEN ELSE structure to determine which path to take in the program. Finally, the concept of a data file is presented, along with techniques for detecting the end of the data file as we are reading data from it.

Starting with this chapter, color is used in FORTRAN programs to highlight new statements and techniques.

3-1 NEW DATA TYPES

Numeric values can be represented by the integer and real types of variables that were presented in the last chapter. In fact, the computer will assume that a variable is numeric if no other information is given. If the name of the variable does not appear on an INTEGER or REAL specification statement, the variable will be assumed to be integer if the name begins with one of the letters I through N; otherwise, the variable will be assumed to be real. Therefore, we must use specific statements to identify variables which are not numeric.

CHARACTER DATA

We often refer to character data as *character strings,* because we usually refer to groups or lists of the characters together. For example, a city is usually given one variable name instead of a variable name for each letter in the city. Using character strings in FORTRAN is similar in many respects to using numeric data. We can have character string constants that will always represent the same information. Character string variables will have names and represent character strings that may remain constant or may change. Generally, these character string constants and variables should contain characters from the *FORTRAN character set,* which is composed of the 26 alphabetic letters, the 10 numeric digits, a blank, and the following 12 symbols:

+ − * / = ( ) , . ' $:

If other symbols are used, a program may not execute the same way on one computer as it does on another.

Character constants are always enclosed in apostrophes. These apostrophes are not counted when determining the *length* or number of characters in a constant. If two consecutive apostrophes (not a double quotation mark) are encountered within a character constant, they represent a single apostrophe. Thus, the character constant for the word LET'S is 'LET''S'. The following list gives several examples of character constants and their corresponding lengths.

`'SOLUTION'`	8 characters
`'TIME AND DISTANCE'`	17 characters
`'ABC'`	3 characters
`'CHANNEL 9'`	9 characters
`' $ AMT.'`	7 characters (note the blanks before and after $)
`'84.56-13.7'`	10 characters
`'THREE '`	6 characters (note the blank at the end of the string)
`'CAN''T'`	5 characters
`''''''`	2 characters

A character string variable must always be specified in a nonexecutable specification statement whose general form is:

```
CHARACTER*n  variable list
```

where *n* represents the number of characters in the variable string. For instance, the following statement,

```
CHARACTER*8 CODE, NAME
```

identifies CODE and NAME as variables containing eight characters each. There is no significance to the first letter of the name of a character variable. Character strings of different lengths can be specified on separate statements or on the same statement, as shown below:

```
CHARACTER*10 TITLE
CHARACTER*15 NAME
```

or

```
CHARACTER TITLE*10, NAME*15
```

There are special operations and intrinsic functions for character strings. We will discuss these in detail in Chapter 6. For now, we only need to be able to use character strings in our input and output statements. When a character string is used in a list-directed output statement, the entire character string is printed. Blanks are automatically inserted around it to separate it from other output on the same line. When a character string variable is used in a list-directed input statement, the corresponding data value must be enclosed in apostrophes. If the character string within the apostrophes is longer than the defined length of the character string variable, any extra characters on the right will be discarded. If the character string within the apostrophes is shorter than the length of the character string variable, the extra positions on the right will automatically be filled with blanks. Thus, the character data is *left-justified* in the character string variable.

EXAMPLE 3-1 Character String I/O

Write a complete FORTRAN program to read a name from the terminal and then print the name. Assume that the length of the name is no more than 20 characters.

Solution

DECOMPOSITION

Read name
Print name

REFINEMENT IN PSEUDOCODE

```
OUTPUT:  BEGIN
           READ name
           PRINT name
         END
```

FORTRAN PROGRAM

```
      PROGRAM OUTPUT
*
*  THIS PROGRAM READS AND PRINTS A NAME
*
      CHARACTER*20 NAME
*
      PRINT*, 'ENTER YOUR NAME'
      READ*, NAME
      PRINT*, 'MY NAME IS', NAME
*
      END
```

A typical interaction when running this program is:

```
ENTER YOUR NAME
?'MANUEL GARCIA'
MY NAME IS MANUEL GARCIA
```

Note that the data entered was not 20 characters in length. The padding of blanks on the end is not noticeable with this output. However, if the output line had been

```
PRINT*, NAME, 'IS MY NAME'
```

the interaction would be different:

```
ENTER YOUR NAME
?'MANUEL GARCIA'
MANUEL GARCIA       IS MY NAME
```

Another interaction that could come from the original program is:

```
ENTER YOUR NAME
?'MADELINE KATHLEEN KENNEDY'
MY NAME IS MADELINE KATHLEEN KE
```

The name exceeded the maximum number of characters and thus part of the name was lost. To avoid this, carefully choose the length of your character variables based on the maximum length that you expect. You can also tell the user of your program what length you are expecting. In this example, you could use the following output statement:

```
PRINT*, 'ENTER YOUR NAME (MAXIMUM OF 20 CHARACTERS)'
```

LOGICAL DATA

Logical variables are useful in defining conditions for IF THEN ELSE structures and WHILE loops. A logical variable can have one of two values: true or false. A logical variable must be specified with a specification statement whose form is:

```
LOGICAL variable names
```

Logical constants are .TRUE. and .FALSE.. Therefore, the statements to identify a logical variable and then give it a value of false are:

```
LOGICAL DONE
DONE = .FALSE.
```

A logical value in list-directed output will be printed as the letter T or the letter F, depending on whether the value is .TRUE. or .FALSE.. For list-directed input, the value for a logical variable depends on the first nonblank character in the character string that is read next. If the first nonblank letter is 'T', then the variable is true. If the first nonblank letter is 'F', then the variable is false. Any other situation causes an execution error.

3-2 IF THEN ELSE STRUCTURE

In Chapter 1 we presented the pseudocode for three forms of the IF THEN ELSE structure. In this section we present the corresponding FORTRAN statements. All forms of the IF THEN ELSE structure use a condition to determine which path to take in the structure. Therefore, before we discuss the forms of these statements, we want to discuss logical expressions which are used as the conditions to be tested.

A *logical expression* is analogous to an arithmetic expression in many ways, but it is always evaluated to either true or false, instead of a number. The simplest form of a logical expression is a logical variable. Logical expressions can also be formed using *relational operators*, which are listed below:

RELATIONAL OPERATOR	INTERPRETATION
.EQ.	is equal to
.NE.	is not equal to
.LT.	is less than
.LE.	is less than or equal to
.GT.	is greater than
.GE.	is greater than or equal to

Numeric variables can be used on both sides of the relational operators to yield a logical expression whose value is either true or false. For example, consider the logical expression

A.EQ.B

where A and B are real values. If the value of A is equal to the value of B, then the logical expression A.EQ.B is true. Otherwise, the expression is false. Similarly, if the value of X is 4.5, then the expression

X.GT.3.0

is true.

We can also combine two logical expressions into a *compound* logical expression with the *connectors* .OR. and .AND.. When two logical expressions are joined by .OR., the entire expression is true if either or both expressions are true. It is false only when both expressions are false. When two logical expressions are joined by .AND., the entire expression is true only if both expressions are true. These connectors (or *logical operators*) can be used only with complete logic expressions on both sides of the connector. For example, A.LT.B.OR.A.LT.C is a valid compound logical expression because .OR. joins A.LT.B and A.LT.C. However, A.LT.B.OR.C is an invalid compound expression because C is a numeric variable, not a complete logical expression.

Logical expressions can also be preceded by the connector .NOT.. This connector changes the value of the expression to the opposite value. Hence, if A.GT.B is true, then .NOT.A.GT.B is false. The following statement

```
IF(.NOT.A.LT.B)X = 1.5
```

is also equivalent to

```
IF(A.GE.B)X = 1.5
```

A logical expression may contain several connectors, as in

```
IF(.NOT.(A.LT.15.0).OR.KT.EQ.ISUM)TOT = 0.0
```

The hierarchy of execution of connectors, from highest to lowest, is .NOT., .AND., .OR.. Thus, in the above statement, the logical expression A.LT.15.0 would be evaluated, and its value, true or false, would be reversed by the .NOT. connector. Then this value would be used, along with the value of KT.EQ.ISUM, with the connector .OR.. For example, if A is 5.0, KT is 5, and ISUM is 5, then the left expression is false and the right expression is true. Since they are connected with .OR., the entire expression is true, and TOT will be set to 0.0.

IF STATEMENT

One form of the IF THEN ELSE structure omitted the ELSE clause. There are two FORTRAN statements that implement this form. One statement handles the situation where only one step is performed when a condition is true; the other statement handles the situation where several steps are to be performed when the condition is true. The general form of the *IF statement* with one step to perform is:

IF(*logical expression*) *executable statement*

Execution consists of the following steps:

1. If the logical expression is true, we execute the statement after the logical expression and then go to the next sequential statement.
2. If the logical expression is false, we jump immediately to the next sequential statement.

A typical IF statement is:

```
IF(A.LT.B)SUM = SUM + A
```

If the value of A is less than the value of B, then the value of A is added to SUM. If the value of A is greater than or equal to B, then control passes to whatever statement follows the IF statement in the program. Some other examples of IF statements are:

```
IF(TIME.GT.1.5)READ*, DIST
IF(DEN.LE.0.0)PRINT*, DEN
IF(-4.NE.NUM)NUM = NUM + 1
```

The executable statement that follows the logical expression is typically a computation or an input/output statement. It cannot be another IF statement.

There are many instances when we would like to perform more than one statement if a logical expression is true. The IF statement that allows us to perform any number of statements if a logical expression is true uses the words THEN and ENDIF to identify these steps. The general form is:

```
IF(logical expression)THEN
   statement 1
   statement 2
      ⋮
   statement n
ENDIF
```

Execution consists of the following steps:

1 If the logical expression is true, we execute statement 1 through statement *n*, and then go to the statement following ENDIF.

2 If the logical expression is false, we jump immediately to the statement following ENDIF.

Although not required, the statements to be performed when the logical expression is true should be indented to indicate that they are a group of statements within the IF statement.

EXAMPLE 3-2 Zero Divide

Assume that you have calculated the numerator NUM (explicitly typed REAL) and the denominator DEN of a fraction. Before dividing the two values, you want to see if DEN is zero. If DEN is zero, you want to print an error message and stop the program. If DEN is not zero, you want to compute the decimal value and print it. Write the statements to perform these steps.

Solution

```
      IF(DEN.EQ.0.0)THEN
         PRINT*, 'DENOMINATOR IS ZERO'
         STOP
      ENDIF
*
      FRACT = NUM/DEN
      PRINT*, 'FRACTION = ', FRACT  ◇
```

IF statements can also be nested. The following construction includes an IF statement within an IF statement.

```
IF(logical expression 1)THEN
   statement 1
   statement 2
      :
   statement n
   IF(logical expression 2)THEN
      statement n + 1
      statement n + 2
         :
      statement m
   ENDIF
   statement m + 1
   statement m + 2
      :
   statement p
ENDIF
statement q
```

Again, the indenting of statements within the construction is not required but makes the logic much easier to follow. If logical expression 1 is true, we then always execute statements 1 through n, and statements $m + 1$ through p. If logical expression 2 is true, then we also execute statements $n + 1$ through m. If logical expression 1 is false, we immediately go to the statement after the second ENDIF, statement q.

Consider the statements below:

```
IF(GPA.GE.3.0)THEN
   PRINT*, 'HONOR ROLL'
   IF(GPA.GT.3.5)THEN
      PRINT*, 'PRESIDENT''S LIST'
   ENDIF
ENDIF
```

If the GPA is less than 3.0, the entire construction is skipped. If the GPA is between 3.0 and 3.5, only HONOR ROLL is printed. If the GPA is greater than 3.5, then HONOR ROLL is printed, followed on the next line by PRESIDENT'S LIST.

IF ELSE STATEMENT

The IF ELSE statement allows us to execute one set of statements if the condition is true, and a different set if the condition is not true. The general form of the IF ELSE statement is:

```
IF(logical expression)THEN
    statement 1
    statement 2
       ⋮
    statement n
ELSE
    statement n + 1
    statement n + 2
       ⋮
    statement m
ENDIF
```

If the logical expression is true, then statements 1 through n are executed. If the logical expression is false, then statements $n + 1$ through m are executed. Any of the statements can also be other IF or IF ELSE statements to provide a nested structure to the statements.

EXAMPLE 3-3 Velocity Computation

Give the statements for calculating the velocity VEL of a cable car. The variable DIST contains the distance of the cable car from the nearest tower. Use

$$\text{vel} = 2.425 + 0.00175d^2 \text{ ft/sec}$$

if the cable car is within 30 feet of the tower. Use

$$\text{vel} = 0.625 + 0.12d - 0.00025d^2 \text{ ft/sec}$$

if the cable car is more than 30 feet from the tower.

Correct Solution

```
IF(DIST.LE.30.0)THEN
   VEL = 2.425 + 0.00175*DIST*DIST
ELSE
   VEL = 0.625 + 0.12*DIST - 0.00025*DIST*DIST
ENDIF
```

Incorrect Solution

```
IF(DIST.LE.30.0)VEL = 2.425 + 0.00175*DIST*DIST
VEL = 0.625 + 0.12*DIST - 0.00025*DIST*DIST
```

This incorrect solution points out a very common error. Let us follow the execution of these two statements to find the error. Suppose DIST is greater than 30. Then the first logical expression is false, and we therefore proceed to the next statement to calculate

VEL. This part works fine. But now suppose the logical expression is true; that is, DIST is less than or equal to 30. We then execute the assignment statement on the IF statement, thus correctly calculating VEL when DIST is less than or equal to 30. But the next statement that is executed is the other assignment statement, which replaces the correct value in VEL with an incorrect value. ◇

IF ELSE IF STATEMENT

When we nest several levels of IF ELSE statements, it can become difficult to determine which conditions must be true (or false) in order to execute a particular set of statements. In these cases, the *IF ELSE IF statement* can often be used to clarify the program logic. The general form of this statement is illustrated below:

```
IF(condition 1)THEN
   statement 1
      ⋮
   statement m
ELSEIF(condition 2)THEN
   statement m + 1
      ⋮
   statement n
ELSEIF(condition 3)THEN
   statement n + 1
      ⋮
   statement p
ELSE
   statement p + 1
      ⋮
   statement q
ENDIF
```

We have shown two ELSE IF clauses, but there may be more or less in an actual construction. If condition 1 is true, then only statements 1 through *m* will be executed. If condition 1 is false and condition 2 is true, then only statements $m + 1$ through *n* will be executed. If conditions 1 and 2 are false and condition 3 is true, then only statements $n + 1$ through *p* are executed. If more than one condition is true, then the first one encountered will be the only one executed.

If none of the conditions are true, then statements $p + 1$ through *q* which follow the ELSE are executed. If there is not a final ELSE clause, and none of the conditions are true, then the entire construction is skipped. The IF ELSE IF form is also called a CASE structure because a number of cases are tested. Each case is defined by its corresponding condition.

EXAMPLE 3-4 Weight Category

An analysis of a group of weight measurements involves converting a weight value into an integer category number that is determined as follows:

Category	Weight (pounds)
1	weight $\leq$ 50.0
2	50.0 $<$ weight $\leq$ 125.0
3	125.0 $<$ weight $\leq$ 200.0
4	200.0 $<$ weight

Write FORTRAN statements that will put the correct value (1, 2, 3, or 4) into CATEGR based on the value of WEIGHT. Assume that CATEGR has been explicitly typed as an integer variable.

Solution 1

```
IF(WEIGHT.LE.50.0)THEN
   CATEGR = 1
ELSE
   IF(WEIGHT.LE.125.0)THEN
      CATEGR = 2
   ELSE
      IF(WEIGHT.LE.200.0)THEN
         CATEGR = 3
      ELSE
         CATEGR = 4
      ENDIF
   ENDIF
ENDIF
```

Solution 2

```
IF(WEIGHT.LE.50.0)THEN
   CATEGR = 1
ELSEIF(WEIGHT.LE.125.0)THEN
   CATEGR = 2
ELSEIF(WEIGHT.LE.200.0)THEN
   CATEGR = 3
ELSEIF(WEIGHT.GT.200.0)THEN
   CATEGR = 4
ENDIF
```

Solution 2, as you can see, is more compact than Solution 1. It combines the ELSE and IF statements into the single statement ELSEIF and eliminates two of the ENDIF statements. The order of the conditions is very important in Solution 2 because the evaluation will stop as soon as a true condition has been encountered. Change the order of the conditions and the category assignments. Find values of WEIGHT which will cause the CATEGR value to be set incorrectly. ◇

3-3 WHILE LOOP

The WHILE loop is a very important structure for repeating a set of statements as long as a certain condition is true. In pseudocode, the WHILE loop structure is:

```
WHILE condition DO
   statement 1
       ⋮
   statement m
END WHILE
```

While the condition is true, statements 1 through *m* are executed. After the group of statements is executed, the condition is again tested. If the condition is still true, the group of statements is executed again. When the condition is false, execution continues with the statement following the WHILE loop. The variables modified in the group of statements in the WHILE loop must involve the variables tested in the condition of the WHILE loop, or the value of the condition will never change.

Unfortunately, standard FORTRAN 77 does not include a WHILE statement. However, we can implement the WHILE loop with the IF statement as shown below:

```
n  IF(condition)THEN
      statement 1
          ⋮
      statement m
      GO TO  n
   ENDIF
```

In this implementation, we have used an unconditional transfer statement, whose general form is:

```
GO TO  n
```

where *n* is the statement number or label of an executable statement in the program. The execution of the GO TO statement causes the flow of program control to transfer or *branch* to statement *n*.

EXAMPLE 3-5 Average Balance

Write a FORTRAN program to read 12 monthly balances from a checking account. Compute the average balance and print it.

Solution

This problem should sound familiar. In Chapter 1 we developed the algorithm for a solution, and we present here the decomposition and pseudocode that we developed. We can now convert the pseudocode into a FORTRAN program.

Decomposition

Read and total the balances from the last 12 bank statements
Divide the total by 12 to get the average
Print the total

Refinement in Pseudocode

```
MONTHLY:  BEGIN
             total ← 0
             count ← 0
             WHILE count < 12 DO
                READ balance
                total ← total + balance
                count ← count + 1
             END WHILE
             average ← total/12
             PRINT 'MONTHLY AVERAGE', average
          END
```

We use a variable to count the number of balances that have been read. After processing 12 balances, we exit the WHILE loop.

FORTRAN Program

```
      PROGRAM MONTH
*
*  THIS PROGRAM COMPUTES A MONTHLY
*  AVERAGE FROM DATA FOR 12 MONTHS
*
      INTEGER COUNT
*
      TOTAL = 0.0
      COUNT = 0
*
    5 IF(COUNT.LT.12)THEN
         READ*, BAL
         TOTAL = TOTAL + BAL
         COUNT = COUNT + 1
         GO TO 5
      ENDIF
*
      AVERG = TOTAL/12.0
*
      PRINT*, 'MONTHLY AVERAGE', AVERG
*
      END ◇
```

3-4 DATA FILES AND END-OF-DATA SIGNALS

Up to this point, we have entered data that our programs needed using READ statements. When the execution of our program reached a READ statement, we would enter the data by hand, usually following a *prompt* or special character such as a question mark. Every time we reran the program, we had to reenter the data. This becomes very tedious if there are several items of data. An alternate way to enter the data is with a *data file*. The data file is built separately, much as you enter your programs (which are really program files); you can use the editing capabilities of your computer system to correct and update the data file. Each line of the file will correspond to a line of data that you would enter by hand.

Some special statements must be used in your program to use data files. We will present them in this section, along with discussions of how to detect when you have reached the end of your data file when you did not know ahead of time how many entries were in it. We will also show you how to write information into a file from your program instead of displaying it on the terminal screen or printing it with a line printer.

DATA FILES

To use data files, the following forms of input and output statements must be used:

READ(*unit number*,*) *variable list*

WRITE(*unit number*,*) *variable list*

The unit number entry is used to specify the number of the file that we wish to read, or the number of the file into which we want to write data. Since a program may use several different data files, this unit number specifies the file that is to be used with a particular statement. The asterisk following the unit number specifies that you are using list-directed input and output.

Most computer systems have several input or output devices attached to them. Each device is assigned a unit number. For example, if a card reader/punch device has been assigned unit number 7, then the following statement would direct that the values of X and Y be punched into data cards.

```
WRITE(7,*)X, Y
```

Many systems assign the standard input device (terminal keyboard for time-sharing, card reader for batch processing) to unit number 5, and the standard output device (terminal screen for time-sharing, line printer for batch processing) to unit number 6. These are the devices used when your program executes PRINT* or READ* statements. Avoid using preassigned unit numbers with your data files. Thus, if your computer system assigns unit numbers 5, 6, and 7 as defined above, do not use these with your data files. Confusion could result if your program assigned a data file to unit 6, and the program then executed a PRINT* statement.

To use a data file, an additional statement that assigns a unit number to the file is required. The general form of this statement that opens the file and assigns the unit number to it is:

OPEN(UNIT=*integer expression*, FILE=*file name*, STATUS=*literal*)

The integer expression designates the unit number to be used in READ/WRITE statements. The file name refers to the name given to the file when it was built. The STATUS literal tells the computer whether we are opening an input file to be used with READ statements or an output file to be used with WRITE statements. If the file is an input file, then it already has data in it and is specified with STATUS='OLD'. If the file is an output file, then it does not contain data yet, and is specified with STATUS='NEW'.

The OPEN statement must precede any READ/WRITE statements that use the file. The OPEN statement should be executed only once, and therefore should not be inside a loop. Some systems require a REWIND statement after opening an input file in order to position the file at its beginning. The REWIND statement and additional information on building and accessing data files are presented in Chapter 7.

EXAMPLE 3-6 Parallel Resistance

A data file RES3 contains three data lines, each containing a resistance value from a resistor in an instrumentation circuit. Write a complete program to read the three resistances and compute their combined resistance R_c for a parallel arrangement, as shown below:

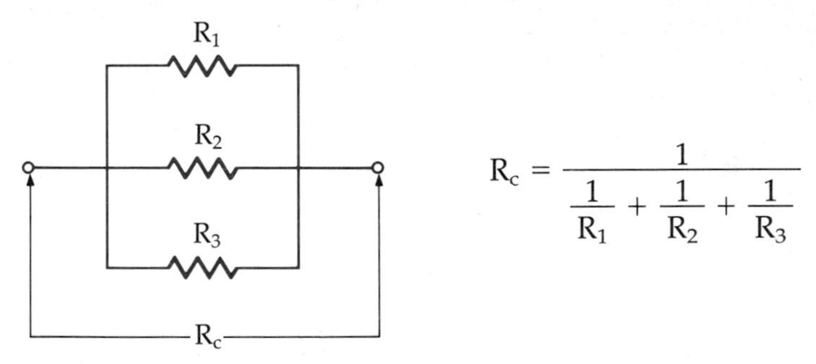

Print the value of R_c. The resistance is measured in ohms.

Solution

Decomposition

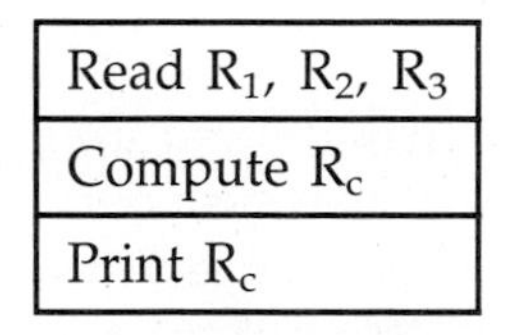

Read R_1, R_2, R_3
Compute R_c
Print R_c

Refinement in Pseudocode

RESIS1: BEGIN
READ R_1, R_2, R_3
PRINT R_1, R_2, R_3

$$R_c \leftarrow \frac{1}{\frac{1}{R_1} + \frac{1}{R_2} + \frac{1}{R_3}}$$

PRINT R_c
END

FORTRAN PROGRAM

```
      PROGRAM RESIS1
*
*   THIS PROGRAM READS A DATA FILE WITH THREE
*   RESISTANCE VALUES AND COMPUTES THEIR
*   EQUIVALENT PARALLEL VALUE
*
      OPEN(UNIT=10, FILE='RES3', STATUS='OLD')
*
      READ(10,*)R1, R2, R3
      PRINT*, 'INPUT VALUES', R1, R2, R3
*
      RC = 1.0/(1.0/R1 + 1.0/R2 + 1.0/R3)
*
      PRINT*, 'COMBINED PARALLEL RESISTANCE =',
     +         RC, 'OHMS'
*
      END
```

DATA FILE RES3

```
1000.0
1100.0
2000.0
```

COMPUTER OUTPUT

```
INPUT VALUES 1000.0000 1100.0000 2000.0000
COMBINED PARALLEL RESISTANCE = 415.0943 OHMS
```

◇

Example 3-6 used a small data file, but the advantages of using a data file become more obvious with large data files. Once the data file is built, no matter how many times you run a program that uses the file, you do not have to reenter the data. Also it is very easy to make changes and updates to a data file with the editing capabilities available on terminal systems. In addition, data files can be shared by various programs, thereby reducing the redundancy of the data and minimizing the memory requirements.

Data files can also be built by a FORTRAN program with WRITE statements. Instead of using the terminal screen or line printer as our output device, we can write the information into a data file. This is often used when plotting data. The data to be plotted is first written into a data file, and the plotter then accesses the data file.

EXAMPLE 3-7 Parallel Resistance with Output File

Modify the program in the solution of Example 3-6 such that the combined resistance R_c is printed and also stored in a file called RESC.

Solution

Since this solution is so similar to that of Example 3-6, we include only the modified FORTRAN program and the input and output from a sample test run.

FORTRAN PROGRAM

```
      PROGRAM RESIS2
*
*  THIS PROGRAM READS A DATA FILE WITH THREE
*  RESISTANCE VALUES AND COMPUTES THEIR EQUIVALENT
*  PARALLEL VALUE WHICH IS STORED IN A FILE
*
      OPEN(UNIT=10, FILE='RES3', STATUS='OLD')
      OPEN(UNIT=11, FILE='RESC', STATUS='NEW')
*
      READ(10,*)R1, R2, R3
      PRINT*, 'INPUT VALUES', R1, R2, R3
*
      RC = 1.0/(1.0/R1 + 1.0/R2 + 1.0/R3)
*
      PRINT*, 'COMBINED PARALLEL RESISTANCE =',
     +        RC, 'OHMS'
      WRITE(11,*)RC
*
      END
```

DATA FILE RES3

```
1000.0
1100.0
2000.0
```

COMPUTER OUTPUT

```
INPUT VALUES 1000.0000 1100.0000 2000.0000
COMBINED PARALLEL RESISTANCE = 415.0943 OHMS
```

DATA FILE RESC

```
415.0943
```

◇

TRAILER SIGNALS

Many applications require the computer to read a number of data values, such as test scores or experimental results. The WHILE loop is a handy structure for the programmer to use to accomplish this task. For instance, if

50 data values are to be read, we could use a WHILE loop of this form:

```
count ← 0
WHILE count <50 DO
   READ value
        ⋮
   count ← count + 1
END WHILE
```

If the number of data values to be read is available in another variable, we can use a WHILE loop of this form:

```
count ← 0
WHILE count <NUM DO
   READ value
        ⋮
   count ← count + 1
END WHILE
```

There are also situations where you do not know prior to executing your program exactly how many data values need to be read. These situations must be handled carefully because, if we execute a READ statement for which there is no data card or data line, an execution error occurs and the execution of our program will be stopped. Two techniques for handling this situation of an unspecified number of input data values are now presented.

The first technique involves the use of a trailer line or a trailer card. These *trailer signals* are data values that signal the end of the data. For example, a valid identification number for a student record may be three digits, ranging from 000 to 500. If we were reading student records, we could use an identification number of 999 as a trailer signal. Thus, as we read each data line, we test the identification number for the value 999. When we find the value 999, we then exit the loop. This process can be structured easily in a WHILE loop, but since the condition will use a value from the data, we must read one student record before entering the WHILE loop.

```
READ ID, student data
WHILE ID ≠ 999 DO
   process student data
   READ ID, student data
END WHILE
```

If we need to know the number of data values read, a counter can be used in the WHILE loop. Be sure not to count the trailer value as a valid data value.

EXAMPLE 3-8 Test Scores with Trailer Signal

A group of test scores have been entered into a data file TESTS1, one score per line. The last line contains a negative value to signal the end of the test scores. Write a complete program to read the data, compute the test average, and print the number of tests and the test average.

Solution

Decomposition

Read and total test scores
Compute average
Print average

Refinement in Pseudocode

```
AVERG1:  BEGIN
            number ← 0
            total ← 0
            READ test
            WHILE test ≥ 0 DO
               number ← number + 1
               total ← total + test
               READ test
            END WHILE
            ave ← total/number
            PRINT number, ave
         END
```

FORTRAN Program

```
      PROGRAM AVERG1
*
*  THIS PROGRAM COMPUTES THE AVERAGE OF A
*  GROUP OF TEST SCORES WHICH ARE FOLLOWED BY A
*  TRAILER LINE IN A DATA FILE
*
      INTEGER TEST, TOTAL
*
      OPEN(UNIT=8, FILE='TESTS1', STATUS='OLD')
*
      NUMBER = 0
      TOTAL = 0
*
      READ(8,*)TEST
*
   20 IF(TEST.GE.0)THEN
         NUMBER = NUMBER + 1
         TOTAL = TOTAL + TEST
         READ(8,*)TEST
         GO TO 20
      ENDIF
*
      AVE = TOTAL/REAL(NUMBER)
*
      PRINT*, 'THE AVERAGE OF', NUMBER,
     +        'TEST SCORES IS', AVE
*
      END
```

Data File TESTS1

```
 85
 92
100
 87
 75
 73
 81
 -1
```

Computer Output

```
THE AVERAGE OF 7 TEST SCORES IS 84.7143
```

◇

END OPTION

If a set of data does not have a trailer signal at the end, and if we do not know the number of data lines in the file, a different technique must be used with the WHILE loop. In pseudocode, we want to perform these steps:

```
WHILE more data DO
   READ ID, student data
   process data
END WHILE
```

To implement this in FORTRAN, we use an option available with the READ statement that tests for the end of the data. A READ statement that uses this option has the following form:

```
READ(*,*,END=20)A, B
```

or

READ(*unit number*,*, END=20)A, B

The first form is the equivalent of a READ* with the END option. The second form has the unit number specification in it to allow you to use this with a data file. The discussion that follows will refer to the first form directly, but also applies to the second form. When this first form is used, as long as there are data lines or data cards, the statement executes exactly like the statement:

```
READ*, A, B
```

However, if the last data line or data card has already been read and we execute the READ statement again, instead of getting an execution error, control will be passed to the statement referenced in the END option. In the previous statement, once the end of the data has been reached, the next execution of the READ statement will cause control to pass to the statement with statement number 20. However, if the READ statement were executed a second time after the end of the data, then an execution error would occur. Using this END option, we can now implement the desired WHILE loop in FORTRAN:

```
 8    READ(*,*,END=20)ID, DATA
             .
             .
             .
        process student data
             .
             .
             .
        GO TO 8
20      .
        .
        .
```

This is a special implementation of the WHILE loop that is used when you do not know the number of data lines to be read and there is not a trailer signal at the end of the file. This technique should be used primarily with files built by another program. When a program builds an output file, the computer system automatically puts an end-of-file indicator at the end of the file. This indicator is the signal that causes the END option to work properly. If you build a data file using an editor, this indicator is not added and thus this technique for detecting the end of a data file will not work properly.

Observe that these two techniques should not be used together. If you have a trailer value, test for that value to exit the loop. If you do not use a trailer value, use the END option to branch out of the loop when you do not know the number of data lines in the data file.

EXAMPLE 3-9 Test Scores without Trailer Signal

A group of test scores has been entered into a data file TESTS2, one score per line, with no trailer line. Write a complete program to read the data, compute the test average, and print the number of tests and the test average.

Solution

DECOMPOSITION

Read and total test scores
Compute average
Print average

REFINEMENT IN PSEUDOCODE

```
AVERG2:  BEGIN
            number ← 0
            total ← 0
            WHILE more tests DO
               READ test
               number ← number + 1
               total ← total + test
            END WHILE
            ave ← total/number
            PRINT number, ave
         END
```

FORTRAN PROGRAM

```
      PROGRAM AVERG2
*
*   THIS PROGRAM COMPUTES THE AVERAGE OF A GROUP
*   OF TEST SCORES WHICH ARE NOT FOLLOWED BY A
*   TRAILER LINE IN A DATA FILE
*
      INTEGER TEST, TOTAL
*
      OPEN(UNIT=8, FILE='TESTS2', STATUS='OLD')
*
      NUMBER = 0
      TOTAL = 0
*
   10 READ(8,*,END=25)TEST
         NUMBER = NUMBER + 1
         TOTAL = TOTAL + TEST
         GO TO 10
*
   25 AVE = TOTAL/REAL(NUMBER)
*
      PRINT*, 'THE AVERAGE OF', NUMBER,
     +        'TEST SCORES IS', AVE
*
      END
```

DATA FILE TESTS2

```
 85
 92
100
 87
 75
 73
 81
```

COMPUTER OUTPUT

```
THE AVERAGE OF 7 TEST SCORES IS 84.7143
```

◇

3-5 PROBLEM SOLVING—ROCKET TRAJECTORY

A small test rocket is being designed for use in testing a retrorocket that is intended to permit soft landings. The designers have derived the following equation that they believe will predict the performance of the test rocket. where t is the elapsed time in seconds:

$$\text{distance} = 90 + 2.13t^2 - .0013t^4 + .000034t^{4.751}$$

The distance equation gives the height above ground level at time t. The first term (90) is the height in feet above ground level of the launch platform that will be used. In order to check the predicted performance, the rocket will be "flown" on a computer, using the derived equations.

Develop an algorithm and use it to write a complete program to cover a maximum flight of 100 seconds. Increments in time are to be 2.0 seconds, from launch through the ascending and descending portions of the trajectory until the rocket descends to within 50 feet of ground level. Below 50 feet the time increments are to be 0.05 seconds. If the rocket impacts prior to 100 seconds, the program is to be stopped immediately after impact. The output is to be in the following form:

```
TIME(SEC.)     DISTANCE(FT.)

0.0000         XXXXXXX
2.0000         XXXXXXX
   .              .
   .              .
   .              .
```

Several possible events could occur as we simulate this flight as shown in the following diagram. The distance above ground should increase for a period and then decrease until the rocket impacts. We can test for impact by testing the distance for a value equal to or less than zero. It is also possible that the rocket will still be airborne after 100 seconds of flight time. Therefore, we must also test for this condition and stop the program if the value of time becomes greater than 100. In addition, we also need to observe the distance above ground. As the rocket gets closer to the ground, we want to monitor its progress more frequently, and thus will need to reduce our time increment from 2 seconds to 0.05 seconds.

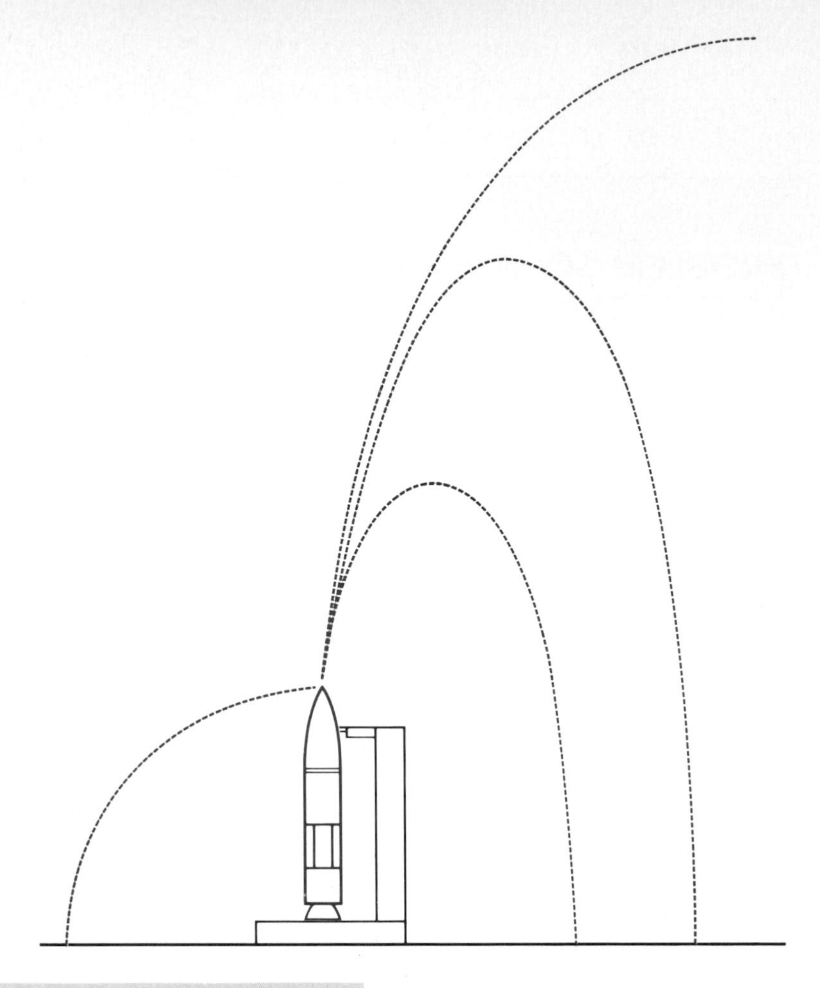

PROBLEM STATEMENT

Using the equation below, compute distance values and print them along with their corresponding time values. Start time at zero and increment it by 2 seconds until the distance is less than 50 feet; then increment time by 0.05 seconds. Stop the program if the rocket impacts or if the total time exceeds 100 seconds.

$$\text{distance} = 90 + 2.13t^2 - .0013t^4 + .000034t^{4.751}$$

INPUT/OUTPUT DESCRIPTION

There is no input to the program. The output is a table of time and distance values, with the following form:

```
TIME(SEC.)    DISTANCE(FT.)

0.0000        XXXXXXX
2.0000        XXXXXXX
```

HAND EXAMPLE

We certainly want to use a calculator for this step. The first three entries in our table are shown below:

```
TIME(SEC.)     DISTANCE(FT.)

0.0000         90.0000
2.0000         98.5001
4.0000         123.7719
```

We are now ready to develop the algorithm so that the computer can compute the rest of the table for us.

ALGORITHM DEVELOPMENT

Decomposition

Set time to zero
Print report

Initial Refinement in Pseudocode

```
ROCKET:  BEGIN
           time ← 0
           WHILE above ground and time ≤ 100 DO
              Compute distance using equation
              PRINT time, distance
              Increment time
           END WHILE
         END
```

Final Refinement in Pseudocode

```
ROCKET:  BEGIN
           time ← 0
           distance ← 90
           WHILE distance > 0 and time ≤ 100 DO
              Compute distance using equation
              PRINT time, distance
              IF distance < 50
                 time ← time + 0.05
              ELSE
                 time ← time + 2.0
              END IF
           END WHILE
         END
```

Notice that the distance variable was initialized to 90.0 before entering the WHILE loop. Why? Could it have been initialized to any value? Since the condition in the WHILE loop used the distance variable, it had to be initialized before the condition was tested. The distance must also be set to a value greater than zero or the loop would never be executed.

FORTRAN PROGRAM 1

```
      PROGRAM ROCKET
*
*  THIS PROGRAM SIMULATES A ROCKET FLIGHT
*
      TIME = 0.0
      DIST = 90.0
*
      PRINT*, 'TIME(SEC.)      DISTANCE(FT.)'
      PRINT*
*
    5 IF(DIST.GT.0.0.AND.TIME.LE.100.0)THEN
         DIST = 90.0 + 2.13*TIME**2 - 0.0013*TIME**4
     +          + 0.000034*TIME**4.751
         PRINT*, TIME, '        ', DIST
         IF(DIST.LT.50.0)THEN
            TIME = TIME + 0.05
         ELSE
            TIME = TIME + 2.0
         ENDIF
         GO TO 5
      ENDIF
*
      END
```

Another solution to this problem is given which uses the logical variables that we introduced in the first section of this chapter. In this solution, we use a logical variable called DONE. As long as neither of the conditions that indicate that we want to stop the program occurs, the value of this variable remains .FALSE.. Thus, as long as .NOT.DONE is true, we want to stay in the WHILE loop, as shown in this statement:

```
IF(.NOT.DONE)THEN
```

It is invalid to compare two logical variables with the relation .EQ. or .NE.. Instead, two new relations, .EQV. and .NEQV., are used to represent equivalent and not equivalent. Thus, if we wanted to compare .NOT.DONE to the value .TRUE., we could also have used this statement:

```
IF(.NOT.DONE.EQV..TRUE.)THEN
```

Whenever arithmetic operators, relational operators, and logical operators are in the same expression, the arithmetic operations are performed first, then the relational operators are applied to yield .TRUE. or .FALSE. values, and these are evaluated with the logical operators whose precedence is .NOT., .AND., .OR.. The relations .EQV. and .NEQV. are evaluated last.

FORTRAN Program 2

```
      PROGRAM FLIGHT
*
*   THIS PROGRAM SIMULATES A ROCKET FLIGHT
*
      LOGICAL DONE
*
      TIME = 0.0
      DIST = 90.0
      DONE = .FALSE.
*
      PRINT*, 'TIME(SEC.)      DISTANCE(FT.)'
      PRINT*
*
    5 IF(.NOT.DONE)THEN
         DIST = 90.0 + 2.13*TIME**2 - 0.0013*TIME**4
     +          + 0.000034*TIME**4.751
         PRINT*, TIME, '       ', DIST
         IF(DIST.LT.50.0)THEN
            TIME = TIME + 0.05
         ELSE
            TIME = TIME + 2.0
         ENDIF
         DONE = DIST.LE.0.0.OR.TIME.GT.100.0
         GO TO 5
      ENDIF
*
      END
```

TESTING

The first few lines of output are shown below, along with the last few. The values are in agreement with the hand example.

```
TIME(SEC.)       DISTANCE(FT.)

0.0000           90.0000
2.0000           98.5001
4.0000           123.7719
6.0000           165.1644
8.0000           221.6590
   .                .
   .                .
   .                .
54.0000          1029.1541
56.0000          857.4203
58.0000          663.2985
60.0000          448.3960
62.0000          214.8096
64.0000          -34.8604
```

Can you think of ways to test different parts of the algorithm? Since we now know that it impacts before 100 seconds of flight time, you could change the cutoff time to 50 seconds. How could you check the change in the increment of the time variable from 2 seconds to 0.5 seconds?

3-6 DO LOOPS

In previous sections we used the IF statement to build WHILE loops. A special case of the WHILE loop is the counting loop or iterative loop. Implementing an iterative loop generally involves initializing a counter before entering the loop, modifying the counter within the loop, and exiting the loop when the counter reaches a specified value. These are then the loops that we execute a specified number of times. The three steps (initialize, modify, and test) can be incorporated in a WHILE loop as we have already seen, but they still require three different statements. A special statement, the DO statement, combines all three steps into one statement. Using the DO statement to construct a loop results in a construction called a *DO loop*.

DO STATEMENT

The general form of the DO statement is

```
DO k, index = initial,limit,increment
```

where *k* is the statement number of the statement that represents the end of the loop,
index is a variable used as the loop counter,
initial represents the initial value given to the loop counter,
limit represents the value used to determine when the DO loop has been completed, and
increment represents the value to be added to the loop counter each time that the loop is executed.

The comma after *k* is optional.

The values of initial, limit, and increment are called the *parameters* of the DO loop. If the increment is omitted, an increment of 1 is assumed. When the value of the index is greater than the limit, control is passed to the statement following the end of the loop. The end of the loop is usually indicated with the CONTINUE statement, whose general form is:

```
k CONTINUE
```

where k is the statement number referenced on the corresponding DO statement. Before we list all the rules that must be followed when using a DO loop, we will look at a simple example.

EXAMPLE 3-10 Integer Sum

The sum of the integers 1 through 50 is represented mathematically as

$$\sum_{i=1}^{50} i = 1 + 2 + \cdots + 49 + 50$$

Obviously we do not want to write one long assignment statement of the form:

```
SUM = 1 + 2 + 3 + 4 + 5 + 6 + ... + 50
```

A better solution is to build a loop that we execute 50 times, and add a number to the sum each time through the loop.

WHILE Loop Solution

```
         INTEGER SUM
             .
             .
             .
         SUM = 0
         NUMBER = 1
      10 IF(NUMBER.LE.50)THEN
            SUM = SUM + NUMBER
            NUMBER = NUMBER + 1
            GO TO 10
         ENDIF
```

DO Loop Solution

```
         INTEGER SUM
             .
             .
             .
         SUM = 0
         DO 10 NUMBER=1,50
            SUM = SUM + NUMBER
      10 CONTINUE
```

The DO statement identifies statement 10 as the end of the loop. The index NUMBER is initialized to 1. The loop will be repeated until the value of NUMBER is greater than 50. Since the third parameter is omitted, the index NUMBER will be automatically incremented by 1 at the end of each loop. Comparing the DO loop solution with the WHILE loop solution, we see that the DO loop solution is shorter than the WHILE loop solution, but both would compute the same value for SUM. ◇

Now that you have seen a DO loop in a simple example, we will summarize the general rules to be followed when building a DO loop. The rules will be divided into two groups: rules relating to the structure of the DO loop and rules relating to the execution of the DO loop.

STRUCTURE OF A DO LOOP

1 The index of the DO loop must be a variable, but it may be either real or integer type.

2 The parameters of the DO loop may be variables or expressions and can also be real or integer type.

3 The increment can be either positive or negative, but it cannot be zero.

4 A DO loop may end on any executable statement that is not a transfer, an IF statement, or another DO. The CONTINUE statement is an executable statement that was designed expressly for the purpose of closing a DO loop. Although other statements may also be used, we strongly encourage the consistent use of CONTINUE to clearly indicate the end of all loops.

5 The pseudocode for a DO loop is:

```
FOR index = initial TO limit STEP increment DO
   (steps in the loop)
END FOR
```

The STEP increment clause is omitted if the increment is 1.

EXECUTION OF A DO LOOP

1 The test for completion is done at the beginning of the loop, as in a WHILE loop. If the initial value of the index is greater than the limit and the increment is positive, the loop will not be executed. For instance, the statement

```
DO 10 I=5,2
```

sets up a loop that ends at statement 10. The initial value of the index I is 5, which is greater than the limit 2. Therefore the statements within the loop will be skipped, and control passes to the statement following statement 10.

2 The value of the index should not be modified by other statements during the execution of the loop.

3 After the loop begins execution, changing the values of the parameters will have no effect on the loop.

4 If the increment is negative, the exit from the loop will occur when the value of the index is less than the limit.

5 You may branch out of a DO loop before it is completed. The value of the index will be the value just before the branch.

6 Upon completion of the DO loop, the index contains the last value that exceeded the limit.
7 Always enter a DO loop through the DO statement so that it will be initiated properly.
8 The number of times that a DO loop will be executed, assuming that the limit is greater than or equal to the initial value, can be computed as follows

$$\left[\frac{\text{limit} - \text{initial}}{\text{increment}}\right] + 1$$

The brackets around the first term represent the greatest integer function. That is, we drop any fractional portion (truncate) in the fraction. Hence, if we had a DO statement

```
DO 35 K=5,83,4
```

the corresponding DO loop would be executed the following number of times.

$$\left[\frac{83 - 5}{4}\right] + 1 = \left[\frac{78}{4}\right] + 1 = 20$$

The value of the index K would be 5, then 9, then 13, and so on until the final value of 81. The loop would not be executed with the value 85 because that value is greater than the limit, 83.

Now that we have summarized the rules for building and describing DO loops, a number of examples are needed to illustrate these rules. The decomposition and psuedocode will not be shown for each example in this group because some of the problems are very similar.

EXAMPLE 3-11 Polynomial Model with Integer Time.

Polynomials are often used to model data and experimental results. Assume that the polynomial

$$3t^2 + 4.5$$

models the results of an experiment where t represents time in seconds. Write a complete program to evaluate this polynomial for the period of time from 1 second to 10 seconds in increments of 1 second (i.e., let t = 1, 2, 3, 4, 5, 6, 7, 8, 9, 10). For each value of time, print the time and the polynomial value.

Solution

Decomposition

Print headings
Print report

Refinement in Pseudocode

```
POLY1:  BEGIN
          PRINT headings
          FOR time = 1 TO 10 DO
             poly ← 3*time^2 + 4.5
             PRINT time, poly
          END FOR
        END
```

FORTRAN Program

```
      PROGRAM POLY1
*
*  THIS PROGRAM PRINTS A TABLE OF VALUES
*  FOR A POLYNOMIAL
*
      INTEGER TIME
*
      PRINT*, 'POLYNOMIAL MODEL'
      PRINT*, 'TIME   POLYNOMIAL'
      PRINT*, '(SEC)'
*
      DO 15 TIME=1,10
         POLY = 3.0*TIME**2 + 4.5
         PRINT*, TIME, '    ', POLY
   15 CONTINUE
*
      END
```

Computer Output

```
POLYNOMIAL MODEL
TIME   POLYNOMIAL
(SEC)
1      7.5000
2      16.5000
3      31.5000
4      52.5000
5      79.5000
6      112.5000
7      151.5000
8      196.5000
9      247.5000
10     304.5000
```

◇

EXAMPLE 3-12 Polynomial Model with Real Time

We again assume that the polynomial $3t^2 + 4.5$ models an experiment where t represents time in seconds. Write a program to evaluate this polynomial for time beginning at zero seconds and ending at 5 seconds in increments of 0.5 second.

Solution

FORTRAN PROGRAM

```
      PROGRAM POLY2
*
*  THIS PROGRAM PRINTS A TABLE OF VALUES
*  FOR A POLYNOMIAL
*
      PRINT*, 'POLYNOMIAL MODEL'
      PRINT*, 'TIME    POLYNOMIAL'
      PRINT*, '(SEC)'
*
      DO 15 TIME=0.0,5.0,0.5
         POLY = 3.0*TIME**2 + 4.5
         PRINT*, TIME, POLY
   15 CONTINUE
*
      END
```

COMPUTER OUTPUT

```
POLYNOMIAL MODEL
TIME    POLYNOMIAL
(SEC)
0.0000 4.5000
0.5000 5.2500
1.0000 7.5000
1.5000 11.2500
2.0000 16.5000
2.5000 23.2500
3.0000 31.5000
3.5000 41.2500
4.0000 52.5000
4.5000 65.2500
5.0000 79.5000
```

◇

EXAMPLE 3-13 Polynomial Model with Variable Time

Assume that we want to evaluate the polynomial $3t^2 + 4.5$, beginning at t equal to zero, in increments of 0.25, for a variable number of seconds. Write a complete program to read an integer NSEC that represents the number of seconds to be used for evaluating the polynomial. Then print the corresponding table.

Solution

DECOMPOSITION

Read number of seconds
Print headings
Print report

REFINEMENT IN PSEUDOCODE

```
POLY3:  BEGIN
            READ nsec
            PRINT headings
            FOR time = 0.0 TO nsec STEP 0.25 DO
                poly ← 3*time^2 + 4.5
                PRINT time, poly
            END FOR
        END
```

FORTRAN PROGRAM

```
      PROGRAM POLY3
*
*  THIS PROGRAM PRINTS A TABLE OF VALUES
*  FOR A POLYNOMIAL
*
      PRINT*, 'ENTER NUMBER OF SECONDS'
      READ*, NSEC
      PRINT*
*
      PRINT*, 'POLYNOMIAL MODEL'
      PRINT*, 'TIME   POLYNOMIAL'
      PRINT*, '(SEC)'
*
      DO 15 TIME=0.0,NSEC,0.25
         POLY = 3.0*TIME**2 + 4.5
         PRINT*, TIME, POLY
   15 CONTINUE
*
      END
```

COMPUTER OUTPUT

```
ENTER NUMBER OF SECONDS
004

POLYNOMIAL MODEL
TIME    POLYNOMIAL
(SEC)
0.0000  4.5000
0.2500  4.6875
0.5000  5.2500
0.7500  6.1875
1.0000  7.5000
1.2500  9.1875
1.5000  11.2500
1.7500  13.6875
2.0000  16.5000
2.2500  19.6875
2.5000  23.2500
2.7500  27.1875
3.0000  31.5000
3.2500  36.1875
3.5000  41.2500
3.7500  46.6875
4.0000  52.5000
```

◇

NESTED DO LOOPS

DO loops may be independent of each other, or they may be *nested* within other DO loops. Overlapping loops, however, are not allowed. Note that we have drawn brackets on the left side of the following statements to connect the beginning and ending of DO loops. These brackets prove to be very helpful in spotting invalid nesting of DO loops. These next structures compare valid and invalid loop structures.

VALID DO LOOP COMBINATIONS — INVALID DO LOOP COMBINATION

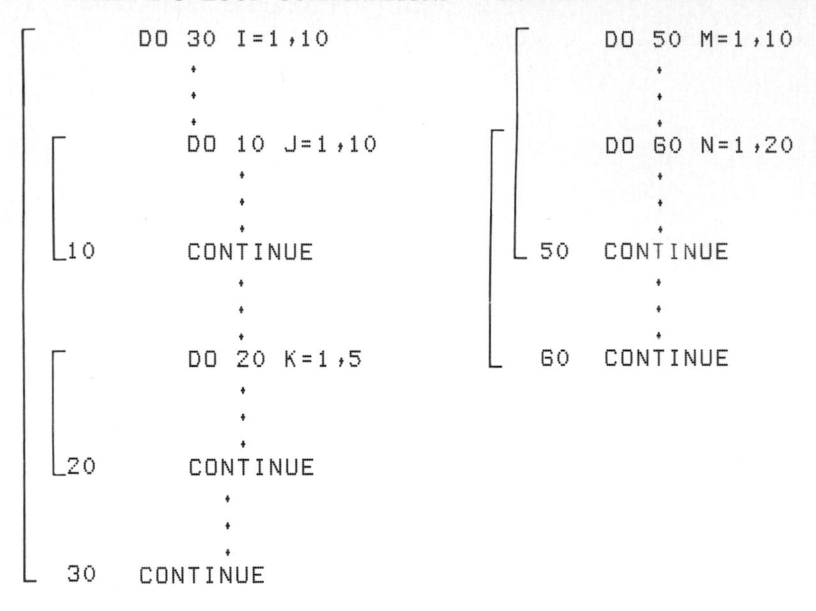

In the valid DO loop construction, the two inside loops, DO 10 and DO 20, are independent of each other. However they are both within the loop DO 30. Independent loops may use the same index. Thus, the DO 10 loop and the DO 20 loop could have used the same index J. However, the DO 30 loop index could not be used on either of the inside loops because the inside loops are not independent of the outside loop.

It is valid for two nested DO loops to end on the same statement, but is not encouraged because of the lack of clarity. With separate CONTINUE statements, each DO statement and its CONTINUE can be indented the same number of positions to emphasize the structure, with the statements inside the loop indented further.

When one loop is nested within another loop, the inside loop is completely executed each pass through the outer loop. To illustrate this, consider the following program.

```
      PROGRAM NEST
*
*   THIS PROGRAM PRINTS THE INDEXES IN NESTED DO LOOPS
*
      PRINT*, 'I   J'
*
      DO 10 I=1,5
         DO 5 J=1,3
            PRINT*, I, J
  5      CONTINUE
         PRINT*, 'END OF PASS'
   10 CONTINUE
*
      END
```

The output from this program is shown below:

```
I  J
1  1
1  2
1  3
END OF PASS
2  1
2  2
2  3
END OF PASS
3  1
3  2
3  3
END OF PASS
4  1
4  2
4  3
END OF PASS
5  1
5  2
5  3
END OF PASS
```

The first time through the outer loop, I is initialized to the value 1. Then we begin executing the inner loop. The variable J is initialized to the value 1. After executing the PRINT statement, we reach statement 5. Since this is the end of the inner loop, control returns to the DO 5 statement, and J is incremented to the value 2. We again write values and return to the DO 5 statement and increment J to the value 3. After writing values, we return to the DO 5 and increment J to the value 4. This value of J is now greater than the test value 3. We have completed the inner loop, so the literal 'END OF PASS' is printed. I is incremented to 2, and we begin the DO 5 loop with J equal to the value 1. The process is repeated until I is greater than 5.

EXAMPLE 3-14 Experimental Sums

Write a complete program to read 100 data values. Each data value has been entered into a data file, one number per line. The name of the data file is RESULT. Compute the sum of the first 20 values, the next 20 values, and so on. Print the five sums. Assume that the values are real values.

Solution

While we need to read 100 values, we will need only 20 at a time, and thus an outer loop is needed to read 5 sets of data. Each set of data is 20 values; the inner loop reads the 20 values. It is very important to set to zero the variable being used to store the sum before the inner loop is begun. Thus, we add 20 values, print the sum, and then set the sum back to zero before we read the next 20 values.

Decomposition

Read data values
Compute sums for 20 values at a time
Print sums

Refinement in Pseudocode

```
SUMS:  BEGIN
          FOR i = 1 TO 5 DO
             sum ← 0
             FOR j = 1 TO 20 DO
                READ value
                sum ← sum + value
             END FOR
             PRINT i, sum
          END FOR
       END
```

FORTRAN Program

```
      PROGRAM SUMS
*
*   THIS PROGRAM READS 100 NUMBERS AND PRINTS
*   THE SUM OF EACH GROUP OF 20 VALUES
*
      OPEN(UNIT=15, FILE='RESULT', STATUS='OLD')
*
      DO 200 I=1,5
         SUM = 0.0
*
         DO 50 J=1,20
            READ(15,*)VALUE
            SUM = SUM + VALUE
   50    CONTINUE
*
         PRINT*, 'SUM', I, '=', SUM
*
  200 CONTINUE
*
      END
```

We will not list a data file with 100 values in it, but here is a sample of the type of output that would be printed from this program.

SAMPLE COMPUTER OUTPUT

```
SUM 1 = 36.4045
SUM 2 = 162.5562
SUM 3 = -2415.2100
SUM 4 = 0.0000
SUM 5 = 25.5100
```

◇

EXAMPLE 3-15 Factorial Computation

Write a complete program to compute the factorial of an integer read from a data card. A few factorials and their corresponding values are shown below (an exclamation point after a number symbolizes a factorial):

$$0! = 1$$
$$1! = 1$$
$$2! = 2 \cdot 1$$
$$3! = 3 \cdot 2 \cdot 1$$
$$4! = 4 \cdot 3 \cdot 2 \cdot 1$$
$$5! = 5 \cdot 4 \cdot 3 \cdot 2 \cdot 1$$

Compute and print the factorial for four different values that are read from cards.

Solution

Since the factorial of a negative number is not defined, we should include in our algorithm an error check for this condition with an appropriate error message. In computing a factorial, we use a DO loop to perform the successive multiplications.

DECOMPOSITION

Read integers
Compute factorials
Print factorials

Refinement in Pseudocode

```
FACT:  BEGIN
          FOR i = 1 TO 4 DO
             READ n
             IF n < 0
                PRINT error message
             ELSE
                nfact ← 1
                IF n > 1
                   FOR k = 1 TO n DO
                      nfact ← nfact*k
                   END FOR
                END IF
                PRINT n, nfact
             END IF
          END FOR
       END
```

FORTRAN Program

```
      PROGRAM FACT
*
*   THIS PROGRAM COMPUTES THE FACTORIAL
*   OF FOUR VALUES READ FROM DATA CARDS
*
      DO 200 I=1,4
*
         READ*, N
*
         IF(N.LT.0)THEN
            PRINT*, 'INVALID N =', N
         ELSE
            NFACT = 1
            IF(N.GT.1)THEN
               DO 50 K=1,N
                  NFACT = NFACT*K
   50          CONTINUE
            ENDIF
            PRINT*, N, '! =', NFACT
         ENDIF
*
  200 CONTINUE
*
      END
```

Data Cards

Card 1	03
Card 2	−2
Card 3	11
Card 4	00

```
3 ! = 6
INVALID N = -2
11 ! = 39916800
0 ! = 1
```

◇

3-7 PROBLEM SOLVING—TIMBER MANAGEMENT ECONOMICS

A problem in timber management is to determine how much of an area to leave uncut so that the harvested area is reforested in a certain period of time. It is assumed that reforestation takes place at a known rate per year, depending on climate and soil conditions. The reforestation rate expresses this growth as a function of the amount of timber standing. For example, if 100 acres are left standing and the reforestation rate is 0.05, then there are $100 + 0.05 \times 100$ or 105 acres forested at the end of the first year. At the end of the second year, the number of acres forested is $105 + 0.05 \times 105$ or 110.25 acres.

Read the name of the area, the total number of acres in the area, the number of acres of uncut area, and the reforestation rate. Print a report that tabulates the number of acres reforested and the total number of acres forested at the end of each year, for 20 years.

PROBLEM STATEMENT

Compute the number of acres forested at the end of each year for 20 years for a given area.

INPUT/OUTPUT DESCRIPTION

The input information consists of the name of the area of land, the total acres, the number of acres with trees, and the reforestation rate. The output is a table with a row of data for each of 20 years. Each row of information contains the number of acres reforested during that year and the total number of acres forested at the end of the year.

HAND EXAMPLE

Assume that there are 14,000 acres total with 2500 acres uncut. If the reforestation rate is 0.02, then we can compute a few entries as shown below:

year 1 $2500 \times 0.02 = 50$ acres of new growth
original 2500 acres + 50 new acres = 2550 acres forested

year 2 $2550 \times 0.02 = 51$ acres of new growth
original 2550 acres + 51 new acres = 2601 acres forested

year 3 $2601 \times 0.02 = 52.02$ acres of new growth
original 2601 acres + 52.02 new acres
= 2653.02 acres forested

ALGORITHM DEVELOPMENT

The overall structure is an iterative loop which is executed 20 times, once for each year. Inside the loop we need to compute the number of acres reforested during that year, and add that number to the acres forested at the beginning of the year in order to compute the total number of acres forested at the end of the year. The PRINT statement should be inside the loop since we want to print the number of acres forested at the end of each year.

Clearly an error condition exists if the uncut area exceeds the total area. We will test for this error condition and exit after printing an error message if it occurs. It is possible to imagine soil conditions that would have a zero or negative reforestation rate so we will not perform any error checking on the rate. However, all the values read will be printed, or *echoed*, so that the user should recognize an error in an input value.

DECOMPOSITION

Read initial information
Print headings
Print report

Initial Refinement in Pseudocode

```
TIMBER:  BEGIN
            READ initial information
            PRINT headings
            FOR year = 1 TO 20 DO
               Compute reforested amount
               Add reforested amount to uncut amount
               PRINT reforested amount, uncut amount
            END FOR
         END
```

Final Refinement in Pseudocode

```
TIMBER:  BEGIN
            READ name, total, uncut, rate
            IF uncut > total
               PRINT error message
            ELSE
               PRINT headings
               FOR year = 1 TO 20 DO
                  refor ← uncut × rate
                  uncut ← uncut + refor
                  PRINT year, refor, uncut
               END FOR
            END IF
         END
```

FORTRAN Program

```
      PROGRAM TIMBER
*
*   THIS PROGRAM COMPUTES A REFORESTATION SUMMARY
*   FOR AN AREA WHICH HAS NOT BEEN COMPLETELY HARVESTED
*
      INTEGER YEAR
      CHARACTER*20 NAME
*
      PRINT*, 'ENTER NAME (MAX 20 CHARACTERS)',
     +        'ENCLOSED IN APOSTROPHES'
      READ*, NAME
      PRINT*, 'ENTER TOTAL NUMBER OF ACRES'
      READ*, TOTAL
      PRINT*, 'ENTER NUMBER OF ACRES UNCUT'
      READ*, UNCUT
      PRINT*, 'ENTER REFORESTATION RATE'
      READ*, RATE
*
      IF(UNCUT.GT.TOTAL)THEN
         PRINT*, 'UNCUT AREA LARGER THAN ENTIRE AREA'
      ELSE
*
         PRINT*
         PRINT*, 'REFORESTATION SUMMARY'
         PRINT*
         PRINT*, NAME
         PRINT*, 'TOTAL ACRES =', TOTAL,
     +           'UNCUT ACRES =', UNCUT
         PRINT*, 'REFORESTATION RATE =', RATE
         PRINT*
         PRINT*, 'YEAR  REFORESTED  TOTAL FORESTED'
*
         DO 10 YEAR=1,20
            REFOR = UNCUT*RATE
            UNCUT = UNCUT + REFOR
            PRINT*, YEAR, '   ', REFOR, '   ', UNCUT
   10    CONTINUE
*
      ENDIF
*
      END
```

TESTING

Using the test data in this program, a typical interaction is:

```
ENTER NAME (MAX 20 CHARACTERS) ENCLOSED IN APOSTROPHES
?'SOUTH MT TAYLOR'
ENTER TOTAL NUMBER OF ACRES
?14000.0
ENTER NUMBER OF ACRES UNCUT
?2500.0
ENTER REFORESTATION RATE
?0.02

REFORESTATION SUMMARY

SOUTH MT TAYLOR
TOTAL ACRES = 14000.0000 UNCUT ACRES = 2500.0000
REFORESTATION RATE = 0.0200

YEAR   REFORESTED   TOTAL REFORESTED

1      50.0000      2550.0000
2      51.0000      2601.0000
3      52.0200      2653.0200
4      53.0604      2706.0803
5      54.1216      2760.2019
6      55.2040      2815.4060
7      56.3081      2871.7141
8      57.4343      2929.1484
9      58.5830      2987.7315
10       59.7546      3047.4861
11       60.9497      3108.4358
12       62.1687      3170.6045
13       63.4121      3234.0166
14       64.6803      3298.6970
15       65.9739      3364.6709
16       67.2934      3431.9643
17       68.6393      3500.6037
18       70.0121      3570.6157
19       71.4123      3642.0280
20       72.8406      3714.8687
```

The numbers match the ones we computed by hand. Try an example to test the error condition by using an uncut area larger than the total area. What happens if the reforestation rate is .00, or −0.02? Should there be an upper limit on the reforestation rate? This information is not given in the original problem so we probably should not arbitrarily set one. What happens if you enter 14,000 instead of 14000? It might be a good idea to remind the program user not to use commas in numbers. How would you do this?

3-8 PROBLEM SOLVING—POPULATION STUDY

The population of Shakespeare, New Mexico, for the years 1880 through 1980, has been entered in a data file IN07. (The names for data files in the problem solving sections have been chosen to match those in the software supplement. Thus, IN07 signifies an input file for the seventh problem solving section.) Each line of the data file contains a year and the corresponding population. The data lines are in ascending order by year. Write a complete program to read the data and determine the two consecutive years in which the percentage increase in population was the greatest.

PROBLEM STATEMENT

Find the two consecutive years in which the percentage increase in population was the greatest for Shakespeare, New Mexico.

INPUT/OUTPUT DESCRIPTION

The input is a data file with 101 lines. Each line contains the year and corresponding population. The data is in ascending order by year. The output is the two consecutive years with the largest percentage increase in population.

HAND EXAMPLE

First, we will look at some typical data and compute the percentage increase in the data each year to be sure that we understand the computations involved.

YEAR	POPULATION	PERCENTAGE INCREASE
1950	82	
		−32% [(56 − 82)/82*100]
1951	56	
		27% [(71 − 56)/56*100]
1952	71	
		21% [(86 − 71)/71*100]
1953	86	
		19% [(102 − 86)/86*100]
1954	102	

In the years above, the largest percentage increase was from 1951 to 1952. Note that this was not the largest increase in actual population. The largest increase in actual population occurred from 1953 to 1954.

ALGORITHM DEVELOPMENT

DECOMPOSITION

Read data
Determine years with largest percentage increase
Print result

As we consider the iterative loop for this algorithm, we realize that we need to read the first line of data outside the loop so that we have old values to use the first time through the loop. The loop is then executed 100 times to read the rest of the data and compute population increases.

INITIAL REFINEMENT IN PSEUDOCODE

```
CENSUS:  BEGIN
            READ first set of data
            year of increase ← first year
            FOR i = 1 TO 100 DO
               READ next set of data
               Compute percentage increase
               IF percentage increase > previous best
                  year of increase ← current year
               END IF
            END FOR
            PRINT year of increase
         END
```

When we read a data line, we need not only the information on that line but also the information on the previous data line in order to compute the population increase. Thus, we will need to use the following variables:

YRNEW: the year just read from a data line
YROLD: the year from the previous data linc
POPNEW: the population just read from a data line
POPOLD: the population from the previous data line
GPIYR: the year in which there was the greatest percentage increase
GPI: the percentage that represents the greatest percentage increase

Note that in the final pseudocode we are initially setting the first pair of years as the ones with the greatest percentage increase. Each time through the loop, we compare this increase with the current increase. If the current increase is higher, this value is placed in the variable GPI (greatest percent increase).

Final Refinement in Pseudocode

```
CENSUS:  BEGIN
            gpi ← 0
            gpiyr ← 0
            READ yrold, popold
            FOR i = 1 TO 100 DO
               READ yrnew, popnew
               perc ← (popnew − popold)∗100/popold
               IF perc > gpi
                  gpi ← perc
                  gpiyr ← yrnew
               END IF
               yrold ← yrnew
               popold ← popnew
            END FOR
            yr1 ← gpiyr − 1
            yr2 ← gpiyr
            PRINT yr1, yr2
         END
```

FORTRAN Program

```
      PROGRAM CENSUS
*
*   THIS PROGRAM READS 101 POPULATION VALUES AND
*   DETERMINES THE YEARS OF GREATEST PERCENTAGE INCREASE
*
      INTEGER YR1, YR2, YRNEW, YROLD,
     +        POPNEW, POPOLD, GPIYR
*
      GPI = 0.0
      GPIYR = 0
*
      OPEN(UNIT=15, FILE='IN07', STATUS='OLD')
*
      READ(15,*)YROLD, POPOLD
*
      DO 50 I=1,100
         READ(15,*)YRNEW, POPNEW
         PERC = (POPNEW - POPOLD)*100.0/POPOLD
         IF(PERC.GT.GPI)THEN
            GPI = PERC
            GPIYR = YRNEW
         ENDIF
         YROLD = YRNEW
         POPOLD = POPNEW
   50 CONTINUE
*
      YR1 = GPIYR - 1
      YR2 = GPIYR
*
      PRINT*, 'GREATEST PERCENT INCREASE OCCURRED',
     +        ' BETWEEN', YR1, 'AND', YR2
*
      END
```

TESTING

We will not print a data file here with 101 sets of data values, but a sample output from this program is shown below:

Sample Computer Output

```
GREATEST PERCENT INCREASE OCCURRED BETWEEN 1890 AND 1891
```

SUMMARY

A number of new topics have been presented in this chapter. The use of IF statements has greatly expanded the types of problems that we can solve in FORTRAN because we can now control the order in which statements are executed. In particular, we can combine an IF statement with an unconditional branch to construct a WHILE loop. The DO loop, which is really a special form of the WHILE loop, was also presented.

An important property of the IF statements and the loops is that they are entered only at the top of the structure and that they have only one exit. Thus, they have *one entrance and one exit*. This type of flow promotes the writing of simpler programs. Another important topic presented in this chapter is the data file. We will use data files frequently throughout the text. They are commonly used for storing information that will be used in other programs or that should be saved for later reference.

KEY WORDS

branch
CASE structure
character string
compound logical expression
connector
control structure
date file
DO loop
echo
END option
FORTRAN character set
IF statement
IF ELSE statement
IF ELSE IF statement
increment value
index
initial value
limit value
logical expression
logical operator
logical value
nested loops
one entrance, one exit
parameter
relational operator
trailer signal
WHILE loop

DEBUGGING AIDS

The most helpful tool in debugging is the PRINT statement. Just knowing that your program is working incorrectly does not really tell you where to begin looking for errors. If you have the computer write the values of key variables at different points in your program, however, it then becomes easier to isolate the parts of the program that are not working correctly. The location of these *checkpoints,* or places to write the values of key variables, depends upon the program. Some of the obvious places are after initializing variables, after completing loops, and after branching.

It is also a good idea to number the checkpoints and then print the checkpoint number along with the other values. For instance, if you print the values of X and Y at several checkpoints, it may not be obvious which set of X and Y values have been printed. However, the following output is very clear:

```
CHECKPOINT 3: X = 14.7623 Y = -3.8211
```

If you have narrowed the problem to an IF statement, then first check the logical expression. Did you use .LT. when you needed .LE.? Be careful when using .NOT. in an expression. It is less confusing to use A.NE.B rather than .NOT.A.EQ.B. Also, note that .NOT.(A.EQ.1.0.OR.B.EQ.2.0) is also equal to A.NE.1.0.AND.B.NE.2.0.

Another possible error with IF statements can be traced to values being very close to, but not exactly, the desired value. For instance, suppose that the result of a mathematical computation should have a real value 5.0. Since computers do have limitations on the number of digits of accuracy, the result might be 4.9999 or 5.0001. Yet, if you check only for 5.0, you may not realize that you really have the correct value. One way to address this problem is to use the IF statement to look for values close to 5.0. For instance, if

$$|5.0 - X| < .001$$

then X is between 4.999 and 5.001. If this is close enough for the particular problem being solved, then replace the statement

```
IF(X.EQ.5.0)PRINT*, TOTAL
```

with the statement

```
IF(ABS(5.0 - X).LT.0.001)PRINT*, TOTAL
```

If you believe that a programming error is within a WHILE loop, then at the beginning of the loop, print the values of key variables. Since this information will be printed each time the loop is executed, you will be able to locate the trouble spot.

Since a DO loop is a special type of loop, an iterative loop, most errors involve the parameters that specify the iterations. Therefore, when a program error seems to involve a DO loop, print the value of the index immediately after the DO statement. After executing the loop with this output statement, you can answer the following questions:

1 Did the index start with the correct value?

2 Did the index increment by the proper amount?

3 Did the index have the correct value during the last execution of the loop?

If the answer to any of these questions is no, check the DO statement itself. You probably have an error in the parameters that you specified.

If the error is not in your original specification of parameters in the DO statement, print the values of the index, both immediately after the DO statement and immediately before the CONTINUE statement. After executing the loop with these two output statements, you will be able to determine if the value of the index is changed by the statements inside the loop. If the index is being modified, you have either used the index inadvertently, which can be corrected, or you do not have an iterative loop and, hence, you should replace the DO loop with a WHILE loop.

Another common error associated with DO loops occurs when a similar variable name is used instead of the index. For instance, if the index of the DO loop is INDEX, use INDEX and not I inside the loop when you intend to use the index value.

STYLE/TECHNIQUE GUIDES

The larger a program grows in size, the more apparent the programmer's style becomes. Not only does bad style/technique become more obvious, it also becomes harder to correct. Therefore, practicing good style/technique in your small programs builds habits that will carry over into all your programming.

One of the best guides to good style is to consistently use the WHILE loop or the DO loop. With a little practice, you will find that all loops fit easily into one of these two forms. An advantage of these types of loops is that each loop has one entrance and one exit. This enhances readability and adds simplicity to your program.

Another characteristic of good style is the utilization of indenting to emphasize the statements in IF THEN ELSE structures and loops. You can convince yourself of the importance of indenting if you try to follow a program written by someone else who has not indented statements within structures.

Comment lines are yet another sign of good style. The use of comment lines, however, can become excessive. Use only as many lines as are needed to show the program's organization and enhance its readability. There should always be initial comments to describe the purpose of the program. If needed, comments may be used throughout the program to identify processes, values, variables, etc. You will also notice that blank comment lines can be very effective in separating different steps within a program. This technique is often used in our example programs.

A final program exhibiting good style will save time in the long run since it is easier to debug. The programmers who may need to follow your program in future projects will also appreciate good style. Changing a few lines of FORTRAN code to achieve this will be time well spent.

PROBLEMS

For problems 1 through 8, use the values given below to determine whether the following logical expressions are true or false.

A = 5.5 B = 1.5 I = −3 K = 12

1 A.LT.10.0

2 A+B.GE.6.5

3 I.NE.0

4 B−I.GT.A

5 .NOT.A.EQ.3*B

6 −I.LE.I+6

7 A.LT.10.0.AND.A.GT.5.0

8 IABS(I).GT.3.OR.K/5.GT.2

For problems 9 through 14, give FORTRAN statements that perform the steps indicated.

9 If TIME is greater than 15.0, increment TIME by 1.0.

10 When the square root of POLY is less than 0.5, print the value of POLY.

11 If the difference between VOLT1 and VOLT2 is larger than 10.0, print the values of VOLT1 and VOLT2.

12 If the value of DEN is less than 0.005, print the message 'DEN IS TOO SMALL'.

13 If the logarithm (base 10) of A is greater than or equal to the logarithm (base e) of Q, set TIME to zero.

14 If DIST is less than 50.0 and TIME is greater than 10.0, increment TIME by 0.05. Otherwise increment TIME by 2.0.

For problems 15 through 22, compute the number of times that the statements inside the DO loop will be executed.

15 `DO 10 J=0,20`

16 `DO 30 KTR=2,20,2`

17 `DO 26 T=5.0,200.0,0.5`

18 `DO 37 LL=5,203,5`

19 `DO 40 N=10,10`

20 `DO 94 I=10,5,4`

21 `DO 150 JI=40,0,-1`

22 `DO 200 RQ=0.0,-5.0,-0.75`

For problems 23 through 28, give the value in COUNTR after each of the following loops is executed. Assume COUNTR represents an integer variable.

23
```
      COUNTR = 0
      DO 5 I=1,10
         COUNTR = COUNTR + 1
    5 CONTINUE
```

24
```
      COUNTR = 0
      DO 5 I=1,10,2
         COUNTR = COUNTR + 1
    5 CONTINUE
```

25
```
      COUNTR = 1
      DO 5 I=2,10,2
         COUNTR = COUNTR + 1
    5 CONTINUE
      COUNTR = COUNTR + 1
```

26
```
      COUNTR = 1
      DO 5 B=5.0,10.0,0.5
         COUNTR = COUNTR + 1
    5 CONTINUE
      DO 10 K=2,6
         COUNTR = COUNTR + 2
   10 CONTINUE
```

27
```
      COUNTR = 1
      DO 5 I=1,10
         DO 4 K=2,10,2
            COUNTR = COUNTR + 1
    4    CONTINUE
    5 CONTINUE
```

28
```
      COUNTR = 0
      DO 5 MM=15,5,-2
         COUNTR = COUNTR + 1
         DO 2 LL=10,20,4
            COUNTR = COUNTR + 1
    2    CONTINUE
    5 CONTINUE
```

For problems 29 through 31, write FORTRAN statements to print tables showing the values of the variables and the function using DO loops to control the loops.

Example: $K = 3M$ for $M = 1, 2, 3, 4$

Solution:
```
      DO 6 M=1,4
         K = 3*M
         PRINT*, M, K
    6 CONTINUE
```

29 $K = I^2 + 2I + 2$ for $I = 0, 1, 2, \ldots, 20$

30 $Y = \dfrac{X^2 - 9}{X^2 + 2}$ for $X = 1.5, 2.0, 2.5, \ldots, 9$

31 $F = \dfrac{X^2 - Y^2}{2XY}$ for $X = 1, 2, \ldots, 9$ and $Y = 0.5, 0.75, 1.0, \ldots, 2.5$

32 Give the statements necessary to compute the salary of a student who works in the University Computer Center. Assume that the hourly rate is RATE and the total number of hours worked is HRS. Pay the student according to the following schedule.

Hours Worked	Hourly Rate
hours ≤ 40	regular rate
$40 <$ hours ≤ 50	regular rate for 40 hours
	1.5 times regular rate for hours above 40
hours > 50	regular rate for 40 hours
	1.5 times regular rate for 10 hours
	2.0 times regular rate for hours above 50

33 Write a complete program to print a table giving consecutive even integers beginning with 2 and squaring each value, until the value of I is greater than 200.

```
I AND I*I
2       4
4      16
.       .
.       .
.       .
```

34 Write a complete program to read a value FINAL from a data card. Print a table that contains values of X and X^2, starting with X = 0.0, in increments of 0.5, until X is greater than FINAL.

```
X         AND    X*X
0.0000        0.0000
0.5000        0.2500
   .             .
   .             .
   .             .
```

35 Write a complete program that reads a data file called EXAMS that has 40 lines of data with three integer numbers per line. Each line represents exam scores on EXAM1, EXAM2, and EXAM3 for a student. There are 40 students. Exam grades can be any integer between 0 and 100. Find the maximum score on each exam and print the following:

```
MAXIMUM SCORE ON EXAM 1 = XXX
MAXIMUM SCORE ON EXAM 2 = XXX
MAXIMUM SCORE ON EXAM 3 = XXX
```

36 Write a complete program that will read a student registration file, called STUDNT, containing a student number and the hours completed, for each student that attends the university. The last line of the data is indicated with student number 9999, which does not represent a student. A student's classification is based on the following table:

CLASSIFICATION	HOURS COMPLETED
FRESHMAN	hours $<$ 30
SOPHOMORE	30 $\leq$ hours $<$ 60
JUNIOR	60 $\leq$ hours $<$ 90
SENIOR	90 $\leq$ hours

Print a report in a form similar to this:

```
REGISTRATION REPORT

STUDENT ID AND CLASSIFICATION

   XXXX           XXXXXXXXX
     .                .
     .                .
     .                .
   XXXX           XXXXXXXXX
```

37 Modify the program of problem 36 so that a final summary report follows the registration report and has the following form:

```
REGISTRATION SUMMARY

FRESHMEN              XXXX
SOPHOMORES            XXXX
JUNIORS               XXXX
SENIORS               XXXX

TOTAL STUDENTS       XXXXX
```

38 Forty-eight temperature measurements for two compounds have been taken at 10-minute intervals over a period of time. The measurements have been put in a data file TEMP, with each pair of temperatures on a new line, in the order that the measurements were made. Write a complete program to read the data and print it in the following manner:

```
TEMPERATURE MEASUREMENTS

TIME ELAPSED
HOURS AND MINUTES     COMPOUND 1    COMPOUND 2

  0          0          XXXXX         XXXXX
  0         10            .             .
  0         20            .             .
  0         30            .             .
  0         40            .             .
  0         50            .             .
  1          0            .             .
  .          .
  .          .
  .          .
  7         50          XXXXX         XXXXX
```

***39** Modify the program of problem 38 so that the following output lines are printed after the temperature measurements:

```
MINIMUM TEMPERATURE AND TIME ELAPSED (HOURS AND MINUTES)
    COMPOUND 1                 XXXXX    X         XX
    COMPOUND 2                 XXXXX    X         XX
```

* Asterisks indicate more challenging problems.

PROBLEM SOLVING—National Park Snowfall

To plan your next ski trip, you are studying average snowfall statistics in a number of national parks. You have available daily snowfall information for each of these locations, but you want to compare them based on the average monthly snowfall. Write a program which will read the daily snowfall averages, compute the monthly average snowfall, and then determine the number of days with snowfall above this monthly average. (See Section 4-3, page 141, for the solution.)

4

ARRAYS

INTRODUCTION

The objective of this chapter is to develop a method for storing groups of values without explicitly giving each value a different name. The group of values have a common name but individual values have a unique subscript. This technique allows us to analyze the data using loops, where the common name remains the same, but the subscript becomes a variable that changes with each pass through the loop. Since the data values are stored in separate memory locations, we can also access the data as often as needed without rereading it. The use of an array to store the snowfall data in the introductory problem is necessary because we need to have all the snowfall data available after we have computed the average. Each snowfall value is then compared to the average, and a counter is incremented if the value is greater than the average snowfall value.

4-1 ONE-DIMENSIONAL ARRAYS

An *array* is a group of storage locations that have the same name. Individual members of an array are called *elements* and are distinguished by using the common name followed by a subscript in parentheses. Subscript numbers are consecutive integers, usually beginning with the integer 1. A one-dimensional array can be visualized as either one column of data or one row of data. The storage locations and associated names for a one-dimensional integer array J of five elements and a one-dimensional real array DIST with four elements are shown below:

J(1)	2
J(2)	−5
J(3)	14
J(4)	80
J(5)	−12

1.2	−0.8	36.9	−0.07
DIST(1)	DIST(2)	DIST(3)	DIST(4)

STORAGE AND INITIALIZATION

The DIMENSION statement, a nonexecutable statement, is used to reserve memory space or storage for an array. In the general form of the DIMENSION statement, a list of array names and their corresponding sizes follows the word DIMENSION.

```
DIMENSION  array1(size), array2(size), . . .
```

A DIMENSION statement that will reserve storage for the two arrays previously mentioned is:

```
DIMENSION J(5), DIST(4)
```

The number in parentheses after the array name gives the total number of values to be stored in that array. Two separate DIMENSION statements, with one array listed in each statement, would also be valid, but not preferable because it requires an extra statement. All DIMENSION statements must be placed before any executable statements in your program because they are specification statements.

The type of values stored in an array can be specified implicitly through the choice of array name, or explicitly with a REAL, INTEGER, LOGICAL, or CHARACTER statement. Character arrays will be discussed in detail in Chapter 6. The following statement specifies that AREA is an array of 15 elements that contains integer values:

```
INTEGER AREA(15)
```

The typing of an array, whether implicit or explicit, applies to all elements of the array; hence, an array cannot contain some real values and some integer values. Explicitly typed array names do not appear on DIMENSION statements because the array size has also been specified in the type statement.

The range of subscripts associated with an array can be specified with a beginning subscript number and an ending subscript number, both of which must be integers separated by a colon and following the array name in the DIMENSION statement. The following statement reserves storage for a real array TAX whose elements are TAX(0), TAX(1), TAX(2), TAX(3), TAX(4), and TAX(5), and an integer array INCOME whose elements are INCOME(−3), INCOME(−2), INCOME(−1), INCOME(0), INCOME(1), INCOME(2), and INCOME(3).

```
DIMENSION TAX(0:5), INCOME(-3:3)
```

Unless stated otherwise, we will assume that all array subscripts begin with the integer 1. There are situations, however, in which the range of subscripts logically starts with an integer other than 1. For instance, in the introductory problem at the beginning of Chapter 3 we discussed a set of population values from the years 1880–1980. If this data were to be stored in an array, it might be very convenient to use the year to specify the corresponding population. We could specify such an array with the following statement:

```
INTEGER POPUL(1880:1980)
```

In all compilers, values can be assigned to array elements in the same way that values are assigned to regular variables. The following are valid assignment statements:

```
J(1) = 36
J(5) = K*L
DIST(2) = 46.2 + SIN(X)
```

We will also find it extremely useful to use variables, instead of constants, as subscripts. The following loop initializes all elements of the array J to the value 10:

```
   DO 13 I=1,5
      J(I) = 10
13 CONTINUE
```

J(1)	10
J(2)	10
J(3)	10
J(4)	10
J(5)	10

The next loop initializes the array J to the values shown on the right:

```
   DO 20 I=1,5
      J(I) = I
20 CONTINUE
```

J(1)	1
J(2)	2
J(3)	3
J(4)	4
J(5)	5

The values of the array DIST are initialized to real values with this set of statements:

```
      DO 5 K=1,4
         DIST(K) = K*1.5
    5 CONTINUE
```

DIST(1)	1.5
DIST(2)	3.0
DIST(3)	4.5
DIST(4)	6.0

The previous examples illustrate that a subscript can be an integer constant or an integer variable. Subscripts can also be integer expressions, as indicated in the following statements:

```
J(2*I) = 3
R(J) = R(J-1)
B1 = TR(2*I) + TR(2*I+1)
```

Whenever an expression is used as a subscript, be sure that the value of the expression is between the starting and ending subscript, which is usually 1 to N, where N is the size of the array. If a subscript is outside the proper range, the program will not work correctly. With some compilers, a logic error message is given if a subscript is out of bounds, but other compilers will use an incorrect value for the invalid array reference, causing errors that are serious and difficult to detect.

INPUT AND OUTPUT

To read data into an array from a terminal or from cards, we use the READ statement. If we wish to read an entire array, we can use the name of the array without subscripts. We can also specify specific elements in a READ statement. If the array A contains three elements, then the following two READ statements are equivalent. If the array A contains eight elements, then the first READ statement will read values for all eight elements and the second READ statement will read values for only the first three elements.

```
READ*, A
READ*, A(1), A(2), A(3)
```

Arrays may also be read with an implied DO loop. Implied DO loops use the indexing feature of the DO statement and may be used only on input and output statements and the DATA statement which is presented in the next section. For example, if we wish to read the first 10 elements of the array R, we can use the following implied DO loop on the READ statement:

```
READ*, (R(I), I=1,10)
```

Further examples illustrate the use of these techniques for reading data into an array.

EXAMPLE 4-1 Temperature Measurements

A set of 50 temperature measurements has been entered into a data file, one value per line. The file is accessed with unit number 9. Give a set of statements to read this data into an array.

TEMP(1)	←	data file line 1
TEMP(2)	←	data file line 2
⋮		⋮
TEMP(50)	←	data file line 50

Solution 1

The READ statement in this solution reads one value, but the READ statement is in a loop executed 50 times and thus will read the entire array.

```
      DIMENSION TEMP(50)
          .
          .
          .
      DO 10 I=1,50
         READ(9,*)TEMP(I)
   10 CONTINUE
```

Solution 2

The READ statement in this solution contains no subscript and hence will read the entire array.

```
      DIMENSION TEMP(50)
          .
          .
          .
      READ(9,*)TEMP
```

Solution 3

The READ statement in this solution contains an implied loop and is equivalent to a READ statement that listed TEMP(1), TEMP(2), . . . , TEMP(50).

```
      DIMENSION TEMP(50)
          .
          .
          .
      READ(9,*)(TEMP(I), I=1,50)
```

Note that solution 2 and solution 3 are exactly the same as far as the computer is concerned; they both represent one READ statement with 50 variables. Solution 1 is the same as 50 READ statements with one variable per READ statement. If the data file contains 50 lines with one temperature measurement, all three solutions will store the same data in the array TEMP. However, suppose that each of the 50 lines in the data file had two numbers: a temperature measurement and a humidity measurement. Solution 1 will read a new data line for each temperature measurement because it is the equivalent of 50 READ statements. However, since solutions 2 and 3 are the equivalent of one READ statement with 50 variables, they will go to a new line only when they run out of data. Thus, the data is stored as shown below:

TEMP(1)	first temperature
TEMP(2)	first humidity
TEMP(3)	second temperature
TEMP(4)	second humidity
⋮	⋮

This is a subtle—but important—distinction between the solutions, because the computer does not recognize that an error has occurred in the last instance shown. It has data for the array and continues processing, assuming it has the correct data. ◇

EXAMPLE 4-2 Snowfall Data

A set of 28 snowfall measurements are stored in a data file, with 1 week of data per line. The unit number is again assumed to be 9. Give statements to read this data into an array called SNOW.

SNOW(1)	SNOW(2)	. . . SNOW(7)	←	data file line 1
SNOW(8)	SNOW(9)	. . . SNOW(14)	←	data file line 2
SNOW(15)	SNOW(16)	. . . SNOW(21)	←	data file line 3
SNOW(22)	SNOW(23)	. . . SNOW(28)	←	data file line 4

Correct Solution

The READ statement in this solution contains no subscript and hence will read the entire array. Since each line contains seven data values, four lines of data are required.

```
DIMENSION SNOW(28)
      .
      .
      .
READ(9,*)SNOW
```

Incorrect Solution

The READ statement in this solution reads 1 value, and the READ statement is in a loop executed 28 times. Thus, 28 lines of data are required. Since the data file is entered on 4 lines, an execution error will occur.

```
      DIMENSION SNOW(28)
           .
           .
           .
      DO 10 I=1,28
         READ(9,*)SNOW(I)
   10 CONTINUE
```

◇

Techniques to print the values in an array are similar to those used to read values into an array. The following examples will illustrate the use of DO loops and implied loops for arrays in PRINT statements.

EXAMPLE 4-3 Mass Measurements

A group of 30 mass measurements are stored in an array MASS. We want to print these values in the following tabulation:

```
MASS( 1  ) = XXX KG
MASS( 2  ) = XXX KG
     .
     .
     .
MASS(  30  ) = XXX KG
```

Solution

For each output line, we need to reference one value in the array. The values of the subscript can be generated with a DO statement that has an index of 1 through 30. The output statement in this solution is important; go through it carefully to be sure you understand the placement of the literals.

```
      DIMENSION MASS(30)
           .
           .
           .
      DO 10 I=1,30
         PRINT*, 'MASS(', I, ') =', MASS(I), 'KG'
   10 CONTINUE
```

Incorrect Solution

This solution includes an implied loop that will print each subscript followed by its corresponding value. However, an entire output line will be filled before the next line is begun. The output will not contain one value per line, but will contain several values per line.

```
DIMENSION MASS(30)
     .
     .
     .
PRINT*, ('MASS(', I, ') =', MASS(I), 'KG', I=1,30)
```

◇

EXAMPLE 4-4 Distance, Velocity, Acceleration

Arrays DIS, VEL, and ACC each contain 50 values. The first value in each array represents the distance, velocity, and acceleration of a test rocket at time equal to 1 second. The second set of values represent data for time equal to 2 seconds, and so on. Print the data in the following tabulation:

```
TIME     DISTANCE     VELOCITY     ACCELERATION
(SEC)    (M)          (M/SEC)      (M/SEC**2)

  1        XXXXX        XXXXX          XXXXX
  2        XXXXX        XXXXX          XXXXX
  .          .            .              .
  .          .            .              .
  .          .            .              .
 50        XXXXX        XXXXX          XXXXX
```

Solution

The index of the DO loop is used as a subscript for each array reference. This solution is the equivalent of 50 PRINT statements, each with 4 output variables.

```
   DIMENSION DIS(50), VEL(50), ACC(50)
       .
       .
       .
   PRINT*, 'TIME   DISTANCE   VELOCITY',
  +         '  ACCELERATION'
   PRINT*, '(SEC)  (M)        (M/SEC) ',
  +         '  (M/SEC**2)'
   DO 20 I=1,50
      PRINT*, I, '    ', DIS(I), '    ',
  +           VEL(I), '    ', ACC(I)
20 CONTINUE
```

Incorrect Solution

```
   DIMENSION DIS(50), VEL(50), ACC(50)
       .
       .
       .
   PRINT*, 'TIME    DISTANCE    VELOCITY',
  +        '  ACCELERATION'
   PRINT*, '(SEC)   (M)          (M/SEC) ',
  +        '  (M/SEC**2)'
   DO 30 I=1,50
      PRINT*, I, '     ', DIS, '     ',
  +           VEL, '     ', ACC
30 CONTINUE
```

This solution is incorrect because each time through the loop, we are printing the index I, the entire DIS array (50 values), the entire VEL array (50 values), and the entire ACC array (50 values). Thus, each time through the loop, we print 151 values! ◇

4-2 DATA STATEMENT

The DATA statement is a specification statement and is therefore nonexecutable. It can be very useful in initializing both simple variables and arrays. The general form of the DATA statement is:

DATA *list of variable names /list of values/*

An example of a DATA statement to initialize simple variables is given below:

```
DATA SUM, VEL, VOLT, LENGTH /0.0, 32.75, -10.0, 10/
```

The number of data values must match the number of variable names. The data values should also be in the correct type so that the computer does not have to convert them. The DATA statement above initializes the following variables:

Variable	Value
SUM	0.0
VEL	32.75
VOLT	−10.0
LENGTH	10

Since the DATA statement is a specification statement, it must precede any executable statements. It is therefore located near the beginning of your program, along with the REAL, INTEGER, LOGICAL, CHARACTER, and DIMENSION statements. Normally, it follows these other specification statements because any changes in the type of variables or the declaration of an array must be done before values are given to the corresponding memory locations.

When using the DATA statement, you should be cautious because the DATA statement initializes values only at the beginning of the program execution. This means that the DATA statement cannot be used in a loop to reinitialize variables. If it is necessary to reinitialize variables, you must use assignment statements.

If a number of values are to be repeated in the list of values, a constant followed by an asterisk indicates a repetition. Thus, the following statement initializes all four locations to zero:

```
DATA A, B, C, D /4*0.0/
```

The next two statements initialize the variables I, J, and K to 1, and X, Y, and Z to −0.5:

```
DATA I, J, K, X, Y, Z /3*1, 3*-0.5/
```

or

```
DATA I, X, J, Y, K, Z /3*(1, -0.5)/
```

A DATA statement can also be used to initialize one or more elements of an array, as follows:

```
DIMENSION J(5), TIME(4)
DATA J, TIME /5*0, 1.0, 2.0, 3.0, 4.0/
```

J	0	0	0	0	0
TIME	1.0	2.0	3.0	4.0	

or

```
DIMENSION HOURS(5)
DATA HOURS(1) /60.0/
```

HOURS	60.0	?	?	?	?

The question marks indicate that some array elements are not initialized by the DATA statement. A syntax error would occur if the subscript were left off the array reference HOURS(1) because the number of variables would then not match the number of data values. That is, HOURS represents five variables, but HOURS(1) represents only one variable.

An implied loop can also be used in a DATA statement to initialize only part of an array, as in:

```
INTEGER YEAR(100)
DATA (YEAR(I), I=1,50) /50*0/
```

The first 50 elements of the array are initialized to zero and the last 50 are not initialized. You must therefore make no assumptions about the contents of the last 50 values in the array.

4-3 PROBLEM SOLVING—National Park Snowfall

The snowfall for the month of January has been stored in a data file called IN08. Each data line contains a snowfall amount recorded in inches. Line 1 contains the data for January 1st, line 2 contains the data for January 2nd, and so on. Determine the daily snowfall average for January and the number of days with snowfall above this daily average.

PROBLEM STATEMENT

Compute the average snowfall for January and the number of days with above-average snowfall.

INPUT/OUTPUT DESCRIPTION

The input data is contained in a file called IN08 which contains the snowfall for each day in January. The output is the average snowfall and the number of days with above-average snowfall.

HAND EXAMPLE

For a hand example, we use 1 week's data instead of 1 month's data. The values are:

Day 1	4.2 inches
Day 2	3.1 inches
Day 3	1.5 inches
Day 4	0.2 inches
Day 5	0.0 inches
Day 6	0.0 inches
Day 7	1.8 inches

To determine the average value, we total the amounts and then divide by 7. This yields 10.8/7, or 1.54 inches. We now compare this value to the original data values and find that three days had snowfalls above the average. Notice that we had to use the data values twice. This is why we must use an array. The array allows us to read all the data to compute the total, and still have all the values accessible for comparing them to the average.

ALGORITHM DEVELOPMENT

After completion of the hand example, the initial decomposition is straightforward.

DECOMPOSITION

Read snowfall data
Compute average snowfall
Determine the number of days with above-average snowfall
Print average, number of days

In the refinement, we need to show two loops: one to read the data and the other to compare the data to the average. Note that the loops are independent. We must complete the first loop and calculate the average before we can compare the individual values to the average.

REFINEMENT IN PSEUDOCODE

```
SNOFAL:  BEGIN
            total ← 0
            FOR i=1 TO 31 DO
               READ snow(i)
               total ← total + snow(i)
            END FOR
            PRINT snow
            ave ← total/31
            PRINT ave
            count ← 0
            FOR i=1 TO 31 DO
               IF snow(i) > ave
                  count ← count + 1
               END IF
            END FOR
            PRINT count
         END
```

FORTRAN PROGRAM

```
      PROGRAM SNOFAL
*
*   THIS PROGRAM COMPUTES THE AVERAGE SNOWFALL
*   FOR JANUARY AND COUNTS THE NUMBER OF DAYS
*   WITH ABOVE-AVERAGE SNOWFALL
*
      DIMENSION SNOW(31)
      INTEGER COUNT
      DATA TOTAL, COUNT /0.0, 0/
*
      OPEN(UNIT=10, FILE='IN08', STATUS='OLD')
*
      DO 10 I=1,31
         READ(10,*)SNOW(I)
         TOTAL = TOTAL + SNOW(I)
   10 CONTINUE
*
      PRINT*, SNOW
*
      AVE = TOTAL/31.0
*
      PRINT*, 'AVERAGE SNOWFALL IS', AVE, 'INCHES'
*
      DO 20 I=1,31
         IF(SNOW(I).GT.AVE)COUNT = COUNT + 1
   20 CONTINUE
*
      PRINT*, COUNT, 'DAYS WITH ABOVE-AVERAGE SNOWFALL'
*
      END
```

TESTING

The program includes a statement to print the original data. This is very useful in debugging a program. How is the snowfall data printed? Is it one value per line or several per line? Since the entire array is listed on a single PRINT statement, as many values as will fit on a line will be printed. This PRINT statement can easily be removed after the program has been carefully tested. Sometimes it is convenient to turn a PRINT statement into a comment by placing an asterisk in column 1. The statement is then ignored during compilation. If you make modifications to the program or if it does not seem to be working properly, it is easy to remove the asterisk and include the PRINT statement again in the program. The computer output on the next page does not include the output from this PRINT statement, but does show the last two lines of output.

A set of data values used in a test run is shown next, seven values per line. When this data is entered in the data file IN08, it should be entered one value per line or the program will not work correctly.

Data Values

4.2	3.1	1.5	0.2	0.0	0.0	1.8
1.1	0.9	0.0	0.0	0.0	0.2	0.0
0.9	1.4	1.2	0.3	0.0	0.0	0.0
0.0	0.0	1.5	1.2	0.4	1.6	0.7
0.3	0.0	0.0				

Computer Output

```
AVERAGE SNOWFALL IS 0.7258 INCHES
12 DAYS WITH ABOVE-AVERAGE SNOWFALL
```

4-4 PROBLEM SOLVING— EARTHQUAKE MEASUREMENTS

In this section we develop an algorithm to sort a one-dimensional array into *ascending*, or low-to-high, order. With minor changes, the algorithm can be changed to one that sorts an array into descending order. The topic of sorting techniques is the subject of entire textbooks; therefore, this text will not attempt to present all the important aspects of sorting. A simple, multi-pass sort, also called a *bubble sort,* is presented because it is straightforward to develop.

The basic step to the sort algorithm is a single pass through the array, comparing adjacent elements in it. If a pair of adjacent elements is in the correct order (that is, the first value less than or equal to the second value), then we go to the next pair. If the pair is out of order, we must switch the values and then go to the next pair.

The single pass through the array can be performed in a DO loop with index I. Each pair of adjacent values will be referred to by the subscripts I and I + 1. If there are N elements in the array, we will make N − 1 comparisons. Thus, the loop will need to be performed N − 1 times. When the value of the index is N − 1, the last pair of adjacent values will still be referenced by I and I + 1, but the actual values of I and I + 1 will be (N − 1) and N, respectively.

The switch of two adjacent values requires three steps, not two as might first be imagined. Consider the statements below:

```
A(I) = A(I+1)
A(I+1) = A(I)
```

Suppose A(I) contained the value 3 and A(I + 1) contained the value −1. The first statement will change the contents of A(I) from the value 3 to the value −1. The second statement will move the value in A(I) to A(I + 1), and then both locations contain −1. These steps are shown below, along with the changes in the corresponding memory locations.

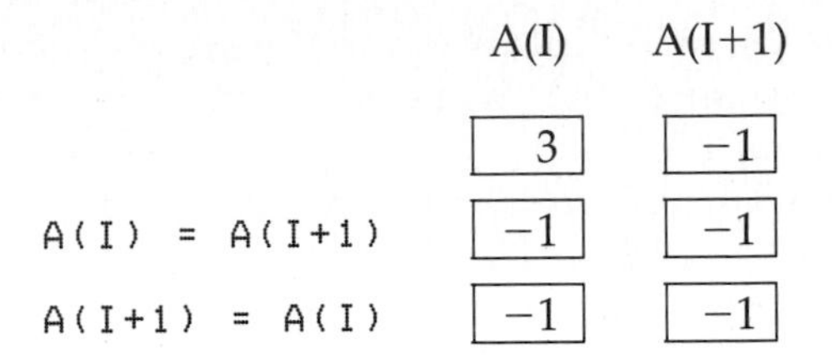

A correct way to switch the two values is shown below, along with the changes in the corresponding memory locations.

	A(I)	A(I+1)	TEMP
	3	−1	?
`TEMP = A(I)`	3	−1	3
`A(I) = A(I+1)`	−1	−1	3
`A(I+1) = A(I)`	−1	3	3

A single pass through a one-dimensional array, switching adjacent elements which are out of order, is not guaranteed to sort the values. Consider a single pass through the following array:

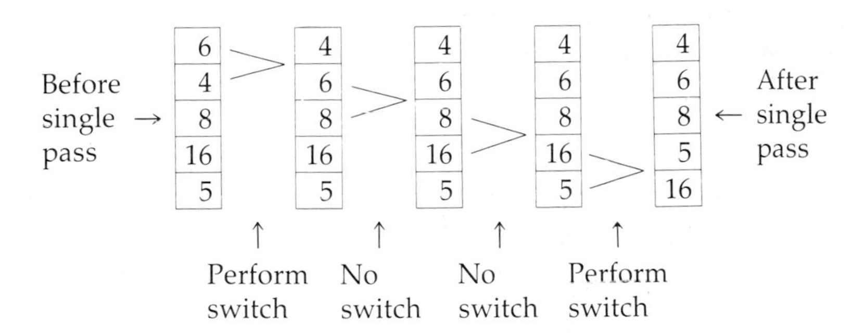

It will take two more complete passes before the array is sorted into ascending order. A maximum of N−1 passes may be necessary to sort an array with this technique. If no switches are made during a single pass through the array, however, it is in ascending order. Thus, our algorithm for sorting a one-dimensional array will be to perform single passes through the array making switches until no elements are out of order. In developing the pseudocode, we use a logical variable SORTED that is initialized to true at the beginning of each pass through the data array. If any values are out of order, we switch the values and change the value of SORTED to false because at least one pair of values was out of order on this pass. Thus, at the end of a pass through the data, if the value of SORTED is still true, the array is in ascending order.

The application that will use this sort routine is one that might be encountered in a field laboratory that monitors seismic, or earthquake, activity. Suppose that a particular location in California has been the site of earthquake activity for a number of years. The magnitude of each event has been recorded using the Richter scale. This data is stored in a data file IN09, in the order in which the earthquakes occurred. Write a program to read this information, sort it into ascending order, and print the data in this new order.

The initial line of the data file contains a 30-character description of the location, enclosed in apostrophes. When new earthquakes occur, the information is added to the end of the file. Therefore, you do not know ahead of time how many data values are in the file. You can, however, assume an upper limit of 200 data values. It should be clear that we need to store the data in an array if we are to sort it; we will need to refer to the data values more than once as we perform the different passes through the data, exchanging values that are out of order.

PROBLEM STATEMENT

Sort a group of earthquake measurements into ascending order, and print the values in the new order.

INPUT/OUTPUT DESCRIPTION

The earthquake measurements are stored in a data file, one value per line. The first line of the data file contains a description of the area. The number of entries in the file is not known ahead of time. The output is to be a listing of the same set of data, but sorted into an ascending order.

HAND EXAMPLE

Using the sort technique presented at the beginning of this section, go through the steps of sorting this group of data:

Original order	
	4.1
	7.3
	1.7
	5.2
	1.3

The first pass through the data is shown in detail, along with the final results from each following pass through the data.

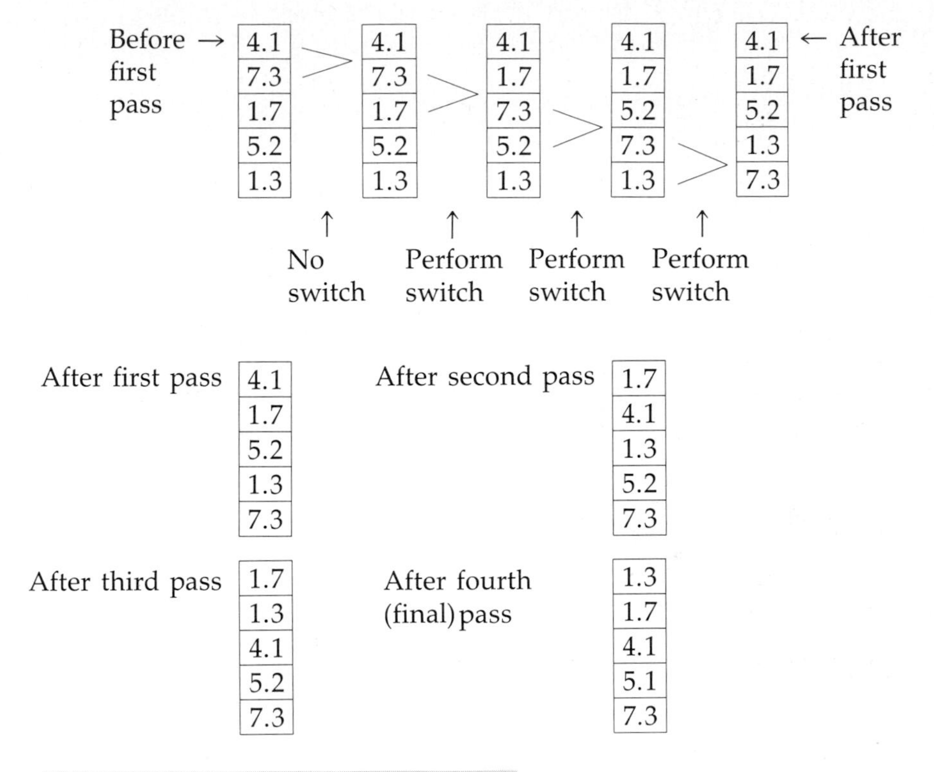

ALGORITHM DEVELOPMENT

Using the ideas about sorting already discussed, we can develop an initial decomposition, and refine that into more detailed pseudocode. In the refined pseudocode, we determine the number of data values, N, when we read the data.

Decomposition

Read description
Print description
Read quake values
Sort quake values
Print quake values

Refinement in Pseudocode

```
EARTH:  BEGIN
           READ description
           PRINT description
           i ← 1
           WHILE more quake data DO
              READ quake(i)
              i ← i + 1
           END WHILE
           n ← i − 1
           Sort quake array
           PRINT quake array
        END
```

We now refine the sort step, using the multiple-pass sort algorithm. Assume that there are N values in the array to be sorted.

Refinement of Sort Algorithm

```
sorted ← false
WHILE not sorted DO
   sorted ← true
   For i=1 TO n−1 DO
      IF quake(i) > quake(i+1)
         Switch values
         sorted ← false
      END IF
   END FOR
END WHILE
```

We are now ready to convert these steps into a FORTRAN program.

FORTRAN Program

```
      PROGRAM EARTH
*
*   THIS PROGRAM WILL READ A FILE OF EARTHQUAKE DATA
*   AND SORT AND PRINT IT IN ASCENDING ORDER
*
      DIMENSION QUAKE(200)
      CHARACTER*30 DESC
      LOGICAL SORTED
*
      OPEN(UNIT=9, FILE='IN09', STATUS='OLD')
*
      READ(9,*)DESC
      PRINT*, DESC
*
      I = 1
    1 READ(9,*,END=20)QUAKE(I)
         I = I + 1
         GO TO 1
*
   20 N = I - 1
*
      SORTED = .FALSE.
   25 IF(.NOT.SORTED)THEN
         SORTED = .TRUE.
         DO 30 I=1,N-1
            IF(QUAKE(I).GT.QUAKE(I+1))THEN
               TEMP = QUAKE(I)
               QUAKE(I) = QUAKE(I+1)
               QUAKE(I+1) = TEMP
               SORTED = .FALSE.
            ENDIF
   30    CONTINUE
         GO TO 25
      ENDIF
*
      DO 50 I=1,N
         PRINT*, QUAKE(I)
   50 CONTINUE
*
      END
```

TESTING

As our programs become longer, testing becomes more of a challenge. A good procedure in testing a program is to test it in pieces. For instance, test the input portion of the program without executing the rest of the program. An easy way to accomplish this is by inserting these statements after statement 20:

```
      PRINT*, DESC, N
      PRINT*, QUAKE
      STOP
```

When you are convinced that this portion is working, take these statements out. We are now ready to look at the sort. Use a small data set initially so that you are not overwhelmed with data. Insert the statement

```
PRINT*, QUAKE
```

just after statement 30. This will print the data values after each pass through the array, just as we did in the hand example. If there are problems here, move the PRINT statement inside the DO loop, just before statement 30. This will allow you to see the results of each comparison. Notice how these pieces of program that we test individually correspond to the overall steps in the initial decomposition.

When you have the algorithm working, be sure to use a variety of test data sets. Use sets that are already in order and sets that are in reverse order, in addition to sequences in random order. The output from a sample set of data would be in this form:

DATA FILE IN09

```
'DATA FROM SANTA PALA, CA'
2.5810
1.5000
1.6200
3.7800
4.2500
1.7330
```

COMPUTER OUTPUT

```
DATA FROM SANTA PALA, CA
1.5000
1.6200
1.7330
2.5810
3.7800
4.2500
```

There is one last point to make. After sorting the array QUAKE, we changed the order of the values from one that was sequential in time to one that is in ascending order. In doing this, we lost the original order within our program. The data file is still in the original order, but our program has the data only in ascending order. If the program also needed the original data, we could move the original data into a second array after it was read. Then, after sorting, we would have two arrays of data—one in the original order and one in ascending order.

In Chapter 6 we extend this sorting technique to include sorting character data into alphabetical order.

4-5 TWO-DIMENSIONAL ARRAYS

If we visualize a one-dimensional array as a single column of data, we can then visualize a group of columns, as illustrated below:

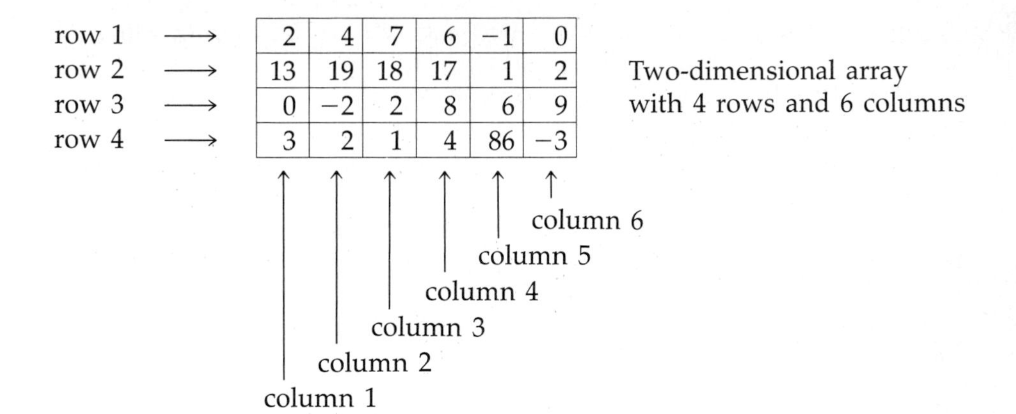

The diagram depicts an integer array with 24 elements. As in one-dimensional arrays, each of the 24 elements has the same array name. However, one subscript is not sufficient to specify an element in a two-dimensional array. For instance, if the array's name is M, it is not clear whether M(3) should be the third element in the first row or the third element in the first column. To avoid any ambiguity, an element in a two-dimensional array will be referenced with two subscripts, one for the row number and one for the column number. The first subscript references the row and the second subscript references the column. Thus, M(2, 3) refers to the number in the second row and third column. In our diagram, M(2, 3) contains 18.

STORAGE AND INITIALIZATION

Two-dimensional arrays must be specified in a DIMENSION statement or a type statement, but not both. The DIMENSION statement below reserves storage for a one-dimensional real array B of 10 elements, a two-dimensional real array C with 3 rows and 5 columns, and a two-dimensional integer array J with seven rows and four columns. The REAL statement reserves storage for a two-dimensional real array NUM with five rows and two columns. If the DIMENSION statement included NUM(5,2) along with the REAL statement, a compilation error would occur.

```
DIMENSION B(10), C(3,5), J(7,4)
REAL NUM(5,2)
```

The statement

```
DIMENSION R(0:2, -1:1)
```

reserves storage for array elements R(0, −1), R(0, 0), R(0, 1), R(1, −1), R(1, 0), R(1, 1), R(2, −1), R(2, 0), R(2, 1).

Two-dimensional arrays can be initialized with assignment statements or with the DATA statement. If the name of the array is used without implied loops, the array will be filled in column order, as illustrated by the next example. When subscripts are used to access a two-dimensional array, it is common notation to use I for the row subscript and J for the column subscript.

EXAMPLE 4-5 Array Initialization, A(5, 4)

Fill the array A as shown:

1.0	1.0	2.0	2.0
1.0	1.0	2.0	2.0
1.0	1.0	2.0	2.0
1.0	1.0	2.0	2.0
1.0	1.0	2.0	2.0

Solution 1

```
      DIMENSION A(5,4)
      DATA A /10*1.0, 10*2.0/
```

Solution 2

```
      DIMENSION A(5,4)
         .
         .
         .
      DO 10 I=1,5
         A(I,1) = 1.0
         A(I,2) = 1.0
         A(I,3) = 2.0
         A(I,4) = 2.0
   10 CONTINUE
```
◇

EXAMPLE 4-6 Array Initialization, M(4, 3)

Fill the array M as shown:

1	1	1
2	2	2
3	3	3
4	4	4

Solution 1

If we observe that each element of the array contains its corresponding row number, then a solution is:

```
      DIMENSION M(4,3)
          .
          .
          .
      DO 10 I=1,4
         DO 5 J=1,3
            M(I,J) = I
    5    CONTINUE
   10 CONTINUE
```

Solution 2

The following DATA statement also initializes the array correctly:

```
      DIMENSION M(4,3)
      DATA M /3*(1, 2, 3, 4)/
```

Again, the DATA statement solution is preferable because only one statement is required. ◇

EXAMPLE 4-7 Identity Matrix

Fill the integer array TOTAL with five rows and five columns with 1's on the main diagonal and 0's elsewhere. This is called a 5 × 5 *identity matrix.* It is also a *square matrix* because it has the same number of rows and columns.

1	0	0	0	0
0	1	0	0	0
0	0	1	0	0
0	0	0	1	0
0	0	0	0	1

Solution

The positions that contain 1's are positions where the row number and column number are the same (TOTAL(1,1), TOTAL(2,2), TOTAL(3,3), TOTAL(4,4), TOTAL(5,5)).

```
      INTEGER TOTAL(5,5)
         .
         .
         .
      DO 10 I=1,5
         DO 5 J=1,5
            IF(I.EQ.J)THEN
               TOTAL(I,J) = 1
            ELSE
               TOTAL(I,J) = 0
            ENDIF
    5    CONTINUE
   10 CONTINUE
```

◇

INPUT AND OUTPUT

The main difference between using values from a one-dimensional array and using values from a two-dimensional array is that the latter requires two subscripts. Most loops used in the reading or printing of two-dimensional arrays are therefore usually nested loops.

EXAMPLE 4-8 Medical Data

Analysis of a medical experiment requires the use of a set of data containing the weight of 100 participants at the beginning of an experiment and at the end of the experiment. The data values have been stored in a data file and will be accessed using unit number 13. Each line in the file contains the initial weight and final weight of a participant. Give statements to read the data into a two-dimensional array.

Solution 1

```
      DIMENSION WEIGHT(100,2)
         .
         .
         .
      DO 10 I=1,100
         READ(13,*)WEIGHT(I,1), WEIGHT(I,2)
   10 CONTINUE
```

Solution 2

```
DIMENSION WEIGHT(100,2)
   .
   .
   .
READ(13,*)(WEIGHT(I,1), WEIGHT(I,2), I=1,100)
```

◇

EXAMPLE 4-9 Terminal Inventory

A large technical firm keeps an inventory of the locations of its computer terminals in a data file. Assume that this data has already been read into a two-dimensional array. There are 4 types of terminals, represented by the 4 columns, and 20 laboratories using the terminals, represented by the 20 rows of the array. Print the data in a form similar to the following:

```
TERMINAL INVENTORY
TYPE         1      2      3      4
-----------------------------------
LAB 1       XX     XX     XX     XX
LAB 2       XX     XX     XX     XX
LAB 3       XX     XX     XX     XX
   .
   .
   .
LAB 20      XX     XX     XX     XX
```

Solution

This solution uses the index of a DO loop as the row subscript. Then the index of an implied loop on the PRINT statement supplies the column subscript. Hence, each time the PRINT statement is executed, one row of data is printed.

```
      DIMENSION INVEN(20,4)
          .
          .
          .
      PRINT*, 'TERMINAL INVENTORY'
      PRINT*, '_____________________'
      PRINT*, 'TYPE    1    2    3    4'
      PRINT*, '_____________________'
*
      DO 200 I=1,20
         PRINT*, 'LAB', I, (INVEN(I,J), J=1,4)
  200 CONTINUE
```

◇

4-6 PROBLEM SOLVING—EXAM STATISTICS

Analyzing data and generating statistics are operations commonly performed by computers. In this section, the data represents exam scores from a university class. In fact, the class is an introductory computing class. It has been so popular that additional sections have been added. The professor in charge of coordinating these classes would like a computer program to generate a few statistics to help her analyze the exam grades.

The particular set of data available is from a summer session which had 8 weeks of classes. The students in each section took a weekly exam. The average grade from each section for each week has been stored in a data file called IN10. The first line of the file contains a 25-character description of the class and semester. The description is enclosed in apostrophes. The next line in the file contains eight numbers, representing the weekly exam averages for section 1. The next line in the file contains the eight weekly exam averages for section 2, and so on.

The coordinator of this class is particularly interested in analyzing the scores by weeks, to see if all sections perform similarly. The first set of data that she would like calculated are weekly averages across the sections, and the maximum and minimum section scores. With this data, she will have the weekly average to compare to the maximum and minimum for that week. If the maximum and minimum values are close to the average, then there is not much difference between the performance of the sections. If the difference is large, then the performance between sections should be studied further. To give a little more information in this analysis, the program should also print the section numbers of the section(s) that had the maximum weekly score and of the section(s) that had the minimum weekly score.

PROBLEM STATEMENT

Compute the average exam grade using scores from six sections, for each week of an 8-week summer session. In addition, determine the maximum and minimum exam averages each week.

INPUT/OUTPUT DESCRIPTION

The exam averages for each section are stored in a data file called IN10 which has the following form:

line 1: description of the class
line 2: averages for the 8 weeks for section 1
line 3: averages for the 8 weeks for section 2
⋮
line 7: averages for the 8 weeks for section 6

The following output will be printed for each week:

```
WEEK X
     AVE = XXXXXX
     MIN = XXXXXX
       SECTION X
     MAX = XXXXXX
       SECTION X
```

HAND EXAMPLE

Since the computations work with 1 week's data at a time, assume that the following is a typical set of data:

section	1	2	3	4	5	6
average	86.1	92.3	85.5	100.0	96.2	100.0

The output information should then be:

```
WEEK 1
     AVE = 93.3500
     MIN = 86.1000
       SECTION 1
     MAX = 100.0000
       SECTION 4
       SECTION 6
```

ALGORITHM DEVELOPMENT

Before we begin decomposing the problem solution into a series of steps, it is important to spend some time considering the best way to store the data that we will need for the program. Unfortunately, once we become comfortable with arrays, we tend to use them all the time. Using an array necessarily complicates our programs, however, because of the subscript handling that becomes necessary. Therefore, we must stop and ask ourselves, "Do we really need an array for this data?"

If the individual data values will be needed more than once, an array is needed. An array is also necessary if the data is not in the order needed. Then we must read all the data before we can go back and begin processing it. However, if an average of a group of data values is all that is to be computed, we probably do not need an array. As we read the values, we can add them to a total, and read the next value into the same location as the previous value. The individual values are not needed again since the information required is now in the total.

Now, let us look at our specific problem and determine whether or not we need to use an array. If we were computing an average for an individual section, we would need only one line of information at a time. Since we are computing the average for a week, we need the first value for section 1 (line 2), the first value for section 2 (line 3), and so on. Therefore, the data is not in the order in which we need it; we will have to read it all, and then return to compute the averages that we need. Even if the data had been stored by weeks instead of by sections, a one-dimensional array would have been needed to store an entire week's data at a time since the data is needed a second time to print the section numbers of the sections whose scores were maximum or minimum for that week.

We are now ready to decompose the problem solution into a series of general steps and then do the initial refinement into pseudocode.

DECOMPOSITION

Read exam data
Compute and print average
Determine and print minimum average and corresponding sections
Determine and print maximum average and corresponding sections

INITIAL REFINEMENT IN PSEUDOCODE

```
STAT:  BEGIN
          READ scores
          FOR week = 1 TO 8 DO
             Compute average
             Find minimum and maximum
             PRINT average
             Determine and print minimum average
                and corresponding sections
             Determine and print maximum average
                and corresponding sections
          END FOR
       END
```

As we refine these steps, we want to be as efficient as possible in searching through the array. Instead of going through the first column of data once to get an average, again to get the maximum, again to get the minimum, and so on, we want to get all the information that we can each time through the column. For instance, we can compute the total for the average at the same time we search for the minimum and maximum values.

After computing and printing the average, we can print the minimum. However, in order to print the number of the section with the minimum average, we need to search through the data again to determine which section (or sections) had the minimum average. After printing these, we can print the maximum average.

We will need to go through the column of data one last time to find the section or sections with the maximum scores. Thus, we will use each column of data three times to get our information: once to compute the average, minimum, and maximum scores, again to find the sections with minimum scores, and finally to find sections with maximum scores.

Certainly there are other ways to get the same information. Remember that the main criterion to use in comparing different solutions is simplicity. Keep your algorithms simple and easy to understand. Clever steps may make the algorithm shorter, but they seldom make it clearer.

We start the search for the minimum by setting the minimum equal to the first value in the data for that week. We then begin comparing the other values to this one, replacing it with any smaller values. This technique is better than starting the minimum with a particular value, such as 100.0, because you do not always know the range of values. A similar technique is used for determining the maximum.

FINAL REFINEMENT IN PSEUDOCODE

```
STAT:  BEGIN
          READ description
          PRINT description
          READ scores array
          FOR week=1 TO 8 DO
             min ← score(1,week)
             max ← score(1,week)
             total ← 0
             FOR sect=1 TO 6 DO
                total ← total + score(sect,week)
                IF score(sect,week) < min
                   min ← score(sect, week)
                END IF
                IF score(sect,week) > max
                   max ← score(sect,week)
                END IF
             END FOR
             ave ← total/6.0
             PRINT ave
             PRINT min
             FOR sect=1 TO 6 DO
                IF score(sect,week) = min
                   PRINT sect
                END IF
             END FOR
             PRINT max
             FOR sect=1 TO 6 DO
                IF score(sect,week) = max
                   PRINT sect
                END IF
             END FOR
          END FOR
       END
```

FORTRAN Program

```
      PROGRAM STAT
*
*  THIS PROGRAM COMPUTES STATISTICS FROM
*  EXAM AVERAGES IN 6 SECTIONS OF A CLASS
*
      DIMENSION SCORES(6,8)
      CHARACTER*25 DESC
      REAL MAX, MIN
      INTEGER WEEK, SECT
*
      OPEN(UNIT=8, FILE='IN10', STATUS='OLD')
*
      READ(8,*)DESC
      PRINT*, DESC
*
      DO 5 SECT=1,6
         READ(8,*)(SCORES(SECT,WEEK), WEEK=1,8)
    5 CONTINUE
*
      DO 50 WEEK=1,8
         TOTAL = 0.0
         MAX = SCORES(1,WEEK)
         MIN = SCORES(1,WEEK)
         DO 10 SECT=1,6
            TOTAL = TOTAL + SCORES(SECT,WEEK)
            IF(SCORES(SECT,WEEK).LT.MIN)MIN = SCORES(SECT,WEE
            IF(SCORES(SECT,WEEK).GT.MAX)MAX = SCORES(SECT,WEE
   10    CONTINUE
*
         PRINT*, 'WEEK', WEEK
         AVE = TOTAL/6.0
         PRINT*, '     AVE =', AVE
*
         PRINT*, '     MIN =', MIN
         DO 20 SECT=1,6
            IF(SCORES(SECT,WEEK).EQ.MIN)PRINT*, '        ',
     +         'SECTION', SECT
   20    CONTINUE
*
         PRINT*, '        MAX =', MAX
         DO 30 SECT=1,6
            IF(SCORES(SECT,WEEK).EQ.MAX)PRINT*, '        ',
     +         'SECTION', SECT
   30    CONTINUE
*
   50 CONTINUE
*
      END
```

TESTING

We suggest testing this program in stages. The obvious places to insert PRINT statements are after reading the data, after computing the total, minimum, and maximum, and after printing the sections that had the maximum and minimum scores. If sections of a program that use arrays are not working properly, print the values of the subscripts to see if you are modifying them properly. For instance, if the total is not correct, just before statement 10 insert the line

```
PRINT*, SECT, WEEK, SCORES(SECT,WEEK)
```

This will print the subscripts and the corresponding array value each time through the loop.

Here is an example set of data, and the output from the program.

DATA FILE IN10

```
'CS105 - SUMMER SESSION'
86.1 91.4 85.5 97.2 94.0 88.4 91.9 95.7
88.3 95.0 87.1 94.4 93.8 90.0 89.9 93.5
84.5 94.6 86.7 95.3 92.2 93.1 90.0 94.1
85.6 93.7 88.2 96.7 91.6 89.2 90.3 92.0
87.7 91.4 89.3 98.1 93.2 91.8 92.0 93.8
90.2 94.1 88.3 93.8 94.7 92.9 89.4 92.6
```

Computer Output

```
CS105 - SUMMER SESSION
WEEK 1
     AVE = 87.0667
     MIN = 84.5000
       SECTION 3
     MAX = 90.2000
       SECTION 6
WEEK 2
     AVE = 93.3667
     MIN = 91.4000
       SECTION 1
       SECTION 5
     MAX = 95.0000
       SECTION 2
WEEK 3
     AVE = 87.5167
     MIN = 85.5000
       SECTION 1
     MAX = 89.3000
       SECTION 5
WEEK 4
     AVE = 95.9167
     MIN = 93.8000
       SECTION 6
     MAX = 98.1000
       SECTION 5
WEEK 5
     AVE = 93.2500
     MIN = 91.6000
       SECTION 4
     MAX = 94.7000
       SECTION 6
WEEK 6
     AVE = 90.000
     MIN = 88.4000
       SECTION 1
     MAX = 93.1000
       SECTION 3
WEEK 7
     AVE = 90.5833
     MIN = 89.4000
       SECTION 6
     MAX = 92.0000
       SECTION 5
WEEK 8
     AVE = 93.6167
     MIN = 92.0000
       SECTION 4
     MAX = 95.7000
       SECTION 1
```

4-7 MULTI-DIMENSIONAL ARRAYS

FORTRAN allows as many as seven dimensions for arrays. We can easily visualize a three-dimensional array, such as a cube. We are also familiar with using three coordinates, X, Y, Z, to locate points. This idea extends into subscripts. The three-dimensional array below would be dimensioned T(3,4,4):

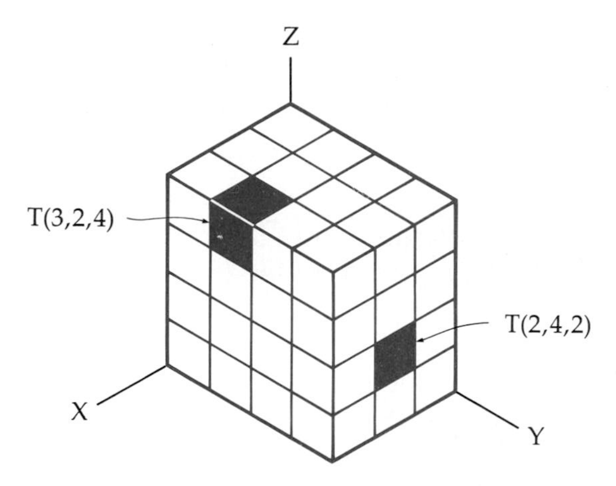

If we use the three-dimensional array name without subscripts, we access the array with the first subscript changing fastest, the second subscript changing next fastest, and the third subscript changing the slowest. Thus, using the array T of the previous diagram, the two statements below would be equivalent:

```
READ(5,*)T
READ(5,*)(((T(I,J,K), I=1,3), J=1,4), K=1,4)
```

It should be evident that three levels of nesting are often needed to access a three-dimensional array.

Most applications do not use arrays with more than three dimensions, probably because visualizing more than three dimensions seems to become abstract. However, here is a simple scheme that allows you to mentally picture even a seven-dimensional array:

Four-dimensional array: Picture a row of three-dimensional arrays. One subscript, the first, specifies a unique three-dimensional array. The other three subscripts specify a unique position in that array.

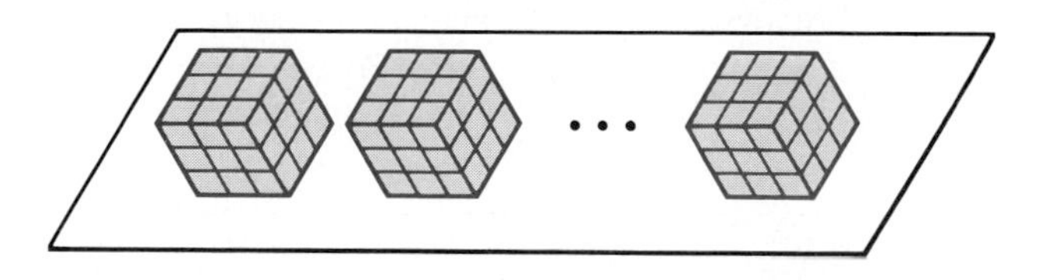

Five-dimensional array: Picture a block or grid of three-dimensional arrays. Two subscripts (first and second) specify a unique three-dimensional array. The other three subscripts specify a unique position in that array.

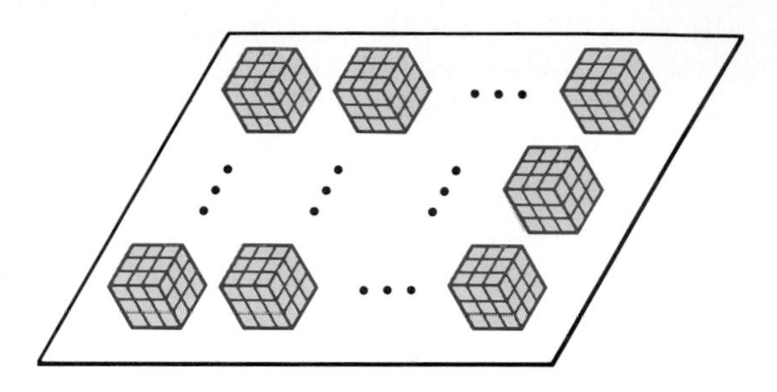

Six-dimensional array: Picture a row of blocks or grids. One subscript specifies the grid. The other five subscripts specify the unique position in the grid.

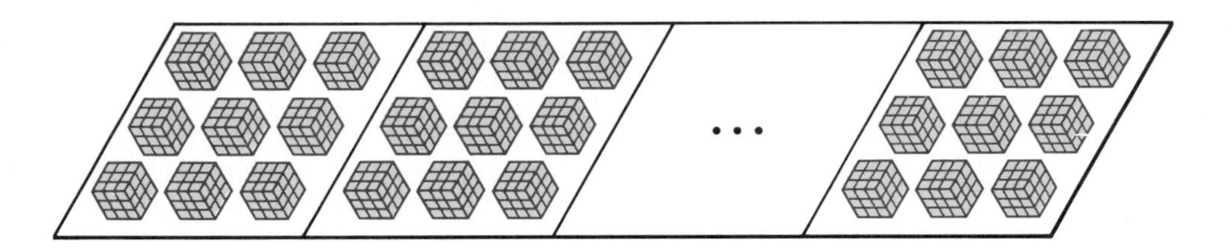

Seven-dimensional array: Picture a grid of grids or a grid of blocks. Two subscripts specify the grid. The other five subscripts specify the unique position in the grid.

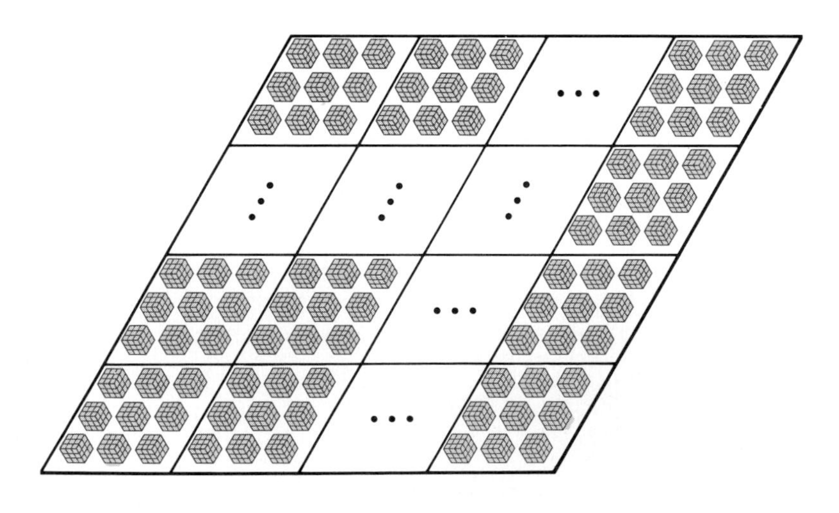

Now that you can visualize multi-dimensional arrays, a natural question is "What dimension array do I use for solving a problem?" There is no single answer. A problem that could be solved with a two-dimensional array of four rows and three columns could also be solved with four one-dimensional arrays of three elements each. Usually, the data fits one array form better than another. You should choose the form that will be the easiest for you to work with in your program. For example, if you have census data from 10 countries over the period 1950–1980, you would probably use an array with 10 rows and 31 columns, or 31 rows and 10 columns. If the data represents the populations of 5 cities from each of 10 countries for the period 1950–1980, a three-dimensional array would be most appropriate. The three subscripts would represent year, country, and city.

SUMMARY

In this chapter we learned how to use an array—a group of storage locations that all have a common name but are distinguished by one or more subscripts. Arrays prove to be one of the most powerful elements of FORTRAN because they allow us to keep large amounts of data easily accessible by our programs. The remaining chapters will rely heavily on arrays for storing and manipulating data. Another important topic that was presented in this chapter is sorting. We will use the sort algorithm developed here in each of the following chapters.

KEY WORDS

array
ascending order
bubble sort
descending order
element
implied DO loop
multi-dimensional array
multi-pass sort
one-dimensional array
subscript
two-dimensional array

DEBUGGING AIDS

Because arrays can be used so conveniently to handle large amounts of data, a natural tendency of new programmers is to use arrays for everything. Unfortunately, using arrays can also introduce new errors. As you debug programs that use arrays, therefore, analyze the decision to use each array. Ask yourself the questions "Will I need this data more than once?" and "Must this data be stored before I can use it?" If the answers to both questions are "No," then you should eliminate the array and replace it with simple variables. You will also probably be eliminating some loops and statements involving subscripts. These changes may not only reduce the number of errors in your program but will also reduce the overall complexity of your program.

If arrays are necessary, then consider each of the following items if your program is working incorrectly:

1 DIMENSION—The DIMENSION statement or type statement must specify the maximum number of elements that are to be stored in the array. While you do not have to use all the elements of an array, you can never use more elements than specified in the DIMENSION statement or type statement.

2 SUBSCRIPT—Check each subscript to be sure that it represents an integer that falls within the proper range of values. Particularly check for subscript values that are one value too small (such as zero) or one value too large (such as N + 1).

3 INDEX—If you are using the index of a DO loop as a subscript, be sure you have used the same variable. That is, if the DO loop index is K, did you use I instead of K as a subscript?

4 REVERSE SUBSCRIPTS—When you are working with multi-dimensional arrays, be sure you have the subscripts in the proper order. Do you want B(K,J) or B(J,K)?

STYLE/TECHNIQUE GUIDES

As we mentioned in Debugging Aids, be sure that you really need an array before implementing an algorithm with an array. If you need arrays to solve your problem, take some time to decide the optimum size. Depending on the application, you may find that a two-dimensional array with 10 rows and 2 columns will be more direct and understandable than two separate arrays of 10 elements each. Choose the array structure that best suits the program.

Be consistent in your choice of subscript names. Common practice is to use the variable I for the first subscript, J for the second subscript, and K for the third subscript. If you follow the same pattern or a similar pattern, it is much easier to decide the nesting of loops and the values of DO loop parameters that are also used as subscripts.

PROBLEMS

For problems 1 through 9, draw the array and indicate the contents of each position in the array after executing the following sets of statements. Assume that each set of statements is independent of the others. If no value is given to a particular position, fill it with a question mark.

1

```
      DIMENSION M(10)
      DO 5 I=1,10
         M(I) = I + 1
    5 CONTINUE
```

2

```
      DIMENSION M(10)
      DO 20 J=1,9
         M(J+1) = 2
   20 CONTINUE
```

3

```
      DIMENSION R(8)
      DO 15 KK=1,8
         R(KK) = 10 - KK
   15 CONTINUE
```

4

```
      DIMENSION LST(6)
      DO 1 K=1,6
         J = 7 - K
         LST(J) = K
    1 CONTINUE
```

5

```
      DIMENSION R(8)
      DO 10 I=1,8
         IF(I.LE.3)THEN
            R(I) = 2.5
         ELSE
            R(I) = -2.5
         ENDIF
   10 CONTINUE
```

6

```
      DIMENSION R(0:9)
      DO 10 I=1,8
         IF(I.GT.4)R(I) = 4.0
   10 CONTINUE
```

7

```
      DIMENSION CH(5,4)
      DO 5 I=1,5
         DO 4 J=1,4
            CH(I,J) = I*J
    4    CONTINUE
    5 CONTINUE
```

8

```
      DIMENSION K(5,4)
      DO 5 M=1,4
         DO 4 N=1,4
            K(M,N) = MOD(M+N,3)
    4    CONTINUE
    5 CONTINUE
```

9

```
      DIMENSION I(8,2)
      I(8,1) = 4
      I(8,2) = 5
      DO 6 L=1,7
         I(L,1) = 2
         I(L,2) = 3
    6 CONTINUE
```

For problems 10 through 13, assume that K, a one-dimensional array of 50 values, has already been filled with data.

10 Give FORTRAN statements to find and print the maximum value of K in the following form:

```
MAXIMUM VALUE IS XXXXX
```

11 Give FORTRAN statements to find and print the minimum value of K, and its position in the array, in the following form:

```
MINIMUM VALUE OF K IS
K(XX) = XXXXX
```

12 Give FORTRAN statements to count the number of positive values, zero values, and negative values in K. The output form should be:

```
XXX  POSITIVE VALUES
XXX  ZERO VALUES
XXX  NEGATIVE VALUES
```

13 Give FORTRAN statements to replace each value of K with its absolute value. Then print the array K, with two values per line.

14 An array TIME contains 30 numbers. Give statements that will print every other value, beginning with the second value, in this form:

```
TIME( 2 ) CONTAINS XXXX SECONDS
TIME( 4 ) CONTAINS XXXX SECONDS
      .
      .
      .
TIME( 30 ) CONTAINS XXXX SECONDS
```

15 An array WIND of 70 integer values represents the average daily wind velocities in Chicago over a 10-week period. Assume the array with 10 rows and 7 columns has been filled. Give FORTRAN statements to print the data so that each week is on a separate line.

```
         CHICAGO WIND VELOCITY (MILES/HOUR)
WIND(1,1)          WIND(1,2)    . . .   WIND(1,7)
WIND(2,1)          WIND(2,2)    . . .   WIND(2,7)
    .
    .
    .
WIND(10,1)         WIND(10,2)   . . .   WIND(10,7)
```

16 Give FORTRAN statements to print the last 10 elements of an array M of size N. For instance, if M contains 25 elements, the output form is:

```
M( 16 ) = XXX
M( 17 ) = XXX
M( 18 ) = XXX
     .
     .
     .
M( 25 ) = XXX
```

17 Give FORTRAN statements to interchange the 1st and 100th elements, the 2nd and 99th elements, and so on, of the array NUM which contains 100 values. See diagram that follows.

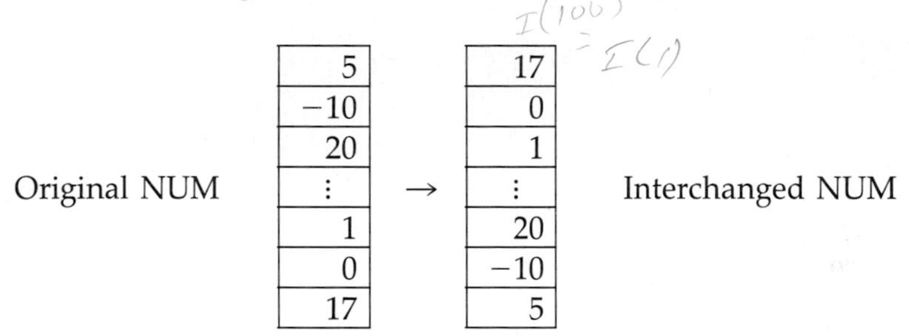

(*Hint:* You will need a temporary storage when you switch values.)

18 An array TEST contains test scores from 100 exams. Give the FORTRAN statements necessary to find the average of the first 50 exams and the second 50 exams. Print the following:

```
           AVERAGES
1ST 50 EXAMS     2ND 50 EXAMS
   XXXXXX           XXXXXX
```

19 Write a complete program that will read as many as 20 integers from a file NUMBR, one integer per line. The last line will contain 9999. Write the data in the reverse order from which it was read. Thus, the value 9999 will be the first value printed.

20 Sometimes, when an x-y plot is made from empirical data, the scatter of the data points is such that it is difficult to select a "best representative line" for the plot. In a case like this, the data can be adjusted to reduce the scatter by using a "moving average" mathematical method of finding the average of three points in succession and replacing the middle value with this average. Write a complete program to read an array X of 20 values from a file EXPR where the values are entered one per line. Build an array Y of 20 values where Y is the array of adjusted values. That is, Y(2) is the average of X(1), X(2), and X(3); Y(3) is the average of X(2), X(3), and X(4); and so on. Notice that the first and last values of X cannot be adjusted and should be moved to Y without being changed. Do not destroy the original values in X. Print the original and the adjusted values next to each other in a table.

21 A life insurance company has 12 salespeople. Each salesperson receives a commission on monthly sales that is dependent on what percentage of overall sales he or she sold. This commission is based on the following table:

PERCENT OF SALES	COMMISSION RATE
0.00– 24.99	.02
25.00– 74.99	.04
75.00–100.00	.06

An identification number and the monthly sales, in dollars, are entered into a data file SALES. Write a complete program to read the data, convert each salesperson's sales to a percentage of the total sales, and compute his or her commission. Print the following report:

```
            MONTHLY COMMISSION REPORT
        ID          SALES        PERCENT    COMMISSION
        XXX      $   XXXXX        XXXX     $   XXXXXXX
13    { .              .            .              .
lines { .              .            .              .
      { .              .            .              .
      TOTALS     $ XXXXXX         XXXX     $ XXXXXXXX
```

Test your program with the following input data:

ID	SALES
002	9000
009	10050
012	550
016	1000
025	15000
036	20000
037	85000
040	4000
043	1250
044	0
045	400
046	850

22 Write a complete program that will read a two-dimensional array called RAIN containing 12 rows (one for each month) and 5 columns (one for each year 1978–1982). Each row is entered on a data line in a file WATER. Print the following table:

```
AVERAGE YEARLY RAINFALL
1978 - XXXXX
1979 - XXXXX
1980 - XXXXX
1981 - XXXXX
1982 - XXXXX

MAXIMUM RAINFALL
MONTH XX    YEAR XXXX

MINIMUM RAINFALL
MONTH XX    YEAR XXXX
```

23 Assume that the reservations for an airplane flight have been stored in a file called FLIGHT. The plane contains 38 rows with six seats in each row. The seats on each row are numbered one through six as follows:

1 Window seat, left side
2 Center seat, left side
3 Aisle seat, left side
4 Aisle seat, right side
5 Center seat, right side
6 Window seat, right side

The file FLIGHT contains 38 lines of information corresponding to the 38 rows. Each line contains six values corresponding to the six seats. The value for any seat is either 0 or 1, representing either an empty or an occupied seat.

Write a complete program to read the FLIGHT information into a two-dimensional array called SEAT. Find and print all pairs of adjacent seats that are empty. Adjacent aisle seats should not be printed. If all three seats on one side of the plane are empty, then two pairs of adjacent seats should be printed. Print this information in the following manner:

```
AVAILABLE SEAT PAIRS

ROW           SEATS
XX            X , X
 .              .
 .              .
 .              .
XX            X , X
```

If no pairs are available, print an appropriate message.

24 Several buyers working for a large international corporation find themselves purchasing computer terminals from several warehouses. Although they can buy the terminals for roughly the same cost from any one warehouse, the shipping cost varies depending upon the location of both the buyer and the warehouse. Therefore, a complete computer program is needed to compute the costs of alternative purchase schemes in order to select the most economical purchase plan.

Assume the program initializes a table called COST for five warehouses and six buyers. Let columns represent the buyers and let rows represent the warehouses. The cost for shipping an item from a particular warehouse I to a particular buyer J is stored in COST(I,J). For example, if COST(3,2) = 15.0, then the cost for shipping each terminal from warehouse 3 to buyer 2 is $15. Use a DATA statement to initialize the following COST table in your program. Output the cost table in an easily understood format (include any necessary headings).

WAREHOUSE	BUYER 1	2	3	4	5	6
1	$12.00	$14.34	$13.45	$12.99	$17.31	$15.81
2	$18.23	$13.09	$21.01	$17.33	$17.76	$ 8.73
3	$ 9.12	$15.00	$14.67	$16.92	$14.03	$19.17
4	$23.23	$ 9.09	$15.87	$17.22	$12.33	$15.75
5	$16.81	$14.03	$21.32	$13.56	$16.63	$10.78

A possible purchasing order can be stored in another table called ORDER with five rows and six columns, where ORDER(I,J) represents the number of terminals from warehouse I that is bought by buyer J. Two possible purchase orders are stored in a file called PURCHS. Each line of the file corresponds to a row in the table ORDER.

Your program should read the first purchase order (five lines) and compute and print the cost of the solution, along with the cost to each buyer, in the following manner:

```
SOLUTION 1

SHIPPING COST TO BUYER 1 = XXXXXXX
SHIPPING COST TO BUYER 2 = XXXXXXX
              .
              .
              .
SHIPPING COST TO BUYER 6 = XXXXXXX

TOTAL SHIPPING COST      =$XXXXXXX
```

Next, repeat the steps to evaluate and print the second solution. Then print a final line that specifies which solution (1 or 2) is more economical. For example, in a situation with two warehouses and three buyers, and if the COST and ORDER tables are those shown below, the cost to buyer 1 is 2*1 + 3*2 or $8, the cost to buyer 2 is 1*3 + 5*0 or $3, and the cost to buyer 3 is 10*0 + 4*4 or $16.

COST

	B1	B2	B3
W1	$ 2	$ 1	$10
W2	$ 3	$ 5	$ 4

ORDER

	B1	B2	B3
W1	1	3	0
W2	2	0	4

***25** Write a complete program to convert a Gregorian date in month-day-year form to a Julian date, which is the year followed by the number of the day in the year. For example, 010982 should be converted to 82009, and 052283 should be converted to 83142. Be sure to take leap years into account. (*Hint:* Use an array to store the number of days in each month.)

***26** Write a complete program to convert a Julian date, which is the year followed by the number of the day in the year, into the Gregorian date, which is in month-day-year form. For example, 82009 should be converted to 010982, and 83142 should be converted to 052283. Be sure to take leap years into account. (*Hint:* Use an array to store the number of days in each month.)

***27** When a certain telephone company monitors local calls from a given phone, it punches a card containing the seven-digit number called. Write a complete program to read the cards and write each number called. Even if a number is called more than once, it should only be printed once. No more than 500 different numbers are ever dialed in one time period. The numbers are punched one per card. The last card (trailer card) has the number 9999999.

French Government Tourist Office

PROBLEM SOLVING—Carbon Dating

Your recent trips have proven expensive, so you have taken a job on Saturdays as an archeologist's assistant. Artifacts from a recent excavation have been sent to a laboratory for carbon analysis. Using this information, and the equation that the archeologist has shown you for carbon dating, it is possible to estimate the age of the artifacts. Write a computer program to perform these calculations. (See Section 5-3, page 185, for the solution.)

5

SUBPROGRAMS

INTRODUCTION

As our programs become longer and more complicated, we frequently need to perform the same set of operations at more than one location in our programs. Rather than actually repeat the statements, we can write a special subprogram, either a *function* or a *subroutine,* that can be referred to as many times as needed by the program. Very commonly used routines, such as the square root or exponential functions, are stored within the computer itself. The type of routine described in the introductory problem is one which could be added to any program that needs to compute an estimated age using carbon dating. Since this type of routine is independent of the programs that use it, a new structure is necessary.

5-1 PROGRAM MODULARITY

In Chapter 1 we stressed the importance of using top-down design techniques in our algorithms and programs. The WHILE loop and IF THEN ELSE structures are essential ingredients in structured programming, but another key element in simplifying program logic is the use of modules. These *modules,* called functions and subroutines in FORTRAN, allow us to write programs composed of nearly independent segments or routines. In fact, when we decompose the problem solution into a series of sequentially executed steps, we are decomposing the problem into a set of modules. Many of the steps in our block diagrams could be structured very easily into functions or subroutines. You should begin to see the advantages of breaking programs into modules or subprograms:

1 You can write and test one module separately from the rest of the program.

2 Debugging is easier because you are working with smaller sections of the program.

3 Modules can be used in other programs without rewriting or retesting.

4 Programs are more readable and thus more easily understood because of the module or *block structure*.

5 More than one programmer can work on a large program independently of other programmers.

6 Programs become shorter and therefore simpler.

7 A subprogram can be used several times by the same program.

5-2 FUNCTIONS

The first type of subprogram that we discuss is the function subprogram. This subprogram computes a single value, such as the square root of a number or the average of an array. You have already had some contact with intrinsic functions, such as SQRT and REAL, which are included in the compiler and are accessible directly from your program. It is also possible to write your own functions that can then be used whenever you need them in your programs.

INTRINSIC FUNCTIONS

A complete list of the *intrinsic functions* (or *library functions,* as they are sometimes called) that are available in FORTRAN 77 is contained in Appendix C. You should read through the list of functions so that you are aware of the types of operations that can be performed with intrinsic functions. Then, when you need to use one of these operations, you can refer to Appendix C to give you the details in using that specific function.

Although we introduced intrinsic functions in Chapter 2, we will summarize the main components of these functions again:

1 The function name and its input values (arguments) collectively represent a single value.

2 A function can never be used on the left side of an equal sign in an assignment statement.

3 The name of the intrinsic function usually determines the type of output from the function (e.g., if the function name begins with I → N, its value is an integer).

4 Generally the arguments of a function are the same type as the function itself. However, there are a few exceptions; refer to the

list of intrinsic functions in Appendix C if you are not sure of the type of arguments used by a function.

5 The arguments of a function must be enclosed in parentheses.

6 The arguments of a function may be constants, variables, expressions, or other functions.

Generic functions accept arguments of any type and return a value of the same type as the argument. Thus the generic function ABS will return an integer absolute value if its argument is an integer, but will return a real absolute value if its argument is real. The table in Appendix C identifies generic functions.

EXAMPLE 5-1 Odd and Even Values

Read an integer and then print the word ODD or EVEN, depending on the value read.

Solution

In this solution we use the intrinsic function MOD. This function has two integer arguments, I and J. The function returns the integer remainder in the division of I by J. This operation is also called *modulo division;* hence the function is called a MOD function. Some example values for I, J, and MOD(I, J) are shown below:

I	J	MOD(I, J)
3	2	1
4	2	0
6	4	2
10	4	2
88	3	1

Thus, if a number K is even, it is a multiple of 2 and MOD(K, 2) will be zero. If K is odd, then MOD(K, 2) will be 1. The statements to determine if an integer is odd or even using this function are shown below:

```
PRINT*, 'ENTER AN INTEGER'
READ*, K
IF(MOD(K, 2).EQ.0)THEN
   PRINT*, K, 'IS EVEN'
ELSE
   PRINT*, K, 'IS ODD'
ENDIF
```

This MOD function can also be used to determine if a number is a multiple of another number. For instance, if MOD(M, 5) is zero, then M is a multiple of 5. ◇

WRITING FUNCTIONS

Since intrinsic functions are contained in a library available to the compiler, you may find that a function in one computer manufacturer's compiler is not available in another's. For example, a function to generate random numbers is frequently used in computer simulations, but not all systems include a function to generate random numbers. You may also find that you would like to use a function that is not available in any compiler. Both these problems can be solved by writing your own function.

A function subprogram, which is a program itself, will be separated from the *main program*. The function subprogram begins with a nonexecutable statement that identifies the function with a name and an argument list:

```
FUNCTION name(arguments)
```

Since a function is compiled separately, it must also end with an END statement. The rules for choosing a function name are the same as those for choosing a program name. In addition, the first letter of the function name specifies the type of value returned unless it is included in an explicit specification. The following statements illustrate a simple example of a main program and a function subprogram.

Main program

```
      PROGRAM TESTS
*
*   THIS IS A SAMPLE MAIN PROGRAM
*
      READ*, TEST1, TEST2, TEST3
      PRINT*, AVE(TEST1, TEST2, TEST3)
      END
```

Function AVE

```
*
*
*
      FUNCTION AVE(TEST1, TEST2, TEST3)
*
*   THIS IS A SAMPLE FUNCTION
*
      AVE = (TEST1 + TEST2 + TEST3)/3.0
      RETURN
      END
```

The following rules must be observed in writing a function:

1 The arguments of the function reference in the main program must match, in type, number, and order, the arguments used in the function statement.

2 If one of the arguments is an array, it must be dimensioned in both the main program and the function subprogram.
3 The value to be returned to the main program is stored in the function name using an assignment statement.
4 When the function is ready to return control to the main program, an executable statement, RETURN, is used. A function may contain more than one RETURN statement, the general form of which is:

```
RETURN
```

5 A function can contain references to other functions, but it cannot contain a reference to itself.
6 A function subprogram is usually placed immediately after the main program, but it may also appear before the main program. In either case, the function is compiled as a separate program. If you have more than one function, the order of the functions does not matter as long as each function is completely separate from the other functions.
7 A main program and its subprograms can be stored together in the same file or they can be stored in separate files. If they are in separate files, it is necessary to link them together before the program can be run.
8 The same statement number may be used in both a function and the main program. No confusion occurs as to which statement is referenced, because the function and main program are completely separate, with only the argument list to link them together. Thus, a function and a main program could use the same variable name, such as SUM, to store different sums as long as the variable is not an argument to the function.
9 If you wish to change the type of value returned by a function, the name of the function must appear in a type statement in both the main program and the function. The following statements include a function AVE, which will return an integer value because it is identified as an INTEGER FUNCTION. The name of the function AVE must also appear in an INTEGER statement in the main program.

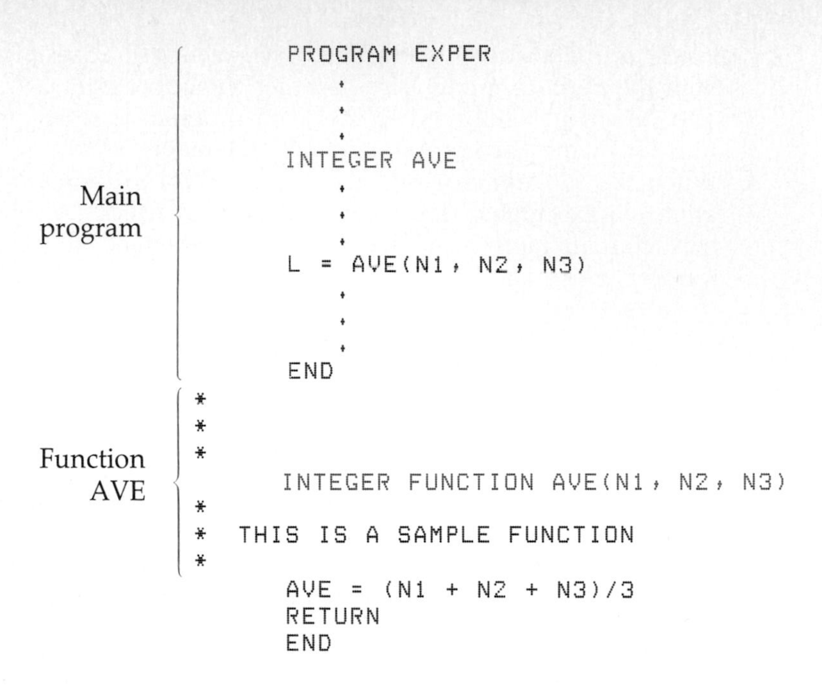


```
      PROGRAM EXPER
         .
         .
         .
      INTEGER AVE
         .
         .
         .
      L = AVE(N1, N2, N3)
         .
         .
         .
      END
*
*
*
      INTEGER FUNCTION AVE(N1, N2, N3)
*
*  THIS IS A SAMPLE FUNCTION
*
      AVE = (N1 + N2 + N3)/3
      RETURN
      END
```

10 Do not change the values of the arguments inside a function. Some compilers will return the new values to the main program when you return, and others will not. If you need to return more than one value, use a subroutine instead of a function.

EXAMPLE 5-2 Sales Commission

A local company has a number of computer programs that are used in maintaining its accounts and preparing payrolls. Several of the programs need to compute the commission earned by salespeople who work for the company. Instead of having each program recompute the sales commission, a subprogram is to be used with each program that needs the sales commission. This commission is computed from the total sales of the salesperson, using the following table:

Total Sales	Commission Percent
sales < $1000	1%
$1000 ≤ sales < $2000	2%
$2000 ≤ sales < $2500	3%
$2500 ≤ sales	5%

The function is to be called SALCOM and has one argument, the total sales for the salesperson. Write a function to compute the sales commission, using the table above.

Solution 1

We show a portion of a main program along with the complete function subprogram. In this function, we set the rate initially to 1%. Then, if a higher rate was warranted, it was changed.

```
      PROGRAM MAIN
          .
          .
          .
      COMM = SALCOM(SALES)
          .
          .
          .
      END
*
*
*
      FUNCTION SALCOM(SALES)
*
*   THIS FUNCTION COMPUTES A SALES COMMISSION
*
      RATE = 0.01
      IF(SALES.GE.1000.0.AND.SALES.LT.2000.0)RATE = 0.02
      IF(SALES.GE.2000.0.AND.SALES.LT.2500.0)RATE = 0.03
      IF(SALES.GE.2500.0)RATE = 0.05
*
      SALCOM = SALES*RATE
*
      RETURN
      END
```

Solution 2

This solution uses the IF ELSE IF statement. The same main program could be used with this solution.

```
      FUNCTION SALCOM(SALES)
*
*   THIS FUNCTION COMPUTES A SALES COMMISSION
*
      IF(SALES.LT.1000.0)THEN
         RATE = 0.01
      ELSEIF(SALES.LT.2000.0)THEN
         RATE = 0.02
      ELSEIF(SALES.LT.2500.00)THEN
         RATE = 0.03
      ELSE
         RATE = 0.05
      ENDIF
*
      SALCOM = SALES*RATE
*
      RETURN
      END
```

Incorrect Solution

The function below is similar to that in Solution 2, but this one does not work correctly. See if you can spot the error before reading the explanation after the function.

```
      FUNCTION SALCOM(SALES)
*
*   THIS FUNCTION COMPUTES A SALES COMMISSION
*
      IF(SALES.GE.2500.0)THEN
         RATE = 0.05
      ELSEIF(SALES.LT.2500.0)THEN
         RATE = 0.03
      ELSEIF(SALES.LT.2000.0)THEN
         RATE = 0.02
      ELSEIF(SALES.LT.1000.0)THEN
         RATE = 0.01
      ENDIF
*
      SALCOM = SALES*RATE
*
      RETURN
      END
```

The key to understanding the problem with this solution is remembering the manner in which an IF ELSE IF statement is executed. As soon as a condition is encountered that is true, the appropriate steps are executed and control passes to the ENDIF at the end of the structure. Thus, even if two conditions are true, the first one encountered is the only one that is tested. Suppose that the SALES amount is $900. Then the commission rate should be 1%. In the function above, though, since SALES is less then 2500.0, the rate is computed to be 3% and control passes to the ENDIF and then to the computation for SALCOM. ◇

When arrays are used as arguments in a function, they must be dimensioned in the function subprogram as well as the main program. Generally, the array will have the same size in the function as it does in the main program. There are situations, however, when the size of an array is an argument to the subprogram. This technique, called *variable dimensioning,* allows us to specify an array of variable size in the subprogram. The argument value then sets the size of the array when the subprogram is executed. We illustrate the use of an array with a fixed size in a function in Example 5-3, and the use of an array with a variable size in a function in Examples 5-4 and 5-5.

EXAMPLE 5-3 Array Average, Fixed Size

Write a function that receives an array of 20 real values. Compute the average of the array and return it as the function value.

Solution

We show a portion of a main program along with the complete function subprogram.

```
      PROGRAM MAIN
          .
          .
          .
      DIMENSION Z(20)
          .
          .
          .
      AVEZ = AVE(Z)
          .
          .
          .
      END
*
*
*
      FUNCTION AVE(Z)
*
*   THIS FUNCTION COMPUTES THE AVERAGE OF A
*   REAL ARRAY WITH TWENTY VALUES
*
      DIMENSION Z(20)
*
      TOTAL = 0.0
      DO 10 I=1,20
         TOTAL = TOTAL + Z(I)
   10 CONTINUE
*
      AVE = TOTAL/20.0
*
      RETURN
      END ◇
```

EXAMPLE 5-4 Array Average, Variable Size

Write a function that receives an array of real values along with an integer variable that gives the size of the array. Compute the average of this array and return it as the function value.

Solution

We show a portion of a main program along with the complete function subprogram.

```
      PROGRAM MAIN
          .
          .
          .
      DIMENSION Z(20)
          .
          .
          .
      AVEZ = AVE(Z, 20)
          .
          .
          .
      END
*
*
*
      FUNCTION AVE(Z, N)
*
*  THIS FUNCTION COMPUTES THE AVERAGE OF A
*  REAL ARRAY WITH N VALUES
*
      DIMENSION Z(N)
*
      TOTAL = 0.0
      DO 10 I=1,N
         TOTAL = TOTAL + Z(I)
   10 CONTINUE
*
      AVE = TOTAL/REAL(N)
*
      RETURN
      END ◇
```

EXAMPLE 5-5 Average of a Two-Dimensional Array

Write a function that computes the average of a two-dimensional real array. The number of rows, NROW, and the number of columns, NCOL, are also arguments to the function.

Solution

We show a portion of a main program along with the complete function subprogram.

```
      PROGRAM MAIN
          .
          .
          .
      DIMENSION A(8,3)
          .
          .
          .
      AVEA = AVE2D(A, 8, 3)
          .
          .
          .
      END
*
*
*
      FUNCTION AVE2D(A, NROW, NCOL)
*
*  THIS FUNCTION COMPUTES THE AVERAGE OF AN
*  ARRAY WITH NROWS (ROWS) AND NCOL (COLUMNS)
*
      DIMENSION A(NROW, NCOL)
*
      SUM = 0.0
      DO 10 I=1,NROW
         DO 5 J=1,NCOL
            SUM = SUM + A(I,J)
    5    CONTINUE
   10 CONTINUE
*
      AVE2D = SUM/REAL(NROW*NCOL)
*
      RETURN
      END  ◇
```

5-3 PROBLEM SOLVING—CARBON DATING

Carbon dating is a method for estimating the age of organic substances such as shells, seeds, and wooden artifacts. The technique compares the amount of a radioactive carbon, carbon 14, that is contained in the remains of the substance with the amount that would have been in the object's environment at the time it was created. The age of the cave paintings at Lascaux, France, has been estimated at 15,500 years using this technique. Assume that you are working as an assistant to an archeologist on Saturdays. Artifacts from a recent excavation have been sent to a laboratory for carbon analysis. The lab will determine the proportion of carbon that remains in the artifact. The archeologist has shown you the following equation that gives the estimated age of the artifact in years:

$$\text{age} = \frac{-\log_e(\text{carbon proportion remaining})}{0.0001216}$$

Recall that $\log_e X$ is the logarithm to the base e of the value X. The archeologist would like you to write a FORTRAN function that will return the estimated age of an artifact given the proportion of carbon that remains in it.

PROBLEM STATEMENT

Write a function to compute the estimated age of an artifact using carbon dating.

INPUT/OUTPUT DESCRIPTION

The input will be a number that represents the proportion of carbon left in the artifact. The output will be a number that estimates in years the age of the artifact.

HAND EXAMPLE

Suppose that no carbon has decayed. Then the carbon proportion is 1.0, and the estimated age is:

$$\text{age} = \frac{-\log_e (1.0)}{0.0001216} = \frac{0}{0.0001216} = 0$$

This age makes sense since the artifact must be relatively young if no carbon decay has occurred.

Suppose that half of the carbon has decayed. The half-life of carbon 14 is 5700 years (we had to look this up in a reference book), so let's use 0.5 as the proportion of carbon left and see what this formula gives for an age:

$$\text{age} = \frac{-\log_e (0.5)}{0.0001216} = 5700.2 \text{ years}$$

ALGORITHM DEVELOPMENT

The decomposition and refinement for the steps to this algorithm are:

DECOMPOSITION

Compute age from proportion of carbon remaining

Refinement in Pseudocode

```
AGE:  BEGIN
        IF proportion of carbon remaining ≤0 or >1
          PRINT error message
          age ← 0.0
        ELSE
```

$$\text{age} \leftarrow \frac{-\log_e (\text{proportion of carbon remaining})}{0.0001216}$$

```
        ENDIF
        RETURN
      END
```

To compute the estimated age in FORTRAN, we need to compute a logarithm to the base e. Using the table in Appendix C, we find that the intrinsic function LOG performs this operation.

FORTRAN Function

```
      FUNCTION AGE(CARBON)
*
*  THIS FUNCTION ESTIMATES THE AGE OF AN ARTIFACT FROM
*  THE PROPORTION OF CARBON REMAINING IN THE ARTIFACT
*
      IF(CARBON.LE.0.0.OR.CARBON.GT.1.0)THEN
         PRINT*, 'ERROR IN CARBON PROPORTION', CARBON
         AGE = 0.0
      ELSE
         AGE = -LOG(CARBON)/0.0001216
      ENDIF
*
      RETURN
      END
```

TESTING

Here is a simple program that allows you to test this function with values both in the proper range and outside the proper range to see if the function is working correctly.

```
      PROGRAM TEST
*
*   THIS IS A PROGRAM TO TEST THE CARBON DATING FUNCTION
*
      DO 10 I=1,5
         PRINT*, 'ENTER CARBON PROPORTION REMAINING'
         READ*, CARBON
         PRINT*, CARBON
         YEARS = AGE(CARBON)
         PRINT*, 'AGE =', YEARS
   10 CONTINUE
*
      END
```

Remember that the function CARBON needs to follow the test program when it is executed.

5-4 SUBROUTINES

FORTRAN supports two types of subprograms—functions and subroutines. A subroutine differs from a function in several ways:

1 A subroutine does not represent a value, and thus the type of the name should be chosen for documentation and not to specify a real or integer value.

2 A subroutine is referenced with an executable statement, CALL, whose form is:

```
CALL name(arguments)
```

3 A subroutine uses the argument list not only for inputs to the subprogram but also for any output from the subprogram. Unlike a function, a subroutine can modify the values of variables or arrays in its argument list. This is how it provides output to the main program. The arguments in the calling statement must match in type, number, and order those on the subroutine statement.

4 A subroutine may return one value, many values, or no value.

LIBRARY SUBROUTINES

Some subroutines are prewritten and are part of a library of subprograms available to the computer system; however, there is not a standard list of library subroutines available similar to the list of intrinsic functions. You will have to examine the documentation for your specific computer system to determine which library subroutines are available and which arguments are needed.

WRITING SUBROUTINES

User-written subroutines are accessed the same as a library subroutine. Writing a subroutine is much like writing a function, except that the first line in a subroutine is the following nonexecutable statement:

```
SUBROUTINE name(arguments)
```

Also, the output of the subroutine is returned by the arguments rather than by the name as is done with a function.

Since the subroutine is a separate program, the arguments are the only link to the main program and the subroutine. Thus, the choice of statement numbers and variable names is independent of the choice of the statement numbers and variable names used in the main program.

The subroutine, like the function, requires:

1 A RETURN statement to return control to the main program.

2 An END statement because it is also a complete program module.

EXAMPLE 5-6 Array Statistics

Information commonly needed from a set of data includes the average, the minimum value, and the maximum value. These values could be computed using three functions. However, if all three are needed, it is more efficient to compute them all at the same time. Write a subroutine that is called with the statement

```
CALL STAT(X, N, XAVE, XMIN, XMAX)
```

where N is the number of elements in the array X.

Solution

We show a portion of a main program along with the complete subroutine subprogram.

```
      PROGRAM MAIN
          .
          .
          .
      DIMENSION X(100)
          .
          .
          .
      CALL STAT(X, 100, XAVE, XMIN, XMAX)
          .
          .
          .
      END
*
*
*
      SUBROUTINE STAT(X, N, XAVE, XMIN, XMAX)
*
*  THIS SUBROUTINE COMPUTES THE AVERAGE, MINIMUM,
*  AND MAXIMUM OF AN ARRAY WITH N VALUES
*
      DIMENSION X(N)
*
      TOTAL = X(1)
      XMIN = X(1)
      XMAX = X(1)
      DO 10 I=2,N
         TOTAL = TOTAL + X(I)
         IF(X(I).LT.XMIN)XMIN = X(I)
         IF(X(I).GT.XMAX)XMAX = X(I)
   10 CONTINUE
*
      XAVE = TOTAL/REAL(N)
*
      RETURN
      END
```

A program might use this subroutine more than once. For instance, suppose a program has exam scores from two different classes. One class has 50 students and the other has 35. The following statements could be used to get the averages, minimums, and maximums of the two arrays. Note that the variables AVE1, AVE2, MIN1, MIN2, MAX1, and MAX2 typically will not have been assigned values before the subroutine is called.

```
      PROGRAM EXAMS
          .
          .
          .
      DIMENSION CLASS1(50), CLASS2(35)
      REAL MIN1, MIN2, MAX1, MAX2
          .
          .
          .
      CALL STAT(CLASS1, 50, AVE1, MIN1, MAX1)
      CALL STAT(CLASS2, 35, AVE2, MIN2, MAX2)
          .
          .
          .
      END
*
*
*
      SUBROUTINE STAT(X, N, XAVE, XMIN, XMAX)
          .
          .
          .
      END ◇
```

EXAMPLE 5-7 Sort Subroutine

We have already written a program which included the steps to sort a one-dimensional array. This operation is used so frequently that we will rewrite it in the form of a subroutine. To make it flexible, we will use a variable in the argument list to specify the number of elements in the array. This is such a useful routine that we suggest that you store it in your file area so that it can be easily accessed. Note in the solution here that we copy the input array X into an array Y before sorting Y. This allows us to keep the original order in X and have the ascending order in Y. If you do not want to use two arrays, use this calling statement:

```
CALL SORT(X, X, N)
```

Solution

We show a portion of a main program along with the complete subroutine subprogram on the following page.

```
      PROGRAM MAIN
          .
          .
          .
      DIMENSION X(25), Y(25)
          .
          .
          .
      CALL SORT(X, Y, 25)
          .
          .
          .
      END
*
*
*
      SUBROUTINE SORT(X, Y, N)
*
*   THIS SUBROUTINE SORTS AN ARRAY X INTO AN ARRAY Y
*   IN ASCENDING ORDER. BOTH ARRAYS HAVE N VALUES.
*
      DIMENSION X(N), Y(N)
      LOGICAL SORTED
*
      DO 10 I=1,N
         Y(I) = X(I)
   10 CONTINUE
*
      SORTED = .FALSE.
   15 IF(.NOT.SORTED)THEN
         SORTED = .TRUE.
         DO 20 I=1,N-1
            IF(Y(I).GT.Y(I+1))THEN
               TEMP = Y(I)
               Y(I) = Y(I+1)
               Y(I+1) = TEMP
               SORTED = .FALSE.
            ENDIF
   20    CONTINUE
         GO TO 15
      ENDIF
*
      RETURN
      END ◇
```

5-5 ADDITIONAL SUBPROGRAM TOPICS

Two additional topics that relate to subprograms are presented in this section. One is the *arithmetic statement function,* which is a special type of function that can be written within the main program. The other topic, *COMMON,* allows you to specify a block of storage that is accessible to all subprograms in a program.

ARITHMETIC STATEMENT FUNCTION

When a user-written function involves only an arithmetic computation that can be written in one statement, it is not necessary to write a function subprogram to incorporate this function in your main program. Instead, an arithmetic statement function can be used that will define the function at the beginning of the main program. It consists of the name of the function followed by the arguments in parentheses on the left side of an equal sign, and the arithmetic expression on the right side. The arithmetic function is nonexecutable and must be placed before any executable statement in the main program.

EXAMPLE 5-8 Sales Tax Computation

The following main program uses a function subprogram to compute the sales tax on purchases. Since the tax computation is a single arithmetic statement, it could also be performed with an arithmetic statement function. Show the main program with an arithmetic statement function instead of the function subprogram.

```
      PROGRAM TAXES
*
*   THIS PROGRAM READS SALES AMOUNTS AND
*   PREPARES A SALES REPORT
*
      READ*, SALES
          .
          .
          .
      TOTAL = SALES + TAX(SALES)
          .
          .
          .
      END
*
*
*
      FUNCTION TAX(SALES)
*
*   THIS FUNCTION COMPUTES THE TAX ON A SALE
*
      TAX = SALES*0.065
*
      RETURN
      END
```

Solution

Using the arithmetic function subroutine, we do not need the separate function subprogram. Instead, the subprogram becomes a single statement at the beginning of the main program, as shown on the following page.

```
      PROGRAM TAXES
*
*   THIS PROGRAM READS SALES AMOUNTS AND
*   PREPARES A SALES REPORT
*
      TAX(SALES) = SALES*0.065
*
      READ*, SALES
         .
         .
         .
      TOTAL = SALES + TAX(SALES)
         .
         .
         .
      END
```
◇

COMMON STATEMENT

As you modularize your programs, you will find that the argument lists can sometimes get long as you pass more and more data to functions and subroutines. FORTRAN allows you to set up a block of storage that is accessible, or common, to the main program and all its subprograms, called a *common block*. The variables in this block of storage do not have to be passed through argument lists. Unless extremely large amounts of data must be passed to subprograms, the use of common blocks is discouraged because they weaken the independence of modules. If you change a variable in a common block, it could conceivably affect all modules using data in the common block.

Blank common is set up with the nonexecutable specification statement

COMMON *variable list*

that goes before any executable statements. Each subprogram that uses data in this common block must also contain a COMMON statement. While the data names do not have to be the same in every subprogram, the order of the names is important. Consider these COMMON statements from a main program and a subprogram, respectively:

```
COMMON A, J, B
COMMON TEMP, KTOT, SUM
```

Here, A and TEMP represent the same value, J and KTOT represent the same value, and B and SUM represent the same value.

Arrays may be dimensioned in either the DIMENSION statement, the COMMON statement, or a type statement, but not in more than one. Variables in common blocks cannot be used as arguments in subprograms. Finally, variables in common cannot be initialized with DATA statements.

Named common is established if the list of variable names in the COMMON statement is preceded by a name set in slashes:

```
COMMON /name/ variable list
```

The purpose of establishing different blocks of common with unique names is to allow subprograms to refer to the named common block with which they wish to share data, without listing all the other variables in the other common blocks. Named common is also referred to as *labeled common*.

Variables in common can be initialized with a special subprogram called a BLOCK DATA subprogram. This subprogram is not executable and serves only to assign initial values to variables in a common block. An example of a block data subprogram that will initialize two named common blocks is given below:

```
BLOCK DATA
COMMON /EXPER1/ TEMP(100)
COMMON /EXPER2/ TIME, DIST, VEL(10)
DATA TEMP, TIME, DIST, VEL /100*0.0, 50.5, 0.5, 10*0.0/
END
```

5-6 PROBLEM SOLVING—MEMBERSHIP LIST

Most organizations keep an active membership list. As new members join they are added to the list, and as others drop their memberships they are deleted from the list. In this section, we will assume that such a list uses social security numbers for identifying members. This list is kept in ascending order in a data file. There is a trailer signal of 999999999 at the end of the file. The number of members varies, but the actual membership will never go over 500.

The computer programs that utilize this file read it into a one-dimensional integer array. Routines are needed to insert members in the array and delete members from it. These routines are needed in several of the programs, so they are to be written as subprograms. Since the subprograms change the contents of an array instead of computing a single value, they should be subroutines instead of functions. One subroutine will insert members in the array, and the other will delete members from the array. Both subroutines will need the membership array and a social security number for the member who is changing status.

PROBLEM STATEMENT

Write two subroutines. INSERT will add a member to a membership array and DELETE will drop a member from the membership array.

INPUT/OUTPUT DESCRIPTION

The social security number of the change is input to the routine, along with the array containing the current membership. This membership array is also an output variable because it will be changed by the subroutine.

HAND EXAMPLE

Assume that the array below represents the membership list. For ease in handling, we use three-digit numbers in our examples instead of the nine-digit social security numbers.

original list

123
247
253
496
999 ← trailer signal

There are four valid members in the array, in addition to the trailer signal. Suppose we want to delete member 247. The array should then contain these values:

modified list

123
253
496
999

This change deletes the value 247, but also moves the rest of the elements back one position in the array. For instance, the trailer signal is now in the fourth position instead of the fifth position. Suppose we now want to add member 297. The array should then contain these values:

modified list

123
253
297
496
999

The items following the one that we inserted are now moved forward in the array. For instance, value 496 is now the fourth item instead of the third item.

ALGORITHM DEVELOPMENT

The two subroutines are similar, so we develop the algorithms in parallel. After going through the hand example, we can describe the initial decomposition:

Decomposition

Insert:

Find location for new member
Move rest of the members forward one position (toward the trailer signal)
Insert new member

Delete:

Find location of old member
Delete old member
Move rest of the members backward one position (away from the trailer signal)

Both routines search for the position that is to be modified. This search is a sequential search, beginning with the first element in the array. We know that the elements in the array are in ascending order. In a deletion, we search until we find the value that matches the one that we want to delete. If, instead, we find a value greater than the one we want to delete, an error condition occurs. We should print an error message that the member we wanted to delete was not in the list. Assuming that we find the value to be deleted, we do not really have to delete it. We just replace it with the next item in the array. We continue moving items backward one position in the array until we have moved the trailer signal. We do not need to move items after the trailer signal because they do not represent valid information.

Suppose we are performing an insertion to the array, and we find a match in the file to the one we wish to add. This then represents another error condition because the one to be added is already in the array. An error message should be printed. If we do not find a match for the insert, we want to stop searching as soon as we find a value greater than the one we want to insert. This is then the position where the new value goes. We have to be careful here that we do not lose a value. Before we can insert the new value, we have to move the current value in that position forward one position in the array, again being careful that we do not destroy the value in that next position. The diagram below illustrates the process that we use to keep from losing any information.

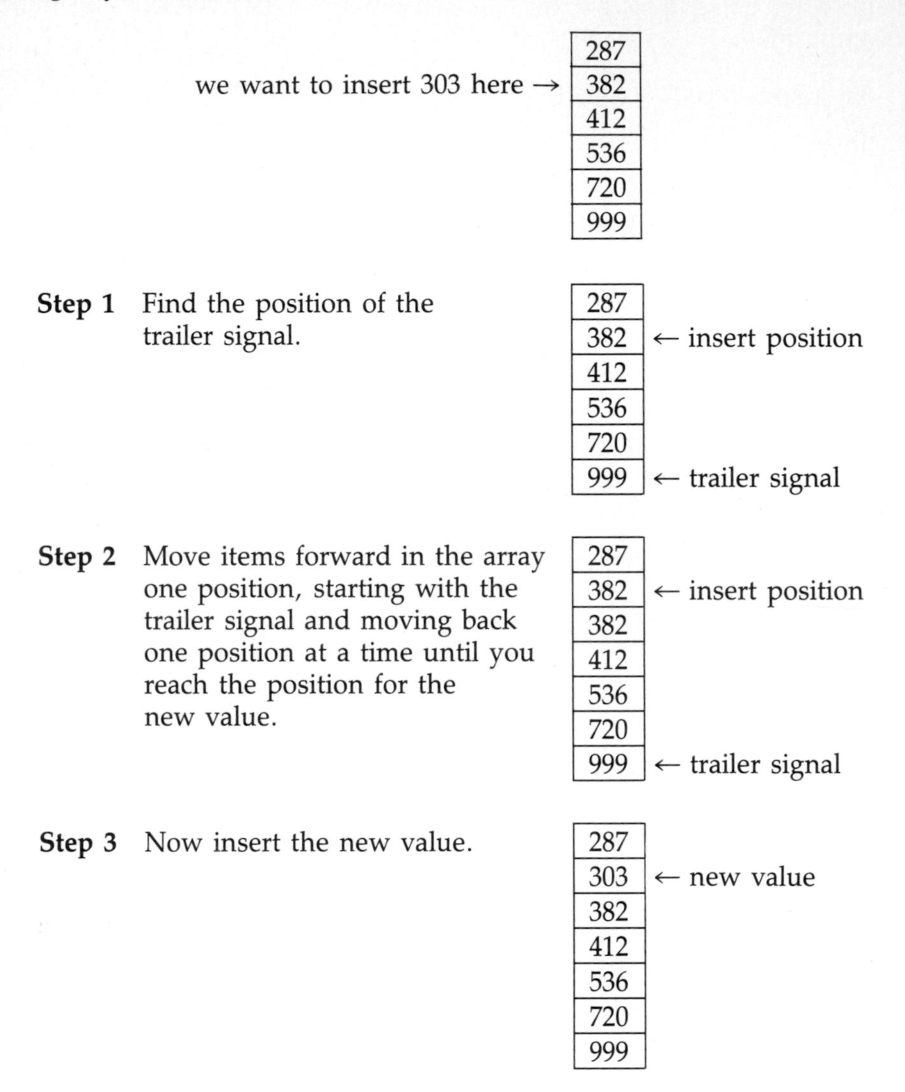

With this illustration, we can now refine the decomposition of the routines into more detailed descriptions.

Refinement in Pseudocode

```
DELETE:  BEGIN
           i ← 1
           WHILE ssn(i) < old DO
             i ← i + 1
           END WHILE
           IF ssn(i) > old
             PRINT error message
           ELSE
             WHILE ssn(i) ≠ 999999999 DO
               ssn(i) ← ssn(i+1)
               i ← i + 1
             END WHILE
           ENDIF
           RETURN
         END

INSERT:  BEGIN
           i ← 1
           WHILE ssn(i) < new DO
             i ← i + 1
           END WHILE
           IF ssn(i) = new
             PRINT error message
           ELSE
             curnt ← i
             WHILE ssn(i) ≠ 999999999 DO
               i ← i + 1
             END WHILE
             trailer ← i
             FOR i = trailer TO curnt STEP −1 DO
               ssn(i+1) ← ssn(i)
             END FOR
             ssn(curnt) ← new
           END IF
           RETURN
         END
```

These routines are not trivial. They require a thorough understanding of arrays and subscript handling. Go through them carefully with data values until you understand the pseudocode. The FORTRAN statements are given below:

FORTRAN SUBROUTINES

```
      SUBROUTINE DELETE(OLD, SSN)
*
*   THIS SUBROUTINE WILL DELETE AN OLD SSN
*   FROM THE SSN ARRAY
*
      INTEGER SSN(501), OLD
*
*   SEARCH FOR OLD VALUE
*
      I = 1
   10 IF(SSN(I).LT.OLD)THEN
         I = I + 1
         GO TO 10
      ENDIF
*
*   IF OLD VALUE NOT IN ARRAY, PRINT ERROR MESSAGE
*
      IF(SSN(I).GT.OLD)THEN
         PRINT*, OLD, 'NOT IN SSN LIST'
      ELSE
*
*   DELETE OLD VALUE
*
   50    IF(SSN(I).NE.999999999)THEN
            SSN(I) = SSN(I+1)
            I = I + 1
            GO TO 50
         ENDIF
      ENDIF
*
      RETURN
      END
```

```
      SUBROUTINE INSERT(NEW, SSN)
*
*  THIS SUBROUTINE WILL INSERT A NEW SSN
*  IN THE SSN ARRAY
*
      INTEGER SSN(501), NEW, CURNT, TRAILR
*
*  SEARCH FOR POSITION FOR INSERT
*
      I = 1
   10 IF(SSN(I).LT.NEW)THEN
         I = I + 1
         GO TO 10
      ENDIF
*
*  IF NEW VALUE ALREADY IN ARRAY, PRINT ERROR MESSAGE
*
      IF(SSN(I).EQ.NEW)THEN
         PRINT*, NEW, 'ALREADY IN SSN LIST'
      ELSE
*
*  INSERT NEW VALUE
*
         CURNT = I
   20    IF(SSN(I).NE.999999999)THEN
            I = I + 1
            GO TO 20
         ENDIF
         TRAILR = I
         DO 30 I=TRAILR,CURNT,-1
            SSN(I+1) = SSN(I)
   30    CONTINUE
         SSN(CURNT) = NEW
      ENDIF
*
      RETURN
      END
```

TESTING

Because subprograms are independent with respect to each other, you can test and debug them separately. In fact, it is really not a good idea to put the main program and all its subprograms together for initial testing. Instead, use a very simple main program (called a *driver*) to initialize the input to the specific subprogram that you are testing. After executing your subprogram, the driving program should print the output of the subprogram. Only after testing each subprogram should you begin combining the complete main program with the subprograms, one subprogram at a time.

The described procedure for testing a main program and its subprograms may seem unnecessarily long. It requires writing some extra driver programs and it requires a specific order to the test. This procedure, however, is very effective in minimizing serious errors in larger programs. A finished subprogram can also be tested before the rest of the modules have been written.

A driver program for testing the INSERT subroutine is given below. It can easily be modified to test the DELETE subroutine.

```
      PROGRAM DRIVER
*
*   THIS PROGRAM WILL TEST THE INSERT SUBROUTINE
*
      INTEGER SSN(501), NEW
*
      PRINT*, 'ENTER ARRAY OF FIVE VALUES AND TRAILER'
      READ*, (SSN(I), I=1,6)
      PRINT*, (SSN(I), I=1,6)
*
      PRINT*, 'ENTER SSN TO INSERT'
      READ*, NEW
    5 IF(NEW.GT.0)THEN
         PRINT*, NEW
         CALL INSERT(NEW, SSN)
         I = 1
    8    IF(SSN(I).NE.999999999)THEN
            PRINT*, SSN(I)
            I = I + 1
            GO TO 8
         ENDIF
         PRINT*, SSN(I)
         PRINT*, 'ENTER SSN TO INSERT, NEGATIVE TO QUIT'
         READ*, NEW
         GO TO 5
      ENDIF
*
      END
```

Note that you enter an initial array of five values plus the trailer. You can then insert as many values as you wish. After each insertion, the entire array is printed. When you are ready to stop the driver program, enter a negative value. In testing both of these routines, be sure to test insertions and deletions at the beginning and end of the array as well as in the middle of the array.

SUMMARY

Functions and subroutines allow us to structure our programs by breaking them into modules that can be written and tested independently of each other. Not only do programs become simpler, but the same module can also be used in other programs without retesting as long as no modifications are made to it. In addition to writing the sort algorithm into a subroutine, we also developed subroutines to insert and delete elements in a one-dimensional array. These two operations will also be useful in the next two chapters as we study character strings and file handling.

KEY WORDS

arithmetic statement function
argument
block structure
common block
deletion
driver
function
generic function
insertion
intrinsic function
library function
library subroutine
main program
module
subprogram
subroutine
variable dimensioning

DEBUGGING AIDS

The testing of an individual module is actually the testing of a complete program; it generally follows the guidelines that have been summarized at the end of the previous chapters. We list here some specific guides to use regarding the communication link between the subprogram and its main program or driver.

FUNCTIONS

1 Be sure that the name of the function reflects the type of value that you want returned. If necessary, use a type statement, REAL or INTEGER.

2 Be sure that each path to a RETURN provides a value for the function.

SUBROUTINES

3 Be sure that all output variables receive new values.

BOTH TYPES OF SUBPROGRAMS

4 Be sure that the variables listed in the main program match the arguments in the subprogram statement. Check the corresponding variables for correct order *and* correct type.

5 Print the values of all variables just before using the subprogram and just after returning from the subprogram as you debug the subprogram.

6 Test several sets of inputs with each subprogram.

7 You can put extra PRINT statements in subprograms just as you do in a main program to help isolate trouble spots.

8 Test subprograms separately from the main program.

9 While a DATA statement can be included in a subprogram, the variables are initialized only at the beginning of the program, and not with each use of the subprogram.

COMMON

Pay particular attention to the order of the variables on all COMMON statements. Also look for omitted variables. If a variable is left out of a COMMON statement in a subprogram, incorrect values will be used for all variables following it in the COMMON statement. Look for misspelled variable names in the COMMON statements. If these suggestions do not work, minimize the number of variables that you keep in common. Either change variables in common to regular subprogram arguments or use labeled common in order to use smaller blocks.

STYLE/TECHNIQUE GUIDES

Separating a long program into modules that transfer control smoothly from one to another becomes easier with practice. While different sets of modules may solve the same problem, some choices will probably be more logical and readable than others; these are the solutions that you want to be able to develop. Once you have selected a segment that is to be made into a module, you must decide whether it is to be a function or a subroutine. Does it have only one value to return? If so, it should probably be a function. But also look at the larger picture. If a loop is used to process each element of an array with a function, it might be better to transfer the whole array to a subroutine, process it in a loop in the subroutine, and return the entire modified array to the main program.

We will now list a few style suggestions for writing subprograms:

1 Choose descriptive names for the subprograms themselves.

2 Use comment lines in the subprograms as you would in the main program. In particular, use comments at the beginning of a subprogram to describe its purpose and define its arguments if necessary.

3 For clarity, use the same variables in the argument list of the subprogram as will be used in the main program if possible. If not, use completely different argument names.

4 List input arguments before output arguments in subroutine argument lists.

PROBLEMS

For problems 1 through 4, give the value of the following function. Assume that A = −5, B = −6.2, C = 0.1, and D = 16.2.

```
      FUNCTION TEST(X, Y, Z)
*
*  THIS FUNCTION RETURNS EITHER 0.5 OR -0.5
*  BASED ON THE VALUES OF X, Y, Z
*
      IF(X.GT.Y.OR.Y.GT.Z)THEN
         TEST = 0.5
      ELSE
         TEST = -0.5
      ENDIF
      RETURN
      END
```

1 TEST(5.2, 5.3, 5.6)

2 TEST(B, C, A)

3 TEST(ABS(A), C, D)

4 TEST(C, C, D*D)

For problems 5 through 9, write the function subprogram whose return value is described below. The input to the function is an integer array K of 100 elements.

5 MAXA(K), the maximum value of the array K.

6 MINA(K), the minimum value of the array K.

7 NPOS(K), the number of values greater than or equal to zero in the array K.

8 NNEG(K), the number of values less than zero in the array K.

9 NZERO(K), the number of values equal to zero in the array K.

For problems 10 through 13, give the values returned in the arguments after each of the following subroutine calls to the subroutine ANSWER. Assume that N(1) = 5, N(2) = 4, N(3) = 1.

```
      SUBROUTINE ANSWER(N, K, L)
*
*  THIS SUBROUTINE RETURNS
*  A VALUE FOR L BASED ON N AND K
*
      DIMENSION N(3)
      IF(K.LT.0)THEN
         L = K
      ELSE
         L = 0
         DO 10 I=1,3
            L = L + N(I)
 10      CONTINUE
      ENDIF
*
      RETURN
      END
```

10 `CALL ANSWER(N, 0, L)`

11 `CALL ANSWER(N, 18, NUM)`

12 `CALL ANSWER(N, -2, L)`

13 `CALL ANSWER(N, N(1), N(2))`

For problems 14 through 17, write the subroutines described below. The input to each subroutine is a two-dimensional array Z of size 5 × 4. The output is another array W of the same size.

14 SUBROUTINE ABSOL(Z, W), where each element of W contains the absolute value of the corresponding element in Z.

15 SUBROUTINE SIGNS(Z, W), where each element of W contains a value based on the corresponding element in Z, where

$$\begin{aligned} W(I,J) &= 0.0 & \text{if} \quad Z(I,J) &= 0 \\ W(I,J) &= -1.0 & \text{if} \quad Z(I,J) &< 0 \\ W(I,J) &= 1.0 & \text{if} \quad Z(I,J) &> 0 \end{aligned}$$

16 SUBROUTINE GREAT(Z, W), where W contains the same values of Z unless the corresponding value was greater than the average value of Z. In these cases, the corresponding value of W should contain the average value.

17 SUBROUTINE ROUND(Z, W), where each element of W is the corresponding value of Z rounded up to the next multiple of 10. Thus, 10.76 rounds to 20.0, 18.7 rounds to 20.0, 0.05 rounds to 10.0, 10.0 rounds to 10.0, and −5.76 rounds to 0.0.

18 Write a function whose input is a two-digit number. The function is to return a two-digit number whose digits are reversed from the input number. Thus, if 17 is the input to the function, 71 will be the output.

19 Write a subroutine that will read a group of test scores until it finds a card with a test score of -1. The subroutine should return the number of test scores read before the -1 was encountered, and the average of the test scores.

20 Write a function FACT that receives an integer value and returns the factorial of the value. Recall, the definition of a factorial is

$$n! = n \cdot (n - 1)(n - 2)\cdots 1;\ n > 0$$
$$0! = 1$$

If $n < 0$, the function should return a value of zero.

21 Write a subroutine that will compute the average $\bar{X}$, the variance σ^2, and the standard deviation σ of an array of 100 real values. Use the following formulas:

$$\bar{X} = \frac{\sum_{i=1}^{100} X_i}{100}$$

$$\sigma^2 = \frac{\sum_{i=1}^{100} (\bar{X} - X_i)^2}{99}$$

$$\sigma = \sqrt{\sigma^2}$$

22 Rewrite the subroutine of problem 21 so that it will compute the average, variance, and standard deviation for an array of size N. The denominator of the expression for σ^2 should then be $N - 1$.

23 Write a subroutine called BIAS that is invoked with the statement:

```
CALL BIAS(X, Y, N)
```

X is an input array of N values. Y is an output array whose values are the values of X with the minimum value of the X array subtracted from each value in the array. For example,

if X =	then Y =
10	8
2	0
36	34
8	6

Thus, the minimum value of Y is always 0. This operation is referred to as *adjusting for bias* in X.

The Folger Shakespeare Library

PROBLEM SOLVING—Average Word Length

In an English literature class you have been reading the works of Shakespeare. An interesting discussion centered on the possibility that Sir Francis Bacon may have authored some of the plays attributed to Shakespeare. One of the suggestions for determining authorship was to compare the average word length of Shakespeare's writing with that of Sir Francis Bacon's to see if there is a significant difference. Write a computer program that will read text information and compute its average word length. (See Section 6-7, page 236, for the solution.)

6

CHARACTER STRINGS

INTRODUCTION

Our use of character data thus far has been limited to input and output of descriptive information. In this chapter we extend our ability to work with character strings by processing them with some familiar operations and also by introducing some new operations that are unique to character strings. A group of intrinsic functions that apply to character strings are also presented. Text processing and word processing applications are illustrated in the examples.

6-1 CHARACTER DATA

In Chapter 2 we learned that computers use a notation internally that is composed of 0's and 1's, called *binary language*. Integers and real numbers are converted into binary numbers when they are used in a computer. If you study computer hardware or computer architecture, you will learn how to convert values such as 56 and −13.25 into binary numbers. To use FORTRAN, however, it is not necessary to learn how to convert numbers from our decimal number system to a binary number system. When characters are used in the computer, they must also be converted into a binary form, or a *binary string*. There are several codes for converting character information into binary strings, but most computers use *EBCDIC* (Extended Binary Coded Decimal Interchange Code) or *ASCII* (American Standard Code for Information Interchange). In these codes, each character can be represented by a binary string. Table 6-1 contains a few characters and their EBCDIC and ASCII equivalents.

TABLE 6-1 Binary Character Codes

CHARACTER	ASCII	EBCDIC
A	1000001	11000001
H	1001000	11001000
Y	1011001	11101000
3	0110011	11110011
+	0101011	01001110
$	0100100	01011011
=	0111101	01111110

You do not need to memorize the binary code for characters in order to use the characters in your FORTRAN programs. You do need, however, to be aware of the fact that the computer will store characters differently than numbers that are to be used in arithmetic computations. That is, the integer number 5 and the character 5 will not be stored the same. Thus, it is not possible to use arithmetic operations with character data even if the characters represent numbers.

The CHARACTER statement presented in Chapter 3 must be used to specify any variables which will contain characters. An array that will contain characters can be defined as shown below:

```
CHARACTER*4 NAME(50)
```

or

```
CHARACTER NAME*4(50)
```

This specification reserves memory for 50 elements in the array NAME, where each element contains four characters. Thus a reference to NAME(18) references the character string which is the 18th element of the array, and it contains four characters.

Character strings can also be used as parameters in subprograms. They need to be specified on a CHARACTER statement in both the main program and in the subprogram. A subprogram can specify a character string STRING without giving a specific length with the statement:

```
CHARACTER*(*) STRING
```

This is a technique similar to specifying the length of an array with an integer variable, as in:

```
DIMENSION NAME(N)
```

In Section 6-3, we combine the statements to define an array of N variables, each of which contains a character string. The length of the character string is not specified in the subprogram. We use the following statement in the subprogram to accomplish all of this:

```
CHARACTER*(*) NAME(N)
```

6-2 CHARACTER STRING OPERATIONS

While character strings cannot be used in arithmetic computations, we can assign values to character strings, compare two character strings, extract a subset of a character string, and combine two character strings into one longer character string. Each of these four operations involving character strings is discussed separately.

ASSIGN VALUES

Values can be assigned to character variables with the assignment statement and a character constant. Thus, the statements below initialize a character string array RANK with the five abbreviations for freshman, sophomore, junior, senior, and graduate.

```
CHARACTER*2 RANK(5)
RANK(1) = 'FR'
RANK(2) = 'SO'
RANK(3) = 'JR'
RANK(4) = 'SR'
RANK(5) = 'GR'
```

If a character constant in an assignment statement is shorter in length than the character variable, blanks will be added to the right of the constant. Thus, if the following statement was executed, RANK(1) would contain letter F followed by a blank.

```
RANK(1) = 'F'
```

That is, an equivalent statement would be the following:

```
RANK(1) = 'F '
```

If a character constant in an assignment statement is larger than the character variable, the excess characters on the right will be ignored. Thus, the following statement,

```
RANK(1) = 'FRESHMAN'
```

would store the letters FR in the character array element RANK(1). The two examples emphasize the importance of using character strings that are the same length as the variables used to store them; otherwise, the statements can be very misleading.

One character string variable can also be used to initialize another character string variable as shown in the following statements:

```
CHARACTER*4 GRADE1, GRADE2
GRADE1 = 'GOOD'
GRADE2 = GRADE1
```

Both variables, GRADE1 and GRADE2, contain the character string 'GOOD'.

Character strings can also be initialized with DATA statements. The examples above could be performed with DATA statements, as shown below:

```
      CHARACTER RANK*2(5), GRADE1*4, GRADE2*4
      DATA RANK, GRADE1, GRADE2 /'FR', 'SO', 'JR', 'SR', 'GR',
     +                           2*'GOOD'/
```

COMPARE VALUES

An IF statement can be used to compare character strings. Assuming that the variable DEPT and the array CH are character strings, the following are valid statements:

```
IF(DEPT.EQ.'EECE')KT = KT + 1
IF(CH(I).GT.CH(I+1))THEN
   CALL SWITCH(I,CH)
   CALL PRINT(CH)
ENDIF
```

To evaluate a logical expression using character strings, you must first look at the length of the two strings. If one string is shorter than the other, add blanks to the right of the shorter string so that you can proceed with the evaluation using strings of equal length.

The comparison of two character strings of the same length is made from left to right, one character at a time. Two strings must have exactly the same characters in the same order to be equal.

A *collating sequence* lists characters from the lowest to the highest value. Partial collating sequences for EBCDIC and ASCII are given in Table 6-2. While the ordering is not exactly the same, there are some similarities that include:

1 Capital letters are in order from A to Z.

2 Digits are in order from 0 to 9.

3 Capital letters and digits do not overlap; digits either precede letters, or letters precede digits.

4 The blank character is less than any letter or number. When necessary for clarity, we use b to represent a blank.

TABLE 6-2 Partial Collating Sequences for Characters

ASCII
b " # $ % & ( ) * + , − . /
0 1 2 3 4 5 6 7 8 9
: ; = ? @
A B C D E F G H I J K L M N O P Q R S T U V W X Y Z
EBCDIC
b . (+ & $ *) ; − / , % ? : # @ = "
A B C D E F G H I J K L M N O P Q R S T U V W X Y Z
0 1 2 3 4 5 6 7 8 9

Several pairs of character strings are now listed, along with their correct relationships.

```
    'A1' < 'A2'
  'JOHN' < 'JOHNSTON'
   '176' < '177'
 'THREE' < 'TWO'
     '$' < 'DOLLAR'
```

If character strings contain only letters, then their order is the same as that which is used in a dictionary. This ordering according to the dictionary is called a *lexicographic ordering*.

EXTRACT SUBSTRINGS

A *substring* of a character string is any string that represents a subset of the original string and maintains the original order. The following list contains substrings of the string 'FORTRAN'.

```
'F'   'FO'   'FOR'   'FORT'   'FORTR'   'FORTRA'   'FORTRAN'
'O'   'OR'   'ORT'   'ORTR'   'ORTRA'   'ORTRAN'
'R'   'RT'   'RTR'   'RTRA'   'RTRAN'
'T'   'TR'   'TRA'   'TRAN'
'R'   'RA'   'RAN'
'A'   'AN'
'N'
```

Substrings are referenced by using the name of the character string followed by two integer expressions in parentheses separated by a colon. The first expression in parentheses is evaluated to give the position in the original string of the beginning of the substring, and the second expression gives the position of the end of the substring. Thus, if the string 'FORTRAN' is stored in a variable LANG, then some of its substring references are shown as follows:

Reference	Substring
LANG(1:1)	'F'
LANG(1:7)	'FORTRAN'
LANG(2:3)	'OR'
LANG(7:7)	'N'

If the first expression in the parentheses is omitted, the substring begins at the beginning of the string. Thus, LANG(:4) refers to the substring 'FORT'. If the second expression in the parentheses is omitted, the substring ends at the end of the string. Thus, LANG(5:) refers to the substring 'RAN'.

The substring operation will not operate correctly if the beginning and ending positions are not integers, are negative, or contain values greater than the number of characters in the substring. The ending position must also be greater than or equal to the beginning position of the substring.

The substring operator is a very powerful tool, as the next two examples illustrate.

EXAMPLE 6-1 Propane-Filled Balloons

Assume that a character array REGNUM contains the registration numbers of 500 hot air balloons. Each registration number is a character string of seven characters. The fifth character specifies balloon type: P, for propane-filled; S, for solar-heated; and H, for helium- or hydrogen-filled. Write a segment of FORTRAN code that counts the number of propane-filled hot air balloons.

Solution

```
      CHARACTER*7 REGNUM(500)
      INTEGER COUNTP
          .
          .
          .
      COUNTP = 0
*
      DO 10 I=1,500
         IF(REGNUM(I)(5:5).EQ.'P')COUNTP = COUNTP + 1
   10 CONTINUE ◇
```

EXAMPLE 6-2 Character Count

A character string CODE of 50 characters contains coded information. The number of occurrences of the letter S represents a special piece of information. Write a loop that counts the number of occurrences of the letter S in CODE.

Solution

```
      CHARACTER*50 CODE
      INTEGER COUNTS
         .
         .
         .
      COUNTS = 0
*
      DO 20 I=1,50
         IF(CODE(I:I).EQ.'S')COUNTS = COUNTS + 1
   20 CONTINUE ◇
```

A reference to a substring can be used anywhere that a string can be used. For instance, if LANG contains the character string 'FORTRAN', the following statement will change the value of LANG to 'FORMATS':

```
LANG(4:7) = 'MATS'
```

If LANG contains 'FORMATS', then the following statement will change the value of LANG to 'FORMASS':

```
LANG(6:6) = LANG(7:7)
```

When modifying a substring of a character string with a substring of the same character string, the substrings must not overlap. That is, do not use LANG(2:4) to replace LANG(3:5). Also, recall that, if a substring is being moved into a smaller string, only as many characters as needed to replace the smaller string will be moved from left to right. If the substring is being moved into a larger string, the extra positions on the right will be filled with blanks.

COMBINE STRINGS

Concatenation is the operation of combining two or more character strings into one character string. It is indicated by two slashes between the character strings to be combined. Thus, the next expression concatenates the constants 'WORK' and 'ED' into one string constant 'WORKED':

```
'WORK'//'ED'
```

The next statement combines the contents of three character string variables MO, DA, and YR into one character string and then moves the combined string into a variable called DATE:

```
DATE = MO//DA//YR
```

If MO='05', DA='15', and YR='84', then DATE='051584'. Since concatenation represents an operation, it cannot appear on the left of an equal sign.

6-3 PROBLEM SOLVING—ALPHABETICAL SORT

We have already seen that characters are compared according to the collating sequence of the computer that is being used. In the collating sequences for codes such as EBCDIC and ASCII, the code for the letter A is less than the code for the letter B, and so on through the alphabet. This ordering of alphabetic characters then implies that an alphabetic sort for character strings is equivalent to an ascending sort for numbers. Thus, the subroutine that we wrote to sort numbers into ascending order will also sort character strings into alphabetical order. The main program and the subroutine will need character specification statements, but otherwise the algorithm remains the same.

If characters other than the alphabetic characters A through Z appear in character strings that are to be sorted, some surprises may occur. For instance, the code for a blank is less than the code for any of the letters. Thus a name that begins with the letter Z would be at the end of an alphabetical list, but a name that begins with a blank followed by a Z would appear at the beginning of the alphabetical list. Therefore, in the sort routine that we present in this section, we will edit the data by removing any leading blanks in the strings that are to be sorted. This operation *left-justifies* the string. A string is right-justified if it contains no blanks on the right side.

PROBLEM STATEMENT

Write a subroutine to sort a character string array into alphabetical order. Remove any leading blanks from the character strings prior to sorting.

INPUT/OUTPUT DESCRIPTION

The input is a character array with N values. The output is the same array, but with the values reordered into alphabetical order and the leading blanks removed.

HAND EXAMPLE

Assume that we are to alphabetize a list of character strings with four characters each. The set of 10 names will be sorted, once with any leading blanks, and again without the leading blanks, to show the difference in the two alphabetical lists. The symbol $_b$ is used to clearly identify blanks in the lists.

Original Order	Alphabetical Order with Blanks	Alphabetical Order without Blanks
SAM$_b$	$_{bb}$ED	AL$_{bb}$
$_{bb}$ED	$_b$AL$_b$	AMY$_b$
$_b$SUE	$_b$SUE	BEV$_b$
MARY	AMY$_b$	ED$_{bb}$
JOSE	BEV$_b$	JOHN
JOHN	JOHN	JOSE
AMY$_b$	JOSE	LISA
$_b$AL$_b$	LISA	MARY
LISA	MARY	SAM$_b$
BEV$_b$	SAM$_b$	SUE$_b$

ALGORITHM DEVELOPMENT

The algorithm for an ascending sort was already developed in Chapter 4. The new feature that we are adding is the removal of leading blanks.

Decomposition

Remove leading blanks from the character strings
Sort the character strings into alphabetical order

Refinement in Pseudocode

```
ALPHA:  BEGIN
            FOR i = 1 TO n DO
                Remove leading blanks from name(i)
            END FOR
            sorted ← false
            WHILE not sorted DO
                sorted ← true
                FOR i = TO n − 1 DO
                    IF name(i) > name(i + 1)
                        Switch name values
                        sorted ← false
                    END IF
                END FOR
            END WHILE
            RETURN
        END
```

Before we translate the refined pseudocode into FORTRAN, we need to consider the step of removing blanks from a character string. For instance, suppose the character string called STRING is four positions long and contains ' SAM'. We can test the first character for a blank with the statement:

```
IF(STRING(1:1).EQ.' ')...
```

Now how do we remove the blank? If we think for a moment, we realize that we really want to shift all the characters one position to the left. This could be done in a loop, but an easier way is possible using the substring operation. Recall that STRING refers to the entire string, but STRING(2:) refers to all except the first character. Thus, we would like to replace STRING with STRING(2:). However, we cannot use the statement:

```
STRING = STRING(2:)
```

The problem with this statement is caused by the overlap of positions. Both sides of the equal sign are referencing some of the same characters. However, if TEMP is a character string with four characters, we can perform the desired step with these statements:

```
IF(STRING(1:1).EQ.' ')THEN
   TEMP = STRING(2:)
   STRING = TEMP
ENDIF
```

The extra position on the right side of TEMP is filled with a blank as discussed when we presented moving character strings into other character strings. Let's go through these steps with a couple of strings. If STRING contained ' SAM', this code would move 'SAM ' into TEMP, and then move 'SAM ' into STRING, resulting in 'SAM ' being stored in STRING. This works nicely, but suppose the initial string had been ' ED', a string with two blanks. Then after the steps above were executed, STRING would contain ' ED ', with one leading blank instead of two leading blanks. Therefore, to account for multiple leading blanks, we need to put these steps in a WHILE loop, such as this one:

WHILE string has a leading blank DO
  Remove leading blank
END WHILE

In FORTRAN, this becomes:

```
5 IF(STRING(1:1).EQ.' ')THEN
     TEMP = STRING(2:)
     STRING = TEMP
     GO TO 5
  ENDIF
```

This seems to work exactly as we desire. As long as there are leading blanks, we remove them and go back to see if there are any more to remove. Do you see any way this loop could "hang up," or get into a loop that it could not get out of by itself? What if STRING contained only blanks? Then we would continue shifting them one position to the left, but a blank would always be in the first position. To keep this from occurring, we can test for a blank string before the WHILE loop.

```
          IF(STRING.NE.' ')THEN
      5      IF(STRING(1:1).EQ.' ')THEN
                TEMP = STRING(2:)
                STRING = TEMP
                GO TO 5
             ENDIF
          ENDIF
```

Now we are ready to combine these statements for removing leading blanks with the statements for an ascending sort to yield an alphabetical sort.

In the FORTRAN program, we will be using the substring reference with elements in our array of character data. Thus, NAME(4) refers to the fourth character string in the array NAME, and NAME(4)(1:1) refers to the first character in the fourth character string.

FORTRAN Subroutine

```
      SUBROUTINE ALPHA(NAME, N)
*
*   THIS SUBROUTINE SORTS A CHARACTER ARRAY WITH N ELEMENTS
*   INTO ALPHABETICAL ORDER, WITH LEADING BLANKS REMOVED
*
      CHARACTER*(*) NAME(N)
      CHARACTER*30 TEMP
      LOGICAL SORTED
*
*   REMOVE LEADING BLANKS
*
      DO 10 I=1,N
         IF(NAME(I).NE.' ')THEN
 5          IF(NAME(I)(1:1).EQ.' ')THEN
               TEMP = NAME(I)(2:)
               NAME(I) = TEMP
               GO TO 5
            ENDIF
         ENDIF
   10 CONTINUE
*
*   PERFORM ALPHABETICAL SORT
*
      SORTED = .FALSE.
   15 IF(.NOT.SORTED)THEN
         SORTED = .TRUE.
         DO 20 I=1,N-1
            IF(NAME(I).GT.NAME(I+1))THEN
               TEMP = NAME(I)
               NAME(I) = NAME(I+1)
               NAME(I+1) = TEMP
               SORTED = .FALSE.
            ENDIF
   20    CONTINUE
         GO TO 15
      ENDIF
*
      RETURN
      END
```

TESTING

A driver to test this subroutine is given below:

```
      PROGRAM DRIVER
*
      CHARACTER*4 NAME(10)
*
      OPEN(UNIT=10, FILE=IN13, STATUS='OLD')
*
      N = 10
      DO 10 I=1,N
         READ(10,*)NAME(I)
   10 CONTINUE
*
      PRINT*, 'BEFORE SORT'
      PRINT*, NAME
*
      CALL ALPHA(NAME, N)
*
      PRINT*, 'AFTER SORT'
      PRINT*, NAME
*
      END
```

Use the data from the hand example to test this subroutine. If you do not want leading blanks removed, the corresponding loop could be removed from the subroutine. No other changes would be needed.

There is a point we would like to make about this solution. Note that by using the statement

```
CHARACTER*(*) NAME(N)
```

we did not have to specify a length for the character strings in the array NAME. This adds a great deal of flexibility to our routine. However, we needed a temporary character string TEMP to store one of the character strings. Since this variable is not sent through the argument list, it must be defined with a specific size. We made the string large (30 characters), but this does add a limitation to the routine. If the strings to be sorted are over 30 characters in length, the size of TEMP would have to be increased or characters would be lost in the sort.

6-4 PROBLEM SOLVING—BAR GRAPH

Bar graphs are frequently used to compare a set of data points. For instance, a company with a sales staff of eight can compare the monthly sales in a bar graph, as shown on the following page.

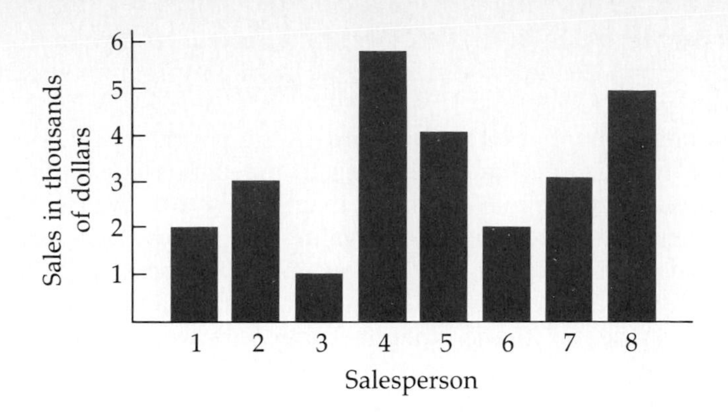

We cannot draw lines on the printer or the terminal screen (unless the terminal is a graphics terminal), so we make the bars with asterisks. The statements to print a bar graph from a set of data could be written such that a number of applications could use the same statements, so we develop the algorithm in the form of a subroutine. The input will be an array of numeric values, and the output from the routine will be a bar graph.

Let's begin by looking at a very simple case. Suppose the data numbers are 1, 4, 2, 3. Then we could print a bar with one asterisk, then one with four asterisks, and so on. This generates something like a bar graph, if you turn the paper sideways.

```
*
****
**
***
```

If the numbers were in an array NUM, the bar graph above could be printed with the following statements:

```
      DIMENSION NUM(4)
      CHARACTER*4 BAR
      DATA BAR /'****'/
          .
          .
          .
      DO 10 I=1,4
         PRINT*, BAR(1:NUM(I))
   10 CONTINUE
```

The value of NUM(1) is used in the substring specification the first time through the loop, and specifies how many asterisks to print. Each time through the loop, another value in the NUM array is used to specify the number of asterisks that will be printed. This solution works fine if we assume that the array of data values contains integer values greater than zero. The data values cannot get too large or we have a problem. The problem has two parts. First, the character string BAR must always have as many asterisks as the largest value in the array NUM. Second, if a value in the array NUM is larger than the number of positions in an output line, we cannot print it in the bar graph form.

The problems mentioned with regard to the previous statements can be solved if we apply some kind of scaling to the data values. For instance, assume that we want the maximum bar length to be 20. We can then look at the data values and match the largest value to a line with 20 asterisks, and then scale the others accordingly. For example, suppose that the values in NUM are 5, 2, 10, 8. Then, since 10 is the maximum value, we would print a bar with 20 asterisks for it, and scale the other bars accordingly. The output would be:

```
**********
****
********************
****************
```

The code to perform this type of scaling is shown below. Note that the scale factor is the length of the maximum bar divided by the maximum data value. If the maximum value is exactly the desired length of the maximum bar, the scale factor is 1, and none of the values are changed. If the maximum data value is less than the length of the maximum bar, then the quotient will be greater than 1, and all the values will increase proportionally. If the maximum data value is greater than the length of the maximum bar, then the quotient will be less than 1, and all the values will decrease proportionally.

```
      DIMENSION NUM(4)
      CHARACTER*20 BAR
      DATA BAR /'********************'/
          .
          .
          .
*
*  FIND MAXIMUM VALUE IN NUM
*
      MAX = NUM(1)
      DO 10 I=2,4
         IF(MAX.LT.NUM(I))MAX = NUM(I)
   10 CONTINUE
*
*  COMPUTE SCALE FACTOR
*
      SCALE = 20.0/REAL(MAX)
*
*  PRINT BAR GRAPH
*
      DO 20 I=1,4
         PRINT*, BAR(1:INT(SCALE*NUM(I)))
   20 CONTINUE
```

Note that SCALE is a real value. To keep from truncating the result of dividing 20 by another integer, MAX, we used the constant 20.0. However, when the scale factor is multiplied by a data value to determine the number of asterisks that we want to print, we want this result to be an integer. Therefore, we used the INT intrinsic function to truncate the result.

If we add two more modifications to the routine, we will have a very flexible bar graph routine. First, we allow the data to be real values. If we want to use the subroutine with an integer array, we can simply move the values into a real array and then call the bar graph routine with the real array. The other modification is in line length. The optimum line length for the maximum bar will depend on the application, and also on the device being used. If the output device is a line printer, we may want to use the entire line of 130 characters. If the output device is a small terminal screen, we may be restricted to 30 characters. Therefore, to accommodate all these possibilities, we let an argument LINE specify the maximum bar length, up to a maximum of 130 characters. Thus, the number of asterisks to be printed for a data value is computed with the following division:

$$K \leftarrow VALUE(I) \times LINE/MAX$$

We will look at this closer in the hand example in case you still have some questions about it.

Before we describe the design steps for pulling all of this together, we want to mention a limitation of the routine that we are developing. Negative data values will not be permitted. We will write the routine such that a value of zero will cause a bar to be skipped, but a negative value will cause the routine to be exited. If you want to modify the routine to handle negative values, you could find the minimum value. If it is negative, add that value to all the values. You then have a set of data values that are non-negative. See problem 23 from Chapter 5 for more information on this technique.

PROBLEM STATEMENT

Write a subroutine that will print a bar graph from a real array of N data values. Assume that the values will be non-negative. A parameter LINE will determine the maximum bar length.

INPUT/OUTPUT DESCRIPTION

The input to the subroutine is the real array of N values, the value of N, and the maximum bar length LINE. There are no output parameters passed back through the subroutine.

HAND EXAMPLE

For our hand example, we will use the data values below:

VALUE(1) = 15.0
VALUE(2) = 26.0
VALUE(3) = 4.0
VALUE(4) = 8.0
VALUE(5) = 15.8

Assume that the maximum line length is to be 30. The first step in computing the scale factor is to find the maximum data value. For our set of data, the maximum value is 26.0. The scale factor can then be computed as the maximum bar length divided by the maximum data value, or 30/26.0, which yields 1.15. We then multiply each data value by the scale factor to determine the number of asterisks to print for each bar. The result will need to be an integer because we cannot print part of an asterisk. Therefore, we can either truncate (drop) the fractional portion or round the fraction portion to the nearest integer. In this example, we choose rounding. The results are shown in the table below:

data value	×	scale factor	=	bar length	→	rounded
15.0	×	1.15	=	17.31	→	17
26.0	×	1.15	=	29.90	→	30
4.0	×	1.15	=	4.60	→	5
8.0	×	1.15	=	9.2	→	9
15.8	×	1.15	=	18.17	→	18

The corresponding bar graph would then be:

```
*****************
******************************
*****
*********
******************
```

ALGORITHM DEVELOPMENT

The earlier discussions on the steps to generate a bar graph are summarized below:

DECOMPOSITION

Scale data values to line size
Print corresponding bars of asterisks

REFINEMENT IN PSEUDOCODE

```
GRAPH:  BEGIN
          IF line > 130 or < 1
            PRINT error message
          ELSE
            neg ← 0
            max ← value(1)
            FOR i=1 TO n DO
              IF value(i) < 0
                neg ← neg + 1
              ELSE
                IF value(i) > max
                  max ← value(i)
                END IF
              END IF
            END FOR
            IF neg = 0
              scale ← line/max
              FOR i=1 TO n DO
                k ← value(i) × scale + 0.5
                PRINT k asterisks
              END FOR
            END IF
          END IF
          RETURN
        END
```

FORTRAN SUBROUTINE

```
      SUBROUTINE GRAPH(VALUE, N, LINE)
*
*   THIS SUBROUTINE PRINTS A BAR GRAPH USING AN ARRAY
*   OF N ELEMENTS WITH MAXIMUM SIZE OF LINE
*
      DIMENSION VALUE(N)
      CHARACTER*130 BAR
      REAL MAX
*
*   FIND MAXIMUM AND CHECK FOR ERROR CONDITIONS
*
      IF(LINE.GT.130.OR.LINE.LT.1)THEN
         PRINT*, 'LINE LENGTH ERROR', LINE
      ELSE
         NEG = 0
         MAX = VALUE(1)
         DO 10 I=1,N
            IF(VALUE(I).LT.0.0)THEN
               NEG = NEG + 1
            ELSE
               IF(VALUE(I).GT.MAX)MAX = VALUE(I)
            ENDIF
   10    CONTINUE
*
*   FILL BAR WITH ASTERISKS
*
         IF(NEG.EQ.0)THEN
            DO 20 I=1,LINE
               BAR(I:I) = '*'
   20       CONTINUE
*
*   SCALE DATA VALUES AND PRINT BAR
*
            SCALE = REAL(LINE)/MAX
            DO 30 I=1,N
               K = VALUE(I)*SCALE + 0.5
               PRINT*, BAR(1:K)
   30       CONTINUE
         ENDIF
      ENDIF
*
      RETURN
      END
```

TESTING

A driver for testing this subroutine is given below:

```
      PROGRAM DRIVER
*
      DIMENSION VALUE(5)
*
      PRINT*, 'ENTER 5 DATA VALUES'
      READ*, VALUE
      PRINT*, VALUE
      PRINT*, 'ENTER LINE SIZE'
      READ*, LINE
      PRINT*, 'LINE = ', LINE
*
      N = 5
      CALL GRAPH(VALUE, N, LINE)
*
      END
```

Here are a few examples of output with different line sizes using the data values in the hand example.

LINE = 10

```
******
**********
**
***
******
```

LINE = 20

```
************
********************
***
******
************
```

LINE = 30

```
*****************
******************************
*****
*********
******************
```

LINE = 40

```
***********************
****************************************
******
************
************************
```

LINE = 50

```
*****************************
**************************************************
********
***************
******************************
```

Can you think of ways to improve the appearance of the bar graph? Double or triple bars instead of single bars would make it larger. These wider bars could be separated by blank lines. Headings and scales on the sides might also help. This bar graph subroutine is general enough to be used with many types of data, but also simple enough to be polished for specific uses. Other types of *printer plots* (ones that do not use a graphics plotter, but instead use the regular keyboard characters) are developed in the problems at the end of the chapter.

6-5 CHARACTER STRING INTRINSIC FUNCTIONS

A number of intrinsic functions were designed to be used with character strings. INDEX is used to locate specific substrings within a given character string. LEN is used to determine the length of a string, and is used primarily in subroutines and functions which have character string arguments. The functions CHAR and ICHAR are used to determine the position of a character in the collating sequence of the computer being used. The functions LGE, LGT, LLE, and LLT allow comparisons to be made based on the ASCII collating sequence, regardless of the collating sequence of the computer being used. We now discuss each group of intrinsic functions separately.

INDEX

The INDEX function has two arguments, both character strings. The function returns an integer value giving the position in the first string of the second string. Thus, if STRGA contained the phrase 'TO BE OR NOT TO BE', INDEX(STRGA, 'BE') would return the value 4, which points to the first occurrence of the string 'BE'. To find the second occurrence of the string, we could use the following statements:

```
      CHARACTER*18 STRGA
            .
            .
            .
      K = INDEX(STRGA,'BE')
      J = INDEX(STRGA(K+1:),'BE') + K
```

After execution of these statements, K would contain the value 4 and J would contain the value 17. Note that we had to add K to the second reference of INDEX in order to get the correct position because the second use of INDEX referred to the substring 'E OR NOT TO BE'. Thus, the second INDEX reference would return a value of 13, not 17. The value of INDEX(STRGA,'AND') would be 0 because the second string 'AND' does not occur in the first string STRGA.

LEN

The input to the function LEN is a character string, and the output is an integer that contains the length of the character string. This function is particularly useful in a subprogram that accepts character strings of any length, but needs the actual length within the subprogram. The statement in the subprogram that allows a character string to be used with any length is

```
      CHARACTER*(*) A, B, STRGA
```

This form can be used only in subprograms. The next example will use both the LEN function and the variable string length parameter in a subprogram.

EXAMPLE 6-3 Frequency of Blanks

Write a function subprogram that accepts a character string and returns a count of the number of blanks in the string.

Solution

```
      INTEGER FUNCTION BLANKS(X)
*
*   THIS FUNCTION COUNTS THE NUMBER
*   OF BLANKS IN A CHARACTER STRING X
*
      CHARACTER*(*) X
*
      BLANKS = 0
*
      DO 10 I=1,LEN(X)
         IF(X(I:I).EQ.' ')BLANKS = BLANKS + 1
   10 CONTINUE
*
      RETURN
      END ◇
```

Character strings may also be used in user-written subroutines. In the next example, we write a subroutine that combines input character strings into an output character string.

EXAMPLE 6-4 Name Editing

Write a subroutine that will receive 3 character strings, FIRST, MIDDLE, and LAST, each containing 15 characters. The output of the subroutine is to be a character string 35 characters long that contains the first name followed by one blank, the middle initial followed by a period and one blank, and finally the last name. Assume that FIRST, MIDDLE, and LAST have no leading blanks and no embedded blanks. Thus, if

```
FIRST = 'JOSEPH         '
MIDDLE = 'CHARLES        '
LAST = 'LAWTON         '
```

then

```
NAME = 'JOSEPH C. LAWTON                   '
```

Solution

The solution to this problem is simplified by the use of the substring operation that allows us to look at individual characters, and the INDEX function that is used to find the end of the first name. We move to NAME the characters in FIRST, then a blank, the middle initial, a period, another blank, and the last name. As you go through the solution, observe the use of the concatenation operation. Also, note that the move of the first name fills the rest of the character string NAME with blanks because FIRST is smaller than the field to which it is moved.

FORTRAN SUBROUTINE

```
      SUBROUTINE EDIT(FIRST, MIDDLE, LAST, NAME)
*
*   THIS SUBROUTINE EDITS A NAME TO THE FORM
*   FIRST, MIDDLE INITIAL, LAST
*
      CHARACTER*15 FIRST, MIDDLE, LAST
      CHARACTER*35 NAME
*
*   MOVE FIRST NAME
*
      NAME = FIRST
*
*   MOVE MIDDLE INITIAL
*
      L = INDEX(FIRST,'  ')
      NAME(L:L+3) = '  '//MIDDLE(1:1)//'. '
*
*   MOVE LAST NAME
*
      NAME(L+4:) = LAST
*
      RETURN
      END ◇
```

CHAR, ICHAR

These functions refer to the collating sequence used in the computer being used to run a program. If a particular computer has 50 characters in its collating sequence, these characters will be numbered from 0 to 49. Assume, for example, that the letter A corresponds to position 12. The function CHAR has an integer argument which specifies the position of a desired character in the collating sequence. The function returns the character in the specified position. Thus, using our example, the following statements will print the character A:

```
N = 12
PRINT*, CHAR(N)
```

The ICHAR function is the inverse of the CHAR function. The argument to the ICHAR function is a character variable that contains one character. The function returns an integer that gives the position in the collating sequence of the character. Thus, the output of the following statements is the number 12:

```
CHARACTER*1 INFO
INFO = 'A'
PRINT*, ICHAR(INFO)
```

Since different systems have different collating sequences, these functions can be used to determine the position of certain characters in the collating sequence.

EXAMPLE 6-5 Collating Sequence

Print each character in the FORTRAN character set along with its position in the collating sequence on your computer. The FORTRAN character set is given on page 72.

Solution

```
      PROGRAM SEQ
*
*   THIS PROGRAM PRINTS THE POSITION IN THE COLLATING
*   SEQUENCE FOR EACH FORTRAN CHARACTER
*
      CHARACTER*49 SET
*
      SET(1:26) = 'ABCDEFGHIJKLMNOPQRSTUVWXYZ'
      SET(27:36) = '0123456789'
      SET(37:49) = ' +-*/=(),.''$:'
*
      DO 10 I=1,49
         PRINT*, SET(I:I), ICHAR(SET(I:I))
   10 CONTINUE
*
      END
```

Why did we put two apostrophes in the assignment for SET(37:49)? Remember that two apostrophes will be converted into a single apostrophe when they are in a literal. If you have several computers available, run this program on each of them to see if they all use the same collating sequence for the FORTRAN character set. ◇

LGE, LGT, LLE, LLT

This set of functions allows you to compare character strings based on the ASCII collating sequence. These functions become useful if a program is going to be used on a number of different computers and is using character comparisons or character sorts. The functions themselves represent a logical value, true or false. Each function has two character string arguments, STRG1 and STRG2. The function reference

LGE(STRG1, STRG2)

is true if STRG1 is lexically greater than or equal to STRG2. Thus, if STRG1 comes after STRG2 in an alphabetical sort, then this function reference is true. Remember, these functions are based on an ASCII collating sequence regardless of the sequence being used on the computer that is running the program. The functions LGT, LLE, and LLT perform comparisons "lexically greater than," "lexically less than or equal to," and "lexically less than."

EXAMPLE 6-6 ASCII Sort

In a sort based on the collating sequence in a computer, we perform the following steps, where STRG represents a character array:

```
IF(STRG(I).GT.STRG(I+1))THEN
   TEMP = STRG(I)
   STRG(I) = STRG(I+1)
   STRG(I+1) = TEMP
   SORTED = .FALSE.
ENDIF
```

Rewrite this loop so that the switch of character strings will occur based on an ASCII collating sequence even if the computer being used does not use an ASCII code.

Solution

```
IF(LGT(STRG(I),STRG(I+1)))THEN
   TEMP = STRG(I)
   STRG(I) = STRG(I+1)
   STRG(I+1) = TEMP
   SORTED = .FALSE.
ENDIF ◇
```

6-6 TEXT PROCESSING

Text processing and *word processing* refer to the processing of character information. The editor that you use to build and edit a program file is an example of a sophisticated text processor. It enables you to perform steps such as deleting information, inserting information, and searching for specific strings. All these capabilities make it easy to prepare and edit files. In fact, we often forget the large number of steps that are actually performed every time that we execute a command such as "change all occurrences of TAX to TAXRT". We will do a couple of examples that show some of the types of steps that are routinely performed in editors and many text processors.

EXAMPLE 6-7 Count Occurrences of Word 'AND'

Give the statements necessary to count the number of times that the string AND appears in a character string called TEXT.

Solution

Since the index function searches for occurrences of a string in another string, we will use it in our solution.

```
    COUNT = 0
    PTR = 1
  5 IF(INDEX(TEXT(PTR:),'AND').NE.0)THEN
       COUNT = COUNT + 1
       PTR = PTR + INDEX(TEXT(PTR:),'AND')
       GO TO 5
    ENDIF
```

This solution requires some time to understand what is happening the first time that you go through it. The best way to start is with a simple example. Suppose TEXT contained 'SAND AND WATER'.

Loop 1 SAND AND WATER
↑

PTR is initialized to 1 so INDEX uses the entire string 'SAND AND WATER' in the search and therefore returns a value of 2. We increment COUNT to 1. We increment PTR to 3.

Loop 2 SAND AND WATER
↑

We return to the INDEX function which is now using the substring 'ND AND WATER' because PTR is 3. The function will return the value 4 because the string 'AND' occurs in the fourth position of the substring that it was using. We increment COUNT to 2. We increment PTR to 7.

Loop 3 SAND AND WATER
↑

We return to the INDEX function which is now using the substring 'ND WATER'. The function will return a 0 so we exit the WHILE loop. TEXT will not be modified and COUNT will contain a value of 2, indicating that two occurrences of 'AND' were found. ◇

EXAMPLE 6-8 Change ? to !

Give the statements necessary to convert all question marks to exclamation points in a character string TEXT.

Solution

We will again use the INDEX function to find the question marks and a pointer PTR to keep track of our location in the character string.

```
    PTR = 1
 10 IF(INDEX(TEXT(PTR:),'?').NE.0)THEN
       PTR = PTR + INDEX(TEXT(PTR:),'?') - 1
       TEXT(PTR:PTR) = '!'
       GO TO 10
    ENDIF
```

This routine is similar to the previous one in that it looks for an occurrence of a specific string. However, when we find it, instead of moving the pointer to the next position, we position the pointer to the desired string, replace it with the new string, and then return to look for the next occurrence. As before, let's take a specific example through the solution. Suppose TEXT contains 'WHAT? WHERE? WHEN?'.

Loop 1 WHAT? WHERE? WHEN?
↑

As we begin, PTR is initialized to 1. The INDEX function is using the entire string and will return to value of 5. PTR is then incremented to 5. The character in position 5 is replaced with '!'.

Loop 2 WHAT! WHERE? WHEN?
↑

We return to the INDEX function which is now using the substring '! WHERE? WHEN?". It returns a value of 8. PTR is incremented to 12. The 12th position of TEXT is replaced by '!'.

Loop 3 WHAT! WHERE! WHEN?
↑

We return to the INDEX function which is now using the substring '! WHEN?'. It returns a value of 7. PTR is incremented to 18. The 18th position of TEXT is replaced with '!'.

Loop 4 WHAT! WHERE! WHEN!
↑

We return to the INDEX function which is now using the substring '!'. We exit the WHILE loop because the INDEX function returns a zero. The TEXT string has been modified from 'WHAT? WHERE? WHEN?' to 'WHAT! WHERE! WHEN!'. ◇

EXAMPLE 6-9 Change 'T' to 'TH'

Give the statements necessary to convert all occurrences of 'T' to 'TH' in a character string TEXT.

Solution

At first, this problem appears to be the same as the previous one which replaces '?' with '!'. However, we now want to put two characters in the place of one character. The rest of the characters will have to be moved one position to the right. The last character of the string will be lost each time a new character is inserted. We do not need a special routine to insert a character, as we did to insert an array value, because of the versatility of the substring operator and the concatenation operator.

```
      PTR = 1
   10 IF(INDEX(TEXT(PTR:),'T').NE.0)THEN
         PTR = PTR + INDEX(TEXT(PTR:),'T')
         TEMP = TEXT(1:PTR-1)//'H'//TEXT(PTR:)
         TEXT = TEMP
         GO TO 10
      ENDIF
```

As before, the best way to be sure that you understand this solution is to go through it with an example character string. Let TEXT contain 'NOW IS THE TIME FOR'.

Loop 1 NOW IS THE TIME FOR
↑

PTR is initialized to 1 so INDEX uses the entire string in the first search and therefore returns a value of 8. We increment PTR to 9. A temporary character string is then formed from the three character strings, 'NOW IS T', 'H', 'HE TIME FOR'. This temporary string is then moved into TEXT as 'NOW IS THHE TIME FO'.

Loop 2 NOW IS THHE TIME FO
↑

We return to the INDEX function which is now using the substring 'HHE TIME FO'. The function will return the value 5. We increment PTR to 14. A temporary character string is then formed from the three character strings, 'NOW IS THHE T', 'H', 'IME FO'. This temporary string is then moved into TEXT as 'NOW IS THHE THIME F'.

Loop 3 NOW IS THHE THIME F
↑

We return to the INDEX function which is now using the substring 'HIME F'. It will return a zero and the WHILE loop is exited with TEXT changed from 'NOW IS THE TIME FOR' to 'NOW IS THHE THIME F'. ◇

6-7 PROBLEM SOLVING—AVERAGE WORD LENGTH

Text material is sometimes analyzed very carefully to determine quantities such as average word length. Such a quantity can be used to recommend the level of reading ability necessary to read the text. Average word length can even be used to help determine authorship of a literary work; it has been applied to the works of Shakespeare in an attempt to indicate whether Sir Francis Bacon authored some of the plays attributed to Shakespeare. Write a function that receives a character string and returns the average word length of the string. Assume that all words are separated from adjacent words by at least one blank. The first and last characters may or may not be blanks.

PROBLEM STATEMENT

Write a function that computes the average word length of a character string.

INPUT/OUTPUT DESCRIPTION

The input is a character string. The output is a number that is the average word length of the input character string.

HAND EXAMPLE

Sometimes the best way to get started on a problem is to work a few cases by hand. Assume that the text is 18 characters long. Then the following strings can be analyzed as shown:

```
'TO BE OR NOT TO BE'
```

6 words, 13 letters, 2.17 average word length

```
'     HELLO         '
```

1 word, 5 letters, 5.0 average word length

```
'IDIOSYNCRATICALLY!'
```

1 word, 18 letters, 18.0 average word length

```
'MR. JOHN P. BUD    '
```

4 words, 12 letters, 3.0 average word length

```
'                   '
```

0 words, 0 letters, 0.0 average word length

ALGORITHM DEVELOPMENT

From the examples done by hand, we see that the text could have no blanks or be all blanks. The words may be separated by one or more blanks, and the text may or may not begin and end with a blank. The key part of the algorithm will be recognizing words. Recognizing a word then is composed of determining where the word begins and where the word ends.

Decomposition

Count number of words
Count number of letters
Average ← number of letters/number of words

Refinement in Pseudocode

```
WORDAV:  BEGIN
            nwords ← 0
            nletrs ← 0
            WHILE more words DO
               Find beginning of next word
               Find end of next word
               Compute number of letters in word
               nletrs ← nletrs + new letters
               nwords ← nwords + 1
            END WHILE
            IF nwords = 0
               wordav ← 0
            ELSE
               wordav ← nletrs/nwords
            END IF
            RETURN
         END
```

We will use NWORDS to store the number of words and NLETRS to store the number of letters. Both of these variables will be initialized to zero. Note that we are counting any nonblank character as a letter. We begin by looking through the text (TEXT) for the first nonblank character, using the substring notation. If we do not find a nonblank character, we will return an average word length of zero. If we do find a nonblank character, call the appropriate position FIRST. Then look for the first blank character in the substring beginning at position FIRST and call this new position NEXTBL. If there are no blanks after FIRST, set NEXTBL to the first position after the end of the string. The number of characters in the word would be NEXTBL − 1. We add this value to NLETRS and 1 to NWORDS. We move the value of NEXTBL to FIRST, and repeat the process until we reach the end of the string. At that point, we compute the average word length, being careful not to lose the fractional portion, and return to the main program.

FORTRAN Function

```
      FUNCTION WORDAV(TEXT)
*
*   THIS FUNCTION COMPUTES THE AVERAGE WORD
*   LENGTH OF THE CHARACTER STRING TEXT
*
      CHARACTER*(*) TEXT
      INTEGER FIRST
*
      NWORDS = 0
      NLETRS = 0
      FIRST = 1
      N = LEN(TEXT)
*
   10 IF(FIRST.LE.N)THEN
         IF(TEXT(FIRST:FIRST).NE.' ')THEN
            NEXTBL = INDEX(TEXT(FIRST:N),' ')
            IF(NEXTBL.EQ.0)NEXTBL = N - FIRST + 2
            LETRS = NEXTBL - 1
            NLETRS = NLETRS + LETRS
            NWORDS = NWORDS + 1
            FIRST = NEXTBL + FIRST - 1
         ELSE
            FIRST = FIRST + 1
         ENDIF
         GO TO 10
      ENDIF
*
      IF(NWORDS.EQ.0)THEN
         WORDAV = 0.0
      ELSE
         WORDAV = NLETRS/REAL(NWORDS)
      ENDIF
*
      RETURN
      END ◇
```

TESTING

A driver program to test this function with the strings used in the hand example is given below:

```
      PROGRAM DRIVER
*
      CHARACTER*18 STRING
*
      OPEN(UNIT=10, FILE='IN15', STATUS='OLD')
*
      DO 20 I=1,5
         READ(10,*)STRING
         PRINT*, STRING
         PRINT*, 'WORD AVERAGE IS', WORDAV(STRING)
   20 CONTINUE
*
      END
```

Suppose we increased the length of STRING from 18 to 30. If the same five example strings from the hand example are used, will the word averages be different? The answer is no, because we are adding only blanks. Suppose the length of STRING is decreased from 18 to 10. If the same five strings are used, will the word averages be different? Try it on the computer. Explain your results.

SUMMARY

The processing of character strings plays an ever-increasing role in the analysis and presentation of information. Solutions to problems are not always numbers, so we must have the ability to handle non-numeric information as effectively as we do numeric information. The CHARACTER data type, its associated substring and concatenation operators, and its intrinsic functions provide the essential ingredients in writing very powerful text processing algorithms.

KEY WORDS

ASCII code
binary string
character string
collating sequence
concatenation
EBCDIC code
FORTRAN character set
left-justify
lexicographical order
printer plotting
right-justify
substring
text processing
word processing

DEBUGGING AIDS

Many errors in character string manipulations occur because the character string is used incorrectly with numeric data. Some typical examples are:

Arithmetic expressions—Even if a character string contains numeric digits, it cannot be used in an arithmetic operation.

Comparisons—Character strings should always be compared to other character strings and not to a numeric constant or variable.

Subprogram arguments—A character string used as an argument to a subprogram must be identified in CHARACTER statements in both the main program and the subprogram.

Another source of errors may be introduced when moving or comparing strings of unequal length. For comparisons, the shorter string will be compared as if it had enough blanks on the right to be equal in length to the longer string. Character strings are always moved character by character from left to right, until the receiving string is filled. If there are not enough characters in the sending string, blanks will be moved into the rightmost characters of the receiving string.

A final caution on the substring operation: Invalid results will occur if the beginning or ending positions of the substring reference are outside the original string itself.

STYLE/TECHNIQUE GUIDES

A programmer who is comfortable and proficient with character string manipulations will find them to be extremely useful. The ability to display information clearly and simply is very valuable in communicating with people, and the use of character strings adds a new dimension to the methods of both reading and displaying information.

Some guides for using character strings in your programs are now listed:

1. Use character strings of the same length where possible.
2. Use the function INDEX instead of writing your own routine to find substrings in a string.
3. Become proficient with the substring and concatenation operators. These are powerful tools in manipulating and analyzing character strings.
4. Take advantage of the printer-plotting techniques that are described in this chapter and in the problems at the end of the chapter.

PROBLEMS

For problems 1 through 12, a character string of length 25 called TITLE is initialized with the statements

```
CHARACTER*25 TITLE
    .
    .
    .
TITLE = 'CONSERVATION OF ENERGY'
```

Tell what substrings are referred to in the following references:

1 `TITLE(1:25)`

2 `TITLE(1:12)`

3 `TITLE(13:23)`

4 `TITLE(16:16)`

5 `TITLE(8:8)`

6 `TITLE(17:)`

7 `TITLE(:12)`

8 `TITLE(:)`

9 `TITLE//'LAW'`

10 `TITLE(1:12)//' IS '//'A'//' LAW'`

11 `TITLE(1:7)//'E'//TITLE(16:)`

12 `''''//TITLE(1:4)//'ID'//TITLE(19:20)//'ATE'//''''`

For problems 13 through 18, WORD is a character string of length 6. What is stored in WORD after each of the following statements?

13 `WORD = 'DESTINY'`

14 `WORD = 'AREA'`

15 `WORD = 'CAN''T'`

16 `WORD = '''''''!'`

17 `WORD = 'FF'//''/SEC'`

18 `WORD = ' VOLUME'`

For problems 19 through 24, tell whether each of the logical expressions is true or false. Assume EBCDIC as the internal code.

19 `'ABC'.EQ.'ABC  '`

20 `'ADAM'.LT.'ABLE'`

21 `'**'.LT.'* *'`

22 `'TWO'.GE.'TWOSOME'`

23 `'138.5'.LE.'138.50'`

24 `' JOE'.NE.'JOE'`

For problems 25 through 30, the character string PHRASE contains 40 characters and has been initialized with the following statement:

```
CHARACTER*40 PHRASE
    .
    .
    .
PHRASE = 'ELECTRONS, NEUTRONS, PROTONS'
```

What value is returned by the following intrinsic functions?

25 `LEN(PHRASE)`

26 `LEN(PHRASE(12:))`

27 `INDEX(PHRASE,'ON')`

28 `INDEX(PHRASE(12:),'ING')`

29 `INDEX(PHRASE(22:),PHRASE(1:1))`

30 `INDEX(PHRASE(:21),' ')`

31 Write a complete program which will read a data file ADDR containing 50 names and addresses. The first line for each person contains the first name (10 characters), the middle name (6 characters), and the last name (21 characters). The next line in the file contains the address (25 characters), the city (10 characters), the state abbreviation (2 characters), and the zip code (5 characters). Print the information in the following label form:

First Initial. Middle Initial. Last Name
Address
City, State ZIP

Skip four lines between labels. The city should not contain any blanks before the comma that follows it. A typical label might be:

```
J. D. DOE
117 MAIN ST.
TAOS, NM  87186
```

For simplicity, assume no embedded blanks in the individual data values. That is, San Jose is punched SANJOSE, not SAN JOSE.

32 Write a subroutine PACK that receives a character string IN of 50 characters and returns a character string OUT that has no adjacent blanks except at the end of the string. Thus, if IN was composed of '$_b$HELLO$_{bbb}$THERE' followed by 36 blanks, then the output OUT from the subroutine PACK should be '$_b$HELLO$_b$THERE' followed by 38 blanks.

33 Write a subroutine DELETE that has an argument list composed of a character string TEXT of 100 characters and a pointer PTR. The subroutine should delete the character in position PTR. The characters in the positions following PTR should be moved one position to the left. A blank should then be added at the end of TEXT to keep the length of TEXT consistent at 100 characters.

34 Write a subroutine INSERT that has an argument list composed of a character string TEXT of 100 characters, a point PTR, and a single character CHAR. The subroutine should insert CHAR in the position pointed to by PTR. The rest of the characters should be moved one position to the right, with the last character truncated to keep the length of TEXT at 100 characters.

35 A data file called CARS contains the license plate number and the number of gallons of gas that can be put into the car for each car in the state of California. The license plate is composed of three characters, followed by three digits. Each line in the file contains a license number and a real number that gives the corresponding gallons of gas. The last line in the file has a license number of ZZZ999 and is not a valid data line. Write a complete program that will help analyze the feasibility of gas rationing based on whether the license plate number is odd or even. The data to be computed and printed is the following:

```
SUM OF GAS FOR ODD CARS     XXXXXX GALLONS    XX X%
SUM OF GAS FOR EVEN CARS    XXXXXX GALLONS    XX X%
```

36 A *palindrome* is a word or piece of text that is spelled the same forward and backward. The word 'RADAR' is an example of a palindrome, but ' RADAR' is not a palindrome because of the unmatched blank. 'ABLE ELBA' is another palindrome. Write a function PALIND that receives a character string X of variable length and returns a 1 if X is a palindrome and a 0 if X is not a palindrome.

37 Write a subroutine ALPHA that receives an array of 50 names, NAME, each four characters long. The subroutine should sort the names into a reverse alphabetical order list and return this list in the array ANAME.

38 Write a subroutine whose input is a character string of length 50. Change all punctuation marks (commas, periods, exclamation points, and question marks) to blanks and return this new string in the same character string. Assume that the main program accesses the subroutine with the following statement:

```
CALL EDIT(STRING)
```

39 Write a subroutine that receives a piece of text called PROSE that contains 200 characters. The subroutine should print the text in lines of 30 characters each. Do not split words between two lines. Do not print any lines that are completely blank. If a word is longer than 30 characters, exit the routine.

40 Write a function CONSNT that receives an array CHAR of 100 elements. Each element contains one character. Count the number of consonants and return that number to the main program. (It might be easiest to count the number of vowels and subtract that number from 100.)

41 Write a subroutine that receives an array of N real values and prints a printer X-Y plot. Use a line of 101 characters. Scale the line from the negative absolute maximum value to the positive absolute maximum value. The first line of output should be 101 periods representing the Y axis. All the following lines should contain a period in column 51 to represent the origin and the letter X to represent the position of each data point, as shown in the following diagram:

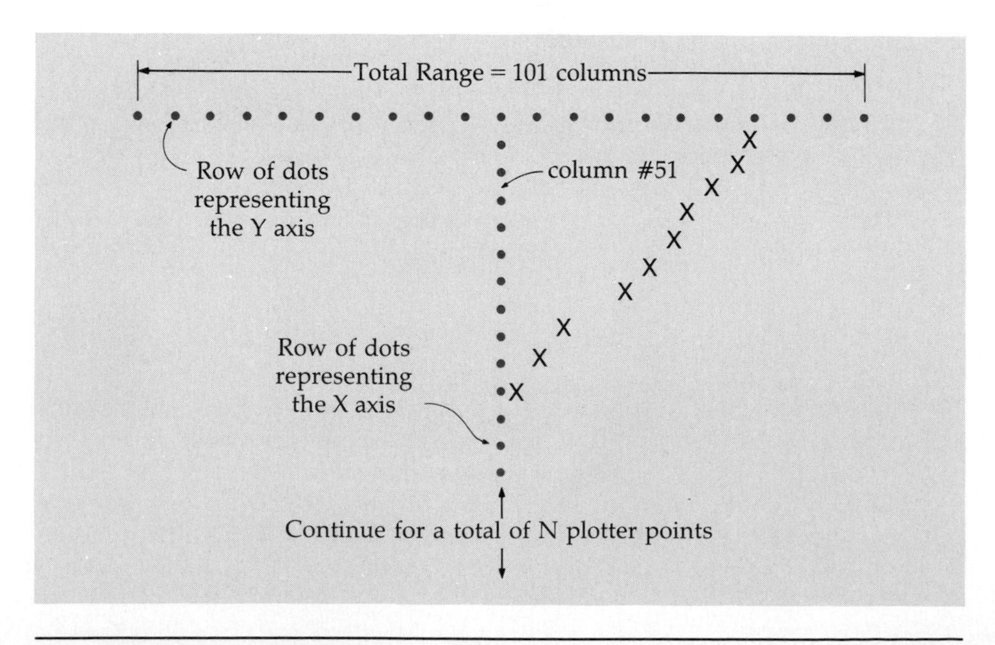

42 Modify the function of Section 6-7 so that punctuation characters are not included in the calculation of average word length. Punctuation characters include:

. , ; : ! ?

***43** Write a complete program that reads and stores the following array of 9 character strings, each string containing 6 characters.

```
ATIDEB
LENGTH
ECPLOT
DDUEFS
OUTPUT
CGDAER
HIRXJI
KATIMN
BHPARG
```

Now read the 11 strings listed below and find the same string in the array above. Print the positions of characters of these hidden words that may appear forward, backward, up, down, or diagonally. For instance, the word EDIT is located in positions 1:5, 1:4, 1:3, and 1:2.

HIDDEN WORDS

```
PLOT      STRING
CODE      TEXT
EDIT      READ
LENGTH    GRAPH
INPUT     BAR
OUTPUT
```

***44** Modify the subroutine of problem 39 such that the length of the output line is an argument to the subroutine. Distribute any blanks at the beginning of a line and the end of a line between words in the line so that every line begins and ends with a nonblank character. Thus, if the character string PROSE contained a portion of the Gettysburg Address, and the line length were 23, then the first few lines of output should be:

```
FOUR  SCORE  AND  SEVEN
YEARS  AGO  OUR  FATHERS
BROUGHT FORTH UPON THIS
```

© Peter Southwick/Stock, Boston

PROBLEM SOLVING—Warehouse Inventory

Summer vacation starts next week. The only response to your job applications has been an offer to maintain inventory information for a large warehouse. At first you were disappointed, but then you remembered the new file-handling techniques that you had just covered in your FORTRAN class. Write a program to maintain an inventory file and update it with daily transactions. (See Section 7-6, page 268, for the solution.)

7

FILE HANDLING

INTRODUCTION

In previous chapters, we have used files extensively. READ statements referred to input from a terminal or a card reader and PRINT statements referred to output on the terminal screen or a line printer. These two files were *automatically* connected to your programs. Using the OPEN statement introduced in Chapter 3, we could also connect other data files. All these types of files are called *external files* because they are external to the memory area reserved by our program.

External files can also be read from other devices, such as *magnetic tape drives* or *magnetic disk drives*. The files on these devices have special properties that determine the types of statements used to process them. Processing magnetic tape or magnetic disk files also requires a knowledge of the concepts involved in *sequential access* and *direct access*. In both of these access methods, we use the term *record* to describe a unit of information in the file. In a card file, one card represents a record. In a data file, one line represents a record. Sequential access of a file involves processing records from the physical beginning of the file. This is the type of access we have used throughout the text with our files. We read the first data line, then the second data line, and so on. In direct access, information is not necessarily accessed in its physical order. We may reference the tenth record, then the last record, and then the second, all without reading the records in between. This type of access is also called *random access* because we can access the records in a random order as opposed to a sequential order. Each record contains *fields* of information. For instance, a payroll file contains individual payroll records. Each record contains fields such as a name, hours worked, and hourly rate.

External files are often used because they are *portable*. This means that they can be used not only on another computer of the same manufacturer, but also on computers made by different manufacturers. For example, a magnetic tape file created on a Digital Equipment Corporation VAX computer can be read on a Control Data Corporation 7600 computer. In order for these files to be portable, there are standard procedures that must be observed when building and using them. One standard applies to the input and output statements that access these files. Since list-directed input and output are system dependent with regard to the number of digits used and the spacing, all input and output on sequential and direct access files that are stored on external devices must use formats to guarantee consistency from one computer to another. Therefore, we will briefly discuss *formatted input and output* in the first section of this chapter before we present the new statements and techniques for sequential and direct access file processing.

In addition to external files, FORTRAN also has a feature called *internal files*. This feature allows us to use a character string as if it were a file in order to manipulate the data internally. This feature is also presented in the chapter.

7-1 SIMPLE FORMATTED INPUT/OUTPUT

Since an extensive discussion of formatted input and output is included in Appendix B, we are going to present only the material on formatting integers, real numbers, and character strings that will be pertinent to the file processing presented in this chapter. If you will be using external files frequently, we suggest that you go through Appendix B in detail.

Recall that the main difference between list-directed statements and formatted statements is in the amount of control that we have in the operation. For example, assume that we execute the statement:

```
X = 3.2167
WRITE(10,*)X
```

The value of X will be printed but we cannot control how many decimal positions are to be printed or what part of the data line is to be used for the output. Suppose we execute these statements:

```
  X = 3.2167
  WRITE(10,8)X
8 FORMAT(F5.3)
```

These statements specify that X is to be printed on a data line with no leading blanks and with three decimal positions. Note that the asterisk in the WRITE statement has been replaced with an integer, 8. This integer is a statement reference to the FORMAT statement which will describe the output line. The general form of the FORMAT statement is:

```
k  FORMAT(specification list)
```

where *k* is a statement number. The specification list then contains *specifications* to describe the output line. We now discuss four specifications. Examples of these specifications will be used in the following sections of this chapter.

X SPECIFICATION

The X specification will skip positions when used with a READ statement and will insert blanks when used with a WRITE statement. The number preceding the X indicates the number of positions to skip or blanks to insert. Thus, 3X in a format that accompanies a READ statement will specify that the next three positions in the line should be skipped.

I SPECIFICATION

The I specification is used for integer variables. Its general form is Iw, where w is the number of positions to use for the variable. Thus, an I4 specification with a READ statement specifies that the next four positions are to be used for reading the value. With a WRITE statement, this specification indicates that the next four positions are to be used for writing the value of the variable.

When reading data, any blanks in the w positions will be interpreted as zeros. Any character besides numbers, plus or minus signs, and blanks will cause an execution error to occur. Thus, 5.0 cannot be read with an I3 specification, but $_{bb}$5 (where $_{b}$ indicates a blank) will be read correctly with an I3 specification. When writing data, the value is always *right-justified* so that there are no blanks on the right of the values in the output positions. Extra positions on the left are filled with blanks. Thus, if the value 16 is printed with an I4 specification, the four positions contain two blanks followed by 16. If there are not enough positions to print the value, including a minus sign if the value is negative, the positions are filled with asterisks. Hence, if we print the value 132 or −12 with an I2 specification, the two positions are filled with asterisks. It is important to recognize that the asterisks do not necessarily indicate that there is an error in the value; instead, the asterisks may indicate that you need to assign a larger width in the corresponding I specification.

F SPECIFICATION

The F specification can be used to read or write a value for a real variable. The form of this specification is Fw.d, where w represents the total number of positions to be used and d represents the number of these that will be interpreted as being to the right of the decimal point. For input, any blanks in the w positions will be interpreted as zeros. If there is a decimal point within the w positions, the value will be stored as it is entered, regardless of what value has been given to d. Thus, if a real value DIST is read with a F4.1 specification and the four characters are 1.26, then the value of DIST is stored as 1.26. If there is no decimal point in the specified positions, then the value of d is used to position a decimal place before storing the value. Thus, if the characters 1246 are read with an F4.1 specification, the value stored is 124.6, a value with one decimal position.

For output, the general form for an F specification is Fw.d, where w represents the total width or number of positions to be used in writing the real value, and d represents the number of those positions that will represent decimal positions to the right of the decimal point. For example, the minimum size F specification that can be used to write 34.186 is F6.3, a total of six positions counting the decimal point with three decimal positions. The form for F6.3 is then

```
XX.XXX
   └┬┘
 DECIMAL
└──┬───┘
 WIDTH
```

If the value to be printed has fewer than d decimal positions, zeros are inserted on the right side. Thus, if the value 21.6 is written with an F6.3 specification, the output is 21.600. If the value to be written has more than d decimal positions, only d decimal positions are written, dropping the rest. Thus, if the value 21.86342 is written with an F6.3 specification, the output is 21.863. Many compilers will round to the last decimal position written. Thus, if the value 18.98662 is written with an F6.3, the output is 18.987.

If the integer portion of a real value requires fewer positions than allotted in the F specification, the extra positions on the left are filled with blanks. Thus, if the value 3.123 is written with an F6.3 specification, the output is $_b$3.123. If the integer portion of a real value, including the minus sign if the value is negative, requires more positions than allotted in the F specification, the entire field is filled with asterisks. Thus, if the value 312.6 is written with an F6.3 specification, the output is ******.

A SPECIFICATION

When a character string is used in formatted input, the specification Aw is used. If w is less than the length of the character string, the rightmost positions in memory will be filled with blanks. If w is greater than the length of the character string, only the first n characters will be stored, where n is the length of the character string. If w is omitted, the length of the string will be used to determine the number of positions to read. Note that apostrophes are not used around a character string data value that is to be read with a formatted READ. The format statement specifies exactly which positions are to be read, so the apostrophes are not necessary to identify the beginning and ending of the string. To illustrate these rules for input, assume that ADDR is a character string with length 15. If a data line contained, in columns 1–15, 962 E. MAIN ST., then the execution of the following READ statement would yield the results shown for various format specifications.

```
CHARACTER*15 ADDR
     .
     .
     .
READ(14,20)ADDR
```

FORMAT	CONTENTS OF ADDR
20 FORMAT(A)	962 E. MAIN ST.
20 FORMAT(A15)	962 E. MAIN ST.
20 FORMAT(A11)	962 E. MAIN$_{bbbb}$
20 FORMAT(A3)	962$_{bbbbbbbbbbbb}$
20 FORMAT(A20)	962 E. MAIN ST.

When a character string is used in formatted output, Aw is used as the specification. If w is omitted, the entire string will be written. If w is less than the length of the character string, the first w positions of the character string will be written. If w is greater than the length of the character string, the extra positions will be filled with blanks on the left of the string. To illustrate these rules for output, assume that the character string variable NAME contains 'JOHN A. SMITH', and that the following statement has been executed:

```
CHARACTER*13 NAME
     .
     .
     .
WRITE(13,10)NAME
```

Beside each of the following format statements is the corresponding output.

FORMAT	CORRESPONDING OUTPUT
10 FORMAT(A)	JOHN A. SMITH
10 FORMAT(A13)	JOHN A. SMITH
10 FORMAT(A4)	JOHN
10 FORMAT(A10)	JOHN A. SM
10 FORMAT(A15)	$_{bb}$JOHN A. SMITH

EXAMPLE 7-1 Read Test Scores

A data file ACCT02 contains test scores for students in an accounting class. Each line in the file has the following format:

columns 1–20	Student name
columns 22–24	Midterm grade (integer)
columns 26–28	Final grade (integer)
columns 30–34	Homework grade (real value with one decimal position)
column 40	Final letter grade

Give the READ and FORMAT statements to read this information. Also show any specification statements needed. Assume that unit 15 is used to refer to this file.

Solution

```
      CHARACTER NAME*20, GRADE*1
      INTEGER FINAL
          .
          .
          .
      READ(15,5)NAME, MIDTRM, FINAL, HW, GRADE
    5 FORMAT(A20,1X,I3,1X,I3,1X,F5.1,5X,A1)  ◇
```

EXAMPLE 7-2 Write Sales Record

At the end of each business day, a summary of the sales transactions are written into a data file. Each record contains the following information:

columns 1–6	Date in month-day-year form (DATE, character)
columns 10–30	Item description (ITEM, character)
columns 31–35	Quantity sold (QUANT, integer)
columns 40–45	Unit price (UNIT, two decimal positions)
columns 50–57	Sales amount with tax (SALES, two decimal positions)

Give WRITE and FORMAT statements to write this set of values. Also show any specification statements necessary. Assume that unit 10 is used to refer to this file.

Solution

```
      CHARACTER DATE*6, ITEM*21
      INTEGER QUANT
          .
          .
          .
      WRITE(10,8)DATE, ITEM, QUANT, UNIT, SALES
    8 FORMAT(A6,3X,A21,I5,4X,F6.2,4X,F8.2)  ◇
```

7-2 INTERNAL FILES

When the unit number of an input or output statement is the name of a character variable, the statement transfers data from one internal storage area to another internal storage area. These storage areas are called *internal files*. For instance, we can read data from a character string instead of a data line or data card. The input and output statements function exactly as if the contents of the character string were actually punched in a data card or entered in a data line, as shown in the following example.

```
      CHARACTER*10 DATA
      DATA = '12.7654217'
          .
          .
          .
      READ(DATA,5)A, B
    5 FORMAT(F4.1,F4.1)
```

After execution of these statements, the value of A is 12.7 and the value of B is 654.2.

This feature is particularly useful if you want to perform some type of editing on the data before using it. For example, suppose you are reading information from a data file that contains amounts which have been entered with dollar signs to the left of the amounts. If the fields are read directly into real variables, execution errors will occur. Using internal files, you can read the data into an internal character file, edit the data by changing all dollar signs to blanks, and then read the numeric values from the internal file. The following statements read 10 positions from a data line, change any leading dollar sign to a blank, and then read the value into a real variable.

```
      INTEGER PTR
      CHARACTER*10 TEMP
          .
          .
          .
      READ(12,5)TEMP
    5 FORMAT(A10)
      IF(INDEX(TEMP,'$').NE.0)THEN
         PTR = INDEX(TEMP,'$')
         TEMP(PTR:PTR) = ' '
      ENDIF
      READ(TEMP,15)AMOUNT
   15 FORMAT(F10.2)
```

A similar use of internal files is useful if you want to edit lines of an output report before they are printed. For example, you might want to insert dollar signs next to real values that are to be printed. With internal files, you can insert the dollar sign next to the digits, as in $_{bbb}\$146.21$, as opposed to next to the output field, as in $\$_{bbb}146.21$.

7-3 SEQUENTIAL FILES

Sequential files are typically built by one program and then accessed by other programs. Once a sequential file is created, individual records cannot be updated. When changes in the information need to be made, the updating is usually done by reading the information in a record, updating it if desired, and then in either case writing the information to an output record. This process is repeated for each record in the file, and is sometimes referred to as *father-son updating* because after the program is run you have the original file (father) and also the updated file (son).

One other form of sequential file updating is allowed in FORTRAN. This type of processing allows you to perform a WRITE statement on an existing file, but all information after that record is lost. Therefore, this processing does not allow you to update a few records, but it does allow you to add information to the end of a file.

When we use sequential files, the same READ and WRITE statements are used, but other new statements may also be needed. An extended form of the OPEN statement is presented, along with statements to close the file, to reposition the record pointer to the first record in the file, to backspace one record in the file, and to add an end-of-file indicator to a new file.

OPEN STATEMENT

The purpose of the OPEN statement is to connect an external file to a program. The OPEN statement is executable but is typically placed at the beginning of the program because it should only be executed once. A simplified form of the OPEN statement was introduced in Chapter 3. The complete form of the OPEN statement is:

```
OPEN(UNIT=integer expression,
     FILE=character expression,
     ACCESS=character expression,
     STATUS=character expression,
     FORM=character expression,
     IOSTAT=integer variable,
     RECL=integer expression,
     BLANK=character expression,
     ERR=integer statement reference)
```

We now discuss each of the specifications that are used with data files.

Unit number: The integer expression in this specification is usually a constant. This value is used in READ or WRITE statements to specify the file to be used. The following example illustrates the use of a unit number to link together a file and the statements specifying that file:

```
      OPEN(UNIT=13, FILE='DIST', STATUS='NEW')
          .
          .
          .
      WRITE(13,10)X, Y
   10 FORMAT(F8.3,F5.1)
```

File: The character expression in this file specification must be the name of the file. All references to a file must use the same name used when the file was originally created. The file names typically consist of 1–6 alphabetic letters or numbers, with an alphabetic letter as the first character.

Access: The character string in this specification must be either 'SEQUENTIAL' or 'DIRECT'. If this specification is omitted, 'SEQUENTIAL' is assumed.

Status: The character string in this specification must be 'NEW', 'OLD', or 'SCRATCH'. 'NEW' is used to specify that the file is being created, through WRITE statements. 'OLD' specifies that the file is already built, and its records are accessed with READ statements. 'SCRATCH' specifies that the file is an output file that is not being used after the program, and hence will be deleted.

Form: The character string in this specification must be either 'FORMATTED' or 'UNFORMATTED'. A FORMATTED file uses either formatted READ and WRITE statements or list-directed input/output statements. All examples used in this text have been formatted examples. UNFORMATTED input/output is used for transfer of data with no conversion of the data. The data is transferred as binary strings, not numbers or characters. One of the main uses of UNFORMATTED input/output is to transfer tape or disk data to another tape or disk file. If this specification is omitted, the default is 'FORMATTED' for sequential files and 'UNFORMATTED' for direct files.

IOSTAT: The IOSTAT specification is not required but can be used to provide error-recovery. If no errors occur in attaching the specified file to the program, the value of the integer variable will be zero. If an error occurs, such as an input file with the proper name is not found, a value specified by the computer system will be stored in the variable. In your program you can test this variable, and if it is nonzero you can specify what action is to be taken. In this next example, an error in opening the file will cause IERR to be nonzero. An error message can be printed, and execution will continue. If the IOSTAT specification had not been used and an error had occurred in opening the file, execution would be terminated with an execution error.

```
      OPEN(UNIT=15, FILE='XYDATA', STATUS='OLD',
     +     IOSTAT=IERR)
      IF(IERR.NE.0)WRITE(*,5)IERR
```

The IOSTAT specification can also be used with READ and WRITE statements.

RECL: The RECL specification is required for direct access files and specifies the record length. It is not used with sequential access files.

BLANK: The character string in this specification must be either 'NULL' or 'ZERO', and cannot be used with unformatted files. If the specification is 'NULL', then blanks will be ignored in numeric fields; if the specification is 'ZERO', then blanks will be assumed to be zeros in numeric fields. If the specification is omitted, then 'NULL' is assumed.

ERR: This is an optional specification that is used to provide error-recovery. If an error occurs during execution of a statement that uses this specification, control will pass to the statement referenced by this specification. The ERR specification can also be used with READ and WRITE statements.

CLOSE STATEMENT

The CLOSE statement is an executable statement that disconnects a file from a program. Its general form is:

```
CLOSE(UNIT=integer expression,
      STATUS=character expression,
      IOSTAT=integer variable,
      ERR=integer statement reference)
```

The CLOSE statement is optional because all files will automatically be closed upon termination of the program's execution. The STATUS, IOSTAT, and ERR specifications are also optional in file-handling statements. If a file has been used and the determination has been made that it will not be needed for any more processing, the file can be deleted with the instruction:

```
CLOSE(UNIT=10, STATUS='DELETE')
```

If an error-recovery is desired from the CLOSE statement, the IOSTAT and/or ERR specifications can be used to detect an error.

REWIND STATEMENT

The REWIND statement is an executable statement that repositions a sequential file at the first record of the file. Its general form is:

```
REWIND(UNIT=integer expression,
       IOSTAT=integer variable,
       ERR=integer statement reference)
```

Some systems require a REWIND statement before reading an input file.

BACKSPACE STATEMENT

The BACKSPACE statement is an executable statement that repositions a sequential file to the last record read. Thus, it *backs up* one record in the file. Its general form is:

```
BACKSPACE(UNIT=integer expression,
          IOSTAT=integer variable,
          ERR=integer statement reference)
```

ENDFILE STATEMENT

When a sequential file is being built, a special *end-of-file* record must be written to specify the end of the file. This special record is written when the ENDFILE statement is executed. The general form of the executable ENDFILE statement is:

```
ENDFILE(UNIT=integer expression,
        IOSTAT=integer variable,
        ERR=integer statement reference)
```

The CLOSE statement automatically performs this function on most systems.

7-4 PROBLEM SOLVING—BANK TRANSACTION MERGE

A number of operations are commonly encountered as we process data. For instance, we have seen a number of applications that use sorting algorithms. Other operations frequently used include finding the minimum value or maximum value in a set of data, computing the average value in a set of data, and inserting or deleting values in a list. Another operation that is very useful is a merge. A *merge* operation is the combining of ordered lists into another list that preserves the same order. We will assume for now that we are merging only two lists, and will extend this to more lists later in the section.

Assume that arrays A and B have each been sorted into ascending order, as shown below:

array A
1
5
8
25
92

array B
7
15
19
106

If these arrays are merged into an array C, the result is:

array C
1
5
7
8
15
19
25
92
106

Note that the array C is larger than either array A or B. In fact, the array C should generally contain N + M elements if A contains N elements and B contains M elements.

Data to be merged must have some order to it, such as an ascending order or descending order. Alphabetical data can also be merged. In either case, one question that arises involves items that appear in both lists. Should the duplicate item appear once or twice in the merged list? The answer depends on the application. If the merged data represents an alphabetical mailing list that has been put together from several sources, then we would not want to duplicate a name that appeared on both lists if it represented the same person. However, if we are merging bank transactions that are received in the mail with transactions processed at the teller windows, we would want to keep transactions with the same account number because they represent different transactions. Therefore, a specific statement on how to handle duplicates needs to be included in the problem statement for a problem that includes a merging operation.

The application in which we will incorporate a merge involves bank transactions. Assume that the data processing office for a local bank receives three tape files of transactions each day. One file (IN16M) contains the transactions processed that day from mail received. Another file (IN16W) contains the transactions processed that day from the teller windows. The third file (IN16A) contains the transactions that were processed by the automatic teller machine. All three files have been sorted into ascending order by account number. Each record contains an integer identification number with three digits, a transaction code, and a transaction amount. The transaction code is 'D' for deposit and 'W' for withdrawal. The transaction amount is the corresponding amount deposited or withdrawn from the account. Assume that each file has a trailer record with an account number of 999. Write a program to read the files and merge them into one transaction file (OUT16), also in account number order, with a trailer record.

PROBLEM STATEMENT

Write a program to merge three files which are already sorted into ascending order by account number. An account number may have multiple transactions.

INPUT/OUTPUT DESCRIPTION

The input to the program is three files. The output is another file. All the files are in ascending order by account number. Each record in the files contains three fields, an account number, a transaction code, and a transaction amount. A trailer record with an account number of 999 is at the end of each file.

HAND EXAMPLE

Suppose that the sorted transaction files for one day were:

```
                    mail transactions    125 D  75.00
                                         147 W 285.00
                                         177 W  50.50
                                         193 D 150.00
                                         999

           teller window transactions     96 W  25.00
                                         101 D 152.76
                                         157 D 262.00
                                         208 W 510.00
                                         252 W 100.00
                                         999

 automated teller window transactions    125 W 100.00
                                         182 D 238.04
                                         193 W  50.00
                                         236 W  50.00
                                         999
```

The file of merged transactions is then:

```
 96 W  25.00
101 D 152.76
125 D  75.00
125 W 100.00
147 W 285.00
157 D 262.00
177 W  50.50
182 D 238.04
193 D 150.00
193 W  50.00
208 W 510.00
236 W  50.00
252 W 100.00
999
```

ALGORITHM DEVELOPMENT

One algorithm for merging two data arrays consists of moving one array (with M elements) into the first part of a large array and moving the other array (with N elements) into the last part of the large array (with M + N elements). Then we could sort the large array, and have the data items in the desired order. This idea could be extended to three arrays. However, there are two reasons why this is not a good algorithm. One reason is that it is very inefficient. Since each individual array is already sorted, there must be a better way to merge the lists without resorting all the data. The other reason that this is not a good algorithm is that it requires that all the data to be merged reside in memory at one time. With very large files, this is not practical. Therefore, we look for a better algorithm.

If you think back to the hand example, you will recall that you only needed the next value on each list in order to determine which record should be moved to the output file. The record with the smallest account number is moved to the output file, and the next record of that input file is read. The trailer signal simplifies the logic development in the algorithm because we do not need to worry about reaching the end of a data file while there are still a number of records left in the other files. When we read the 999 trailer signal (remember, this is not the end-of-file condition that causes an execution error), it will be larger than the other valid account numbers and thus it will force the rest of the records to be moved to the output file until we are positioned at the trailer signals of each file. We then write a trailer signal to the output file. Let's take some simple data through this algorithm. Assume that we want to merge File 1 and File 2. Both files contain a trailer signal 999. The arrows point to the current record (the one we have just read for input files or the one we have just written for output files).

File 1	File 2	Output File
→ 5	→ 2	
10	51	
82	999	
107		
999		

File 1	File 2	Output File
→ 5	2	→ 2
10	→ 51	
82	999	
107		
999		

File 1	File 2	Output File
5	2	2
→ 10	→ 51	→ 5
82	999	
107		
999		

File 1	File 2	Output File
5	2	2
10	→ 51	5
→ 82	999	→ 10
107		
999		

File 1	File 2	Output File
5	2	2
10	51	5
→ 82	→999	10
107		→ 51
999		

File 1	File 2	Output File
5	2	2
10	51	5
82	→999	10
→107		51
999		→ 82

(continued)

File 1	File 2	Output File
5	2	2
10	51	5
82	→999	10
107		51
→999		82
		→107

File 1	File 2	Output File
5	2	2
10	51	5
82	→999	10
107		51
→999		82
		107
		→999

We first develop the pseudocode and FORTRAN program to merge two files, to be sure that we understand the fundamental steps. We then develop the pseudocode and a FORTRAN program to merge three files. Generally, if you need to merge more than three files, you perform several smaller merges. For example, suppose you need to merge FILE1, FILE2, FILE3, FILE4, and FILE5. Assume that you have a program to merge three files. Use that program to merge FILE1, FILE2, and FILE3 into FILEA. Then merge FILEA, FILE4, and FILE5 to get the desired file.

DECOMPOSITION

Read account information from two files
Merge information
Write new file

Initial Refinement in Pseudocode

```
MERGE2:  BEGIN
            READ account information from both files
            WHILE more data DO
               WRITE information from file with
                        minimum account number
               READ information from file with
                        minimum account number
            END WHILE
         END
```

Final Refinement in Pseudocode

```
MERGE2:  BEGIN
            READ acct1, info1
            READ acct2, info2
            WHILE not at end of both files DO
               IF acct1 < acct2
                  WRITE acct1, info1
                  READ acct1, info1
               ELSE
                  WRITE acct2, info2
                  READ acct2, info2
               END IF
            END WHILE
            WRITE trailer signal
         END
```

FORTRAN Program

```
      PROGRAM MERGE2
*
*   THIS PROGRAM MERGES TWO FILES IN ACCOUNT ORDER
*   INTO ONE FILE IN ACCOUNT ORDER
*
      INTEGER ACCTM, ACCTW
      CHARACTER*10 INFOM, INFOW
*
      OPEN(UNIT=11, FILE='IN16M', ACCESS='SEQUENTIAL',
     +     STATUS='OLD', FORM='FORMATTED')
      OPEN(UNIT=12, FILE='IN16W', ACCESS='SEQUENTIAL',
     +     STATUS='OLD', FORM='FORMATTED')
      OPEN(UNIT=13, FILE='OUT16A', ACCESS='SEQUENTIAL',
     +     STATUS='NEW', FORM='FORMATTED')
*
      READ(11,5)ACCTM, INFOM
      READ(12,5)ACCTW, INFOW
    5 FORMAT(I3,A10)
*
   10 IF(ACCTM.NE.999.OR.ACCTW.NE.999)THEN
*
         IF(ACCTM.LT.ACCTW)THEN
            WRITE(13,5)ACCTM, INFOM
            READ(11,5)ACCTM, INFOM
         ELSE
            WRITE(13,5)ACCTW, INFOW
            READ(12,5)ACCTW, INFOW
         ENDIF
*
         GO TO 10
*
      ENDIF
*
      WRITE(13,5)ACCTM
      ENDFILE(UNIT=13)
*
      END
```

The solution that we present for a three-file merge will use a logical variable to determine when we have reached the trailer signals of all three files. We also use the intrinsic function MIN to determine the minimum value in the three account numbers.

Decomposition

Read account information from three files
Merge information
Write new file

Refinement in Pseudocode

```
MERGE3:  BEGIN
           READ acct1, info1
           READ acct2, info2
           READ acct3, info3
           WHILE not at end of all three files DO
              Find minimum of acct1, acct2, acct3
              WRITE account number and information for minimum
              READ account number and information for minimum
           END WHILE
           WRITE trailer signal
         END
```

FORTRAN Program

```
      PROGRAM MERGE3
*
*  THIS PROGRAM MERGES THREE FILES IN ACCOUNT ORDER
*  INTO ONE FILE IN ACCOUNT ORDER
*
      INTEGER ACCTM, ACCTW, ACCTA
      CHARACTER*10 INFOM, INFOW, INFOA
      LOGICAL ENDM, ENDW, ENDA, ENDALL
      DATA ENDM, ENDW, ENDA, ENDALL /4*.FALSE./
*
      OPEN(UNIT=11, FILE='IN16M', ACCESS='SEQUENTIAL',
     +     STATUS='OLD', FORM='FORMATTED')
      OPEN(UNIT=12, FILE='IN16W', ACCESS='SEQUENTIAL',
     +     STATUS='OLD', FORM='FORMATTED')
      OPEN(UNIT=13, FILE='IN16A', ACCESS='SEQUENTIAL',
     +     STATUS='OLD', FORM='FORMATTED')
      OPEN(UNIT=14, FILE='OUT16B', ACCESS='SEQUENTIAL',
     +     STATUS='NEW', FORM='FORMATTED')
*
      READ(11,5)ACCTM, INFOM
      READ(12,5)ACCTW, INFOW
      READ(13,5)ACCTA, INFOA
    5 FORMAT(I3,A10)
*
      IF(ACCTM.EQ.999)ENDM = .TRUE.
      IF(ACCTW.EQ.999)ENDW = .TRUE.
      IF(ACCTA.EQ.999)ENDA = .TRUE.
      ENDALL = ENDM.AND.ENDW.AND.ENDA
*
   10 IF(.NOT.ENDALL)THEN
*
         IF(MIN(ACCTM, ACCTW, ACCTA).EQ.ACCTM)THEN
            WRITE(14,5)ACCTM, INFOM
            READ(11,5)ACCTM, INFOM
            IF(ACCTM.EQ.999)ENDM = .TRUE.
         ELSEIF(MIN(ACCTM, ACCTW, ACCTA).EQ.ACCTW)THEN
            WRITE(14,5)ACCTW, INFOW
            READ(12,5)ACCTW, INFOW
            IF(ACCTW.EQ.999)ENDW = .TRUE.
         ELSE
            WRITE(14,5)ACCTA, INFOA
            READ(13,5) ACCTA, INFOA
            IF(ACCTA.EQ.999)ENDA = .TRUE.
         ENDIF
*
         ENDALL = ENDM.AND.ENDW.AND.ENDA
*
         GO TO 10
*
      ENDIF
*
      WRITE(14,5)ACCTM
      ENDFILE(UNIT=14)
*
      END
```

TESTING

Test the program first with the data from the hand example. Then test different combinations of data. A very important part of program testing with files involves end-of-file situations. Remember that each of our files will contain the trailer signal, even if there is no other data in the file. Since we have three files, a number of situations could occur if we assume that some files could have only the trailer signal. The table below shows the different possibilities.

TEST CASE	FILE 1	FILE 2	FILE 3
1	data	data	data
2	data	data	no data
3	data	no data	data
4	no data	data	data
5	data	no data	no data
6	no data	data	no data
7	no data	no data	data
8	no data	no data	no data

If we were merging 4 files, the corresponding table would have 16 test cases. You can now see the increase in time involved in testing a program with a large number of files. Therefore, we try to minimize the number of files needed in a program while still being realistic about the practical use of it.

7-5 DIRECT ACCESS FILES

Direct access files do not access records sequentially; they access them in the order specified. You could read them sequentially by specifying that you want the first record, then the second record, and so on. However, you can also access them by specifying that you want the tenth record, then the second record, and so on.

When a direct file is opened, the ACCESS specification in the OPEN statement must be set to 'DIRECT' and a record length must be given with the RECL specifier. The READ and WRITE statements must include a REC specification to give the record number of the record to be addressed. Thus, the general form of a direct access READ or WRITE is:

```
READ(unit number, format reference,
        REC=integer expression)   variable list
```

```
WRITE(unit number, format reference,
        REC=integer expression)   variable list
```

The integer expression on the REC specification is evaluated to give the record number that is to be accessed. The ERR and IOSTAT specifications may also be used with the direct access READ or WRITE statement, while the END option may be used only with READ statements.

Applications that use direct files usually have an account number or identification number that is part of each record, that can also be used as the record number. For example, student identification numbers in a university often start at 00001 and increase in steps of 1. Thus, the information for student number 00210 could be stored in record 210. Sometimes a numerical computation is performed on a field in the record to yield its record number. Suppose an inventory file contains records for items with stock numbers 500 through 1000. Then, if 499 is subtracted from the stock number, we have the record number for the record that will store information about that stock item. When the steps to convert a value into a record number for a direct file reference become more complicated, the steps are called a *hash code*. The value computed as the record number is often called a *key*.

A direct file is usually built by loading the information into the file sequentially, with the record number starting at 1 and increasing by 1 each time a new record is written. The file can be accessed in a sequential order by varying the record number from 1 through the total number of records. However, the real power of a direct file is apparent when we want to update information in some of its records. Instead of reading each record sequentially, looking for the one we want to update, we specify the record number and that record is automatically accessed. Once we have updated the information in that record, we can write that new information into the record. Note that this is not father-son updating. We are actually updating information in the direct file itself, which can be considered to be a *master file* because it contains all the updated information. If we specify a record number in a READ statement for a record that does not exist, an error occurs. To recover from this error, the ERR specification can be included in the WRITE statement to provide a branch in control to an error routine. These concepts are illustrated in the example in the next section.

7-6 PROBLEM SOLVING—WAREHOUSE INVENTORY

In this section we develop a program to update the inventory file IN17I for a warehouse. The inventory file is a direct access file with the following record format:

stock number	item description	quantity on hand	unit price

Stock number is a numeric value that can range from 001 to 999. Item description is a 10-character description of the item. The number of items currently in the warehouse is stored in quantity on hand, which is a four-digit integer. The unit price of one item is stored in a real value with a format of F6.2. Thus the total record length is 23 characters.

The file that we use to update the inventory file is a *transaction file* IN17T which contains the daily transactions of items shipped out of the warehouse or items received by the warehouse. The order of the transactions is the order in which they occurred. The transaction record consists of a stock number and a quantity. If the quantity is positive, the transaction represents items received. If the transaction is negative, the transactions represent items shipped. The transaction file is a sequential file with the following record format:

stock number	2 blanks	quantity

The stock number is a three-digit integer and the quantity is a four-digit integer. Two blanks separate the two fields. Assume that a trailer line in the transaction file contains 999 in the stock number. Write a program to update the inventory file using this transaction file.

PROBLEM STATEMENT

Write a program to update the quantity on hand in a direct access file.

INPUT/OUTPUT DESCRIPTION

The input to the program is two files, the direct access master inventory file IN17I and the sequential transaction file IN17T.

HAND EXAMPLE

Assume that the two files contain the following records:

Master inventory file:

Stock Number	Item Description	Quantity on Hand	Unit Price
1	terminal	10	586.92
2	modem	5	85.00
3	printer	3	299.50
4	cable	12	24.95

Transaction file:

Stock Number	Quantity
1	−2
3	−1
2	8
1	15
1	−2
2	−2

After the update, the master inventory file should be updated to contain the following information:

Master inventory file:

Stock Number	Item Description	Quantity on Hand	Unit Price
1	terminal	21	586.92
2	modem	11	85.00
3	printer	2	299.50
4	cable	12	24.95

ALGORITHM DEVELOPMENT

The steps to solving this problem are very straightforward, as shown in the decomposition. The primary reason that this solution is so simple is because of the power in direct access file processing.

Decomposition

Read transaction records
Update corresponding inventory records

Initial Refinement in Pseudocode

```
UPDATE:  BEGIN
           WHILE more transactions DO
             READ transaction record
             READ corresponding inventory record
             Update quantity
             WRITE updated inventory record
           END WHILE
         END
```

In refining the solution further, we add an error routine to print a message on the terminal screen if a match cannot be found between the inventory stock number and the transaction stock number.

Final Refinement in Pseudocode

```
UPDATE:  BEGIN
           READ key, change
           IF key = 999
             more ← false
           ELSE
             more ← true
           END IF
           WHILE more DO
             READ inventory record using key
             IF no match
               PRINT error message
             ELSE
               new quantity ← old quantity + change
               WRITE inventory record using key
             END IF
             READ key, change
             IF key = 999
               more ← false
             END IF
           END WHILE
         END
```

FORTRAN PROGRAM

```
      PROGRAM UPDATE
*
*   THIS PROGRAM UPDATES A DIRECT FILE
*   USING A STOCK NUMBER AS THE KEY
*
      INTEGER STOCK, CHANGE, QUANT
      CHARACTER*10 DESC
      LOGICAL MORE
      DATA MORE /.TRUE./
*
      OPEN(UNIT=10, FILE='IN17T', ACCESS='SEQUENTIAL',
     +      STATUS='OLD', FORM='FORMATTED')
      OPEN(UNIT=11, FILE='IN17I', ACCESS='DIRECT',
     +      STATUS='OLD', FORM='FORMATTED', RECL=23)
*
      READ(10,5)KEY, CHANGE
    5 FORMAT(13,2X,I4)
      IF(KEY.EQ.999)MORE = .FALSE.
*
   10 IF(MORE)THEN
         READ(11,15,REC=KEY,ERR=20, END=20)
             STOCK, DESC, QUANT, PRICE
   15    FORMAT(I3,A10,I4,F6.2)
         QUANT = QUANT + CHANGE
         WRITE(11,15,REC=KEY)STOCK, DESC, QUANT, PRICE
   20    IF(KEY.NE.STOCK)THEN
            PRINT*. 'NO MATCH FOR TRANSACTION', KEY
         ENDIF
         READ(10,5)KEY, CHANGE
         IF(KEY.EQ.999)MORE = .FALSE.
         GO TO 10
      ENDIF
*
      END
```

TESTING

Before you can test this program, you need to create the direct access file. A program to build the direct access file from a sequential file is shown below. The program closes the file after it is built, reopens it as an input file, and prints the data. Try this with the initial set of hand data. Then try the update program. After you are comfortable with the steps, develop some new test data. Be sure to try transactions without a match in the master inventory file.

FORTRAN Program

```
      PROGRAM CREATE
*
*   THIS PROGRAM CREATES AN INVENTORY DIRECT FILE
*   FROM A SEQUENTIAL FILE
*
      INTEGER STOCK, QUANT
      CHARACTER*10 DESC
*
      OPEN(UNIT=8, FILE='IN17C', ACCESS='SEQUENTIAL',
     +     STATUS='OLD', FORM='FORMATTED')
      OPEN(UNIT=9, FILE='IN17I', ACCESS='DIRECT',
     +     STATUS='NEW', FORM='FORMATTED', RECL=23)
*
      DO 10 I=1,4
         READ(8,5)STOCK, DESC, QUANT, PRICE
 5       FORMAT(I3,A10,I4,F6.2)
         WRITE(9,5,REC=STOCK)STOCK, DESC, QUANT, PRICE
   10 CONTINUE
*
      CLOSE(UNIT=9)
      OPEN(UNIT=9, FILE='IN17I', ACCESS='DIRECT',
     +     STATUS='OLD', FORM='FORMATTED', RECL=23)
*
      DO 15 I=1,4
         READ(9,5,REC=I,ERR=12,END=12)STOCK, DESC,
     +     QUANT, PRICE
         PRINT*, STOCK, DESC, QUANT, PRICE
   12    IF(I.NE.STOCK)PRINT*, 'NO RECORD', I
   15 CONTINUE
*
      END
```

A number of interesting problems can be easily solved with direct access files. The problems at the end of the chapter will include some of these, along with some suggested modifications to the update program presented in this section.

7-7 INQUIRE STATEMENT

The final new statement that is used with files is the INQUIRE statement. It has two general forms, which are given below:

> INQUIRE(FILE=*character expression, inquiry specifier list*)

> INQUIRE(UNIT=*integer expression, inquiry specifier list*)

The purpose of this executable statement is to gain information about a file or a unit number. For instance, by using the inquiry specifier OPENED, the following statement can be used to determine whether or nor a file has been opened.

INQUIRE(FILE=*file name,* OPENED=*logical variable*)

The logical variable is true if the file has been opened; otherwise, it is false. A specific example is:

```
      LOGICAL USED
          .
          .
          .
      INQUIRE(FILE='TEMP', OPENED=USED)
      IF(.NOT.USED)OPEN(UNIT=19, FILE='TEMP',
     +    STATUS='NEW')
```

Table 7-1 contains a complete list of the INQUIRY specifiers.

TABLE 7-1 Inquiry Specifiers

INQUIRY SPECIFIER	VARIABLE TYPE	VALUE FOR FILE INQUIRY	VALUE FOR UNIT INQUIRY
ACCESS=	Character	'SEQUENTIAL' 'DIRECT'	'SEQUENTIAL' 'DIRECT'
BLANK=	Character	'NULL' 'ZERO'	'NULL' 'ZERO'
DIRECT=	Character	'YES' 'NO' 'UNKNOWN'	—
ERR=	Integer	Statement number of error routine	Statement number of error routine
EXIST=	Logical	.TRUE. .FALSE.	.TRUE. .FALSE.
FORM=	Character	'FORMATTED' 'UNFORMATTED'	'FORMATTED' 'UNFORMATTED'
FORMATTED=	Character	'YES' 'NO' 'UNKNOWN'	—
IOSTAT=	Integer	Error code	Error code
NAME=	Character	—	Name of the file if it is not a scratch file
NAMED†=	Logical	—	.TRUE. .FALSE.
NEXTREC=	Integer	Next record number in direct access file	Next record number in direct access file
NUMBER†=	Integer	Unit number	—
OPENED=	Logical	.TRUE. .FALSE.	.TRUE. .FALSE.
RECL=	Integer	Record length	Record length
SEQUENTIAL=	Character	'YES' 'NO' 'UNKNOWN'	—
UNFORMATTED=	Character	'YES' 'NO' 'UNKNOWN'	—

†These specifiers do not refer to scratch files.

SUMMARY

This chapter has presented the statements and techniques for processing both sequential and direct access files. Both techniques are very powerful and give you the capability to handle large amounts of data with simple programs.

KEY WORDS

direct access file	key
external file	master file
father-son update	merge
field	random access
formatted I/O	record
format specification	sequential access file
hash code	transaction file
internal file	

DEBUGGING AIDS

When processing files, a very handy subroutine is one which prints the data in the file in a highly readable form. You might call this routine SNAP because it gives you a snapshot of the file at a particular time. When you are debugging a program that uses the file, call the routine every time that you want to check the file. If the subroutine has already been written, then this becomes a very simple procedure for checking the contents of the file.

Another point we want to emphasize relates to proper handling of files when there is no data. Circumstances can occur such that one of the files that we are using will be empty. Be sure that this does not cause your program to work incorrectly. Using trailer signals will simplify this logic. Then, even if a file is empty, the trailer signal will be in the file and should keep the program executing properly. The INQUIRE statement can also be very useful in detecting files that do not exist without causing the program to get an execution error.

STYLE/TECHNIQUE GUIDES

Good documentation is very important when working with data files. The record format and field descriptions for the record should be the same in all programs that use the file. For example, if a file contains a stock number, call it the same name in each program that uses it. It is also a good idea to use all the specifications that relate to the file in the OPEN statement. They do not need to be repeated in the other statements that refer to the file, but they should all be included once at the beginning.

PROBLEMS

Problems 1 through 5 refer to the merge algorithms developed in Section 7-4.

1 Convert the two-file merge into a subroutine. The names of the files should be subroutine parameters.

2 Convert the three-file merge into a subroutine. The names of the files should be subroutine parameters.

3 Using one of the merge subroutines from problems 1 or 2, write a program to perform a five-file merge.

4 Write a program that will accept the merged bank transaction file and split it into two files, one for deposits and one for withdrawals.

5 Modify the two-file merge program so that a final summary is printed that gives the number of records (not counting the trailer record) in the two input files and in the output file.

Problems 6 through 14 refer to the inventory update program developed in Section 7-6.

6 Write a program to create the initial direct access file from data entered from the terminal.

7 Write a subroutine to print the data in the inventory file in stock number order.

8 Write a program to compute and print the total value of the items in stock using the inventory file.

9 Write a program to add records to the inventory file.

10 Write a program to delete records from the inventory file. Assume that the stock numbers of records to be deleted will be entered in ascending order. (*Hint:* This will require building a new inventory file.)

11 Write a program to change the description for selected stock items in the inventory file.

12 Write a program to change the unit price for selected stock items in the inventory file.

13 Modify the program in Section 7-6 such that an error message is printed if the quantity goes below zero.

14 Write a program to print a reorder report for items whose quantity has gone below 5 units. Include the number of items to be ordered to bring the total quantity to 10.

15 Write a subroutine DECODE that receives a character string KEY containing 26 characters, and a character string TEXT containing 50 characters. The subroutine should decode TEXT, which has been encoded with a substitution key where the first letter in KEY was substituted for the letter A, the second letter in KEY was substituted for the letter B, and so on. Blanks were not changed in the coding process. Thus, if KEY contains the following character string

```
'YXAZKLMBJOCFDVSWTREGHNIPUQ'
```

and TEXT contained the character string

```
'DKKG YG YJRWSRG EYGHRZYU'
```

then the decoded character string would be,

```
'MEET AT AIRPORT SATURDAY'
```

The decoded character string should be written into a file whose name is stored in the character string NFILE. The subroutine will be called by the statement,

```
CALL DECODE(KEY, TEXT, NFILE)
```

Use the INQUIRE statement to determine if the file has been opened. If it has, then determine the appropriate unit number to use. If it has not been opened, then use the OPEN statement to open it.

16 Write a subroutine ENCODE that receives a character string KEY containing 26 characters, and a character string TEXT containing 50 characters. The subroutine should encode TEXT, using a substitution code where the first letter in KEY is substituted for the letter A in TEXT, and the second letter in KEY is substituted for the letter B in TEXT, and so on. Thus, if KEY contains the following character string

```
'YXAZKLMBJOCFDVSWTREGHNIPUQ'
```

and TEXT contained the character string

```
'MEET AT AIRPORT SATURDAY'
```

then the encoded character string would be

```
'DKKG YG YJRWSRG EYGHRZYU'
```

The encoded character string should be written into a file whose name is stored in the character string NFILE. Use the INQUIRE statement to determine if the file has been opened. If it has, then determine the appropriate unit number to use. If it has not been opened, then use the OPEN statement to open it. The subroutine will be called by the statement

```
CALL ENCODE(KEY, TEXT, NFILE)
```

17 Write a main program that will read a character string KEY of 26 characters from columns 1–26 of a data card. From the next data card, read two file names, FILE1 and FILE2, from columns 1–6 and columns 11–16 and a character called CONVRT from column 20. The main program should read records from FILE1, where each record is a character string of 50 characters. If CONVRT contains the letter E, the main program should call the subroutine ENCODE from problem 16. If CONVRT contains the letter D, the main program should call the subroutine DECODE from problem 15. In either case, the subroutine should write its output on FILE2. Thus, the main program will either encode all the messages in FILE1 and write them in FILE2, or it will decode all the messages in FILE1 and write them in FILE2.

National Aeronautics and Space Administration

PROBLEM SOLVING—Distances to the Sun

The summer job is fine, but you need a hobby. Astronomy has always interested you, so you are attending weekly presentations at the local planetarium. A recent lecturer gave very precise measurements of the distances of a number of objects from the sun. Write a program to read this data and print the name of the object that is the closest to the sun and the name of the object that is the farthest from the sun. (See Section 8-2, page 285, for the solution.)

8

ADDITIONAL FEATURES OF FORTRAN 77

INTRODUCTION

This chapter summarizes a number of features of FORTRAN that were not introduced in earlier chapters but should be included for completeness. The topics generally fall into two categories. One contains features that are seldom used but are necessary for certain applications, such as double precision and complex numbers. The other category contains features from older versions of FORTRAN that are seldom used. In general, the use of these features is discouraged because they make programs more difficult to debug and to understand. For example, the control structures that we discuss employ multiple branches from a single statement and thus no longer yield structures with one entrance and one exit. We have divided the additional features in this last chapter into data types, specification statements, control statements, and subprogram features.

8-1 DATA TYPES

We have used a variety of data types in our programs. For numerical values we use real and integer data types, for logical values we use the logical data type, and for character strings we use the character data type. Two additional data types, double precision and complex, are also available for numeric data.

DOUBLE PRECISION

In some applications, more precision is needed than is available through real variables. In these cases, a special type of *double precision* variable or constant is used. Typically, this type of constant or variable has more than twice as many digits of accuracy as are available for real variables. If 7 digits of accuracy correspond to real values, then usually 16 digits of accuracy correspond to double precision values.

A double precision constant is written in an exponential form, with a D in place of E. Some examples of double precision constants are:

```
0.378926542D+04
1.4762D-02
0.25D+00
```

Always use the exponential form with the letter D for double precision constants, even if seven or fewer digits of accuracy are used in the constant. Otherwise, you may lose some accuracy because a fractional value that can be expressed evenly in decimal notation may not be evenly expressed in binary notation.

Double precision variables are specified with a specification statement, whose general form is:

> `DOUBLE PRECISION` *variable names*

A double precision array is specified as shown below:

```
DOUBLE PRECISION DTEMP(50)
```

A double precision value can be used in list-directed output similarly to a real value. The only distinction will be that more digits of accuracy can be stored in a double precision value; therefore more digits of accuracy can be written from a double precision value.

When an arithmetic operation is performed with two double precision values, the result will be double precision. If an operation involves a double precision value and a single precision value or an integer, the result will be a double precision result. In such a mixed-mode operation, do not assume that the other value is converted to double precision. Instead, think of the other value as being extended in length with zeros. To illustrate this point, the first two assignment statements below will yield exactly the same values. The third assignment statement, however, adds a double precision constant to DX and yields the most accurate result of three statements.

```
DOUBLE PRECISION DX, DY1, DY2, DY3
    .
    .
    .
DY1 = DX + 0.3872
DY2 = DX + 0.38720000000000
DY3 = DX + 0.3872D+00
```

The most accurate way to obtain a constant that cannot be written in a fixed number of decimal places is to perform an operation in double precision that will yield the desired value. For instance, to obtain the double precision constant one-seventh, use the following expression:

```
1.0D+00/7.0D+00
```

If a double precision argument is used in a generic function, the function value will also be double precision. Many of the common intrinsic functions for real numbers can be converted to double precision functions by preceding the name with the letter D. For instance, DSQRT, DABS, DMOD, DSIN, DEXP, DLOG, and DLOG10 all require double precision arguments and yield double precision values. Double precision functions can also be used to compute constants with double precision accuracy. For instance, the following statements compute π with double precision accuracy:

```
DOUBLE PRECISION DPI
    .
    .
    .
DPI = 4.0D+00*DATAN(1.0D+00)
```

While Appendix C contains a complete list of the functions that relate to double precision values, there are two functions, DBLE and DPROD, that are specifically designed for use with double precision variables. DBLE converts a REAL argument to a double precision value. DPROD has two REAL arguments and returns the double precision product of the two arguments.

EXAMPLE 8-1 Spherical Mirror Sag

Assume that DR and DS represent double precision values for the radius r of a spherical mirror and the distance s from the center of the spherical mirror to its tangent plane. These two values have already been computed in a program. Write the section of code to compute the sag to at least 10 digits of accuracy (assuming real values have 7 digits of accuracy), where

$$\text{sag} = \frac{rs^2}{1 + \sqrt{1 - r^2s^2}}$$

Solution

```
DOUBLE PRECISION DR, DS, DSAG
    .
    .
    .
DSAG = DR*DS*DS/(1.0D+00 + DSQRT(1.0D+00
+                                - DR*DR*DS*DS))
```
◇

COMPLEX

Since *complex numbers* are needed to solve many problems in science and engineering, particularly in physics and electrical engineering, FORTRAN includes a special type for these complex variables and constants. These complex values are stored as an ordered pair of real values, the real portion of the value and the imaginary portion of the value.

A complex constant is specified by two real constants separated by a comma and enclosed in parentheses. The first constant represents the real part of the complex value, and the second constant represents the imaginary part of the complex value. Thus, the complex constant $3.0 - i1.5$, where i represents $\sqrt{-1}$, is written in FORTRAN as the complex constant (3.0,−1.5).

Complex variables are specified with a specification statement, whose general form is:

`COMPLEX` *variable names*

A complex array is specified as shown below:

```
COMPLEX CX(100)
```

A complex value in list-directed output will be printed as two real values separated by a comma and enclosed in parentheses. Also, two real values will be read for each complex value in a list-directed input statement.

When an arithmetic operation is performed between two complex values, the result will also be a complex value. Expressions containing both complex values and double precision values are not allowed. In an expression containing a complex value and a real or integer value, the real or integer value is converted to a complex value whose imaginary part is zero.

The rules of complex arithmetic are not as familiar as those for integers or real values; we list below the results of basic operations on two complex numbers C_1 and C_2, where $C_1 = a_1 + ib_1$ and $C_2 = a_2 + ib_2$:

$$C_1 + C_2 = (a_1 + a_2) + i(b_1 + b_2)$$
$$C_1 - C_2 = (a_1 - a_2) + i(b_1 - b_2)$$
$$C_1 * C_2 = (a_1a_2 - b_1b_2) + i(a_1b_2 + a_2b_1)$$
$$\frac{C_1}{C_2} = \frac{a_1a_2 + b_1b_2}{a_2^2 + b_2^2} + i\frac{a_2b_1 - b_2a_1}{a_2^2 + b_2^2}$$
$$|C_1| = \sqrt{a_1^2 + b_1^2}$$
$$e^{C_1} = e^{a_1} \cos b_1 + ie^{a_1} \sin b_1$$
$$\cos C_1 = 1 - \frac{C_1^3}{3!} + \frac{C_1^5}{5!} - \frac{C_1^7}{7!} + \cdots$$

If a complex value is used in one of the generic functions such as SQRT, ABS, SIN, COS, EXP, or LOG, the function value will also be complex. The functions CSQRT, CABS, CSIN, CCOS, CEXP, and CLOG are all intrinsic functions with complex arguments. These function names begin with the letter C to emphasize that they are complex functions.

While Appendix C contains a complete list of the functions that relate to complex values, there are four functions, REAL, AIMAG, CONJ, and CMPLX, that are specifically designed for use with complex variables. REAL yields the real part of its complex argument and AIMAG yields the imaginary part of its complex argument. CONJ converts a complex number to its conjugate, where the conjugate of $a + ib$ is $a - ib$. CMPLX is a function that converts two real arguments, a and b, into a complex value $a + ib$.

8-2 PROBLEM SOLVING—DISTANCES TO THE SUN

Double precision variables are necessary any time we want to keep more significant digits than are stored in real variables. Assume that a real variable can store seven significant digits. This means that the real variable will keep seven digits of accuracy, beginning with the first nonzero digit, in addition to remembering where the decimal point goes. A double precision value will store more digits, with the exact number of digits dependent on the computer being used. For this example, assume that double precision variables store 14 digits. The table on the next page then compares values that can be stored in real values (also called *single precision* values) and those stored in double precision.

Value to be Stored	Single Precision	Double Precision
37.6892718	37.68927	37.689271800000
−1.60003	−1.600030	−1.6000300000000
820000000487.	820000000000.	820000000487.00
.0000001869	.0000001869000	.00000018690000000000
18268296.300405079	18268290.	18268296.300405

Note that we are doubling (or at least increasing) the precision of our values, but we are not doubling the range of numbers that can be stored. The same range of numbers apply to both single and double precision values, but double precision values have more digits of precision.

Many science and engineering applications use double precision to get the accuracy needed. A number of other applications also need double precision values. For instance, suppose you are working on an economic model for predicting the gross national debt. The numbers that you must use exceed a trillion dollars. Integer variables on most machines cannot exceed a few billion, so you have to use real values. But with single precision, you cannot store the values with an accuracy to the nearest dollar. If you use double precision, you can then use amounts up to ten trillion and still have significant digits for all dollar amounts. We find this example of the national debt depressing, so we will switch to an example whose subject is distances in the universe.

The study of solar systems, galaxies, and stars involves storing distances that need as much precision as possible. A data file has been generated that contains two data values per line. The first value on the line is a character string that gives the name of the object, such as VENUS; the second value represents the distance of the object in millions of miles from the sun. This file is updated as new stars and planets are discovered. Write a subroutine which receives two arrays that contain this information, NAME and DIST, and an integer N that contains the number of items in each array. The NAME array contains character strings with 20 characters each and DIST is a double precision array. The subroutine should print the name of the object closest to the sun and the name of the object farthest from the sun, along with the corresponding distances.

PROBLEM SOLVING

Write a subroutine to print the names of the objects closest to the sun and farthest from the sun, using data arrays.

INPUT/OUTPUT DESCRIPTION

The subroutine will receive two arrays and an integer N that specifies the size of the arrays. One array contains character strings of 20 characters each that represent names of objects in space. The other array contains the corresponding double precision distances of the objects from the sun.

HAND EXAMPLE

Suppose the arrays contained the planet names and their approximate average distances from the sun, as shown below:

Array Position	NAME Array Value	DIST Array Value (in millions of miles)
1	JUPITER	438.6371766
2	MARS	141.6175158
3	SATURN	886.740654
4	VENUS	67.2356964
5	PLUTO	3666.2718
6	URANUS	1783.42374
7	MERCURY	35.9791758
8	NEPTUNE	2794.444794
9	EARTH	92.9617392

The subroutine should then print:

```
CLOSEST TO SUN IS MERCURY (35.979175800000 MILLION MILES)
FARTHEST FROM SUN IS PLUTO (3666.2718000000 MILLION MILES)
```

ALGORITHM DEVELOPMENT

We are familiar with finding the maximum and minimum values in arrays. The only new step in this solution involves referencing the names that correspond to the maximum and minimum distances. Look back to the table used for the hand example and assume that we want to find the minimum value. We search through the array one time comparing values until we have the minimum, which is 35.9791758 in this case. In addition to printing this value, we also want to print the corresponding name. Therefore, we locate the minimum value and then go to the corresponding name, which is MERCURY. In order to go to the corresponding position in the name array, we need a position value or subscript. Thus, in the algorithm, instead of keeping the minimum value in a separate location, we will keep the subscript of the minimum value. We can then reference either the distance array or the name array.

Decomposition

Find positions of minimum and maximum distances
Print corresponding names and distances

Refinement in Pseudocode

```
SOLAR:  BEGIN
           minsub ← 1
           maxsub ← 1
           FOR i=2 TO n DO
              IF dist(i) < dist(minsub)
                 minsub ← i
              END IF
              IF dist(i) > dist(maxsub)
                 maxsub ← i
              END IF
           END FOR
           PRINT name(minsub), dist(minsub)
           PRINT name(maxsub), dist(maxsub)
           RETURN
        END
```

FORTRAN Subroutine

```
      SUBROUTINE SOLAR(NAME, DIST, N)
*
*  THIS SUBROUTINE DETERMINES THE OBJECTS THAT ARE
*  NEAREST THE SUN AND FARTHEST FROM THE SUN
*  USING TWO DATA ARRAYS
*
      DOUBLE PRECISION DIST(N)
      CHARACTER*20 NAME(N)
*
      MINSUB = 1
      MAXSUB = 1
      DO 10 I=2,N
         IF(DIST(I).LT.DIST(MINSUB))MINSUB = I
         IF(DIST(I).GT.DIST(MAXSUB))MAXSUB = I
   10 CONTINUE
*
      PRINT*, 'CLOSEST TO SUN IS ', NAME(MINSUB),
     +        '(', DIST(MINSUB), 'MILLION MILES)'
      PRINT*, 'FARTHEST FROM SUN IS ', NAME(MAXSUB),
     +        '(', DIST(MAXSUB), 'MILLION MILES)'
*
      RETURN
      END
```

TESTING

A driver to test this subroutine is given below:

```
      PROGRAM DRIVER
      DOUBLE PRECISION DIST(9)
      CHARACTER*20 NAME(9)
*
      OPEN(UNIT=12, FILE='IN18', STATUS='OLD')
*
      DO 10 I=1,9
         READ(12,*) NAME(I), DIST(I)
   10 CONTINUE
*
      N = 9
      CALL SOLAR(NAME, DIST, N)
*
      END
```

Use the data given in the hand example to test the program. Does the program handle ties? Suppose two planets were exactly the same distance from the sun, but in different directions. Would one or both names be printed? The subroutine presented here would find the subscript of the first minimum in the list. Since the subscript is updated only when a smaller value is found, it would not be updated if another value that was the same was encountered. Hence, only the first minimum would be printed, no matter how many more distances were the same value. Suppose you wanted to change the algorithm to print all values with the minimum. What would you change? The loop that finds the subscript with the minimum value could be left alone. Then the single print statement that prints the name of the minimum could be replaced with a loop that printed every name that had a distance equal to the minimum. Another similar loop could print any names that had a distance equal to the maximum.

8-3 SPECIFICATION STATEMENTS

Three specification statements, and thus nonexecutable statements, have not yet been covered. The IMPLICIT statement is used to specify the beginning letters of variable names that are to be associated with a particular type, such as REAL or CHARACTER. The PARAMETER statement is used to initialize constants. The EQUIVALENCE statement allows the sharing of data storage.

IMPLICIT STATEMENT

We have discussed six different specification statements: INTEGER, REAL, CHARACTER, DOUBLE PRECISION, COMPLEX, and LOGICAL. Only two of these statements, INTEGER and REAL, have default values. That is, variable names beginning with letters I $\rightarrow$ N specify integer variables by default, and all other variable names specify real variables by default. The IMPLICIT statement allows us to specify defaults for variables of all types. Its general form is:

```
IMPLICIT type1(default), type2(default), . . .
```

For instance, if a program contained only integers, you might want to specify that any variable is an integer with this statement:

```
IMPLICIT INTEGER(A-Z)
```

Or you might want to specify that the first half of the alphabet should represent beginning letters of integer names and the last half should represent real values:

```
IMPLICIT INTEGER(A-M), REAL(N-Z)
```

If you are following the convention of beginning all double precision variable names with the letter D, instead of listing all the names in a DOUBLE PRECISION statement you could use the following:

```
IMPLICIT DOUBLE PRECISION(D)
```

An implicit declaration can be overridden with a specification statement, as shown below:

```
IMPLICIT COMPLEX(C), LOGICAL(L)
CHARACTER*10 CHAR
```

The variable CHAR should be a complex variable according to the IMPLICIT statement, but instead it is defined to be a character string by the CHARACTER statement.

PARAMETER STATEMENT

The PARAMETER statement is a specification statement used to assign constant values to variable names, with the following general form:

```
PARAMETER (name1 = expression, name2 = expression, . . .)
```

The expression after the equal sign typically is a constant, but it may be an expression that contains variables that have already been defined in a DATA statement or a PARAMETER statement. A specific example of the PARAMETER statement is:

```
PARAMETER (PI=3.14159, N=75)
```

This statement cannot be used in a subprogram.

The DATA statement and PARAMETER statement can both be used to initialize variables, but there are some differences between the two statements. A variable defined in a PARAMETER statement cannot be redefined in another statement such as a READ or an assignment. However, a variable defined in a PARAMETER statement can be used anywhere in a program that a constant is used except in FORMAT statements. It is particularly useful in conjunction with other specification statements, as seen in the following pair of statements:

```
PARAMETER (M=50)
DIMENSION TEMP(M,M)
```

If a variable is to be initialized with a PARAMETER statement, any other specification statements that affect the variable must precede the PARAMETER statement. For example, if a PARAMETER statement is used to initialize a character string, the CHARACTER statement must precede the PARAMETER statement.

```
CHARACTER*6 DATE
PARAMETER (DATE='010184')
```

EQUIVALENCE STATEMENT

The EQUIVALENCE statement, a specification statement that permits data storage to be shared by several variables, has the following general form:

EQUIVALENCE (*variable list 1*), (*variable list 2*), . . .

The variable list may contain variable names, array names, and character substring names. The EQUIVALENCE statement causes all the names enclosed in a set of parentheses to reference the same storage location. Character variables cannot be equivalenced with noncharacter variables. In fact, it is best to use the same type in all equivalence lists. When array elements are equivalenced, the entire arrays are involved, as will be shown in the next example, because an array is always stored sequentially in memory. Two variables in a common block or in two different common blocks cannot be made equivalent, and two variables in the same array cannot be made equivalent.

Consider the following EQUIVALENCE statement:

```
DIMENSION A(5), B(9), C(2,2)
EQUIVALENCE (HEIGHT,DIST), (A(1),B(4),C(1,1))
```

The first variable list specifies that HEIGHT and DIST are to occupy the same location that is referenced by either variable name. The equivalence of storage locations specified by the second variable list is best explained using the following diagram of computer memory:

	B(1)		
	B(2)		
	B(3)		
A(1)	B(4)	C(1,1)	← All three variables share the same storage location
A(2)	B(5)	C(2,1)	
A(3)	B(6)	C(1,2)	
A(4)	B(7)	C(2,2)	
A(5)	B(8)		
	B(9)		

By specifying that A(1) and B(4) share the same location, we also have implicitly specified that A(2) and B(5) share the same location, and so on through A(5) and B(8). Furthermore, we have equated the location that stores A(1) and B(4) with C(1,1), and hence other implicit equivalences have been specified as shown in the diagram. When using two-dimensional arrays in equivalence statements, it is important to remember that they are stored by columns.

8-4 CONTROL STATEMENTS

The control structures mentioned in this section contain *multiple branches* and therefore have multiple exits. Since these statements do not follow a one entrance, one exit path of execution, we discourage their use. The IF statements provide alternatives that still incorporate the one entrance, one exit path of execution. The main reason that multiple branch statements are included in the language is so that programs written in earlier versions can still be used without modifications. Older versions of FORTRAN did not include all forms of the IF statements, and thus multiple branching could not always be avoided.

ARITHMETIC IF STATEMENT

The general form of the arithmetic IF statement is:

```
IF(arithmetic expression)label 1, label 2, label 3
```

Label 1, label 2, and label 3 must be references to executable statements in the program. The arithmetic expression is evaluated, and if it represents a negative value, control passes to the statement referenced by label 1. If the expression represents zero, then control passes to the statement referenced by label 2. Finally, if the expression represents a positive value, control passes to the statement referenced by label 3. In the following arithmetic IF statement, control will pass to statement 10 if A is greater than B, to statement 15 if A is equal to B, and to statement 20 if A is less than B.

```
IF(B - A)10, 15, 20
```

Thus, the arithmetic IF statement is a three-way branch, equivalent to the following statements:

```
IF(arithmetic expression.LT.0.0)GO TO label 1
IF(arithmetic expression.EQ.0.0)GO TO label 2
GO TO label 3
```

Early versions of FORTRAN did not include the logical IF statement. Hence, all IF statements were in the form of arithmetic IF statements at that time.

COMPUTED GO TO STATEMENT

The general form of the computed GO TO statement is:

```
GO TO(label 1,label 2, . . . , label n),integer expression
```

Label 1, label 2, . . ., and label n must be references to executable statements in your program. The computed GO TO statement is used for a multi-way branch of control. For example, if we wish to execute a different set of statements dependent on the rank (RANK) of a student, we could use the following computed GO TO statement, where RANK = 1 for freshman, 2 for sophomore, 3 for junior, 4 for senior, and 5 for graduate. Assume RANK is an integer variable.

```
      INTEGER RANK
        .
        .
        .
      GO TO(11, 15, 20, 17, 17), RANK
      PRINT*, 'RANK VALUE IN ERROR'
```

If RANK = 1 (representing a freshman), then the computed GO TO will be executed as if it were:

```
GO TO 11
```

Similar branches would occur for RANK = 2 and RANK = 3. For seniors and graduate students (RANK = 4 and RANK = 5), control will transfer to statement 17, thus illustrating the fact that the statement labels do not have to be unique. If the value of RANK is such that it does not cause a branch (in this case, less than 1 or greater than 5), control passes to the next statement, which we have used to print an error message.

ASSIGNED GO TO STATEMENT

The ASSIGN statement and the assigned GO TO statement work together to yield a multi-branch structure. The general forms of these two statements are given below:

> ASSIGN *integer constant* TO *integer variable*

> GO TO *integer variable,(label 1,label 2, . . .,label n)*

The assigned GO TO statement looks very similar to the computed GO TO statement but there are some significant differences.

1 The integer variable referenced in the assigned GO TO must have been initialized with the ASSIGN statement.

2 The integer variable can be used only to store statement references.

3 If the value of the integer variable is not in the list of labels, an error occurs.

In the next example, the value 3 has been initially assigned to K. The IF statements may change the value stored in K to either 1 or 2. When the assigned GO TO statement is executed, control will transfer to statement 1 if K = 1, statement 2 if K = 2, or statement 3 if K = 3. Otherwise, an execution error occurs.

```
ASSIGN 3 TO K
   .
   .
   .
IF(A.LT.B)ASSIGN 2 TO K
IF(A.GE.C)ASSIGN 1 TO K
   .
   .
   .
GO TO K,(1, 2, 3)
```

8-5 SUBPROGRAM FEATURES

This section discusses additional features of FORTRAN that relate to subprograms. The SAVE, INTRINSIC, and EXTERNAL statements are not frequently used but can be very useful, as pointed out in the discussions following. The ENTRY statement and alternate return point from a subprogram are covered in order that the coverage of FORTRAN 77 be complete, but their use is discouraged, again because they do not support a one entrance, one exit path of execution.

SAVE

Local variables are those used in a subprogram that are not arguments. Thus, they tend to be totals, loop indexes, and counters. The values of these local variables are generally lost when a RETURN statement is executed. However, a SAVE specification statement will save the values of local variables so that they will contain the same values as they had at the end of the previous reference. This nonexecutable statement appears only in the subprogram. The general form of the SAVE statement is:

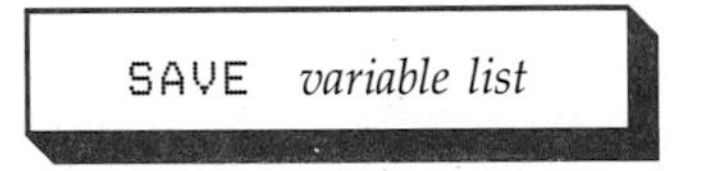

If the list of variables is omitted, the values of all local variables will be saved.

To illustrate the use of the SAVE statement, suppose you wanted to know how many times a subprogram was accessed. The following statements would initialize the counter COUNTR to zero at the beginning of the program and increment COUNTR each time the subprogram was used. Recall that the DATA statement does not reinitialize COUNTR each time the function is used.

```
FUNCTION AVE(X, Y)
INTEGER COUNTR
SAVE COUNTR
DATA COUNTR /0/
    .
    .
    .
COUNTR = COUNTR + 1
    .
    .
    .
END
```

INTRINSIC, EXTERNAL

The INTRINSIC and EXTERNAL statements are specification statements used when subprogram names are to be used as arguments in another subprogram. The general forms of these nonexecutable statements are:

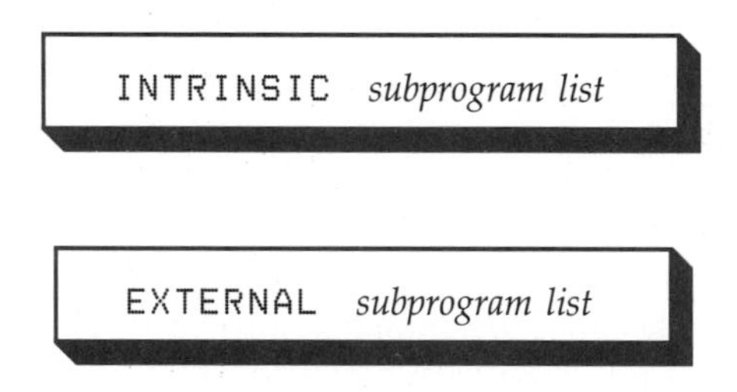

These statements appear only in the module that sends the arguments representing the subprogram names. If the argument is an intrinsic function, use the INTRINSIC statement. If the argument is a user-written function or a subroutine, use the EXTERNAL statement.

In the following statements, we reference a subroutine twice. With one reference, the subroutine replaces each value in an array with its natural logarithm. The other reference replaces each value in an array with its logarithm, using base 10.

Main program

```
      PROGRAM TEST5
      DIMENSION X(10), TIME(10)
      INTRINSIC ALOG, ALOG10
         .
         .
         .
      CALL COMPUT(X, ALOG)
         .
         .
         .
      CALL COMPUT(TIME, ALOG10)
         .
         .
         .
      END
```

Subroutine COMPUT

```
*
*
*
      SUBROUTINE COMPUT(R, F)
*
*  THIS SUBROUTINE APPLIES A
*  FUNCTION TO THE ARRAY R
*
      DIMENSION R(10)
*
      DO 10 I=1,10
         R(I) = F(R(I))
   10 CONTINUE
*
      RETURN
      END
```

ENTRY

The ENTRY statement is used to define entry points into a subprogram other than the entry point at the beginning of the subprogram. The general form of the statement is:

> ENTRY *entry name* (*argument list*)

The ENTRY statement is placed at the point in the subprogram that is to be an alternative entry. The argument list does not have to be the same as that for the original entry point. The ENTRY statement is nonexecutable and will not affect execution of the subprogram if it is in the statements being executed from a previous entry point.

The following statements illustrate references to a subroutine through two different entry points.

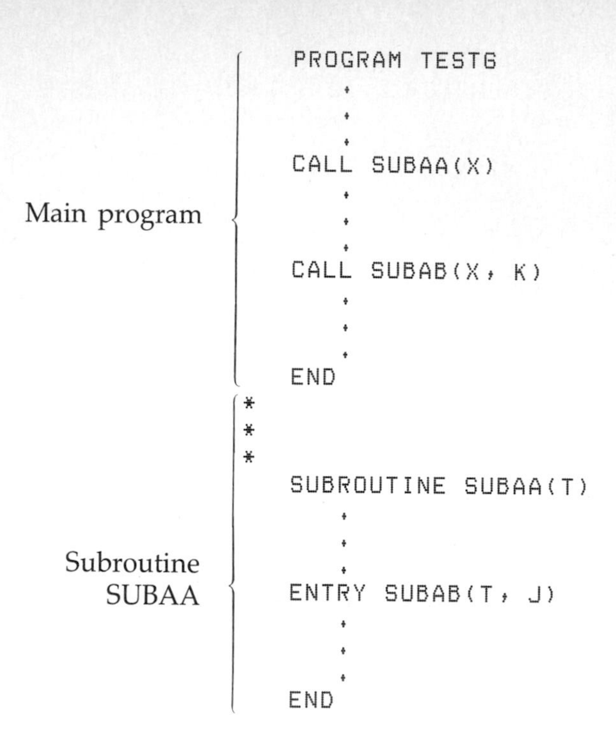

One of the fundamental advantages of structured programming lies in the simplicity of linkages between modules. The use of *multiple entry* points to a subprogram complicates that linkage; their usage is therefore not generally recommended.

ALTERNATE RETURNS

Normally, the execution of a RETURN statement in a subroutine returns control to the first statement below the CALL statement. A return point, however, can be specified with an argument in the subroutine. The argument list in the SUBROUTINE statement contains asterisks in the locations of arguments that are the *alternate return* points. The RETURN statement has this expanded general form:

RETURN *integer expression*

If the value of the integer expression is 1, the return point is the statement number that corresponds to the first asterisk in the argument list. If the value of the integer expression is 2, the return point is the statement number that corresponds to the second asterisk, and so on. The following statements will help clarify this process:

Main program

```
      PROGRAM TEST7
          .
          .
          .
      CALL SUB1(A, B, *20, *50)
          .
          .
          .
   20 WRITE(6,5)A
          .
          .
          .
   50 COUNT = COUNT + 1
          .
          .
          .
      END
*
*
*
      SUBROUTINE SUB1(X, Y, *, *)
          .
          .
          .
      RETURN I
      END
```

Subroutine SUB1

If the value of I is 1 in the subroutine, then control will return to statement 20. If the value I = 2, then control returns to statement 50. An error occurs if the value of I is not 1 or 2.

Multiple return points also complicate the linkage between modules and generally should be avoided.

SUMMARY

The various new features of this section complete the set of statements available in the FORTRAN 77 language. As you refine an algorithm and begin to choose FORTRAN statements to implement the algorithm, keep in mind the goals of structured programming. A program should be as straightforward and easy to understand as is reasonable. Techniques that are very useful in achieving these goals include breaking the solution into modules, and then writing the modules with a one entrance, one exit path of execution.

KEY WORDS

alternate return
complex value
double precision value
local variable
multiple branch
multiple entry
single precision

DEBUGGING AIDS

The primary debugging tool that will be discussed in this section is the PRINT statement. The usefulness of this statement cannot be overemphasized. Since several different topics were discussed in this chapter, we address them separately.

Double precision: If an error is related to a double precision value, print it each time that it is used to be sure that you are not losing the extra accuracy. Also, be sure that you are not moving the value into a single precision variable in an intermediate step in your program.

Complex: If your program errors relate to complex values, write the values of the complex numbers as soon as they are initialized and after each modification. Remember that if you move a complex value into a real variable, the imaginary part is lost.

Implicit: When a program is not giving the desired results, carefully check the type of your variables. Remember that if a variable is not listed in a type statement or an IMPLICIT statement, the default typing of real and integer variables occurs.

Parameter: Remember that a variable initialized with a PARAMETER statement cannot have its value modified. The variable must be considered to be a constant throughout the program.

Equivalence: Whenever you plan to use an EQUIVALENCE statement, draw a diagram similar to that shown on page 292, to be sure that you understand which variables will be equivalent. Do not equate variables with different types.

Control statements: The best debugging advice that we can give you with regard to control statements is always to structure control statements so that they incorporate a one entrance, one exit path of execution. This may require rewriting sections of code that do not adhere to this advice.

Subprograms: If your subprograms are not working correctly, minimize the interaction of different modules. Do not use multiple entry points and multiple returns in a program, because tracking all possible entries and exits becomes very complex. Another suggestion to help debug modules again involves using the PRINT statement. Print the values of all variables used as you come into the module and again as you leave the module.

STYLE/TECHNIQUE GUIDES

When you use a feature of FORTRAN that is not commonly used, good documentation is very important. More comment lines may be necessary to clarify your code. If a computation uses complex numbers, explain the computations in more detail than you would in regular arithmetic computations. Good documentation also includes choosing descriptive names.

Since this is the last style/technique guide, it is important to emphasize three guidelines that have been stressed throughout the text. First, if there are several ways to solve the same problem, choose the simplest solution. Second, use the five design phases to develop an algorithm. Finally, use the structures (SEQUENCE, IF THEN ELSE, WHILE loop) presented in Chapter 1 and illustrated in the rest of the text to design your programs. These rules will become more important as your programs become longer, solve more complicated problems, and use more files.

PROBLEMS

For problems 1 through 6, show how to represent the following constants as double precision constants.

1 .25	**2** .58	**3** $\frac{1}{3}$
4 $\frac{1}{13}$	**5** 108.3	**6** 2.0

For problems 7 through 12, compute the value stored in CX if CY = 1.0 + i3.0 and CZ = 0.5 − i1.0. Assume CX, CY, and CZ are complex variables.

7 `CX = CY + CZ`

8 `CX = CY - CZ`

9 `CX = CONJ(CZ)`

10 `CX = REAL(CY) + AIMAG(CZ)`

11 `CX = CMPLX(5.0,0.2)`

12 `CX = EXP(CY)`

Problems 13 through 17 use the data arrays NAME and DIST from Section 8-2. The variable N specifies the number of values in the arrays.

13 Write a subroutine which prints the data arrays NAME and DIST so that the name and corresponding distance are printed on the same line. The subroutine is referenced by:

```
CALL PRDATA(NAME, DIST, N)
```

14 Write a subroutine which reads the data file containing the data for the arrays NAME and DIST, and determines the value of N. Assume that the name of the file is IN18. The file does not have a trailer line. The subroutine is referenced by:

```
CALL RDDATA(NAME, DIST, N)
```

Note that the arguments are all output parameters.

15 Modify the subroutine developed in Section 8-2 so that it will print the names of all objects that are the minimum or maximum distances from the sun in case there is more than one object with the minimum or maximum distance.

16 Write a subroutine to sort the distances in the array DIST into ascending order. Be sure to sort the names in the array NAME into a corresponding order.

17 Write a subroutine to sort the names in the array NAME into alphabetical order. Be sure to sort the distances in the array DIST into a corresponding order.

18 Write a complete program to compute π using double precision variables. The algorithm to be used should compute the area of a quarter circle with a radius of 1 and multiply that area by 4 to get an approximation to π. To compute the area of a quarter circle, called AREAQ, we sum the areas of 2000 subsections of the quarter circle. The area of a subsection is approximately the area of a trapezoid and will be called SUB. The basic relationships needed, and a diagram, are shown below:

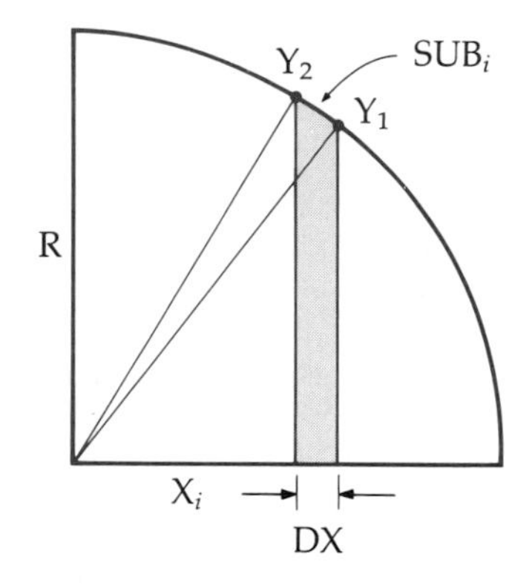

$$AREAQ = \sum_{i=1}^{2000} SUB_i$$

$$SUB_i = \frac{Y_2 + Y_1}{2} \cdot DX$$

$$Y_2 = \sqrt{R^2 - X_i^2}$$

$$Y_1 = \sqrt{R^2 - (X_i + DX)^2}$$

$$X_i = R - i \cdot DX$$

$$DX = R/2000$$

No arrays are needed. Print the value of π. Compare your value to the real value of π, which is approximately 3.14159265358979.

19 Write a complete program that will read the coefficients A, B, and C of a quadratic equation from a data line. The variables A, B, and C represent the coefficients of the equation below:

$$AX^2 + BX + C = 0$$

Write a program to print the variables in an equation form, as above. Then print the two roots, X_1 and X_2, of the equation, where:

$$X_1 = \frac{-B + \sqrt{B^2 - 4AC}}{2A} \qquad X_2 = \frac{-B - \sqrt{B^2 - 4AC}}{2A}$$

Remember that the roots may be complex variables. If the value of A is zero, print an error message.

APPENDIX A

FLOWCHARTS

INTRODUCTION

Flowcharts are occasionally used instead of pseudocode to describe the steps in an algorithm. While pseudocode uses English-like statements to define these steps, flowcharts use a graphic method. Your choice of which tool you use to describe your algorithms should be based on which form works best for you. Most people consistently use either one or the other, although some switch back and forth depending on which form seems to best fit a particular algorithm. We suggest that you try both so that you are able to read algorithms in either form. Then choose the form that you find easiest to use. In this appendix we first present the basic flowchart symbols and illustrate their use in IF THEN ELSE structures and WHILE loops. This is followed by a section with flowcharts to accompany each problem solving section in the text.

A-1 FLOWCHART SYMBOLS AND STRUCTURES

Algorithms are described in terms of steps such as input, output, and computations. Decisions are made by testing conditions or asking questions. The flowchart symbols for these processes, along with a symbol to indicate the beginning or end of a flowchart, are shown below:

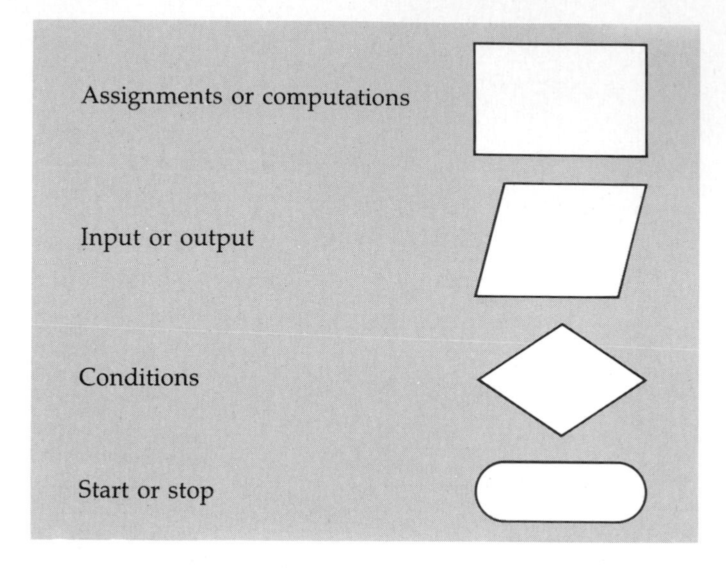

These symbols can be combined to show the steps in IF THEN ELSE structures and WHILE loops as shown below. The FORTRAN statements that correspond to the structures are shown above the flowchart segments.

IF FORMS

IF(*logical expression*)*executable statement*

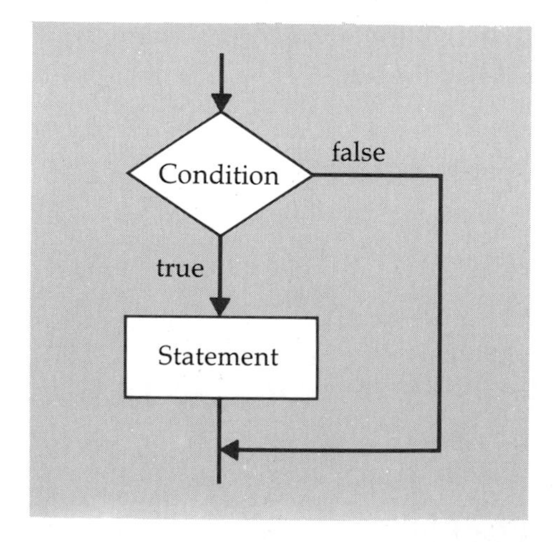

```
IF(logical expression)THEN
    statement 1
    statement 2
        ⋮
    statement n
ENDIF
```

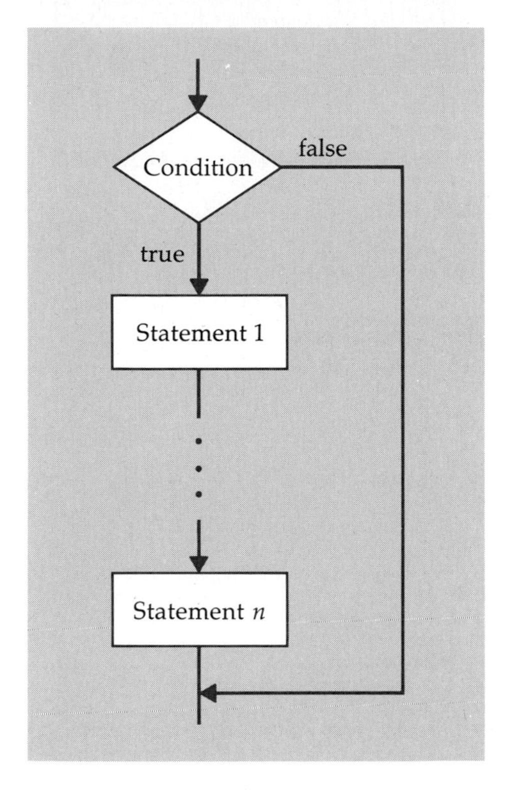

IF ELSE FORM

```
IF(logical expression)THEN
    statement 1
    statement 2
        ⋮
    statement n
ELSE
    statement n+1
    statement n+2
        ⋮
    statement m
ENDIF
```

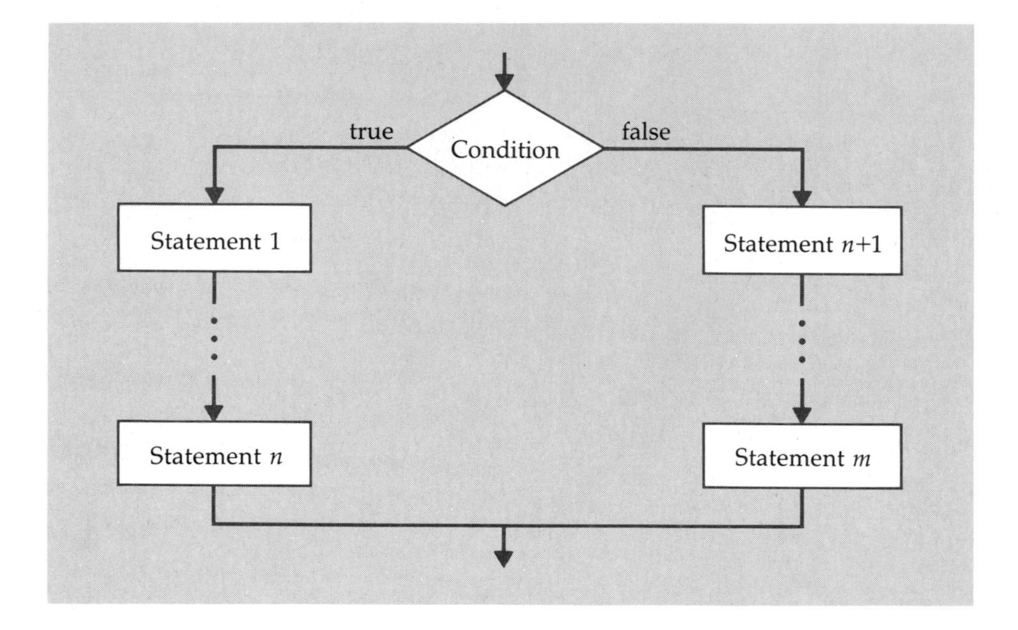

IF ELSE IF FORM

(This form can also have a final ELSE clause.)

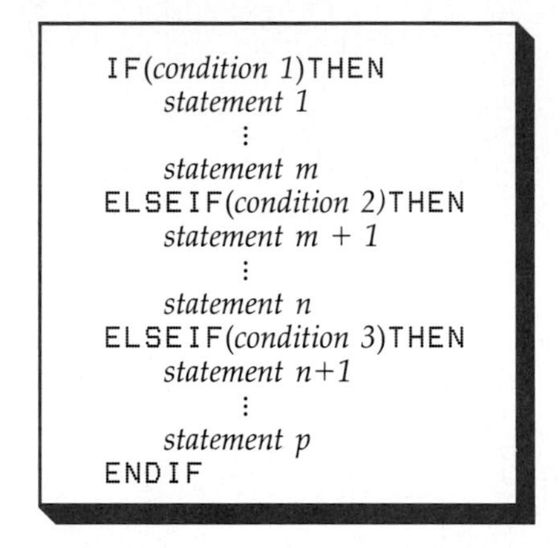

```
IF(condition 1)THEN
    statement 1
        ⋮
    statement m
ELSEIF(condition 2)THEN
    statement m + 1
        ⋮
    statement n
ELSEIF(condition 3)THEN
    statement n+1
        ⋮
    statement p
ENDIF
```

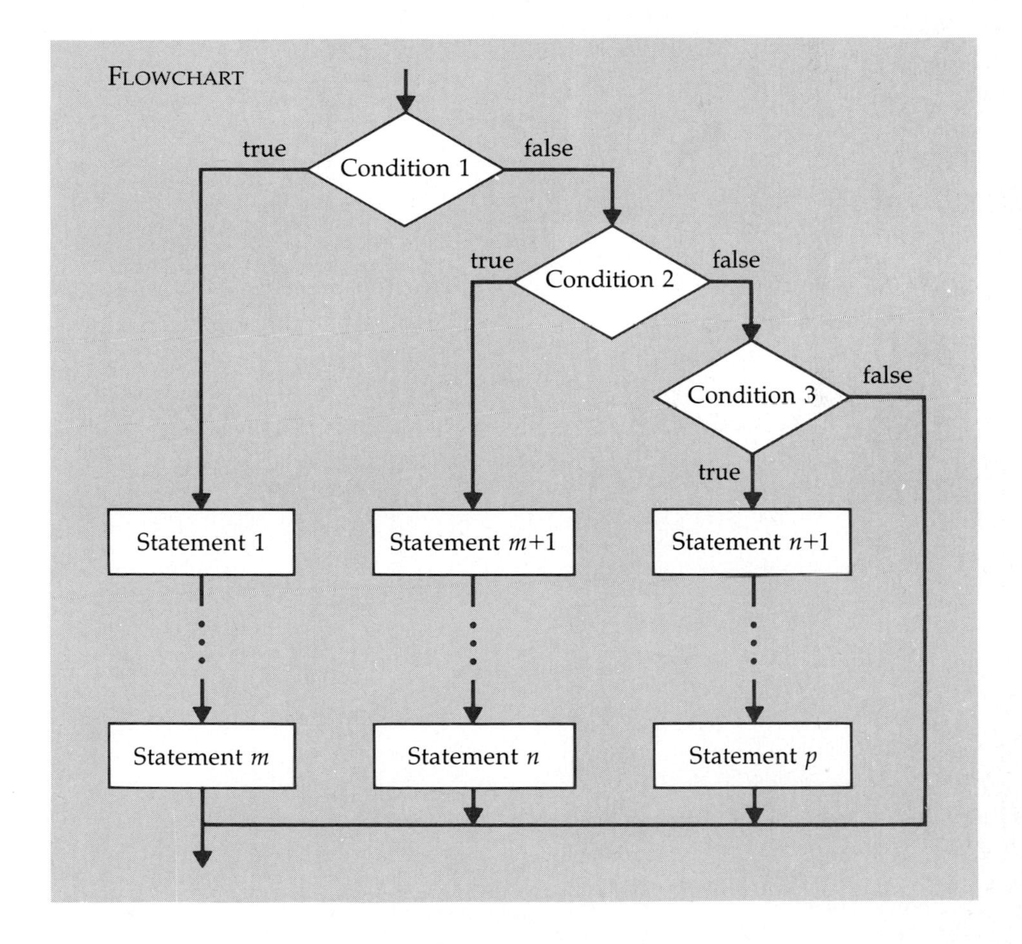

A nested structure can also be shown graphically.

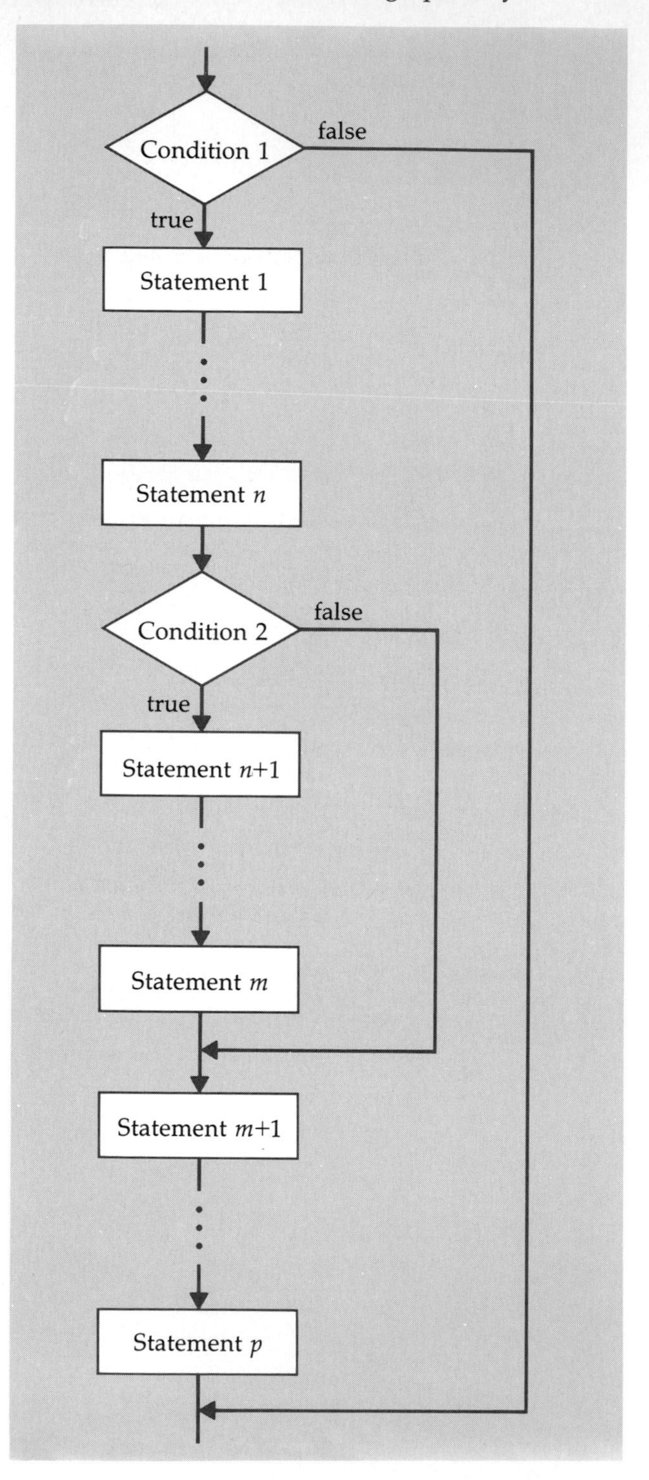

The WHILE loop is shown below:

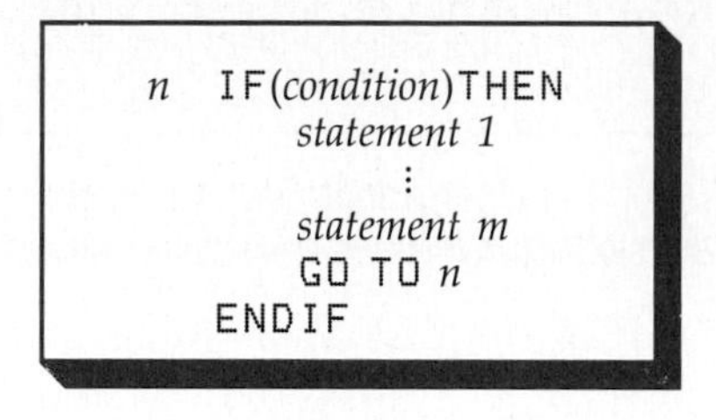

```
n   IF(condition)THEN
        statement 1
            ⋮
        statement m
        GO TO n
    ENDIF
```

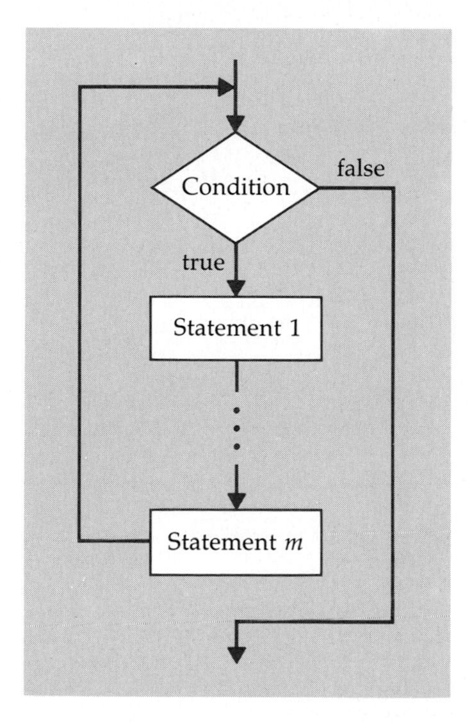

The flowchart symbol for an iterative loop represents the three steps of initializing the index, testing the index, and incrementing the index. In FORTRAN, this iterative loop corresponds to a DO loop.

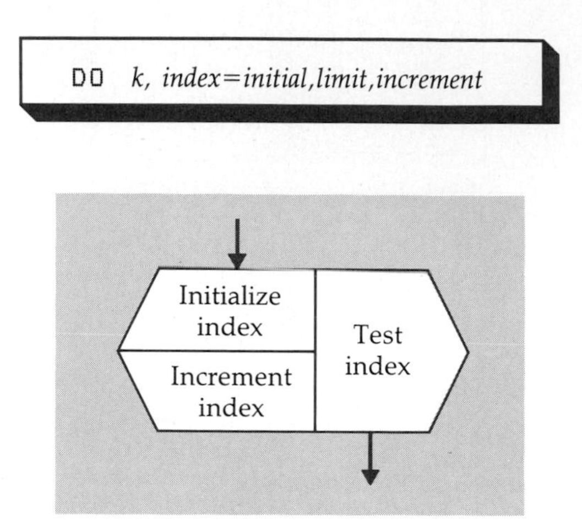

An example iterative loop and its corresponding DO loop are shown below:

```
      DO 10 I=1,50
         statement 1
             ⋮
         statement n
   10 CONTINUE
```

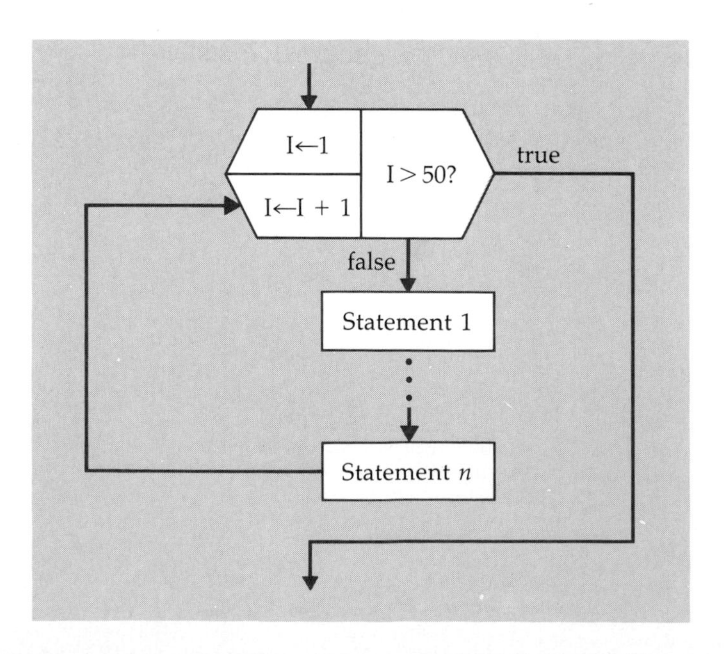

Functions and subroutines are described by the following symbol in the main program. A separate flowchart can also be done for the individual subprograms, as will be shown in the next section.

```
CALL SORT(X)
```

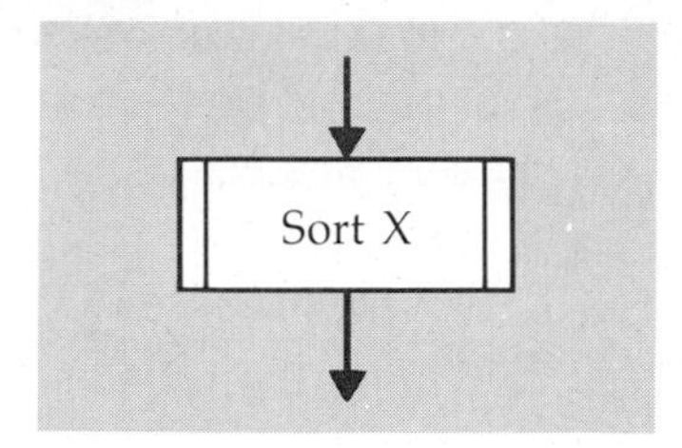

These symbols describe all basic operations needed to develop algorithms. Just as many algorithms can be developed to solve the same problem, many flowchart solutions also exist. Therefore, do not be surprised if your flowchart is somewhat different from one developed by another student to describe the same algorithm. The flowchart is a tool to aid you in describing your algorithms, and if too many rules are applied to it, the tool is no longer a quick and easy one to use.

A-2 FLOWCHARTS FOR PROBLEM SOLVING SECTIONS

The following flowcharts accompany the problem solving sections from the text. The algorithm development process still starts with the decomposition. The decomposition steps are then refined into a flowchart. Just as several pseudocode solutions may be necessary to refine the algorithm into sufficient detail, several flowcharts may also be necessary. The flowcharts shown here represent the final algorithm description before proceeding to the FORTRAN solution.

GRADE POINT AVERAGE (Section 1-7)

PROGRAM GPA

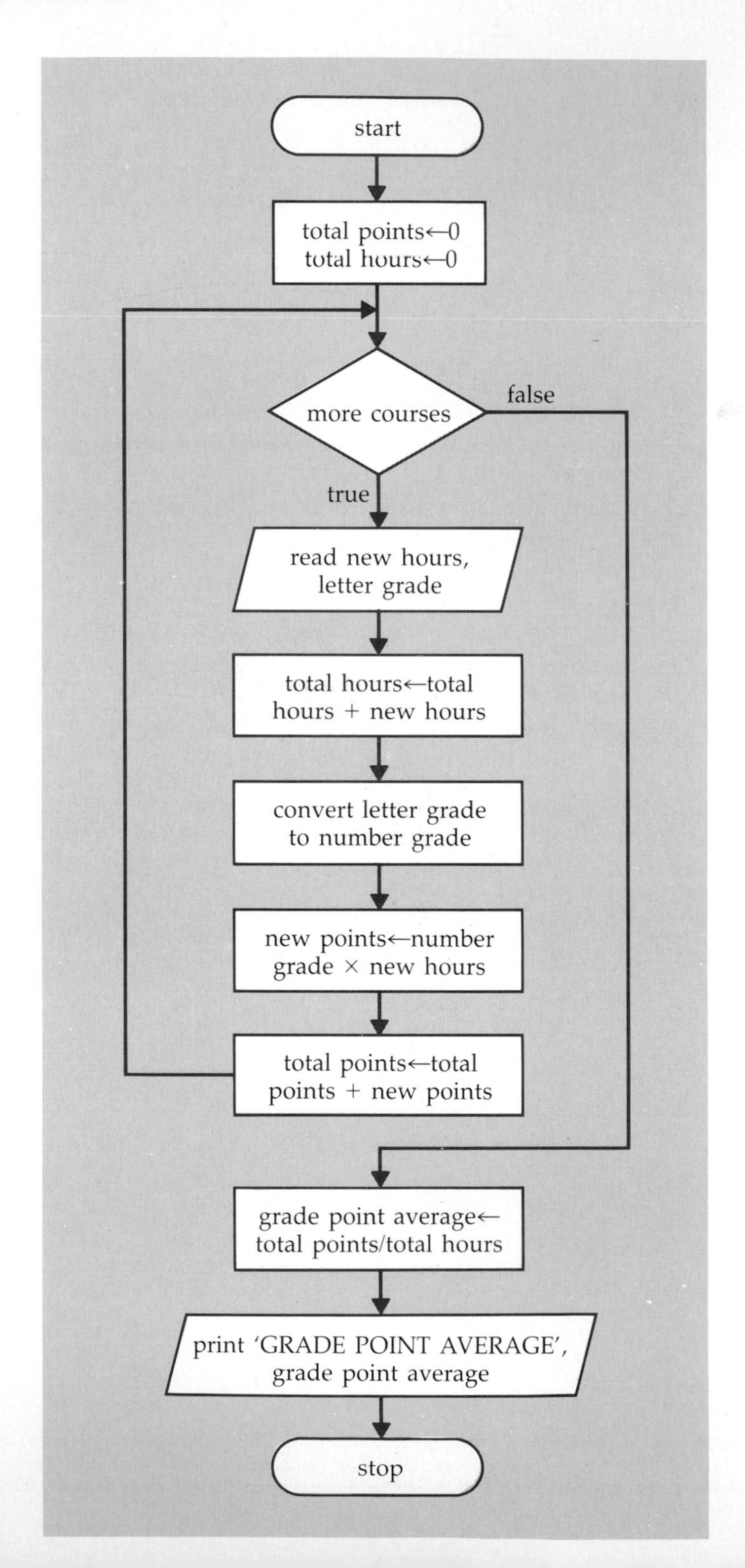

STATE TAX TABLE (Section 1-8)

PROGRAM TAXTBL

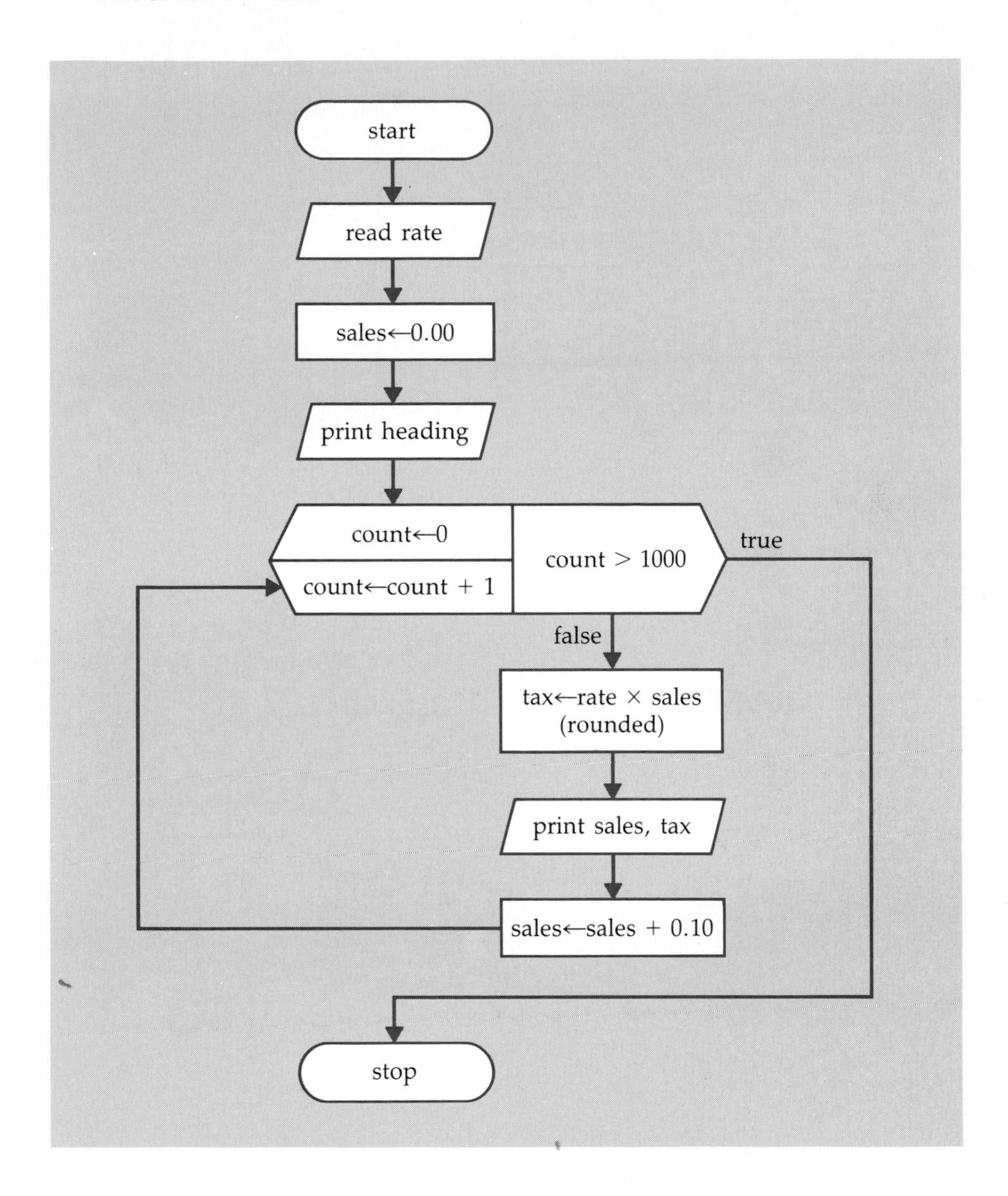

FOREIGN CURRENCY EXCHANGE (Section 2-6)

PROGRAM CONVRT

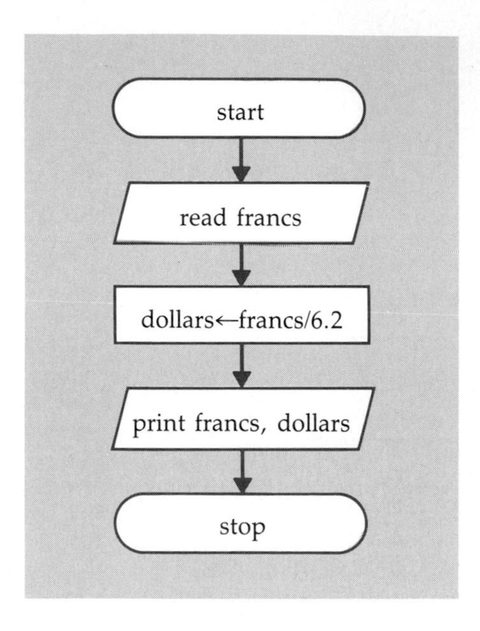

BACTERIA GROWTH (Section 2-7)

PROGRAM GROWTH

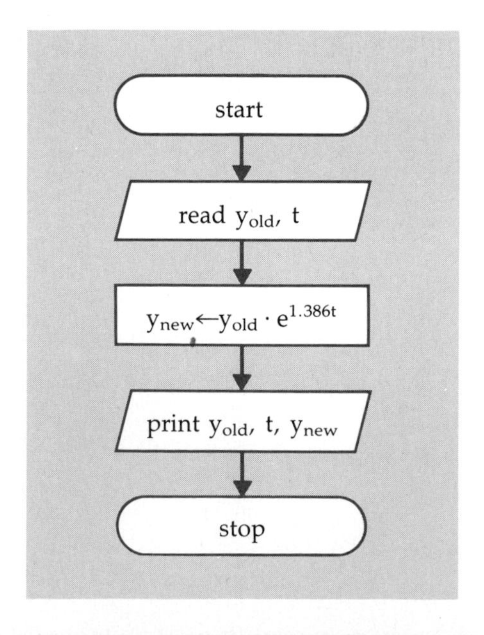

ROCKET TRAJECTORY (Section 3-5)

PROGRAM ROCKET

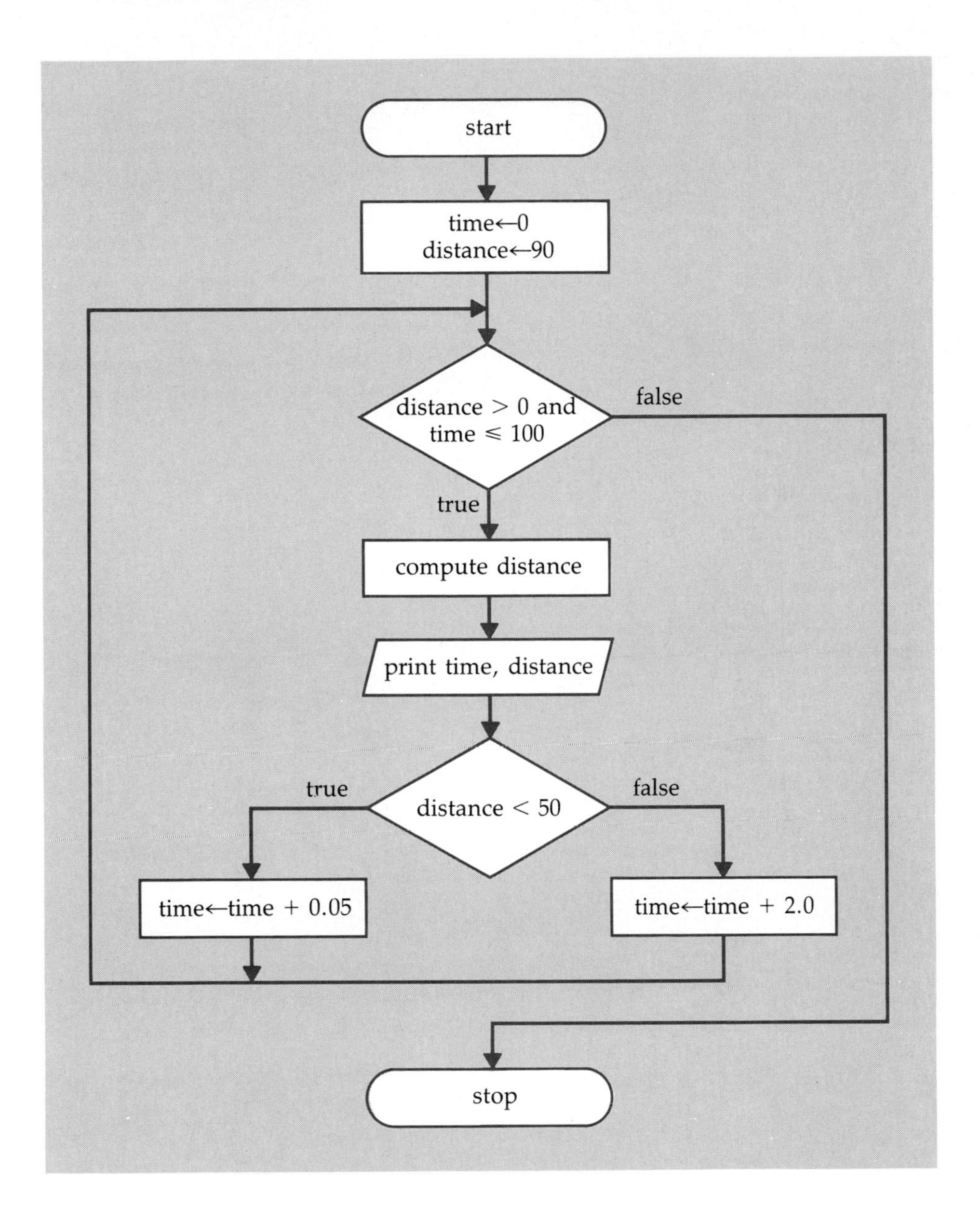

TIMBER MANAGEMENT ECONOMICS (Section 3-7)

PROGRAM TIMBER

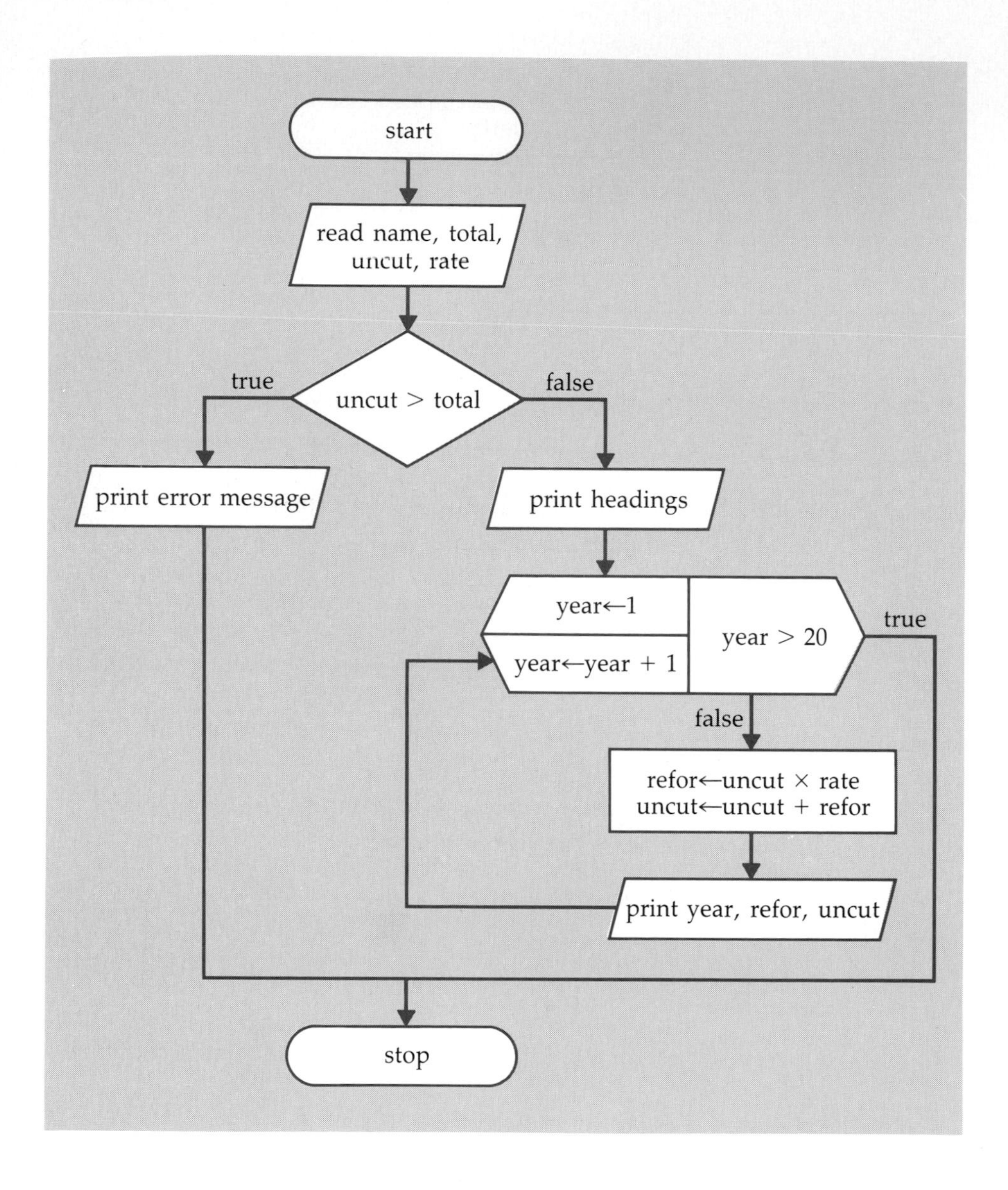

POPULATION STUDY (Section 3-8)

PROGRAM CENSUS

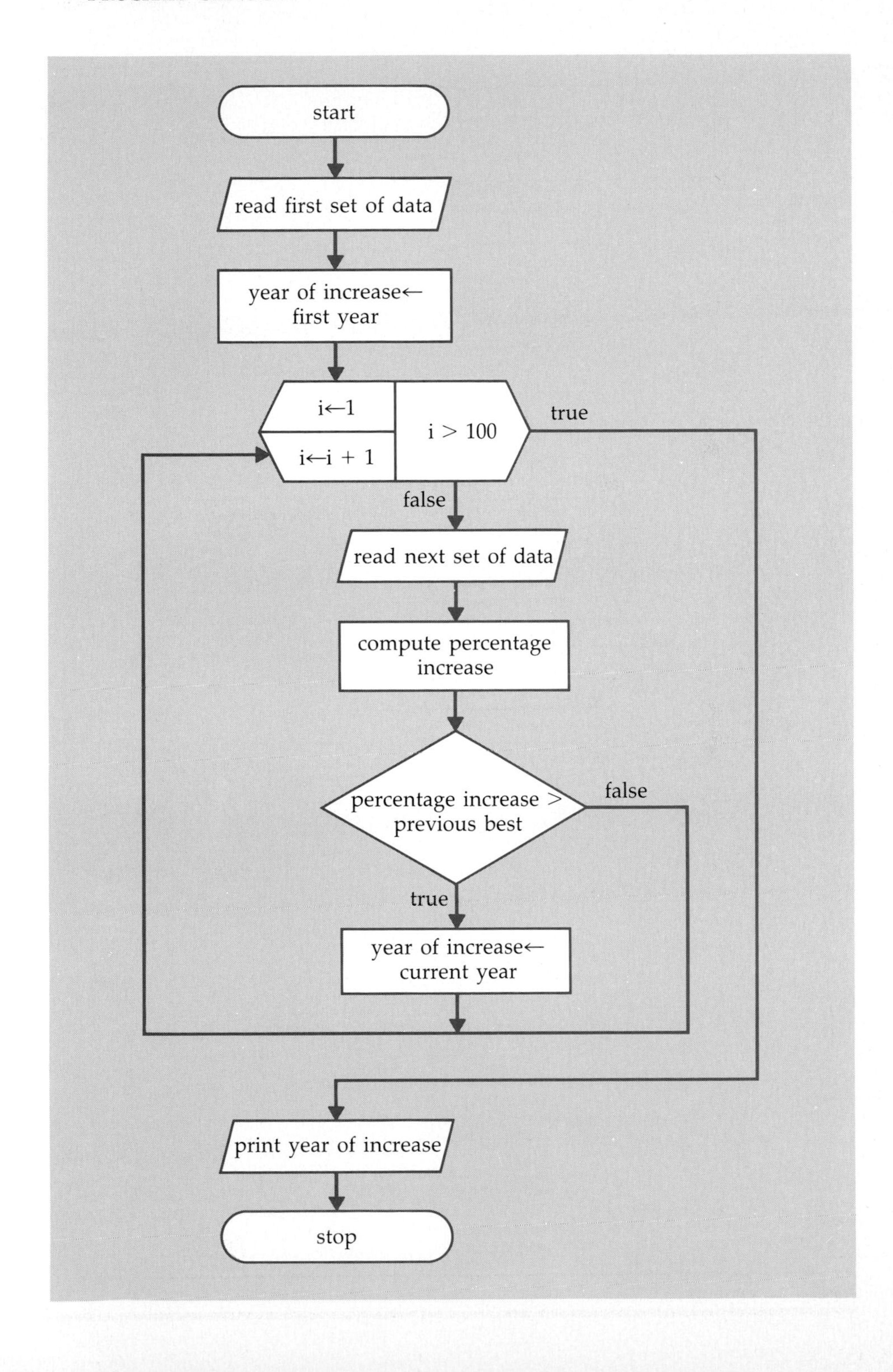

NATIONAL PARK SNOWFALL (Section 4-3)

PROGRAM SNOFAL

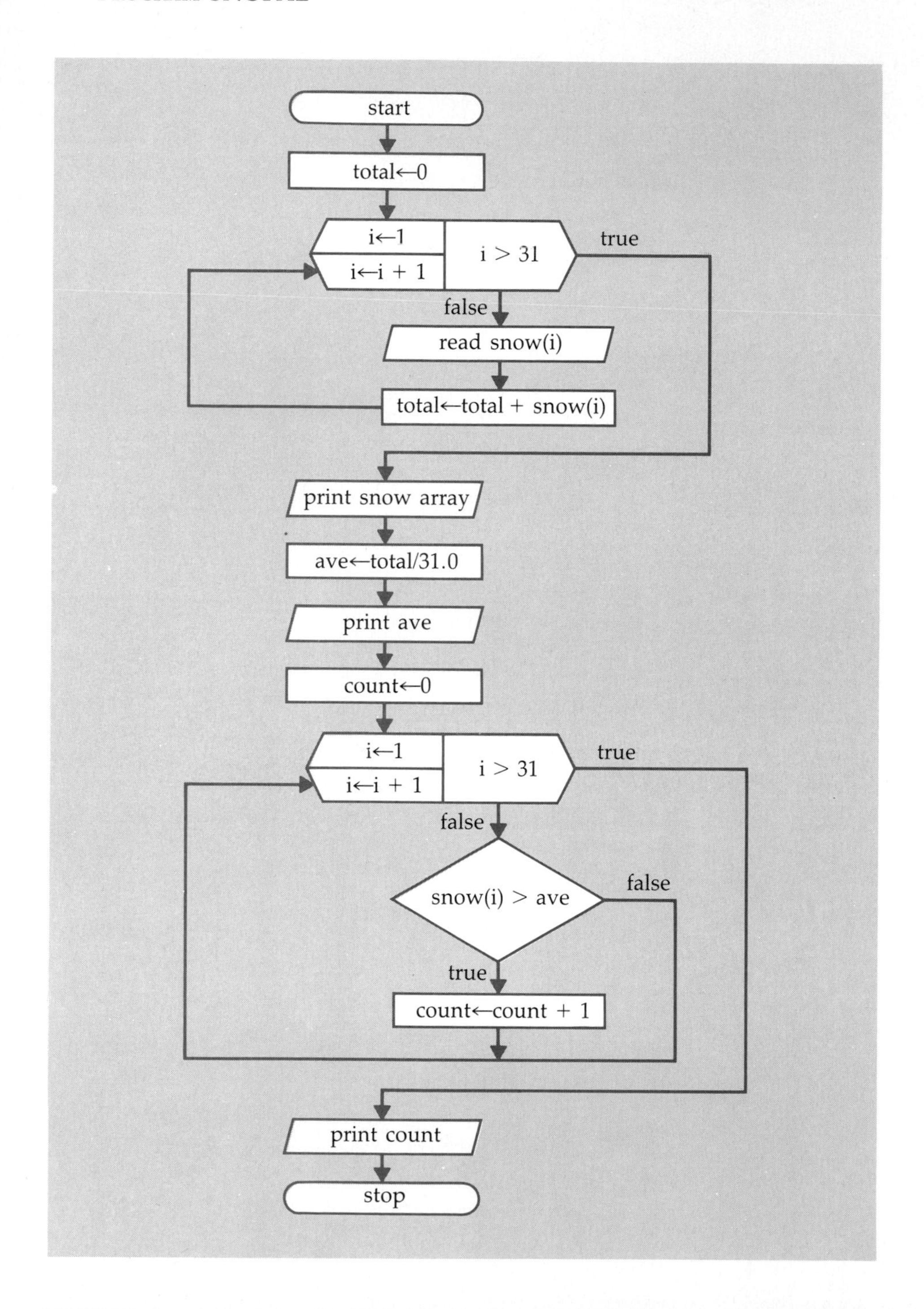

EARTHQUAKE MEASUREMENTS (Section 4-4)

Program EARTH

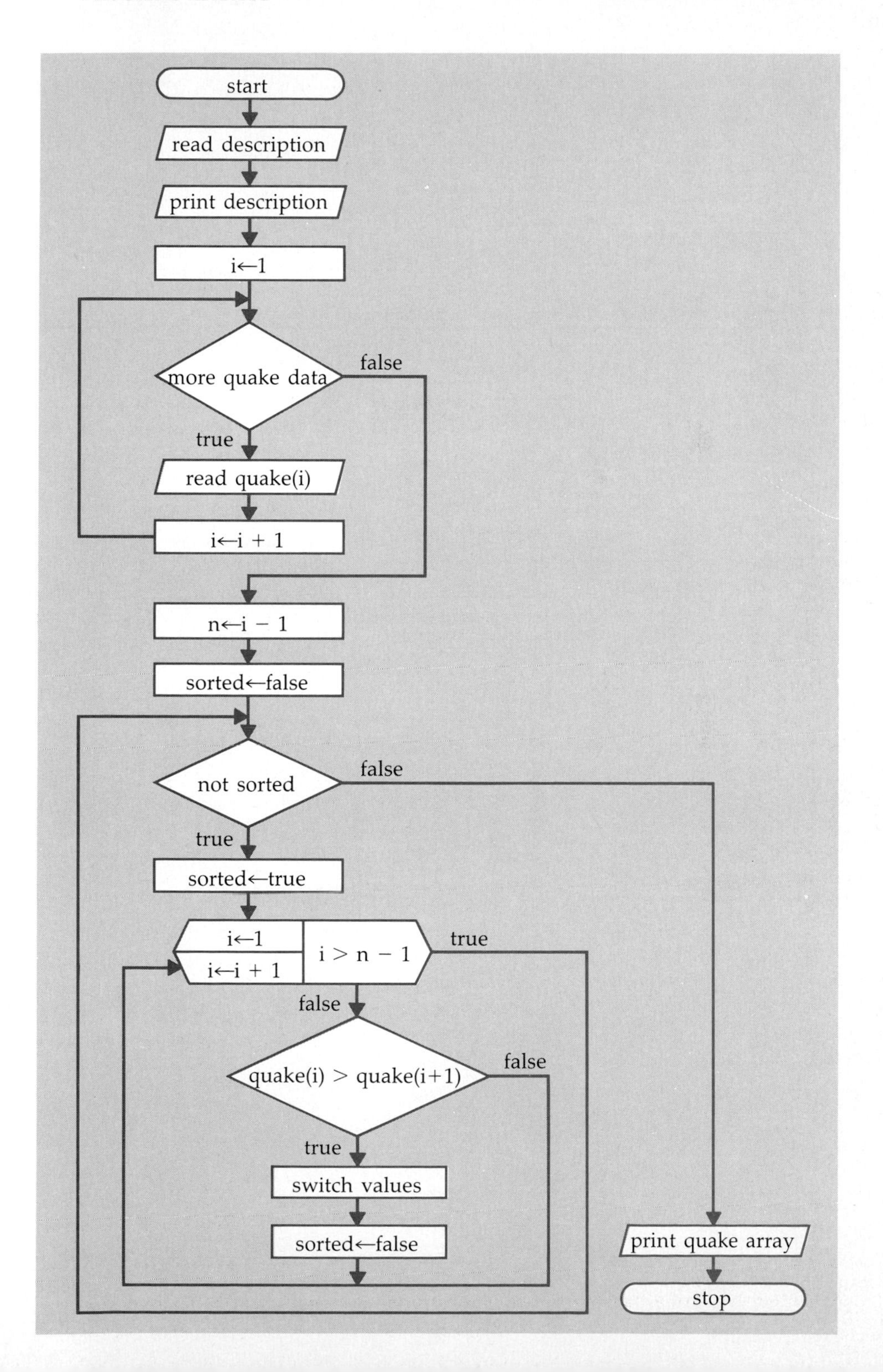

EXAM STATISTICS (Section 4-6)

PROGRAM STAT

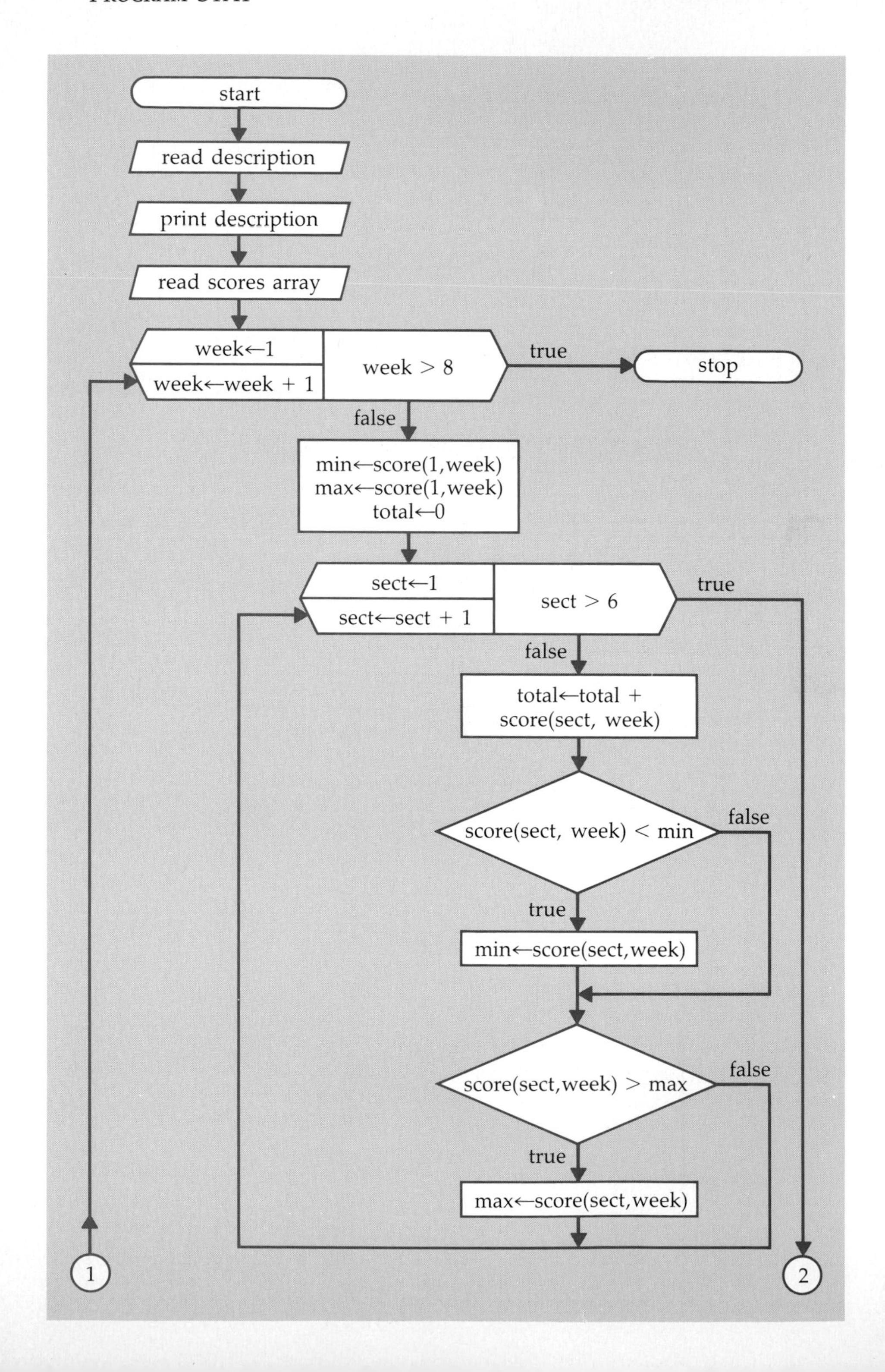

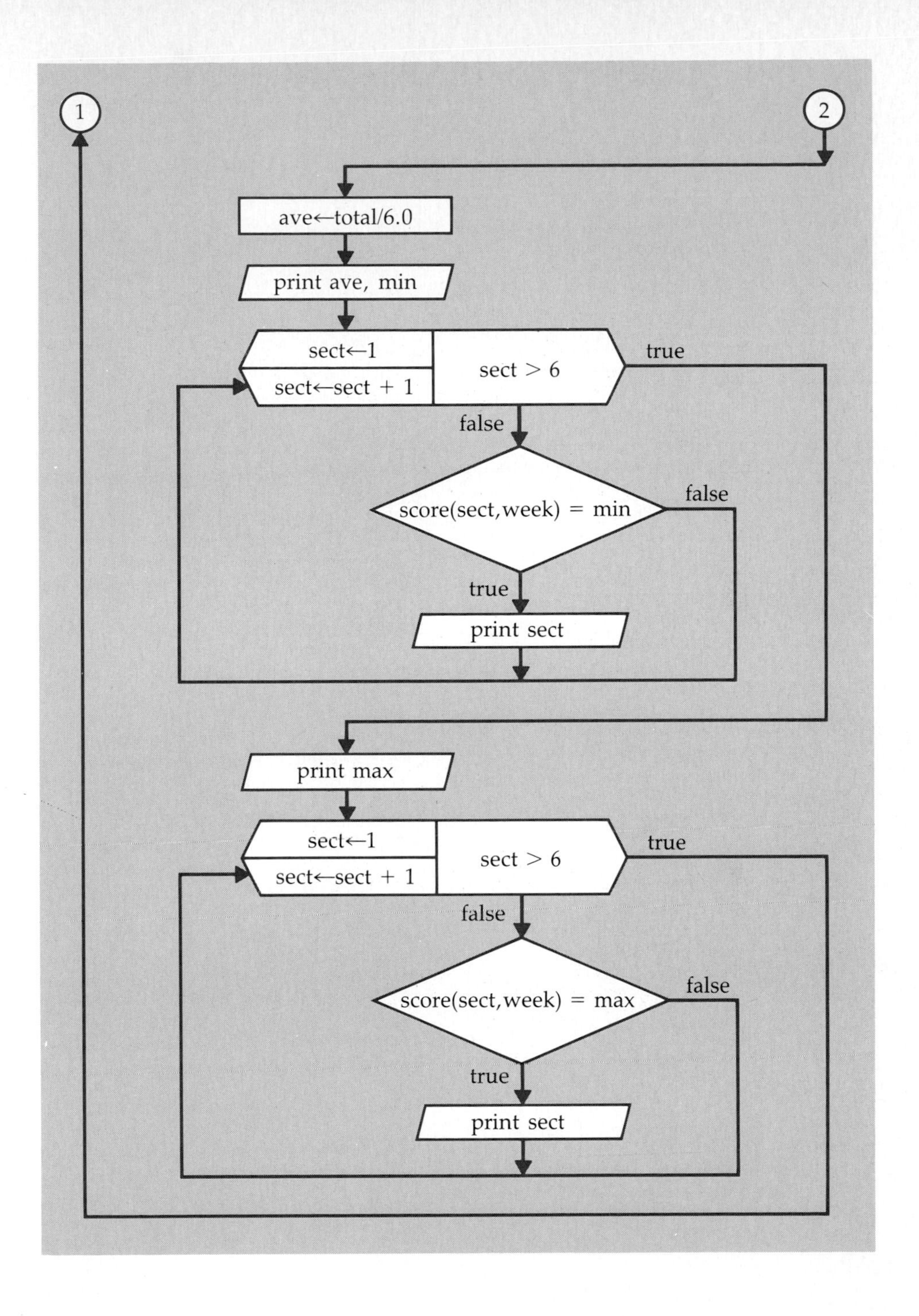
1
2
ave←total/6.0
print ave, min
sect←1
sect←sect + 1
sect > 6
true
false
score(sect,week) = min
false
true
print sect
print max
sect←1
sect←sect + 1
sect > 6
true
false
score(sect,week) = max
false
true
print sect

CARBON DATING (Section 5-3)

FUNCTION AGE

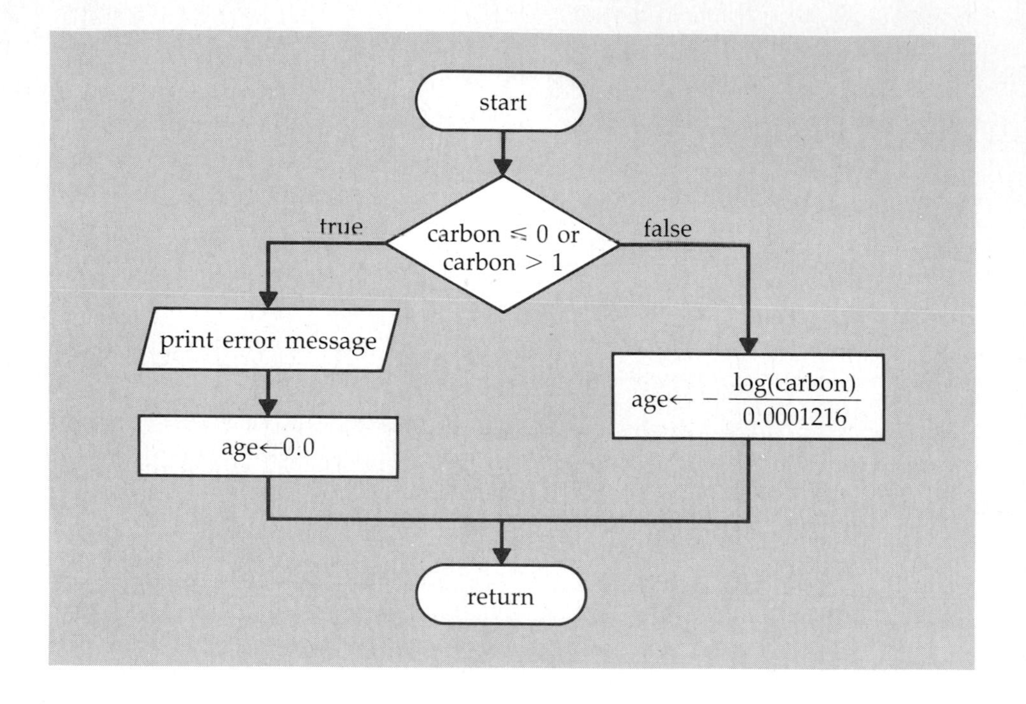

MEMBERSHIP LIST (Section 5-6)

SUBROUTINE DELETE

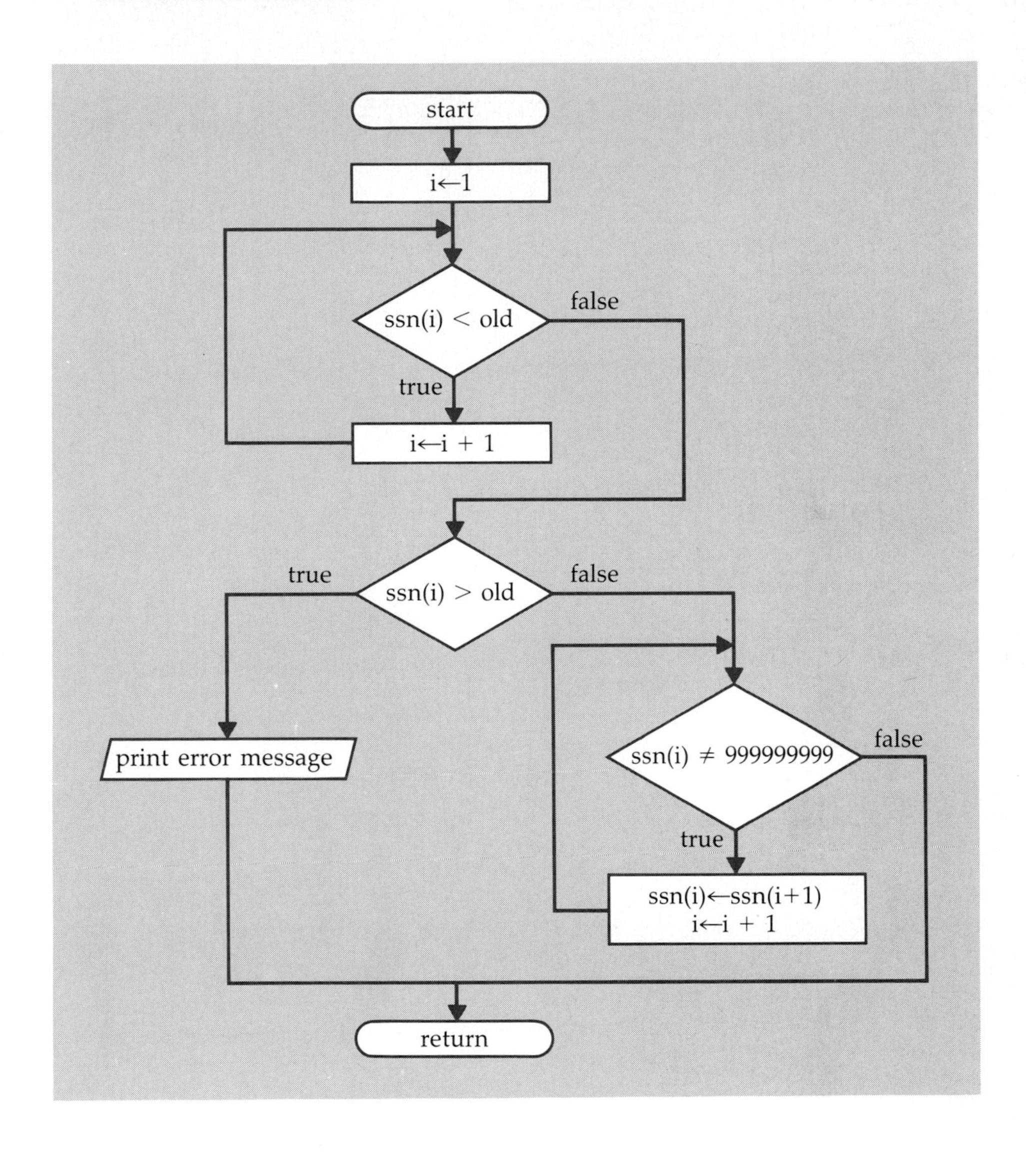

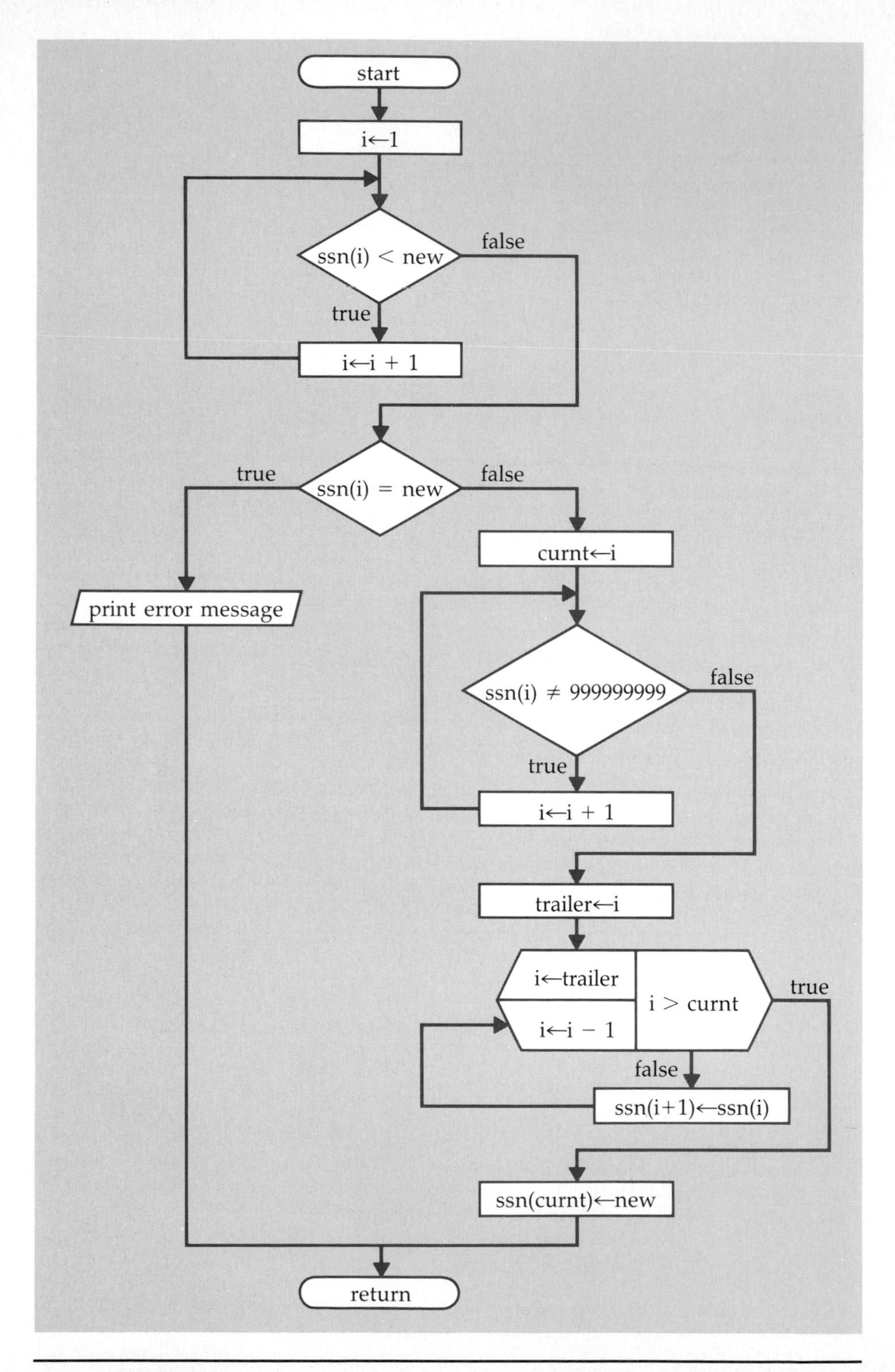
start
i←1
ssn(i) < new
false
true
i←i + 1
true
ssn(i) = new
false
curnt←i
print error message
ssn(i) ≠ 999999999
false
true
i←i + 1
trailer←i
i←trailer
i > curnt
true
i←i − 1
false
ssn(i+1)←ssn(i)
ssn(curnt)←new
return

ALPHABETICAL SORT (Section 6-3)

SUBROUTINE ALPHA

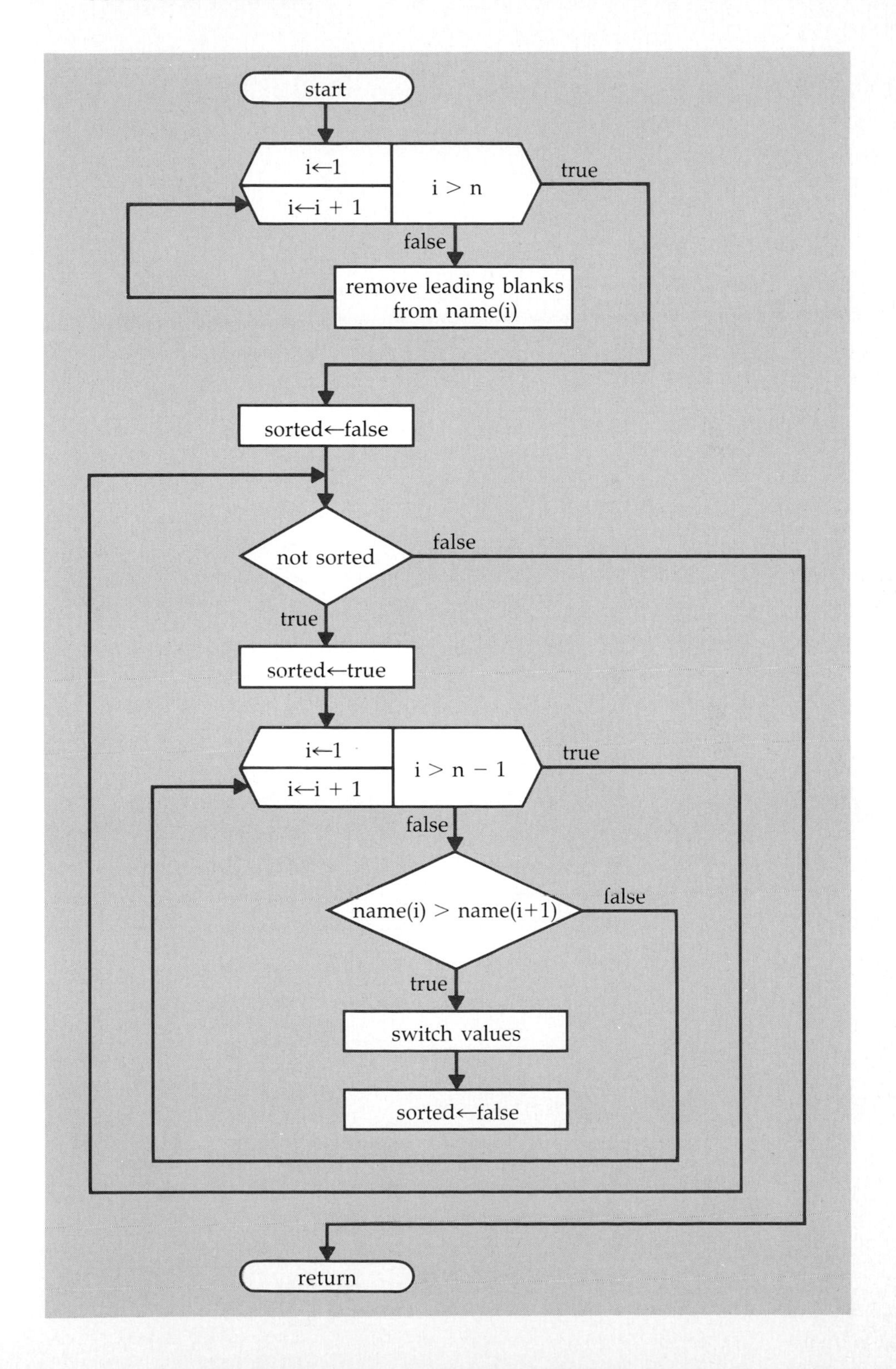

BAR GRAPH (Section 6-4)

Subroutine GRAPH

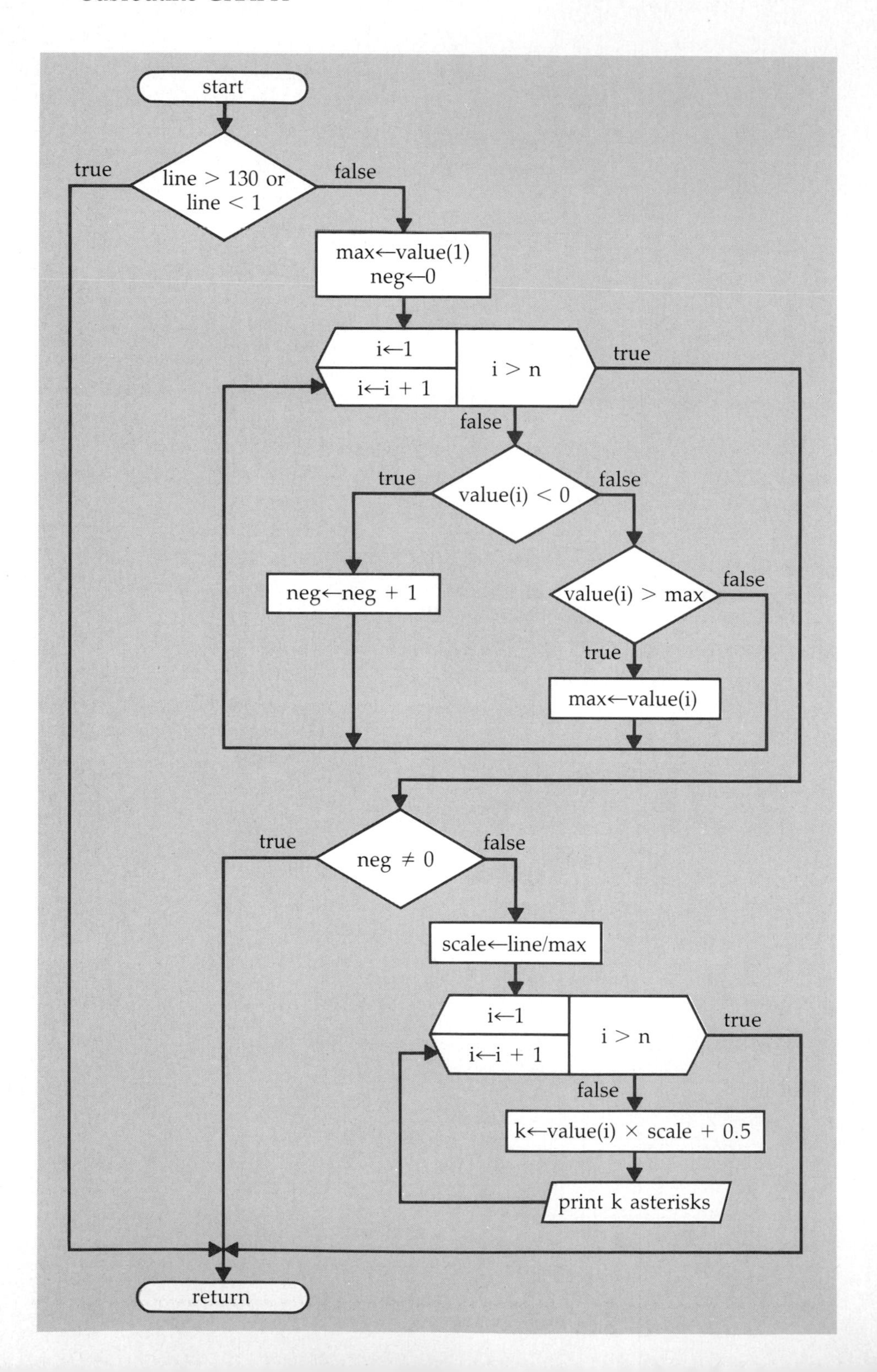

AVERAGE WORD LENGTH (Section 6-7)

FUNCTION WORDAV

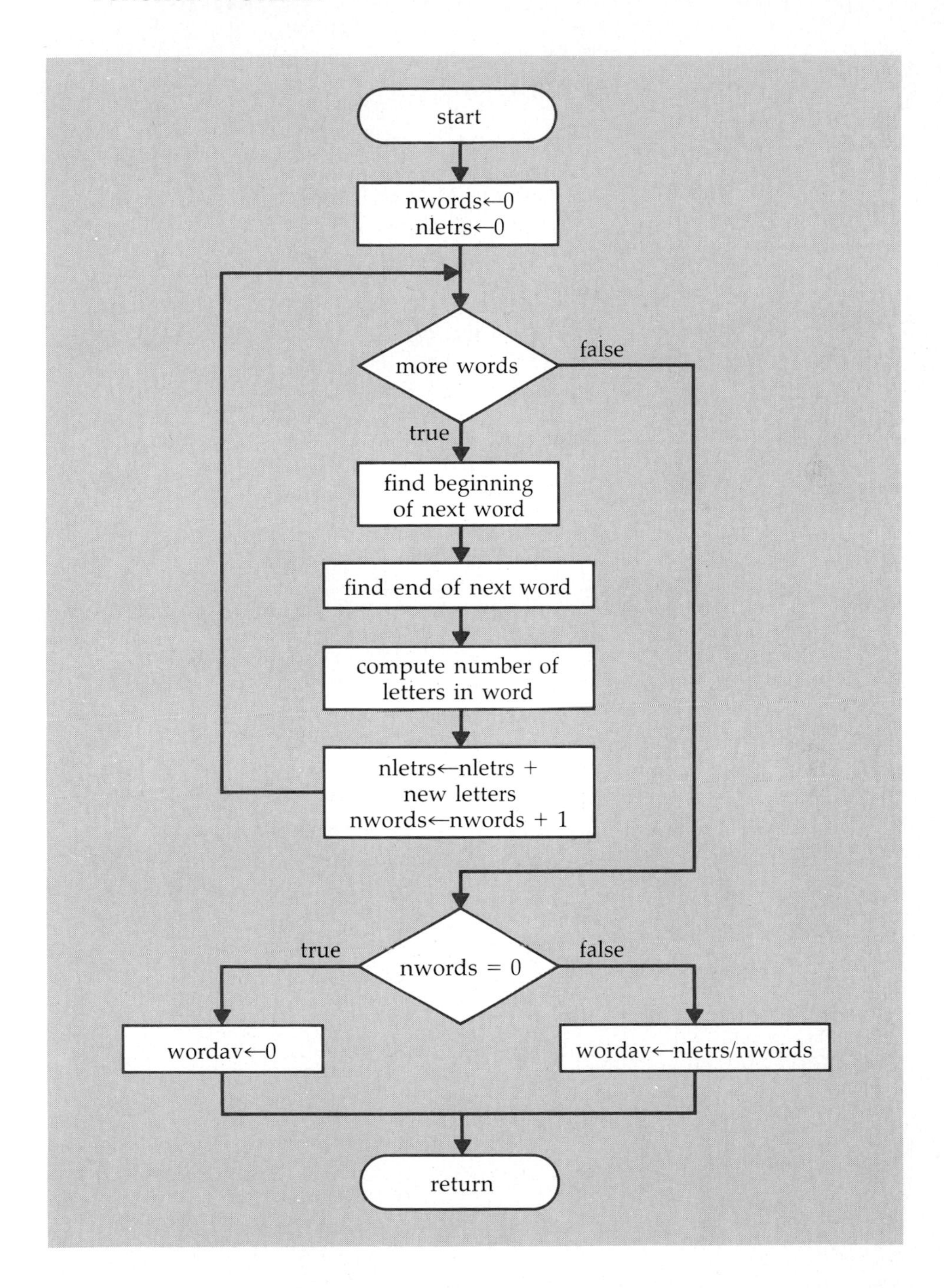

BANK TRANSACTION MERGE (Section 7-4)

PROGRAM MERGE3

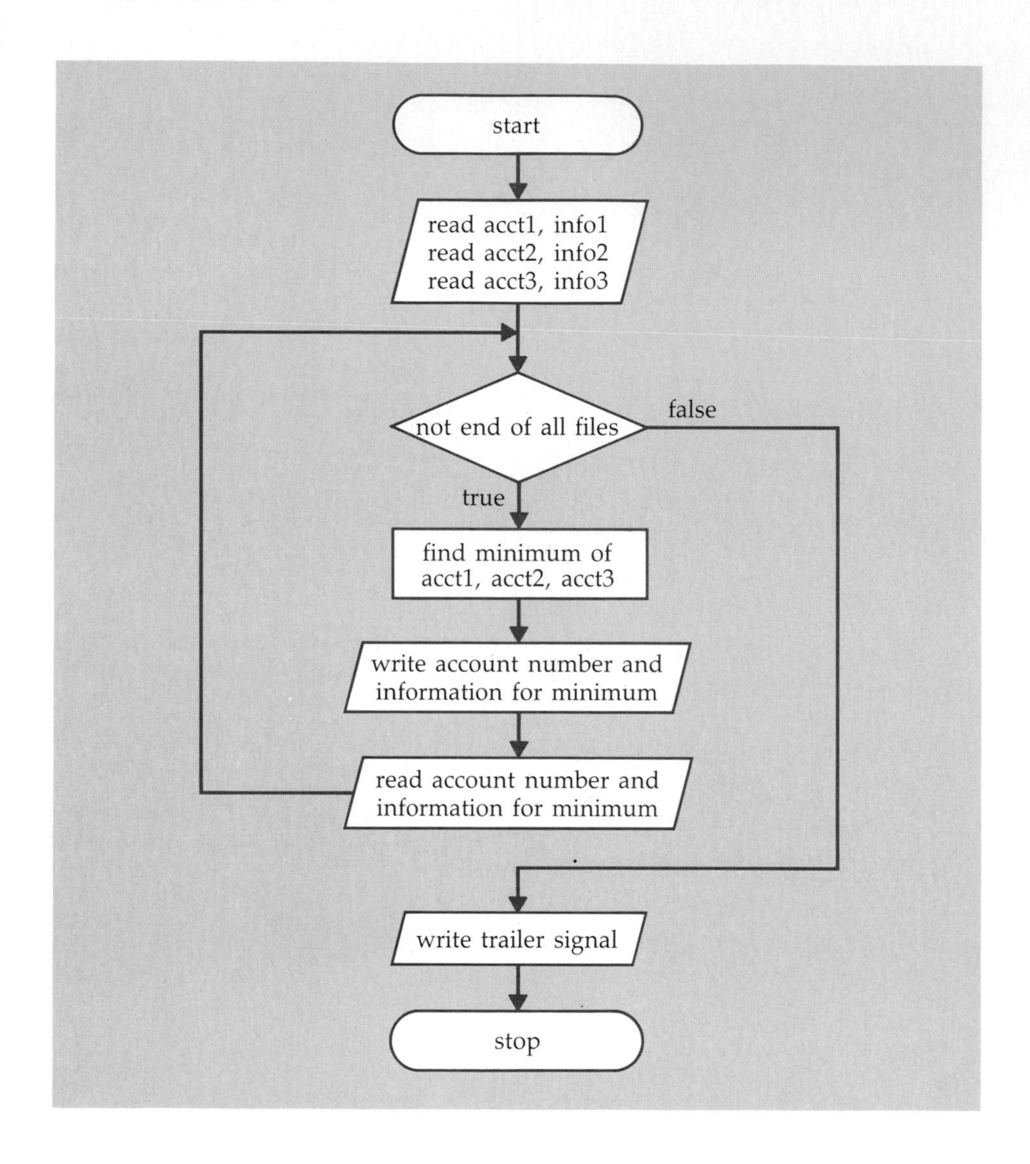

WAREHOUSE INVENTORY (Section 7-6)

PROGRAM UPDATE

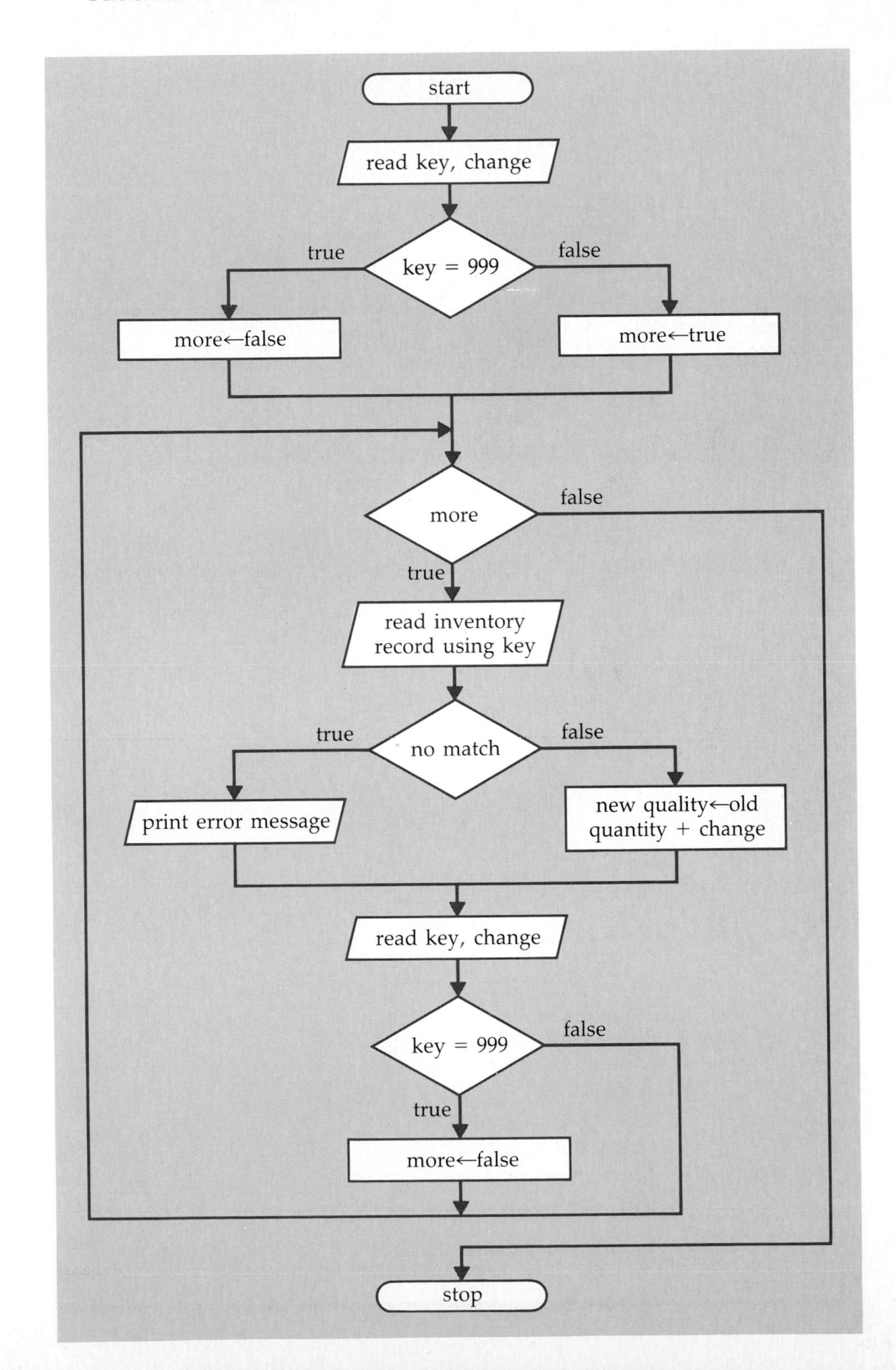

DISTANCES TO THE SUN (Section 8-2)

SUBROUTINE SOLAR

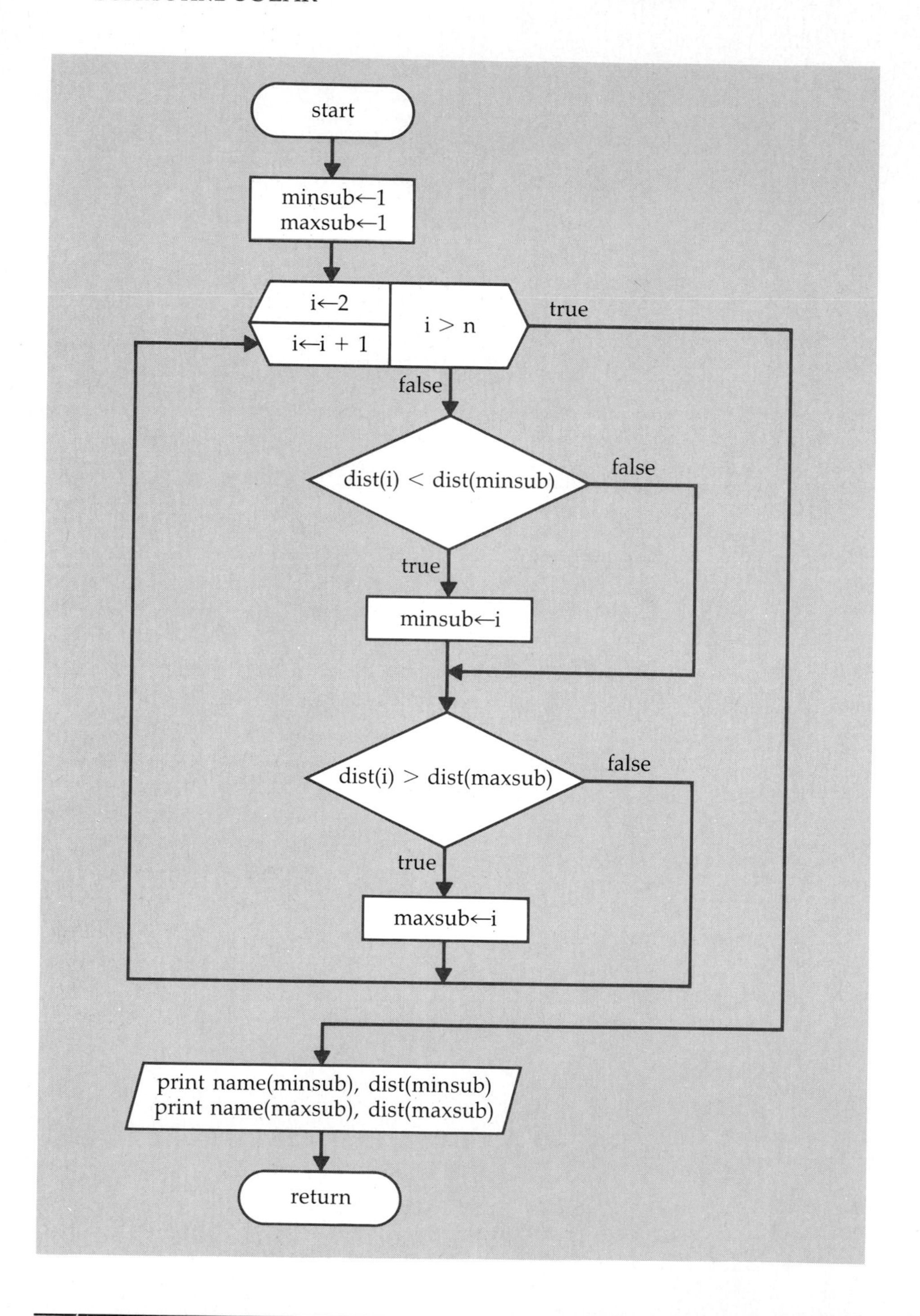

APPENDIX B

FORMATTED INPUT AND OUTPUT

INTRODUCTION

A fundamental part of a computer program is the input and output of information. FORTRAN has two types of statements that allow us to perform these operations in our programs. *List-directed input/output* statements are easy to use, but give us little control over the exact spacing used in the input and output lines. *Formatted input/output,* while more involved, allows us to control the input and output forms with great detail. The formatted output statements (WRITE and PRINT) are presented first, followed by formatted input statements (READ). A short discussion on using formatted statements with data files and some additional format features are also presented. A number of problems are included at the end of the appendix for practice.

B-1 FORMATTED OUTPUT WITH REAL AND INTEGER DATA

If we want to specify the form in which data values are printed, and where on the output line they are printed, formatted statements are necessary. The general form of a formatted WRITE statement is

WRITE(*, *format reference number*)*variable list*

where the variable list is optional. The asterisk specifies that a system-determined device will be used. Generally, this will be the terminal screen for time-sharing and a printer for batch processing. The list of variables designates the storage locations whose contents will be printed or arithmetic expressions whose values will be printed. The list of variables also determines the order in which the data values will be printed. The other information still needed is the spacing desired between variables, what part of the page (top, bottom, next line, etc.) is to be used when printing the line, and how many digits are to be printed for the variable values. This information is all given in the FORMAT statement. Each FORMAT statement has a statement number that is used in the WRITE statement to tie the two together. A sample WRITE/FORMAT combination would thus be:

```
      WRITE(*,5)TIME, DIST
    5 FORMAT(1X,F5.1,2X,F7.2)
```

Note that the WRITE statement identifies the statement with reference number 5 as the FORMAT to be used with it. Also note that the variable names in the list must be separated by commas.

The general form of the FORMAT statement is:

k FORMAT(*specification list*)

where *k* is a statement number. The specification list tells the computer the vertical spacing and horizontal spacing to be used when printing the variables. The vertical spacing options include printing on the top of a new page, the next line (single spacing), double spacing, and no spacing. Horizontal spacing includes indicating how many digits will be used for each value, how many blanks will be between numbers, and how many values are to be printed per line.

In order to understand the specifications that are used to describe the vertical and horizontal spacing, we must first examine the output from a line printer or terminal. These are the most common output devices, but other forms of output have similar characteristics.

The line printer prints on computer paper that is a series of connected pages, each separated by perforations so that it is easy to separate the pages. A common size for a computer page is 11 inches by 14 7/8 inches. Typically 55 to 75 lines of information can be printed per page, and each line can contain up to 132 characters. In our discussion of printed output, we will assume that an output line contains 132 characters. Most line printers print either 6 lines per inch or 8 lines per inch. The WRITE/FORMAT combination describes specifically how each line is to be printed on the page (vertical spacing) and which positions, in the 132 possible positions, will contain data (horizontal spacing).

The computer uses the specification list to construct each output line internally in the memory before actually printing the line. This internal memory region, which contains 133 characters, is called a *buffer*. The buffer is automatically filled with blanks before it is used to construct a line of output. The first character of the buffer is called the *carriage control* character. It determines the vertical spacing for the line. The remaining 132 characters represent the line to be printed.

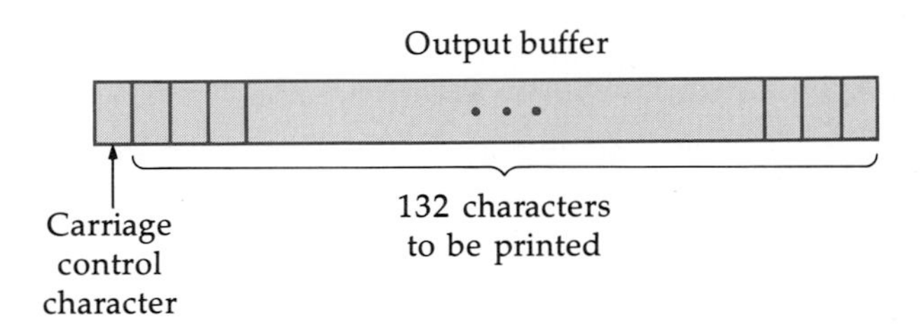

The following table shows some of the valid carriage control characters and the vertical spacing that they generate. When needed for clarity in either FORMAT statements or buffer contents, a blank will be indicated by the character b placed one-half space below the regular line.

Carriage Control	Vertical Spacing
1	new page
blank, b	single spacing
0	double spacing
+	no vertical spacing

When a plus sign is in carriage control, no spacing will occur and the next line of information will print over the last line printed. Some of the examples to follow will contain applications for this *overprinting*. On most computers, an invalid carriage control character will cause single spacing.

When a terminal is used as the output device, the width of the line may be less than 132 positions. Although terminal systems do not always use carriage control, the internal buffer will contain one character more than the line width if carriage control applies. Since a terminal does not have the same capability as a line printer for spacing to a new page, a 1 in carriage control usually becomes an invalid control character and causes single spacing.

We will now examine five FORMAT specifications that will describe how to fill the output buffer. Commas are used to separate specifications in the FORMAT statement.

LITERAL SPECIFICATION

The literal specification allows you to put characters directly into the buffer. The characters must be enclosed in single quote marks or apostrophes. These characters can represent the carriage control character or the characters in a literal. The following examples illustrate the use of the literal specification in FORMAT statements.

EXAMPLE B-1 Title Heading

Print a title heading, TEST RESULTS, on the top of a new page, *left-justified* (i.e., no blanks to the left of the heading).

Solution

FORTRAN STATEMENTS

```
      WRITE(*,4)
    4 FORMAT('1','TEST RESULTS')
```

BUFFER CONTENTS

1TEST$_b$RESULTS

COMPUTER OUTPUT

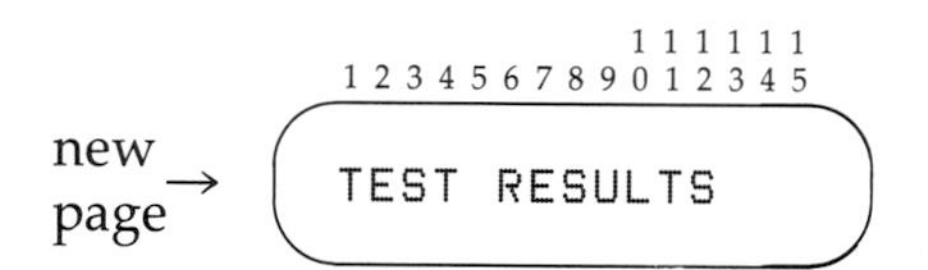

The buffer is filled according to the FORMAT. No variable names were listed on the WRITE statement; hence, no values are printed. The literal specifications cause the characters 1TEST RESULTS to be put in the buffer, beginning with the first position in the buffer. After filling the buffer as instructed by the FORMAT, the carriage control is examined to determine vertical spacing. The character 1 in the carriage control position tells the computer to space the computer paper to the beginning of a new page. The rest of the buffer, 132 positions, is then printed. Notice that the carriage control character is not printed. The row of small numbers above the computer output shows the specific column of the output line. That is, the first T is in column 1, the second T is in column 4, and the third T is in column 11. ◇

EXAMPLE B-2 Column Headings

Double-space from the last line printed, and then print column headings 1979 SALES and 1980 SALES, with no blanks on the left side of the line and five blanks between the two column headings.

Correct Solution

FORTRAN STATEMENTS

```
      WRITE(*,3)
    3 FORMAT('0','1979bSALESbbbbb1980bSALES')
```

BUFFER CONTENTS

01979$_b$SALES$_{bbbbb}$1980$_b$SALES

COMPUTER OUTPUT

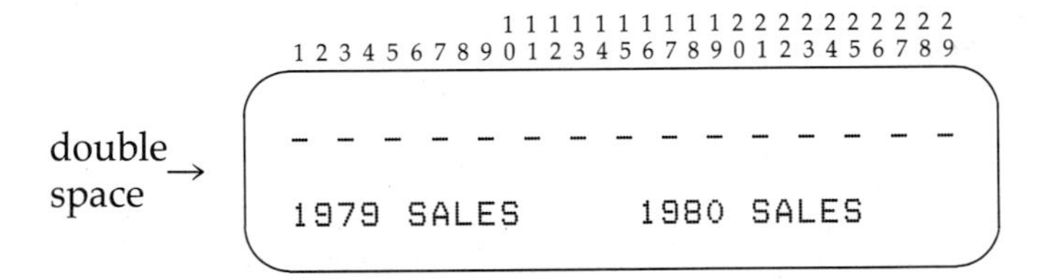

The line of dashes in the computer output represents the previous line of output. The first character inserted in the buffer is a zero, to indicate double spacing from the previous line of output. Then the column headings are specified with five blanks between them.

Incorrect Solution

FORTRAN STATEMENTS

```
      WRITE(*,3)
    3 FORMAT('1979bSALESbbbbb1980bSALES')
```

BUFFER CONTENTS

1979$_b$SALES$_{bbbbb}$1980$_b$SALES

COMPUTER OUTPUT

```
                    1 1 1 1 1 1 1 1 1 1 2 2 2 2 2 2 2 2 2
  1 2 3 4 5 6 7 8 9 0 1 2 3 4 5 6 7 8 9 0 1 2 3 4 5 6 7 8
new  →
page    979 SALES      1980 SALES
```

In this example we forgot to specify the carriage control; however, the computer does not forget. The first position of the buffer contains a 1, which indicates spacing to a new page. The rest of the buffer, 979$_b$SALES$_{bbbbb}$1980$_b$SALES, is then printed. ◇

X SPECIFICATION

The X specification will insert blanks into the buffer. Its general form is nX, where n represents the number of blanks to be inserted in the buffer. An example using both the X specification and the literal specification follows.

EXAMPLE B-3 Centered Heading

Print the heading EXPERIMENT NO. 1, centered at the top of a new page.

Solution

FORTRAN STATEMENTS

```
      WRITE(*,35)
   35 FORMAT('1',58X,'EXPERIMENT NO. 1')
```

BUFFER CONTENTS

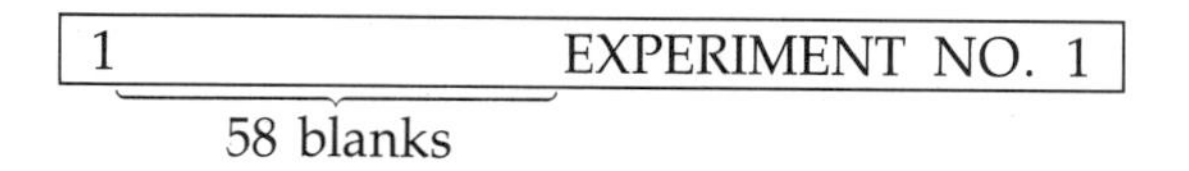

COMPUTER OUTPUT

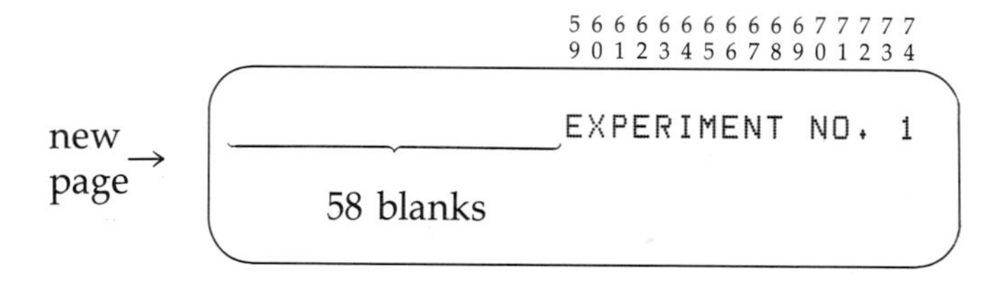

This heading could have been done without the 58X specification, but would require a literal specification of a 1, followed by 58 blanks, followed by EXPERIMENT NO. 1. ◇

I SPECIFICATION

The literal specification and the X specification already discussed allow us to specify carriage control and to print headings. They cannot, however, be used to print variable values. We will now look at a specification that is used for printing the contents of integer variables. The form of the specification is Iw, where w represents the number of positions (width) to be assigned in the buffer for printing the value of an integer variable. The value is always *right-*

justified (no blanks to the right of the value) in those positions in the buffer. Extra positions on the left are filled with blanks. Thus, if the value 16 is printed with an I4 specification, the four positions contain two blanks followed by 16. If there are not enough positions to print the value, including a minus sign if the value is negative, the positions are filled with asterisks. Hence, if we print the value 132 or −12 with an I2 specification, the two positions are filled with asterisks. It is important to recognize that the asterisks do not necessarily indicate that there is an error in the value; instead, the asterisks may indicate that you need to assign a larger width in the corresponding I specification.

Often, more than one variable name will be listed on the WRITE statement. When interpreting a WRITE/FORMAT combination, the compiler will match the first variable name to the first specification for printing values, the second variable name to the second specification for printing values, and so on. There should therefore generally be the same number of specifications for printing values as there are variables on the WRITE statement list.

EXAMPLE B-4 Integer Values

Print the values of the integer variables SUM, MEAN, and N on the same line, single-spaced from the previous line.

Solution

COMPUTER MEMORY

SUM	12
MEAN	−14
N	−146

FORTRAN STATEMENTS

```
      WRITE(*,30)SUM, MEAN, N
   30 FORMAT(1X,I3,2X,I2,2X,I4)
```

BUFFER CONTENTS

$_{bb}$12$_{bb}$**$_{bb}$−146

COMPUTER OUTPUT

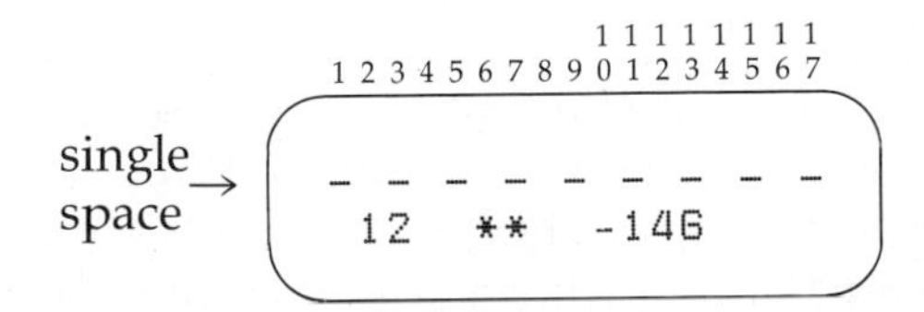

The computer will print SUM with an I3 specification, MEAN with an I2 specification, and N with an I4 specification. The value of SUM is 12, so the three corresponding positions are $_b$12. The value of MEAN, −14, requires at least three positions, so the two specified positions are filled with asterisks. The value of N fills all four allotted positions. The carriage control character is a blank and thus the line of output is single-spaced from the previous line. ◇

EXAMPLE B-5 Literal and Variable Information

On separate lines, print the values of MEAN and SUM, along with an indicator of the name of each of the integer variables.

Solution

COMPUTER MEMORY

SUM	12
MEAN	−14

FORTRAN STATEMENTS

```
  WRITE(*,2)MEAN
2 FORMAT(1X,'MEAN = ',I4)
  WRITE(*,3)SUM
3 FORMAT(1X,'SUM = ',I4)
```

BUFFER CONTENTS

$_b$MEAN$_b$=$_{bb}$−14

$_b$SUM$_b$=$_{bbb}$12

COMPUTER OUTPUT

```
          1 1 1 1 1 1 1 1
1 2 3 4 5 6 7 8 9 0 1 2 3 4 5 6 7

                   - - - - - - - - - - -
single  →          MEAN =   -14
space              SUM =    12
```

◇

F SPECIFICATION

The F specification is used to print real numbers in a decimal form (e.g., 36.21), as opposed to an exponential form (0.3621E+02). The general form for an F specification is Fw.d, where w represents the total width or number of positions to be used in printing the real value, and d represents the number of those positions that will represent decimal positions on the right of the decimal point. For example, the minimum size F specification that can be used to print 34.186 is F6.3, a total of six positions counting the decimal point with three decimal positions. Before the value is inserted in the buffer, the decimal point is located in the specified position. The form for F6.3 is then

$$\underbrace{XX.\underbrace{XXX}_{\text{DECIMAL}}}_{\text{WIDTH}}$$

If the value to be printed has fewer than d decimal positions, zeros are inserted on the right side. Thus, if the value 21.6 is printed with an F6.3 specification, the output is 21.600. If the value to be printed has more than d decimal positions, only d decimal positions are printed, dropping the rest. Thus, if the value 21.86342 is printed with an F6.3 specification, the output is 21.863. Many compilers will round to the last decimal position printed. Thus, if the value 18.98662 is printed with an F6.3 specification, the output is 18.987.

If the integer portion of a real value requires fewer positions than allotted in the F specification, the extra positions on the left are filled with blanks. Thus, if the value 3.123 is printed with an F6.3 specification, the ouput is $_b$3.123. If the integer portion of a real value, including the minus sign if the value is negative, requires more positions than allotted in the F specification, the entire field is filled with asterisks. Thus, if the value 312.6 is printed with an F6.3 specification, the output is ******.

If a value is between −1 and +1, positions must usually be allowed for both a leading zero to the left of the decimal point and a minus sign if the value can be negative. Thus, the smallest F specification that could be used to print −.127 is F6.3, which would be output as −0.127. If a smaller specification width were used, all the positions would be filled with asterisks.

EXAMPLE B-6 Angle THETA

Print the value of an angle called THETA. Construct the Greek symbol for theta (θ) and print in this form:

$$\theta = XX.XX$$

Solution

COMPUTER MEMORY

THETA	3.184

FORTRAN Statements

```
      WRITE(*,1)
    1 FORMAT(' ','-')
      WRITE(*,2)THETA
    2 FORMAT('+','0 = ',F5.2)
```

Buffer Contents

$_b-$
$+0_b = {}_{bb}3.18$

Computer Output

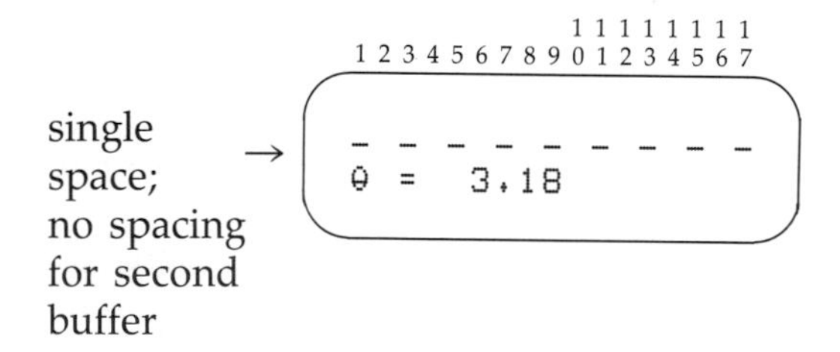

The first WRITE printed a dash in the first position of the output line after single-spacing. The second WRITE had a plus sign in the carriage control which caused no vertical spacing. The character zero is therefore printed on top of the character dash, giving the Greek symbol θ. The value of THETA is printed on the same line. ◇

EXAMPLE B-7 Sine and Cosine Computation

Print the values of the sine of the angle THETA and the cosine of the angle THETA. Assume that THETA is in radians. Use descriptive literals.

Solution

Computer Memory

THETA | 1.26 |

FORTRAN Statements

```
      WRITE(*,1)
    1 FORMAT('1',3X,'0',3X,'SINEb0',
     +           3X,'COSINE 0')
      WRITE(*,2)
    2 FORMAT('+',3X,'-',8X,'-',10X,'-')
      WRITE(*,3)THETA, SIN(THETA), COS(THETA)
    3 FORMAT(2X,F4.2,3X,F4.2,5X,F4.2)
```

Buffer Contents

1$_{bbb}$0$_{bbb}$SINE$_{b}$0$_{bbb}$COSINE$_{b}$0

+$_{bbb}$¯$_{bbbbbbbb}$¯$_{bbbbbbbbbb}$¯

$_{bb}$1.26$_{bbb}$0.95$_{bbbbb}$0.31

Computer Output

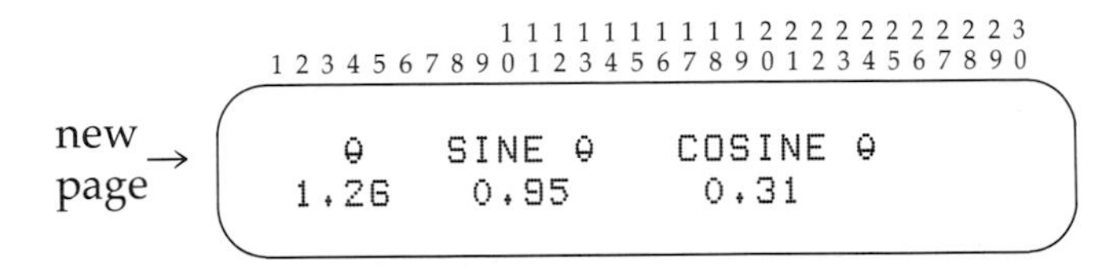

The first line was printed on a new page, the second line was over-printed on the same line as the first to build the symbol θ, and the third line was printed after single-spacing. Note that if either the sine or cosine of THETA had been negative, the corresponding output field would have been filled with asterisks because there is not room for a minus sign. ◇

E SPECIFICATION

Real numbers may be printed in an exponential form with the E specification. This specification is primarily used for very small values, very large values, or when you are uncertain of the magnitude of a number. If you use an F format or an I format that is too small for a value, the output field will be filled with asterisks. In contrast, a real number will always fit in an E specification field.

The general format for an E specification is Ew.d. The w again represents the total width or number of positions to be used in printing the value. The d represents the number of positions to the right of the decimal point assuming that the value is in exponential form. The framework for printing a real value in an exponential specification with three decimal places is:

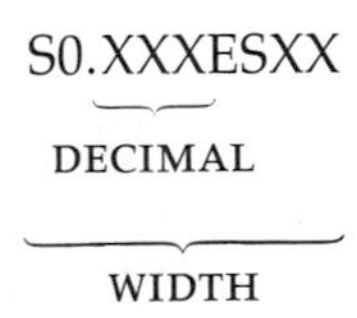

The symbol S indicates that positions must be reserved for the sign of the value and the sign of the exponent in case they are negative. Note that with all the extra positions, the total width becomes 10 positions. Three of the 10 positions are the decimal positions and the other 7 are positions that are always needed for an E format. Thus, the total width of an E specification must be at least d + 7. The above specification is then E10.3.

If there are more decimal positions in the specification than are in the exponential form of the value, the extra decimal positions are filled on the right with zeros.

If the total width of the E specification is more than 7 plus the decimal positions, the extra positions appear as blanks on the left side of the value.

EXAMPLE B-8 Exponential Value

Print the value of TIME in an exponential form with four decimal positions.

Solution 1

COMPUTER MEMORY

TIME | −0.00125 |

FORTRAN STATEMENTS

```
      WRITE(*,105)TIME
  105 FORMAT(1X,'TIME = ',E11.4)
```

BUFFER CONTENTS

| $_b$TIME$_b$=$_b$−0.1250E−02 |

COMPUTER OUTPUT

```
         111111111
123456789012345678
single  → 
space     TIME = -0.1250E-02
```

Solution 2

COMPUTER MEMORY

TIME | −0.00125 |

FORTRAN STATEMENTS

```
      WRITE(*,110)TIME
  110 FORMAT(1X,'TIME = ',E13.4)
```

BUFFER CONTENTS

| $_b$TIME$_b$=$_{bbb}$−0.1250E−02 |

COMPUTER OUTPUT

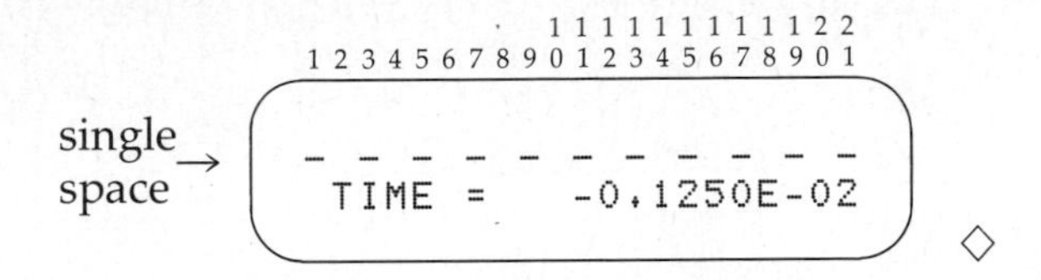

◇

EXAMPLE B-9 Polynomial Computation

Calculate and print the value of the polynomial $X^6 + 2X^4 - 6X$ for the number stored in the variable X. Since X may be a small number, use an E format to print both the value of X and the value of the polynomial.

Correct Solution

COMPUTER MEMORY

(Before execution) X | 0.00143 |

FORTRAN STATEMENTS

```
   POLY = X**6 + 2.0*X**4 - 6.0*X
   WRITE(*,5)X, POLY
 5 FORMAT('0','X = ',E11.3,' POLYNOMIAL = ',E11.3)
```

COMPUTER MEMORY

(After execution) X | 0.00143 |

POLY | −0.00858 |

BUFFER CONTENTS

0X$_b$=$_{bbb}$0.143E−02$_b$POLYNOMIAL$_b$=$_{bb}$−0.858E−02

COMPUTER OUTPUT

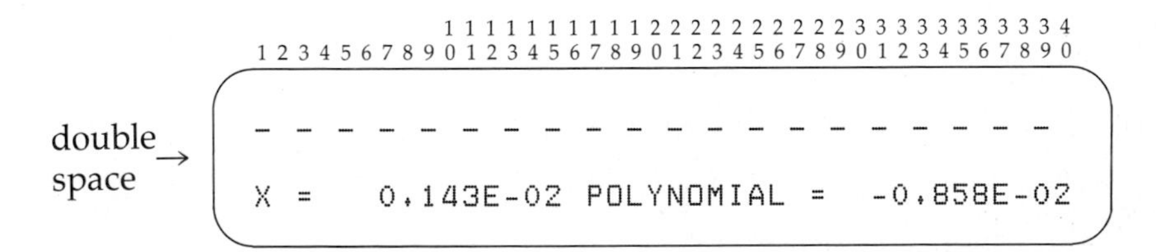

Incorrect Solution

COMPUTER MEMORY

(Before execution) X | 0.00143 |

FORTRAN STATEMENTS

```
   POLY = X**6 + 2.0*X**4 - 6.0*X
   WRITE(*,6)POLY, X
 6 FORMAT('0','X = ',E11.3,' POLYNOMIAL = ',E11.3)
```

COMPUTER MEMORY

(After execution) X | 0.00143 |

POLY | −0.00858 |

BUFFER CONTENTS

| $0X_b=_{bb}-0.858E-02_b\text{POLYNOMIAL}_b=_{bbb}0.143E-02$ |

COMPUTER OUTPUT

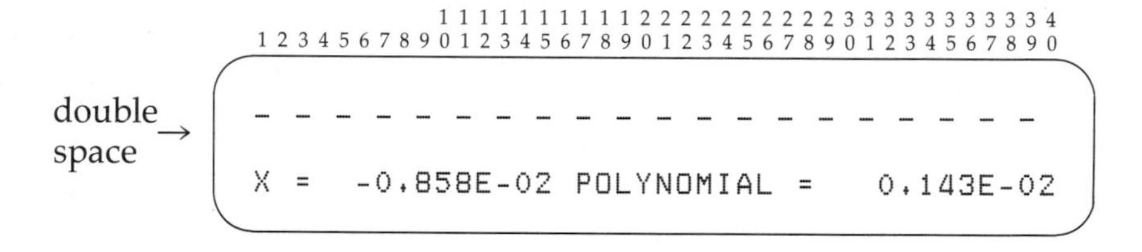

Note that the only difference between the correct solution and the incorrect solution is the order of the variables in the WRITE statement. Thus, in the incorrect solution, the output has the values interchanged. This is obviously a serious error but, unfortunately, one that the computer cannot detect. ◇

The PRINT statement can also be used with formats, as shown in these statements:

```
   PRINT 10, X
10 FORMAT(1X,'X = ',F4.2)
```

B-2 READ/FORMAT COMBINATIONS WITH REAL AND INTEGER DATA

To specify the columns to be used in reading data from a data line or a data card, we use a formatted READ statement. The general form of a formatted READ statement is:

> READ(*, *format reference number*)*variable list*

The asterisk again specifies that a system-determined device will be used. Generally, this will be the terminal keyboard for time-sharing and a card reader for batch processing. The list of variable names determines the order in which new values are stored, and the format reference number refers to a FORMAT statement that will describe the positions to be read. A typical READ/FORMAT combination is:

```
      READ(*,2)DIST, VEL
    2 FORMAT(F4.1,3X,F4.2)
```

The form of the FORMAT appears to be the same as that used with WRITE statements. Even the specifications in the FORMAT look familiar. There are, however, differences between the specifications used for reading data values and those used to write data values. Also, no carriage control is needed with READ statements. Each READ statement begins reading at column 1 of a new terminal input line or a new card. The new values must agree in type (integer or real) with the variables in the list. Time-sharing systems usually print a special character such as a question mark when a READ statement is executed, to tell you when to enter the data. You then enter the new values for the variables.

We now look at each specification individually, as we did for the WRITE statement specifications. We start with the X specification instead of the literal specification because it is invalid to use a literal specification when reading data.

X SPECIFICATION

The X specification will skip positions on the data line. Its general form is nX, where n represents the number of positions to skip. Thus, we can skip over unnecessary values.

I SPECIFICATION

The I specification is required when reading a value into an integer variable. The form of this specification is Iw where w represents the number of positions to use on the data line. Any blanks in the w positions will be interpreted as zeros. Any character besides numbers, plus or minus signs, and blanks will cause an execution error to occur. Thus, 5.0 cannot be read with an I3 specification, but ${}_{bb}5$ will be read correctly with an I3 specification.

EXAMPLE B-10 MEAN and NORM

Read the values of the variables MEAN and NORM from a data line. MEAN is in columns 1–4 and NORM is in columns 10–11.

Correct Solution

FORTRAN Statements

```
      READ(*,1)MEAN, NORM
    1 FORMAT(I4,5X,I2)
```

Data Line

${}_{b}123_{bbbbb}10$

Computer Memory

MEAN	123
NORM	10

The first four columns, ${}_{b}123$, are used to assign a value to MEAN. The first blank is interpreted as a zero, and thus 0123 is stored in MEAN. We then skip the next five columns. From columns 10–11 we pick up the value 10 for NORM. ◇

Incorrect Solution

FORTRAN Statements

```
      READ(*,2)MEAN, NORM
    2 FORMAT(1X,I4,5X,I2)
```

Data Line

${}_{b}123_{bbbbb}10_{b}$

Computer Memory

MEAN	1230
NORM	0

If carriage control is used with READ statements, incorrect values may be stored in memory. Using the above format, we skip the first column and use the next four columns for determining the value of MEAN. These columns contain 123_b, which is interpreted as 1230. We then skip five columns, and use the next two columns for determining the value of NORM. The contents 0_b will be interpreted as 0. ◇

F SPECIFICATION

The F specification can be used to read a value for a real variable. The form of this specification is Fw.d, where w represents the total number of positions to use on the data line and d represents the number of decimal positions. As with the I specification, any blanks in the w positions will be interpreted as zeros. If there is a decimal point punched in the w positions, the value will be stored as it is punched, regardless of what value has been given to d. Thus, if a real value DIST is read with a F4.1 specification, and the four characters are 1.26, then the value of DIST is 1.26. If there is no decimal point punched in the specified positions, then the value of d is used to position a decimal place before storing the value. Thus, if the characters 1246 are read with an F4.1 specification, the value stored is 124.6, a value with one decimal position. Note that printing this value would require an F5.1 specification. The same specification will therefore not always work for both input and output.

EXAMPLE B-11 TIME and TEMP

Read two variables, TIME and TEMP. TIME will be in columns 10–13, with two decimal positions, and TEMP will be in columns 16–18, with one decimal position.

Solution

FORTRAN STATEMENTS

```
          READ(*,200)TIME, TEMP
      200 FORMAT(9X,F4.2,2X,F3.1)
```

DATA LINE

$_{bbbbbbbbb}4.66_{bb}125$

COMPUTER MEMORY

TIME	4.66
TEMP	12.5

Since there was no decimal point in the TEMP field, which was read with F3.1, one was positioned in the three numbers so that one position was a decimal position. ◇

When running a program with computer cards there is additional information required by your particular computer and compiler. This *job control information* is unique to your computer system. It consists of information such as your name, the compiler you are using, and other additional data about your program. Your instructor or the computer center documentation will provide you with the job control requirements for your computer system.

The placement of the control cards, along with a program to calculate the slope of the line between two points, is given in Figure B-1.

JOB CONTROL CARDS { (system dependent)

FORTRAN PROGRAM {

```
      PROGRAM SLOPE1
*
*   THIS PROGRAM COMPUTES THE SLOPE
*   OF A STRAIGHT LINE THROUGH TWO POINTS
*
      READ(*,10)X1, Y1, X2, Y2
   10 FORMAT(F4.1,F4.1,F4.1,F4.1)
*
      SLOPE = (Y2 - Y1)/(X2 - X1)
*
      WRITE(*,20)X1, Y1, X2, Y2, SLOPE
   20 FORMAT('1','THE SLOPE OF THE ',
     +        'LINE THROUGH (',F4.1,',',
     +         F4.1,') AND (',F4.1,',',
     +         F4.1,') IS',F4.1)
*
      END
```

JOB CONTROL CARDS { (system dependent)

DATA { $_b$5.5$_b$3.1$_b$0.5–1.6

JOB CONTROL CARDS { (system dependent)

FIGURE B-1 Job control information placement and FORTRAN program with data.

The output from the program of Figure B-1 is:

```
                    1111111111222222222233333333334444444444555555555566666
           1234567890123456789012345678901234567890123456789012345678901234
new
page →   THE SLOPE OF THE LINE THROUGH ( 5.5, 3.1) AND ( 0.5,-1.6) IS 0.9
```

E SPECIFICATION

The E specification is used in a READ/FORMAT combination when a variable is entered in an E format, or exponential form. The general form is Ew.d, where w represents the total number of positions that are being considered, and d represents the number of decimal positions when the value is expressed in exponential form. If a decimal point is included, then its placement will override the value of d. If no decimal point is included, then one is located, according to d, before storing the value. It is not necessary that the width be at least seven positions greater than the number of decimal positions as was necessary for output with an E format. In fact, for READ statements, the E format will accept many forms of input. The following list shows some of the different ways in which the value 1.26 can be entered in a field read with E9.2. Note that the data can even be in an F specification form.

DATA CARD	VALUE STORED
0.126E$_b$01	1.26
1.26$_b$E$_b$00	1.26
1.126$_{bbbb}$	1.26
12.60E-01	1.26
$_{bbb}$.126E1	1.26
$_{bbbbbb}$126	1.26

Remember that the system will use two positions for the exponent if they are available. Thus $_{bbb}$.126E1 will be interpreted as 1.26, but $_{bb}$.126E1$_b$ will be interpreted as $_{bb}$.126E10, or 0.126×10^{10}.

EXAMPLE B-12 Job Number and Computer Time

Read two values. The first value, in columns 2–6, represents an integer job number assigned to a computer run, and the second value, in columns 10–16, represents the number of computer seconds used to run the program. This computer time will be entered in an exponential form, with two decimal places.

Solution

FORTRAN STATEMENTS

```
      READ(*,10)NUM, CTIME
   10 FORMAT(1X,I5,3X,E7.2)
```

DATA LINE

$_b$13034$_{bbb}$.36E-02

Computer Memory

NUM	13034
CTIME	0.0036

◇

EXAMPLE B-13 Nutrition Research Results

A research scientist performed nutrition tests using three animals. Data on each animal includes an identification number, the weight of the animal at the beginning of the experiment, and the weight of the animal at the end of the experiment. The data values for one animal are on one line, with each data value separated from other values by commas. Write a complete program to read this information and print a report. The report is to include both the original information and the percentage increase in weight for each test animal.

Solution

Decomposition

Read data
Compute percentage increases in weights
Print original data and percentage increases in weights

Refinement in Pseudocode

```
RESRCH:  BEGIN
            READ ID number, beginning weight, final weight for
               each animal
            percent increase ← (final weight − beginning weight)/
                               beginning weight × 100.0 for
                               each animal
            PRINT ID number, beginning weight, final weight,
               percent increase for each animal
         END
```

FORTRAN Program

```
      PROGRAM RESRCH
*
*   THIS PROGRAM PRINTS A REPORT ON THE RESULTS OF
*   AN EXPERIMENT INVOLVING THREE TEST ANIMALS
*
      READ*, N1, BWT1, FWT1
      READ*, N2, BWT2, FWT2
      READ*, N3, BWT3, FWT3
*
      PERC1 = (FWT1 - BWT1)/BWT1*100.0
      PERC2 = (FWT2 - BWT2)/BWT2*100.0
      PERC3 = (FWT3 - BWT3)/BWT3*100.0
*
      WRITE(*,5)
    5 FORMAT('1','TEST RESULTS')
      WRITE(*,10)
   10 FORMAT('0','NUMBER  INITIAL WT  FINAL
     +       'WT  PERCENTAGE INCREASE')
*
      WRITE(*,20)N1, BWT1, FWT1, PERC1
      WRITE(*,20)N2, BWT2, FWT2, PERC2
      WRITE(*,20)N3, BWT3, FWT3, PERC3
   20 FORMAT(1X,I4,6X,F4.1,7X,F4.1,6X,F10.5)
*
      END
```

Data Input

```
10, 5.3, 6.2
11, 5.2, 5.2
12, 5.3, 5.1
```

Computer Output

```
                  1 1 1 1 1 1 1 1 1 1 2 2 2 2 2 2 2 2 2 2 3 3 3 3 3 3 3 3 3 3 4 4 4 4 4 4 4 4 4 4 5
1 2 3 4 5 6 7 8 9 0 1 2 3 4 5 6 7 8 9 0 1 2 3 4 5 6 7 8 9 0 1 2 3 4 5 6 7 8 9 0 1 2 3 4 5 6 7 8 9 0

TEST RESULTS

NUMBER   INITIAL WT   FINAL WT   PERCENTAGE INCREASE
  10         5.3         6.2         16.98112
  11         5.2         5.2          0.00000
  12         5.3         5.1         -3.77359
```

In this example, we used list-directed input and formatted output. This is a very common way of performing I/O on terminals. ◇

B-3 DATA FILES

Another form for READ and WRITE statements is shown below:

> `WRITE(`*unit number, format reference number*`)` *variable list*

> `READ(`*unit number, format reference number*`)` *variable list*

This form includes a unit number designation instead of an asterisk. The asterisk referred to the input or output device automatically assigned to your program by your computer system (usually a terminal for time-sharing and the card reader and line printer for batch processing). Most systems have other input and output devices that can also be used. Each device is assigned a number. If you use that number instead of an asterisk, you will be specifying a particular device. For example, if unit number 7 is a card punch, then the following statements will direct that the output is to be punched into computer cards. Note that carriage control is not used for punched cards.

```
      WRITE(7,5)X, Y
    5 FORMAT(F4.1,1X,F6.2)
```

In addition to being able to specify other input or output devices, you can also use this feature to build and use *data files*. In a time-sharing system these files will be stored in your workspace. In a batch system these files will probably be on magnetic tape or disk and will require additional job control information.

There are many advantages to using data files. More than one program can access a data file to obtain information. Thus, the data does not have to be entered by hand every time that it is needed. You only have to build the data file once, and use the editing capabilities of the computer system to correct and update the file. To use this feature, a statement that assigns the file to a unit number is required. READ/WRITE statements that use this device number can then access the data file directly. The general form of the statement that assigns a file to a unit number is:

> `OPEN(UNIT=`*integer expression,* `FILE=`*file name,* `STATUS=`*literal*`)`

The integer expression designates the unit number to be used in READ/WRITE statements. Do not use the device numbers assigned to the standard input and output devices on your system. For example, if your system assigns the terminal input device to unit number 5, then you should not use unit number 5 for a data file. Typically units 5 and 6 are reserved for the system input and output devices. In our examples, we will not assign data files to units 5 and 6. The file name refers to the name given to the file. The STATUS literal tells the computer whether we are opening an input file to be used with READ statements or an output file to be used with PRINT or WRITE statements. If the file is an input file, then it already has data in it and is specified with STATUS = 'OLD'. If the file is an output file, then it does not contain data yet, and is specified with STATUS = 'NEW'. Some systems require a REWIND statement after opening an input file. This statement and additional information on building and accessing data files are presented in Chapter 7.

EXAMPLE B-14 Parallel Resistance

A data file RES3 contains three data lines, each containing a resistance value from a resistor in an instrumentation circuit. Write a complete program to read the three resistances and compute their combined resistance R_c for a parallel arrangement, as shown below:

$$R_c = \frac{1}{\frac{1}{R_1} + \frac{1}{R_2} + \frac{1}{R_3}}$$

Print the value of R_c.

Solution

DATA FILE RES3

```
1000.0
1100.0
2000.0
```

FORTRAN PROGRAM

```
      PROGRAM RESIS1
*
*  THIS PROGRAM READS A DATA FILE WITH THREE
*  RESISTANCE VALUES AND COMPUTES THEIR EQUIVALENT
*  PARALLEL VALUE
*
      OPEN(UNIT=10, FILE='RES3', STATUS='OLD')
*
      READ(10,*)R1, R2, R3
*
      RC = 1.0/(1.0/R1 + 1.0/R2 + 1.0/R3)
*
      WRITE(*,5)RC
    5 FORMAT(1X,F6.2,1X,'OHMS')
*
      END
```

Example B-14 used a small data file, but the advantages of using a data file become more obvious with large data files. Once the data file is built, no matter how many times you run a program that uses the file, you do not have to reenter the data. Also, it is very easy to make changes and updates to a data file with the editing capabilities available on terminal systems.

Data files can also be built by a FORTRAN program with WRITE statements. Thus, instead of using a printer as our output device, we can write the values in a data file. This is often used when plotting data. The data to be plotted is first entered into a data file, and the plotter then accesses the data file. Carriage control is not used with a formatted WRITE to a data file because the output is not actually being printed, but instead is being stored internally in the computer.

EXAMPLE B-15 Parallel Resistance with Files

Modify the program in the solution of Example B-14 so that the combined resistance R_c is printed and also stored in a file called RESC.

Solution

DATA FILE RES3

```
1000.0
1100.0
2000.0
```

FORTRAN Program

```
      PROGRAM RESIS2
*
*  THIS PROGRAM READS A DATA FILE WITH THREE
*  RESISTANCE VALUES AND COMPUTES THEIR EQUIVALENT
*  PARALLEL VALUE
*
      OPEN(UNIT=10, FILE='RES3', STATUS='OLD')
      OPEN(UNIT=11, FILE='RESC', STATUS='NEW')
*
      READ(10,*)R1, R2, R3
*
      RC = 1.0/(1.0/R1 + 1.0/R2 + 1.0/R3)
*
      WRITE(*,5)RC
    5 FORMAT(1X,F6.2,1X,'OHMS')
      WRITE(11,*)RC
*
      END
```

Computer Output

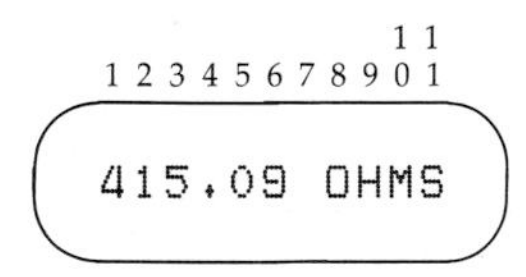

Data File RESC

415.09 ◇

B-4 ADDITIONAL DATA TYPES

In this section we present a discussion of formatted input and output for character data, logical data, double precision data, and complex data.

CHARACTER DATA

When a character string is used in formatted output, Aw is used as the specification. If w is omitted, the entire string will be printed. If w is less than the length of the character string, the first w positions of the character string will be printed. If w is greater than the length of the character string, the extra positions will be filled with blanks on the left of the string.

When the specification Aw for formatted input is used, if w is less than the length of the character string, the rightmost positions in memory will be filled with blanks. If w is greater than the length of the character string, only the first w characters will be stored. If w is omitted, the length of the string will be used to determine the number of positions to read.

To illustrate the rules for output, assume that the character string variable NAME contains 'JOHN A. SMITH', and that the following statement has been executed:

```
CHARACTER*13 NAME
      .
      .
      .
WRITE(*,10)NAME
```

Beside each of the following format statements is the corresponding output.

FORMAT	CORRESPONDING OUTPUT
`10 FORMAT(1X,A)`	`JOHN A. SMITH`
`10 FORMAT(1X,A13)`	`JOHN A. SMITH`
`10 FORMAT(1X,A4)`	`JOHN`
`10 FORMAT(1X,A10)`	`JOHN A. SM`
`10 FORMAT(1X,A15)`	`bbJOHN A. SMITH`

To illustrate further the rules for input, assume that ADDR is a character string with length 15. If a computer card contained 962 E. MAIN ST., in columns 1–15, then the execution of the following READ statement would yield the results shown:

```
CHARACTER*15 ADDR
      .
      .
      .
READ(*,20)ADDR
```

FORMAT	CONTENTS OF ADDR
`20 FORMAT(A)`	`962 E. MAIN ST.`
`20 FORMAT(A15)`	`962 E. MAIN ST.`
`20 FORMAT(A11)`	`962 E. MAINbbbb`
`20 FORMAT(A3)`	`962bbbbbbbbbbbb`
`20 FORMAT(A20)`	`962 E. MAIN ST.`

LOGICAL DATA

In formatted input, a logical value is read with the specification Lw, where w represents the width of the input field. The first nonblank character in the field must be T or F. In formatted output, the Lw specification is also used. All w positions will be blanks except the rightmost position, which will contain T or F, depending on the value of the logical variable.

As an example of formatted input and output, consider the following segment from a program:

```
      LOGICAL LX
         .
         .
         .
      READ(*,1)LX
    1 FORMAT(L5)
      WRITE(*,2)LX
    2 FORMAT(1X,L5)
```

If the data card read with this segment contained the word FALSE in columns 1–5, the value of LX would be .FALSE.. The corresponding output line would contain four blanks followed by the letter F.

DOUBLE PRECISION

In formatted input and output, double precision values may be referenced with the F or E format specifications. A new specification, Dw.d, may also be used. It functions essentially like the E specification but the D emphasizes that it is being used with a double precision value. In output, the value in exponential form is printed with a D instead of an E. Thus, if the following statements were executed,

```
      DOUBLE PRECISION DX
         .
         .
         .
      DX = 1.66587514521D+00
      WRITE(*,10)DX
   10 FORMAT(1X,D17.10)
```

the output would contain the value

```
b0.1665875145D+01
```

COMPLEX DATA

In formatted input, a complex value is read with two real specifications. For output, a complex value is printed with two real specifications. The real part of the complex value will be read or printed before the imaginary portion. It is good practice to enclose the two parts printed in parentheses and separate them by a comma, or print them in the a + *i*b form. Both of these forms are illustrated in the statements below:

```
      COMPLEX CX, CY
          .
          .
          .
      CX = (1.5, 4.0)
      CY = (0.0, 2.4)
      WRITE(*,5)CX, CY
    5 FORMAT(1X,'(',F4.1,',',F4.1,')'/1X,F4.1, ' + I',F4.1)
```

The output from thc WRITE statement would be:

```
(b1.5,b4.0)
b0.0b+bIb2.4)
```

B-5 ADDITIONAL FORMAT FEATURES

REPETITION

If we have two specifications in a row that are the same, we can use a constant in front of the specification (or sets of specifications) to indicate repetition. For instance, I2, I2, I2 can be replaced by 3I2. Often our FORMAT statements can be made shorter with repetition constants. The following pairs of FORMAT statements illustrate the use of repetition constants.

```
10 FORMAT(3X,I2,3X,I2)
10 FORMAT(2(3X,I2))

20 FORMAT(1X,F4.1,F4.1,1X,I3,1X,I3,1X,I3)
20 FORMAT(1X,2F4.1,3(1X,I3))
```

SLASH

The FORMAT statement may also contain the character slash, /. Commas around the slash in a FORMAT are optional. If the slash is in a READ statement, a new data line or a new data card will be read when the slash is encountered.

EXAMPLE B-16 Real Values

Read the values of HT1 and HT2 from one data line, TIME from a second line, and VEL from a third data line. Each number is entered in four columns, with one decimal position. There are no extra columns between HT1 and HT2.

Solution 1

FORTRAN STATEMENTS

```
      READ(*,15)HT1, HT2, TIME, VEL
   15 FORMAT(2F4.1/F4.1/F4.1)
```

DATA LINES

```
16.518.2
00.5
-4.6
```

COMPUTER MEMORY

HT1	16.5
HT2	18.2
TIME	0.5
VEL	−4.6

Solution 2

In this solution, we do not use the slash. Notice the extra READ statements that are required.

FORTRAN STATEMENTS

```
      READ(*,15)HT1, HT2
   15 FORMAT(2F4.1)
      READ(*,16)TIME
      READ(*,16)VEL
   16 FORMAT(F4.1)
```

DATA LINES

```
16.518.2
00.5
-4.6
```

COMPUTER MEMORY

HT1	16.5
HT2	18.2
TIME	0.5
VEL	−4.6

◇

The slash can be used with WRITE statements also. It is very important, however, to interpret the slash as a signal that says "print the current buffer and start a new one." If you interpret it this way, you see that the carriage control character following the slash will determine whether the spacing between lines is single-spacing, double-spacing, or some other spacing.

EXAMPLE B-17 Title and Headings

Print the heading TEST RESULTS followed by column headings TIME and HEIGHT. Start on a new page.

Solution 1

FORTRAN STATEMENTS

```
      WRITE(*,5)
    5 FORMAT('1','bbTEST RESULTS'/
     +       1X,'TIMEbbbbbHEIGHT')
```

BUFFER CONTENTS

1$_{bb}$TEST RESULTS
$_{b}$TIME$_{bbbbb}$HEIGHT

COMPUTER OUTPUT

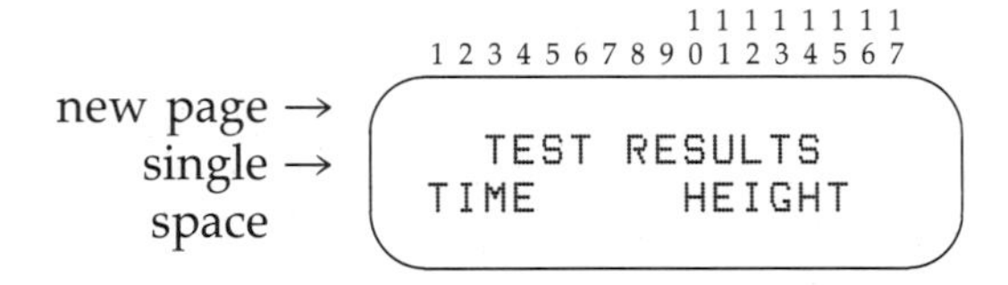

When the slash is encountered, we "print the current buffer." The carriage control character is a 1, and thus the first line is printed on a new page. We then "start a new buffer." The 1X specification puts a blank first in the buffer. Thus, when we reach the end of the FORMAT this line will be single-spaced from the first line. If the 1X had been omitted, the character T would have been used for carriage control. This is an undefined carriage control character and thus also causes single-spacing. However, the computer output would be:

```
                  1 1 1 1 1 1 1 1
1 2 3 4 5 6 7 8 9 0 1 2 3 4 5 6 7
new page →      TEST  RESULTS
single →    IME         HEIGHT
space
```

Solution 2

FORTRAN STATEMENTS

```
      WRITE(*,20)
   20 FORMAT('1','bbTEST RESULTS'/
     +       '0','TIMEbbbbbHEIGHT')
```

BUFFER CONTENTS

1bbTEST RESULTS
0TIMEbbbbbHEIGHT

COMPUTER OUTPUT

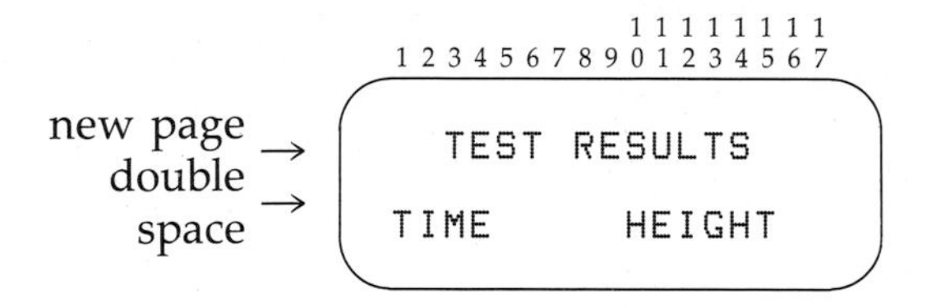

The only difference between the statements in this solution and the first solution is that the carriage control character for the second buffer is a 0. Thus, we have double-spacing between the lines instead of single-spacing. ◇

TAB SPECIFICATION

The tab specification, Tn, allows you to shift directly to a specified position, n, in the input or output buffer. The following pairs of FORMAT statements function exactly the same.

```
500 FORMAT(58X,'EXPERIMENT NO. 1')
500 FORMAT(T59,'EXPERIMENT NO. 1')

550 FORMAT('1','SALES',10X,'PROFIT',10X,'LOSS')
550 FORMAT('1','SALES',T17,'PROFIT',T33,'LOSS')

600 FORMAT(F6.1,15X,I7)
600 FORMAT(F6.1,T22,I7)
```

The TLn and TRn specifications tab left or right for n positions from the current position. The following formats are therefore equivalent:

```
85 FORMAT(1X,25X,'HEIGHT',5X,'WEIGHT')
85 FORMAT(T27,'HEIGHT',TR5,'WEIGHT')
```

The tab specifications are particularly useful in aligning column headings and data.

NUMBER OF SPECIFICATIONS

Suppose there are more FORMAT specifications than variables on a READ or WRITE list, as shown below:

```
  READ(*,1)SPEED, DIST
1 FORMAT(4F5.2)
```

In these cases, the computer uses as much of the specification list as is needed, and ignores the rest. Thus, in our example, SPEED and DIST would be matched to the first two specifications, and the last two specifications would be ignored. This rule allows us occasionally to use the same FORMAT with several statements.

Suppose there are fewer FORMAT specifications than variables on a READ or WRITE list, as shown below:

```
   WRITE(*,20)TEMP, VOL
20 FORMAT(1X,F6.2)
```

In these cases, we match variables and specifications until we reach the end of the FORMAT. Then, two events occur:

1. With a READ instruction, we go to the next data line or data card; with a WRITE instruction, we print the current buffer and start a new one.
2. We back up in the FORMAT specification list with both READ and WRITE statements until we reach a left parenthesis, and we again begin matching the remaining variables to the specifications at that point. If a repetition constant is in front of this left parenthesis, it applies to the FORMAT specifications being reused.

Thus, in the previous statements, TEMP would be matched to the F6.2 specification. Since there is not a specification for VOL, we do the following:

1. Print the value of TEMP after single spacing.
2. Back up to the beginning of the FORMAT specification list (first left parenthesis) and match the F6.2 to the value of VOL. We then reach the end of the list and single space to print the value of VOL. Thus TEMP and VOL are printed on separate lines.

ADDITIONAL FORMAT SPECIFICATIONS

The following FORMAT specifications are not routinely used, but occasionally these specifications will simplify the input and output steps in a program.

Gw.d—The G format code is a generalized code used to transmit real data. The width w specifies the number of positions in the input or output that are used. Input data can be entered in an F or E format. The real advantage of the G format is in output formats. If the exponent of the data value is negative or larger than d, the output is performed with an Ew.d specification. If the exponent is between 0 and d, the output is performed with an (F(w − 4).d, 4X) specification. Thus, very large or small values are automatically printed with an E format, and values of reasonable size are printed with an F format. For example, if the G specification is G10.3, then the value 26.8 is printed as 26.800_{bbbb} while the value 1248.1 is printed as $_{b}0.125_{b}E04$.

wH—Literal data can be specified in an output format with an H, or Hollerith, specification. The width w specifies the total number of positions in the literal, and the literal itself immediately follows the H. The following two formats are equivalent:

```
10 FORMAT(1X,'EXPERIMENT NO. 1')
10 FORMAT(1X,16HEXPERIMENT NO. 1)
```

Specifying literals with apostrophes is easier because we do not need to count the characters in the literal, and hence H formats are rarely used.

FORMAT EXTENSIONS

The following FORMAT extensions are not specifications that correspond to a variable, but instead are modifiers that affect the performance of the specifications already presented.

Ew.dEe and Gw.dEe—The addition of Ee to an exponential or generalized format specifies that e positions are to be printed in the exponent. The Ee affects only output specifications.

nP—The addition of nP to an F, E, D, or G format code specifies a scale factor n that is applied to subsequent specifications until another scale factor is encountered. The actual value stored will be multiplied by 10**n to give the number read or printed when the scale factor n is in effect. For instance, if the following READ statement is executed,

```
  READ(*,5)A, B
5 FORMAT(2PF4.1,F5.1)
```

and the data line read is

12.1362.4

then the value stored in A is 0.121 and the value stored in B is 3.624. Thus, any computations with A and B use the values 0.121 and 3.624. The output statement

```
   WRITE(*,10)A, B
10 FORMAT(1X,F4.1,1X,F5.1)
```

generates the following data line:

$$00.1_{bbb}3.6$$

The scale factor might be useful in applications that use percentages. The input could be in the form XX.X but the internal values used in calculations and the output would use the form .XXX. If a scale factor is used, document its use carefully in the program.

S, SP, and SS—These options affect I, F, E, G, and D specifications during the execution of output statements. If a numerical value is negative, the minus sign is printed in the first position to the left of the data value. If the numerical value is positive, the printing of the plus sign is system-dependent. If SP precedes a specification, in the value to be printed and all subsequent values a sign will be printed, whether the value is positive or negative. If SS precedes a specification, in the value to be printed and all subsequent values only a minus sign will be printed. If S precedes a specification, the system designation of producing signs is restored. The following example illustrates the use of the SP modifier. If these statements are executed,

```
      A = 36.2
      WRITE(*,5)A, A, A
    5 FORMAT(1X,F5.1,1X,SPF5.1,1X,F5.1)
```

the output line is:

$${}_{b}36.2_{b}{+}36.2_{b}{+}36.2$$

BN and BZ—The BN and BZ modifiers specify the interpretation of nonleading blanks in numeric data fields during the execution of input statements. Normally, leading and nonleading blanks are converted to zeros in numeric input fields. The modifier BN, however, specifies that blanks be considered to be null characters or ignored in the current and all succeeding specifications. The BZ modifier restores the interpretation of all blanks as zeros in numeric fields. If the data line

$${}_{b}21_{bb}21_{b}$$

is read with the statement

```
      READ(*,15)I, J
   15 FORMAT(I4,BNI4)
```

the value stored in I is 210 and the value stored in J is 21.

Colon—A colon terminates the format if there are no more items in the input or output list. The following statements and their corresponding output illustrate the usefulness of this feature.

```
      MAX = 20
      MIN = -5
      WRITE(*,10)MAX
      WRITE(*,10)MAX, MIN
   10 FORMAT(1X,'MAX =',I3,:,2X,'MIN =',I3)
```

The output from the first WRITE statement is

```
MAXb=b20
```

while the output from the second WRITE statement is

```
MAXb=b20bbMINb=b-5
```

Without the colon, the output from the first WRITE statement would be

```
MAXb=b20bbMINb=
```

VARIABLE FORMATTING

The format identifier in input and output statements up to this point has always been a statement number reference. However, this format identifier can also be an integer variable that has been initialized by an ASSIGN statement with the number of the desired FORMAT statement. The format identifier can also be a character constant, character array element, character array, or character expression. The power of variable formatting with character strings is illustrated in the following statements:

```
      CHARACTER*20 CHAR
         .
         .
         .
      IF(COUNTR.EQ.1)THEN
         CHAR = '(1X,''X = '',F4.1)'
      ELSE
         CHAR = '(1X,4X,F4.1)'
      ENDIF
      WRITE(*,CHAR)X
```

If the value of COUNTR is 1, then the output line will include the literal 'X = '. All other lines will include only data values, allowing us to use the same WRITE statement to obtain reports of the following form:

```
X =  1.5
    17.2
    -8.6
     8.1
```

SUMMARY

In this appendix we have presented in detail formatted input and output statements. The only way to become proficient with them is to use them frequently. We suggest that you use formatted input and output all the time until you are comfortable with it. Then use list-directed input and output in your testing and debugging phases. Once you get correct answers, use formatted output statements to give a neat and attractive form to your answers.

KEY WORDS

buffer
carriage control
data file
FORMAT specification
formatted I/O
job control information
left-justified
list-directed I/O
literal
overprinting
right-justified
variable formatting

DEBUGGING AIDS

The following steps will help you correct input and output statements that are not working properly.

1. Check to be sure you have given values to all variables on a WRITE list.
2. *Echo* values that you read. That is, immediately after reading values, print them for a comparison check.
3. If any of your output contains asterisks, enlarge the width w of the corresponding specifications or use an E format.
4. Be sure that the order of variables on the input or output list matches the order you used when writing the format.
5. Check *every* line of output to be sure that you have correctly specified carriage control. Look for incorrect spacing between lines or missing first letters or numbers.
6. Be sure that you have as many FORMAT specifications as variable names in the READ/WRITE list. In general, do not try to share FORMAT statements.
7. Always print integer values with I specifications, and real values with F or E specifications.
8. Be sure you do not have the characters I and 1 interchanged, or the characters O (letter) and 0 (number) interchanged.
9. Be sure that you have not gone past column 72 on long statements.

10 Do not try to combine too many lines of output in a single WRITE statement.

11 Use unformatted statements to print values first. After you have determined that the values are correct, then change to formatted statements, if needed.

12 Check input formats to be sure that you have not included carriage control.

13 Do not split a literal specification when continuing a long format to the next line. For example, consider the following FORMAT statement:

```
10 FORMAT('1',20X,'EXPERIMENTAL RESULTS
  +   FROM PROJECT #1')
```

Any blanks between the word RESULTS and column 72 of the first line, and the blanks between the continuation character + and the word FROM, will be inserted in the literal. Thus, the heading would appear something like this:

```
EXPERIMENTAL RESULTS     FROM PROJECT #1
```

STYLE/TECHNIQUE GUIDES

1 Develop the habit of echo printing values that you have read.

2 Print the physical units that correspond to numerical values that are being printed. This information is vital for proper interpretation of results.

3 Be consistent about your placement of FORMAT statements. Either put the FORMAT immediately after the READ or WRITE that uses it, or place them all just before the END statement in your program.

4 Label FORMAT numbers so that they are in ascending order, and fit into the order of other statements in your program. Do not, however, number statements sequentially. Leave a difference of at least 10 between statement numbers in case you need to insert additional statements later.

5 Make your carriage control evident. For instance, use (1X,F4.1) instead of (F5.1).

6 Label values printed. Use (1X,'X=',F3.1) instead of (1X,F3.1).

7 Use an E format to print values for which you cannot approximate the size. Then, if desired, after seeing the answer, you can change the E specification to an F specification that will accommodate the value.

8 Do not print more significant digits than you have. For instance, if you computed sums with values that had one decimal position, do not print the result with three decimal positions.

9 Generally, it is best to use the same number of specifications in the FORMAT as there are variable names on the READ/WRITE variable list.

10 Do not use extremely long FORMAT statements. Instead, use additional READ or WRITE statements with separate FORMAT statements.

11 Remember that the slash character must always be followed by carriage control in WRITE statements.

PROBLEMS

In problems 1 through 5, express the following values with the specified format. Be sure to indicate blanks when needed. The first is done as an example.

	VALUE	FORMAT	OUTPUT
	1000.3	F8.2	$_b$1000.30
1	.0004	E9.2	
2	136	I4	
3	−16	I2	
4	163.21	F8.1	
5	−7.6	F4.2	

In problems 6 through 8, show the output from the following WRITE statements. Be sure to indicate the vertical spacing as well as the horizontal spacing. Use the following variables and corresponding values:

TIME	4.55
RESP1	0.00074
RESP2	56.83

6
```
     WRITE(*,5)TIME, RESP1, RESP2
   5 FORMAT('0',F6.2,5X,2F7.4)
```

7
```
     WRITE(*,4)TIME, RESP1, TIME, RESP2
   4 FORMAT(' ','TIME = ',F5.2,2X,'RESPONSE 1 = ',F8.5/
    +       ' ','TIME = ',F5.2,2X,'RESPONSE 2 = ',F8.5)
```

8
```
     WRITE(*,1)TIME, RESP1, RESP2
   1 FORMAT('1','EXPERIMENT RESULTS'/1X, 'TIME',2X,
    +       'RESPONSE 1',2X,'RESPONSE 2'/
    +       1X,F4.2,2E12.3)
```

In problems 9 and 10, show the values that will be stored in the variables after execution of the following READ statements.

9

```
   READ(*,15)ID, HT, WIDTH
15 FORMAT(I4,2X,2F4.1)
```

DATA LINE 1456$_{bb}$14.6$_{bb}$.7

ID	
HT	
WIDTH	

10

```
   READ(*,7)ID, HT, WIDTH
7 FORMAT(I2,F4.1,2X,F4.2)
```

DATA LINE $_{bb}$13.7$_{bb}$.865

ID	
HT	
WIDTH	

In problems 11 through 14, tell how many data lines or data cards are required for the following READ/WRITE combinations to work correctly. Indicate which variables are on each line or card and the columns that must be used.

11

```
  READ(*,4)TIME, DIST, VEL, ACCEL
4 FORMAT(4F6.3)
```

12

```
   READ(*,14)TIME, DIST, VEL, ACCEL
14 FORMAT(F6.2)
```

13

```
  READ(*,2)TIME, DIST, VEL, ACCEL
2 FORMAT(F3.2/F4.1)
```

14

```
  READ(*,3)TIME, DIST
  READ(*,3)VEL, ACCEL
3 FORMAT(4F6.3)
```

For problems 15 through 18, assume that a data line contains the following characters, beginning in the first position,

ENERGY ALTERNATIVE AND SOURCES

and that the line is read with these statements:

```
CHARACTER*20 TITLE
     .
     .
     .
READ(*,5)TITLE
```

Give the contents of TITLE for each of the following formats:

15 `5 FORMAT(A)`

16 `5 FORMAT(A20)`

17 `5 FORMAT(A5)`

18 `5 FORMAT(A25)`

In problems 19 through 22, what is written by the following statements with the different formats indicated?

```
CHARACTER*10 UNIT
     .
     .
     .
UNIT = 'METERS'
     .
     .
     .
WRITE(*,20)UNIT
```

19 `20 FORMAT(1X,A)`

20 `20 FORMAT(1X,A10)`

21 `20 FORMAT(1X,A15)`

22 `20 FORMAT(1X,A5)`

In problems 23 through 28, show the ouput of the following WRITE statements. Assume that DX = 14.17862459, LX = .FALSE., and CX = 2.3 + 0.2.

23
```
    WRITE(*,4)DX
  4 FORMAT(1X,D14.6)
```

24
```
    WRITE(*,4)DX
  4 FORMAT(1X,D19.12)
```

25
```
    WRITE(*,5)LX
  5 FORMAT(1X,L1)
```

26
```
    WRITE(*,5)LX
  5 FORMAT(1X,L5)
```

27
```
    WRITE(*,6)CX
  6 FORMAT(1X,2F4.1)
```

28
```
    WRITE(*,6)CX
  6 FORMAT(1X,F4.1)
```

29 Write a complete program to read the diameter of a circle from columns 1–5 of a data card, in the form XX.XX. Compute the radius, circumference, and area of the circle. Print these new values in the following form:

```
new
page → PROPERTIES OF A CIRCLE WITH DIAMETER XX.XX
                (1) RADIUS = XX.XX
                (2) CIRCUMFERENCE = XXX.XX
                (3) AREA = XXXX.XXXX
```

30 Write a complete program to read the coordinates of three points (X_1, Y_1), (X_2, Y_2), (X_3, Y_3) from one data line with

columns	1–4	X_1	XX.X
	6–9	Y_1	XX.X
	11–14	X_2	XX.X
	16–19	Y_2	XX.X
	21–24	X_3	XX.X
	26–29	Y_3	XX.X

Assume that the name of the file is POINTS. Compute the area of the triangle formed from these points using

$$AREA = \tfrac{1}{2}|X_1Y_2 - X_2Y_1 + X_2Y_3 - X_3Y_2 + X_3Y_1 - X_1Y_3|$$

Print the coordinates and the area in the following form:

```
double space →  TRIANGLE VERTICES:
                  (1) XX.X, XX.X
                  (2) XX.X, XX.X
                  (3) XX.X, XX.X
                TRIANGLE AREA:
                     XXXX.XX
```

31 Write a complete program to read an integer value from columns 10–13 on a data card. This value represents a measurement in meters. Print the value read followed by the units, 'METERS'. Convert the measurement to kilometers, and print on the next line, again with the correct units. Convert the measurement to miles, and print on the third line, with correct units. Give some careful thought to both the type of variables that you should use and the size of output field that you will need.

32 Write a complete program to read the following integer information from one line in a data file called LABOR:

columns	1–4	year
	10–17	number of people in civilian labor force
	20–27	number of people in military labor force

Compute the percentage of the labor force that is civilian and the percentage that is military. Print the following information:

```
                      LABOR FORCE-YEAR XXXX

                  NUMBER OF WORKERS
                   (IN THOUSANDS)        PERCENTAGE OF WORKERS

CIVILIAN              XXXXX.X                   XX.X
MILITARY              XXXXX.X                   XX.X
TOTAL                XXXXXX.X                  XXX.X
```

APPENDIX C

FORTRAN 77 INTRINSIC FUNCTIONS

In the following table of intrinsic functions, the names of the arguments specify their type as indicated below:

ARGUMENT		TYPE
X	⟶	real
CHX	⟶	character
DX	⟶	double precision
CX	⟶	complex, a + *i*b
LX	⟶	logical
IX	⟶	integer
GX	⟶	generic

Function type, the second column of the table of intrinsic functions, specifies the type of value returned by the function.

Generic function names will be preceded by the dagger sign, †. Any type argument that is applicable can be used with generic functions, and the function value returned will be the same type as the input arguments, except for type conversion functions such as REAL and INT.

Function Name	Function Type	Definition
†SQRT(X)	Real	$\sqrt{X}$
DSQRT(DX)	Double precision	$\sqrt{DX}$
CSQRT(CX)	Complex	$\sqrt{CX}$
†ABS(X)	Real	$\|X\|$
IABS(IX)	Integer	$\|IX\|$
DABS(DX)	Double precision	$\|DX\|$
CABS(CX)	Complex	$\|CX\|$
†EXP(X)	Real	e^{X}
DEXP(DX)	Double precision	e^{DX}
CEXP(CX)	Complex	e^{CX}
†LOG(GX)	Same as GX	$\log_e GX$
ALOG(X)	Real	$\log_e X$
DLOG(DX)	Double precision	$\log_e DX$
CLOG(CX)	Complex	$\log_e CX$
†ALOG10(X)	Real	$\log_{10} X$
DLOG10(DX)	Double precision	$\log_{10} DX$
†REAL(GX)	Real	Convert GX to real value
FLOAT(IX)	Real	Convert IX to real value
SNGL(DX)	Real	Convert DX to single precision
†ANINT(X)	Real	Round to nearest whole number
DNINT(DX)	Double precision	Round to nearest whole number
†NINT(X)	Integer	Round to nearest integer
IDNINT(DX)	Integer	Round to nearest integer
†AINT(X)	Real	Truncate X to whole number
DINT(DX)	Double precision	Truncate DX to whole number
†INT(GX)	Integer	Truncate GX to an integer
IFIX(X)	Integer	Truncate X to an integer
IDINT(DX)	Integer	Truncate DX to an integer
†SIGN(X, Y)	Real	Transfer sign of Y to $\|X\|$
ISIGN(IX, IY)	Integer	Transfer sign of IY to $\|IX\|$
DSIGN(DX, DY)	Double precision	Transfer sign of DY to $\|DX\|$
†MOD(IX, IY)	Integer	Remainder from IX/IY
AMOD(X, Y)	Real	Remainder from X/Y
DMOD(DX, DY)	Double precision	Remainder from DX/DY
†DIM(X, Y)	Real	X − (minimum of X and Y)
IDIM(IX, IY)	Integer	IX − (minimum of IX and IY)
DDIM(DX, DY)	Double precision	DX − (minimum of DX and DY)

Function Name	Function Type	Definition
†MAX(GX,GY,...)	Same as GX, GY,...	Maximum of (GX,GY,...)
MAX0(IX,IY,...)	Integer	Maximum of (IX,IY,...)
AMAX1(X,Y,...)	Real	Maximum of (X,Y,...)
DMAX1(DX,DY,...)	Double precision	Maximum of (DX,DY,...)
AMAX0(IX,IY,...)	Real	Maximum of (IX,IY,...)
MAX1(X,Y,...)	Integer	Maximum of (X,Y,...)
†MIN(GX,GY,...)	Same as GX, GY,...	Minimum of (GX,GY,...)
MIN0(IX,IY,...)	Integer	Minimum of (IX,IY,...)
AMIN1(X,Y,...)	Real	Minimum of (X,Y,...)
DMIN1(DX,DY,...)	Double precision	Minimum of (DX,DY,...)
AMIN0(IX,IY,...)	Real	Minimum of (IX,IY,...)
MIN1(X,Y,...)	Integer	Minimum of (X,Y,...)
†SIN(X)	Real	Sine of X, assumes radians
DSIN(DX)	Double precision	Sine of DX, assumes radians
CSIN(CX)	Complex	Sine of CX
†COS(X)	Real	Cosine of X, assumes radians
DCOS(DX)	Double precision	Cosine of DX, assumes radians
CCOS(CX)	Complex	Cosine of CX
†TAN(X)	Real	Tangent of X, assumes radians
DTAN(DX)	Double precision	Tangent of DX, assumes radians
†ASIN(X)	Real	Arcsine of X
DASIN(DX)	Double precision	Arcsine of DX
†ACOS(X)	Real	Arccosine of X
DACOS(DX)	Double precision	Arccosine of DX
†ATAN(X)	Real	Arctangent of X
DATAN(DX)	Double precision	Arctangent of DX
†ATAN2(X,Y)	Real	Arctangent of X/Y
DATAN2(DX,DY)	Double precision	Arctangent of DX/ DY
†SINH(X)	Real	Hyperbolic sine of X
DSINH(DX)	Double precision	Hyperbolic sine of DX
†COSH(X)	Real	Hyperbolic cosine of X
DCOSH(DX)	Double precision	Hyperbolic cosine of DX
†TANH(X)	Real	Hyperbolic tangent of X
DTANH(DX)	Double precision	Hyperbolic tangent of DX
DPROD(X,Y)	Double precision	Product of X and Y
†DBLE(X)	Double precision	Convert X to double precision

Function Name	Function Type	Definition
†CMPLX(X)	Complex	X + i·0
†CMPLX(X,Y)	Complex	X + i·Y
AIMAG(CX)	Real	Imaginary part of CX
†REAL(CX)	Real	Real part of CX
CONJ(CX)	Complex	Conjugate of CX, a − ib
LEN(CHX)	Integer	Length of character string CHX
INDEX(CHX,CHY)	Integer	Position of substring CHY in string CHX
CHAR(IX)	Character string	Character in the IXth position of collating sequence
ICHAR(CHX)	Integer	Position of the character CHX in the collating sequence
LGE(CHX,CHY)	Logical	Value of (CHX is lexically greater than or equal to CHY)
LGT(CHX,CHY)	Logical	Value of (CHX is lexically greater than CHY)
LLE(CHX,CHY)	Logical	Value of (CHX is lexically less than or equal to CHY)
LLT(CHX,CHY)	Logical	Value of (CHX is lexically less than CHY)

GLOSSARY OF KEY WORDS

algorithm a stepwise procedure for solving a problem

alternate return a technique for modifying the return location of a subprogram; not a structured programming construction

argument a variable or constant used in a function or subroutine reference

arithmetic expression an expression of variables, constants, and arithmetic operations that can be evaluated as a single numerical value

arithmetic logic unit (ALU) a fundamental computer component that performs all the arithmetic and logic operations

arithmetic statement function a function that can be defined in a single arithmetic statement that is placed before any executable statement in a program

array a group of variables that share a common name and are specified individually with subscripts

ascending order an order from lowest to highest

ASCII code a binary code (American Standard Code for Information Interchange) commonly used by computers to store information

assembler a program that converts an assembly language program into machine language

assembly language a programming language that is unique to an individual computer system

assignment statement a FORTRAN statement that assigns a value to a variable

batch processing a method of interacting with the computer in which programs are executed one at a time, in the order in which they are submitted

binary a term used to describe something that has two values, such as a binary digit which can be 0 or 1

binary string a string or group of binary values, such as 11011000

blank common a single group of storage locations that is accessible to subprograms without being specified as subprogram arguments

block structure a manner of describing algorithms such that the solution becomes a series of sequentially executed steps

branch a change in the flow of a program such that the steps are not executed in the sequential order in which they are written

bubble sort a technique for sorting an array of values which makes several passes through the array

buffer an internal storage area used to store input and output information

bug an error in a computer program

carriage control a character used at the beginning of a formatted line of printed output that specifies the page spacing desired before the line is printed

CASE structure a structure that specifies steps to be performed on the basis of a series of conditions that are tested

cathode ray tube (CRT) terminal a terminal that uses a video screen for its input and output

central processing unit (CPU) the combination of processor unit, ALU, and internal memory that forms the basis of a computer

character string a string or group of characters that contains numerical digits, alphabetical letters, or special characters

checkpoint a strategic location in a program for printing the values of important variables when debugging the program

collating sequence the ascending order of characters specified by a particular code

comment statement a statement included in FORTRAN programs to document the program which is not translated into machine language

common block a block or group of storage locations that is accessible to subprograms without being specified as subprogram arguments

compilation the process of converting a program written in a high-level language into machine language

compiler the program that converts a program written in a high-level language into machine language

complex value a numerical value that is of the form a + ib, where $i = \sqrt{-1}$

composition of functions the nesting of functions; the argument of one function is another function

compound logical expression a logical expression formed by combining two single logical expressions with the connectors .AND. or .OR.

concatenation an operation that connects two strings together to form one string

connectors the operators .NOT., .AND., and .OR. that are used with logical expressions

constant a specific value used in an expression

control structure a structure that controls the order of execution of a series of steps

conversational computing a method of interacting with the computer in which the computer seems to converse with the user in an English-like language

counter a variable used in a program to store a count

counting loop a loop that is executed a specific number of times

data information used by, or generated by, a program

data file a file used to store information used by, or generated by, a program

debugging the process of eliminating bugs or errors from a program

decomposition the first step in top-down design; the process involves breaking a problem into a series of smaller problems

deletion a common routine for removing an item in an ordered list

design phases a set of five phases that begins with a problem statement and ends with a computer program that solves the problem

descending order an order from highest to lowest

diagnostic a message that describes an error in a program that has been located in either the compilation or execution step

direct access file a file whose records can be accessed in nonsequential order using a record key

DO loop an iterative loop specified in FORTRAN with the DO statement

double precision value a real value that has been specified to have more significant digits than the standard real value

driver a main program written specifically to test a subprogram

EBCDIC code a binary code (Extended Binary Coded Decimal Interchange Code) commonly used by computers to store information

echo a debugging aid in which the values of variables are printed immediately after being read

editor a major program in a computer system such as ones that allow you to modify programs entered into the system or that link subprograms to a main program

element a specific storage location in an array

ELSE clause a clause in the IF THEN ELSE structure which is executed if the condition is false

END option an option in a READ statement that allows the program to detect the end of a data file

error condition data values in a program that are not desirable or valid and require special error routines

executable statement a statement specifying action to be taken in a program that is translated into machine language by the compiler

execution the process of executing the steps specified by a program

explicit typing a specification of the type of information to be stored in a variable with a REAL, INTEGER, CHARACTER, LOGICAL, COMPLEX, or DOUBLE PRECISION statement

exponential notation a notation for real values that uses an E to separate the mantissa and the exponent

external file a file that is available to a program through an external device such as a card reader or tape drive

father-son update an update procedure which generates a new output file with updated information

field a piece of information in a record

fixed-point value a numerical value that may represent only integers

floating-point value a numerical value that may contain decimal positions

flowchart a graphical diagram used to describe the steps in an algorithm

formatted I/O the input or output statements that use FORMAT statements to describe the spacing

format specification a specification in a FORMAT statement used to describe the output line

FORTRAN character set the set of characters accepted by FORTRAN compilers

FORTRAN 77 a version of FORTRAN established in 1977 that includes a number of new features

function a subprogram that returns a single value to the main program

generic function a function that returns a value of the same type as its input argument

hard-copy terminal a terminal whose output is printed on paper

hardware the physical components of a computer

hash code a code used with direct access files to convert a key into a record number

high-level language an English-like language that has to be converted into machine language before it can be executed

IF THEN ELSE structure a structure that specifies steps to be performed based on the evaluation of a single condition

implicit typing the specification of the type of information (real or integer) to be stored in a variable by the beginning letter of the variable name

implied DO loop a DO loop that can be specified completely on an I/O statement or a DATA statement

increment value the parameter in a DO loop that specifies the increment to be added to the index each time the loop is executed

index the variable used as a loop counter in a DO loop

infinite loop a loop that does not have an exit when it is executed

initial value the parameter in a DO loop that specifies the initial value of the index

initialize the assignment of an initial value to a variable

input/output (I/O) information that a program reads or writes

insertion a common routine for adding an item in an ordered list

integer value a value that contains no fractional portion

interactive computing a mode of interaction with the computer in which the user can interact with a program as it is executing

interface a connection between two devices

intermediate result a result used in evaluating an expression to get the final result

internal file a file that is defined on information stored in the internal memory of the computer

intrinsic function a function used so frequently that its code is included in a library available to the compiler

iterative loop a loop that is executed a specific number of times

job control information the information that must accompany a program submitted to a batch-processing system

key a value that is used to specify a desired record in a direct access file

left-justify to adjust characters by removing blanks on the left side

lexicographic order a dictionary order

library function a function used so frequently that its code is available in a library available to the compiler

library subroutine a subroutine whose code is included in a library available to the compiler

limit value the parameter in a DO loop that specifies the value used to determine completion of the DO loop

linkage the step that prepares a compiled program and its subprograms for the execution step

list-directed I/O input or output statements that do not use FORMAT statements to describe their spacing

literal a character string

local variable a variable that is not an argument in all subprogram references and is not in a common block

logic error an error in the logic used to define an algorithm

logical expression an expression of variables, constants, and operations that can be evaluated as a single logical value

logical operator an operator that is used with logical expressions; .AND., .OR., and .NOT.

logical value a value that is either true or false

loop a group of statements that are executed more than once

machine language a binary language understood by a computer

main program a complete program that may access functions and subroutines

master file a file that contains updated information

memory the storage available for the variables and constants needed in a program

merge a common routine for combining sorted files into one sorted file

microcomputer a microprocessor with input and output capabilities

microprocessor a central processing unit contained in one or more integrated circuit chips

minicomputer a small computer system that is usually contained in small, portable consoles

mixed-mode operation an operation between values that are not of the same type

module a function or a subroutine

multi-dimensional array a group of variables that share the same name and whose elements are specified by more than one subscript

multi-pass sort a sort technique that performs several passes through the data to be sorted

multiple branch a branch that contains different paths which do not come back together; not a structured programming construction

multiple entry a technique for entering a block of code or a module through more than one location; not a structured programming construction

named common a group of storage locations that is accessible to subprograms by name without being specified as subprogram arguments

nested loop a loop that is completely contained within another loop

nested function a function argument that is the value of another function

nonexecutable statement a statement that affects the way memory is used by a program although it is not converted into machine language by the compiler

object program a program in machine-language form

one-dimensional array a group of variables that share the same name and whose elements are specified by one subscript

one entrance, one exit a technique that requires that a section of a program maintain only one entrance and one exit for simplicity

overprinting printing a new line of information over a line of information that has already been printed

parameter a value or variable used in the DO statement to specify the DO loop

path a set of steps that can be taken to go from the beginning of a program to the end of the program

permanent workspace workspace available in a time-sharing system that is not erased each time the user logs off the system

printer plotting plotting that uses print characters to generate plots

problem statement a clear, concise statement of the problem to be solved

processor a fundamental computer component that controls the operation of the other parts of the computer

program a set of statements that specify a complete algorithm in a computer language

prompt a symbol used by a computer program to tell the user when to enter information

pseudocode English-like statements used to describe the steps in an algorithm

random access file a file whose records can be accessed in nonsequential order using a record key

real value a value that may contain a fractional or decimal portion

record the basic unit of information related to a data file

relational operator an operator used to compare two arithmetic expressions

REPEAT UNTIL loop a set of statements that are repeated until a condition is true

right-justify to adjust characters by removing blanks on the right side

rounding a technique that approximates a value, usually to the nearest integer

scientific notation a notation for real values that expresses a value as a number between 1 and 10 multiplied by a power of 10

SEQUENCE structure a set of steps that are performed sequentially (or one after another)

sequential access file a file whose records are accessed in a sequential order

single precision the standard precision used for real values in a computer; typically the precision is expressed with a number of significant digits and an allowable range for the exponent of the real value when it is expressed in an exponential form

software computer programs used to specify the steps in algorithms

source program a program in a high-level language

specification statement a statement that specifies the nature of the values to be stored in a variable

stepwise refinement a process for converting a general algorithm to one that is detailed enough to be converted into a computer language

structured algorithm an algorithm composed of steps which form SEQUENCE structures, IF THEN ELSE structures, or WHILE loops

structured program a program composed of steps which form SEQUENCE structures, IF THEN ELSE structures, or WHILE loops

style the characteristics that distinguish one person's programs from another

subprogram a function or subroutine

subroutine a subprogram that may return many values, a single value, or no value to the main program

subscript an integer variable or constant used to specify a unique element in an array

substring a string that is a subset of another string and maintains the original order of characters

syntax error an error in a FORTRAN statement

technique the methods used to describe an algorithm

temporary workspace the workspace available in a time-sharing system that is erased each time the user logs off the system

testing the design phase that includes developing test data and testing an algorithm or program thoroughly

text processing processing of character information

time-sharing a method of interacting with the computer in which a number of programs are executed at the same time, although the user appears to have the complete attention of the computer

top-down design a design process which decomposes a problem into a series of smaller problems, and then refines the solution to each of the smaller pieces

trailer signal a signal at the end of a data file that indicates that no more data follows

transaction file a file that contains update information for a master file

truncation a technique which approximates a value by dropping its fractional value and using only the number's integer portion

two-dimensional array a group of variables that share the same name and whose elements are specified by two subscripts

variable a memory location referenced with a name whose value can be changed within a program

variable dimensioning a technique that permits the size of an array in a subprogram to be specified by an argument to the subprogram

variable formatting a technique that permits the format for a formatted I/O statement to be specified by a character string

WHILE loop a loop that is executed as long as a specified condition is true

word processing the processing of character information

ANSWERS TO SELECTED PROBLEMS

Answers that contain FORTRAN statements are not always unique. Although these answers represent good solutions to the problems, they are not necessarily the only valid solutions.

Chapter 1

1
```
CHECKING1:  BEGIN
               balance ← old balance
               WHILE more transactions DO
                  READ type, amount
                  IF type = 'DEPOSIT' or 'INTEREST EARNED'
                     balance ← balance + amount
                  ELSE IF type = 'CHECK' or 'NEW CHECKS PRINTED'
                     balance ← balance − amount
                  ELSE
                     PRINT 'ERROR IN TRANSACTION TYPE'
                  END IF
               END WHILE
               balance ← balance − $5.00
               PRINT 'FINAL BALANCE', balance
            END
```

3 CHECKING1:

```
BEGIN
   balance ← old balance
   WHILE more transactions DO
      READ type, amount
      IF type = 'DEPOSIT' or 'INTEREST EARNED'
         balance ← balance + amount
      ELSE IF type = 'CHECK'
         balance ← balance − amount
      ELSE
         PRINT 'ERROR IN TRANSACTION TYPE'
         PRINT type, amount
      END IF
   END WHILE
   balance ← balance − $5.00
   PRINT 'FINAL BALANCE', balance
END
```

5 CHECKING1:

```
BEGIN
   balance ← old balance
   count ← 0
   WHILE more transactions DO
      READ type, amount
      IF type = 'DEPOSIT' or 'INTEREST EARNED'
         balance ← balance + amount
      ELSE IF type = 'CHECK'
         balance ← balance − amount
         count ← count + 1
      ELSE
         PRINT 'ERROR IN TRANSACTION TYPE'
      END IF
   END WHILE
   balance ← balance − $5.00
   PRINT 'FINAL BALANCE', balance
   PRINT 'NUMBER OF CHECKS', count
END
```

7 CHECKING1:

```
BEGIN
   balance ← old balance
   minimum ← old balance
   WHILE more transactions DO
      READ type, amount
      IF type = 'DEPOSIT'
         balance ← balance + amount
      ELSE IF type = 'CHECK'
         balance ← balance − amount
      ELSE
         PRINT 'ERROR IN TRANSACTION TYPE'
      END IF
      IF balance < minimum
         minimum ← balance
      END IF
   END WHILE
   balance ← balance − $5.00
   IF minimum > 0
      balance ← balance + 0.005 × minimum
   END IF
   PRINT 'FINAL BALANCE', balance
END
```

9 MONTHLY:

```
BEGIN
   total ← 0
   count ← 0
   WHILE count < 24 DO
      READ balance
      total ← total + balance
      count ← count + 1
   END WHILE
   average ← total/24
   PRINT 'MONTHLY AVERAGE', average
END
```

11 MONTHLY:

```
BEGIN
   total ← 0
   count ← 0
   maximum ← 0
   WHILE count < 12 DO
      READ balance
      total ← total + balance
      count ← count + 1
      IF balance > maximum
         maximum ← balance
      END IF
   END WHILE
   average ← total/12
   PRINT 'MONTHLY AVERAGE', average
   PRINT 'MAXIMUM BALANCE', maximum
END
```

13 MONTHLY:

```
MONTHLY: BEGIN
            total ← 0
            count ← 0
            WHILE count < 12 DO
               READ balance
               IF count = 1
                  incr ← balance − old
               ELSE IF count > 1
                  IF balance − old > incr
                     incr ← balance − old
                  END IF
               END IF
               old ← balance
               total ← total + balance
               count ← count + 1
            END WHILE
            average ← total/12
            PRINT 'MONTHLY AVERAGE', average
            PRINT 'LARGEST INCREMENT', incr
         END
```

15 GPA:

```
GPA: BEGIN
        total points ← 0
        total hours ← 0
        WHILE more courses DO
           READ new hours, letter grade
           total hours ← total hours + new hours
           IF letter grade = A
              number grade ← 4.0
           ELSE IF letter grade = B
              number grade ← 3.0
           ELSE IF letter grade = C
              number grade ← 2.0
           ELSE IF letter grade = D
              number grade ← 1.0
           ELSE IF letter grade = F
              number grade ← 0.0
           ELSE
              PRINT 'ERROR IN LETTER GRADE'
              PRINT new hours, letter grade
              number grade ← 0.0
              total hours ← total hours − new hours
           END IF
           new points ← number grade × new hours
           total points ← total points + new points
        END WHILE
        grade point average ← total points/total hours
        PRINT 'GRADE POINT AVERAGE', grade point average
     END
```

```
17 GPA:   BEGIN
            total points ← 0
            total hours ← 0
            WHILE more courses DO
              READ new hours, letter grade
              IF letter grade ≠ I
                total hours ← total hours + new hours
                IF letter grade = A
                  number grade ← 4.0
                ELSE IF letter grade = B
                  number grade ← 3.0
                ELSE IF letter grade = C
                  number grade ← 2.0
                ELSE IF letter grade = D
                  number grade ← 1.0
                ELSE IF letter grade = F
                  number grade ← 0.0
                ELSE
                  PRINT 'ERROR IN LETTER GRADE'
                  number grade ← 0.0
                  total hours ← total hours − new hours
                END IF
                new points ← number grade × new hours
                total points ← total points + new points
              END IF
            END WHILE
            grade point average ← total points/total hours
            PRINT 'GRADE POINT AVERAGE', grade point average
          END
```

19 GPA:

```
GPA:  BEGIN
        total points ← 0
        total hours ← 0
        count ← 0
        WHILE more courses DO
           READ new hours, letter grade
           count ← count + 1
           total hours ← total hours + new hours
           IF letter grade = A
              number grade ← 4.0
           ELSE IF letter grade = B
              number grade ← 3.0
           ELSE IF letter grade = C
              number grade ← 2.0
           ELSE IF letter grade = D
              number grade ← 1.0
           ELSE IF letter grade = F
              number grade ← 0.0
           ELSE
              PRINT 'ERROR IN LETTER GRADE'
              number grade ← 0.0
              total hours ← total hours − new hours
           END IF
           new points ← number grade × new hours
           total points ← total points + new points
        END WHILE
        grade point average ← total points/total hours
        PRINT 'GRADE POINT AVERAGE', grade point average
        PRINT 'NUMBER OF CLASSES', count
      END
```

21 TAX:

```
TAX:  BEGIN
        READ rate, increment
        sales ← 0.00
        PRINT 'TAX TABLE'
        PRINT 'SALES TAX'
        count ← 0
        WHILE count < 1001 DO
           tax ← rate × sales (rounded)
           PRINT sales, tax
           sales ← sales + increment
           count ← count + 1
        END WHILE
      END
```

23 TAX: BEGIN

```
        READ rate
        sales ← 0.00
        PRINT 'TAX TABLE'
        PRINT 'SALES  TAX  TOTAL'
        count ← 0
        WHILE count < 1001 DO
            tax ← rate × sales (rounded)
            total ← sales + tax
            PRINT sales, tax, total
            sales ← sales + 0.10
            count ← count + 1
        END WHILE
    END
```

Chapter 2

1 valid—real variable name

3 valid—real variable name

5 invalid—illegal character (dash)

7 invalid—illegal characters (parentheses)

9 valid—real variable name

11 `DUE = ORIG - PAYNO*PAYMNT`

13 `TOTAL = SALES + 0.065*SALES`

15 gross = commission × sales + bonus

17 check = salary − state taxes − federal taxes

19 K [1]

21 T [5.0]

23 NUM [2]

25 TOT [16.6]

27 IBASE [14]

29 The contents of A and B are switched. The original value of C is lost, and it now contains the original value of A.

31

```
      PROGRAM CONVRT
*
*  THIS PROGRAM CONVERTS DOLLARS TO FRANCS
*
      PRINT*, 'ENTER AMOUNT IN DOLLARS'
      READ*, DOLLAR
      FRANCS = DOLLAR*6.2
      PRINT*, DOLLAR, 'DOLLARS =', FRANCS, 'FRANCS'
      END
```

33

```
      PROGRAM CONVRT
*
*  THIS PROGRAM CONVERTS DEUTSCHE MARKS TO DOLLARS
*
      PRINT*, 'ENTER AMOUNT IN DEUTSCHE MARKS'
      READ*, DMARKS
      DOLLAR = DMARKS/2.4
      PRINT*, DMARKS, 'DEUTSCHE MARKS =', DOLLAR,
     +              'DOLLARS'
      END
```

35

```
      PROGRAM CONVRT
*
*  THIS PROGRAM CONVERTS FRANCS TO DEUTSCHE MARKS
*
      PRINT*, 'ENTER AMOUNT IN FRANCS'
      READ*, FRANCS
      DOLLAR = FRANCS/6.2
      DMARKS = DOLLAR*2.4
      PRINT*, FRANCS, 'FRANCS =', DMARKS,
     +        'DEUTSCHE MARKS'
      END
```

37

```
      PROGRAM GROWTH
*
*  THIS PROGRAM PREDICTS BACTERIA GROWTH
*
      PRINT*, 'ENTER INITIAL POPULATION'
      READ*, YOLD
      PRINT*, 'ENTER TIME ELAPSED IN DAYS'
      READ*, TIME
      YNEW = YOLD*EXP(1.386*(TIME*24.0))
      PRINT*, 'TIME ELAPSED(DAYS) =', TIME
      PRINT*, 'PREDICTED POPULATION =', YNEW
      END
```

39

```
      PROGRAM GROWTH
*
*  THIS PROGRAM PREDICTS BACTERIA GROWTH
*
      PRINT*, 'ENTER TIME1 (HOURS)'
      READ*, TIME1
      PRINT*, 'ENTER TIME2 (GREATER THAN TIME1)'
      READ*, TIME2
      POP1 = EXP(1.386*TIME1)
      POP2 = EXP(1.386*TIME2)
      CHANGE = POP2 - POP1
      PRINT*, 'AMOUNT OF GROWTH =', CHANGE
      END
```

41

```
      PROGRAM GROWTH
*
*  THIS PROGRAM PREDICTS BACTERIA GROWTH
*
      PRINT*, 'ENTER TWO INITIAL POPULATIONS'
      READ*, START1, START2
      PRINT*, 'ENTER TIME(HOURS)'
      READ*, TIME
      POP1 = START1*EXP(1.386*TIME)
      POP2 = START2*EXP(1.386*TIME)
      PRINT*, START1, 'YIELDS POPULATION OF', POP1
      PRINT*, START2, 'YIELDS POPULATION OF', POP2
      END
```

Chapter 3

1 true

3 true

5 true

7 true

9 `IF(TIME.GT.15.0)TIME = TIME + 1.0`

11

```
IF(ABS(VOLT1 - VOLT2).GT.10.0)THEN
   PRINT*, 'VOLT1 =', VOLT1
   PRINT*, 'VOLT2 =', VOLT2
ENDIF
```

13 `IF(ALOG10(A).GE.ALOG10(Q))TIME = 0.0`

15 21 times

17 391 times

19 1 time

21 41 times

23 COUNTR [10]

25 COUNTR [7]

27 COUNTR [51]

29

```
      DO 10 I=0,20
         K = I*I + 2*I + 2
         PRINT*, I, K
   10 CONTINUE
```

31

```
      DO 20 X=1.0,9.0
         DO 10 Y=0.5,2.5,0.25
            F = (X*X - Y*Y)/(2.0*X*Y)
            PRINT*, X, Y, F
   10    CONTINUE
   20 CONTINUE
```

Chapter 4

1 M

2	3	4	5	6	7	8	9	10	11

3 R

9.0	8.0	7.0	6.0	5.0	4.0	3.0	2.0

5 R

2.5	2.5	2.5	−2.5	−2.5	−2.5	−2.5	−2.5

7 CH

1.0	2.0	3.0	4.0
2.0	4.0	6.0	8.0
3.0	6.0	9.0	12.0
4.0	8.0	12.0	16.0
5.0	10.0	15.0	20.0

9 I

2	3
2	3
2	3
2	3
2	3
2	3
2	3
4	5

11
```
      DIMENSION K(50)
         .
         .
         .
      MINSUB = 1
      DO 10 I=2,50
         IF(K(I).LT.K(MINSUB))MINSUB = I
   10 CONTINUE
      PRINT*, 'MINIMUM VALUE OF K IS'
      PRINT*, 'K(', MINSUB, ')=', K(MINSUB)
```

13
```
      DIMENSION K(50)
         .
         .
         .
      DO 10 I=1,50
         K(I) = IABS(K(I))
   10 CONTINUE
      DO 20 I=1,50,2
         PRINT*, K(I), K(I+1)
   20 CONTINUE
```

15
```
      INTEGER WIND(10,7)
         .
         .
         .
      PRINT*, 'CHICAGO WIND VELOCITY (MILES/HOUR)'
      DO 10 I=1,10
         PRINT*, (WIND(I,J), J=1,7)
   10 CONTINUE
```

17

```
      DIMENSION NUM(100)
          .
          .
          .
      DO 10 I=1,50
         K = NUM(I)
         NUM(I) = NUM(101-I)
         NUM(101-I) = K
   10 CONTINUE
```

Chapter 5

1 −0.5

3 0.5

5

```
      FUNCTION MAXA(K)
*
*  THIS FUNCTION RETURNS THE MAXIMUM VALUE
*  OF AN INTEGER ARRAY WITH 100 ELEMENTS.
*
      DIMENSION K(100)
*
      MAXA = K(1)
      DO 5 I=2,100
         IF(K(I).GT.MAXA)MAXA = K(I)
    5 CONTINUE
*
      RETURN
      END
```

7

```
      FUNCTION NPOS(K)
*
*  THIS FUNCTION COUNTS THE NUMBER OF VALUES GREATER
*  THAN OR EQUAL TO ZERO IN AN ARRAY OF 100 ELEMENTS.
*
      DIMENSION K(100)
*
      NPOS = 0
      DO 10 I=1,100
         IF(K(I).GE.0)NPOS = NPOS + 1
   10 CONTINUE
*
      RETURN
      END
```

9

```
      FUNCTION NZERO(K)
*
*  THIS FUNCTION COUNTS THE NUMBER OF ZEROS
*  IN AN ARRAY OF 100 ELEMENTS.
*
      DIMENSION K(100)
*
      NZERO = 0
      DO 10 I=1,100
         IF(K(I).EQ.0)NZERO = NZERO + 1
   10 CONTINUE
*
      RETURN
      END
```

11 N

5	4	1

NUM

10

13 N

5	4	10

15

```
      SUBROUTINE SIGNS(Z, W)
*
*  THIS SUBROUTINE PUTS THE SIGN(1,0,-1)
*  OF THE ELEMENTS OF Z INTO THE
*  CORRESPONDING POSITIONS OF W
*
      DIMENSION Z(5,4), W(5,4)
*
      DO 10 I=1,5
         DO 5 J=1,4
            IF(Z(I,J).GT.0.0)THEN
               W(I,J) = 1.0
            ELSEIF(Z(I,J).EQ.0.0)THEN
               W(I,J) = 0.0
            ELSE
               W(I,J) = -1.0
            ENDIF
    5    CONTINUE
   10 CONTINUE
*
      RETURN
      END
```

17

```
      SUBROUTINE ROUND(Z, W)
*
*  THIS SUBROUTINE ROUNDS EACH ELEMENT OF
*  Z UP TO THE NEXT MULTIPLE OF 10 AND
*  STORES THAT IN THE CORRESPONDING
*  POSITION OF W
*
      DIMENSION Z(5,4), W(5,4)
*
      DO 10 I=1,5
         DO 5 J=1,4
            IF((INT(Z(I,J)/10))*10.0.EQ.Z(I,J))THEN
               W(I,J) = Z(I,J)
            ELSE
               IF(Z(I,J).LT.0.0)THEN
                  W(I,J) = INT(Z(I,J))/10*10
               ELSE
                  W(I,J) = INT(Z(I,J) + 10.0)/10*10
               ENDIF
            ENDIF
    5    CONTINUE
   10 CONTINUE
*
      RETURN
      END
```

Chapter 6

1 CONSERVATION OF ENERGY$_{bbb}$

3 $_{b}$OF ENERGY$_{b}$

5 A

7 CONSERVATION

9 CONSERVATION OF ENERGY$_{bbb}$LAW

11 CONSERVE ENERGY$_{bbb}$

13 WORD | DESTIN |

15 WORD | CAN'T$_{b}$ |

17 WORD | FT/SEC |

19 true

21 false

23 true

25 40

27 7

29 0

Chapter 7

1

```
      SUBROUTINE MERGE2(FILE1, FILE2, FILE3)
*
*  THIS SUBROUTINE MERGES TWO FILES IN ACCOUNT ORDER
*  INTO ONE FILE IN ACCOUNT ORDER
*
      INTEGER ACCTM, ACCTW
      CHARACTER*10 INFOM, INFOW
      CHARACTER*6 FILE1, FILE2, FILE3
*
      OPEN(UNIT=11, FILE=FILE1, ACCESS='SEQUENTIAL',
     +     STATUS='OLD', FORM='FORMATTED')
      OPEN(UNIT=12, FILE=FILE2, ACCESS='SEQUENTIAL',
     +     STATUS='OLD', FORM='FORMATTED')
      OPEN(UNIT=13, FILE=FILE3, ACCESS='SEQUENTIAL',
     +     STATUS='NEW', FORM='FORMATTED')
*
      READ(11,5)ACCTM, INFOM
      READ(12,5)ACCTW, INFOW
    5 FORMAT(I3,A10)
*
   10 IF(ACCTM.NE.999.OR.ACCTW.NE.999)THEN
*
         IF(ACCTM.LT.ACCTW)THEN
            WRITE(13,5)ACCTM, INFOM
            READ(11,5)ACCTM, INFOM
         ELSE
            WRITE(13,5)ACCTW, INFOW
            READ(12,5)ACCTW, INFOW
         ENDIF
*
         GO TO 10
*
      ENDIF
*
      WRITE(13,5)ACCTM
      ENDFILE(UNIT=13)
*
      RETURN
      END
```

3

```
      PROGRAM MERGE5
*
*  THIS PROGRAM MERGES 5 FILES INTO A SINGLE FILE
*
      CHARACTER*6 FILE1, FILE2, FILE3, FILE4, FILE5, FILE6
*
      PRINT*, 'ENTER NAMES OF 5 FILES TO MERGE'
      READ*, FILE1, FILE2, FILE3, FILE4, FILE5
      PRINT*, 'ENTER NAME OF OUTPUT FILE'
      READ*, FILE6
*
      CALL MERGE2(FILE1, FILE2, 'TEMP1')
      CALL MERGE2(FILE3, FILE4, 'TEMP2')
      CALL MERGE2('TEMP1', 'TEMP2,' 'TEMP3')
      CALL MERGE2('TEMP3', FILE5, FILE6)
*
      END
```

5

```
      PROGRAM MERGE2
*
*  THIS PROGRAM MERGES TWO FILES IN ACCOUNT ORDER
*  INTO ONE FILE IN ACCOUNT ORDER
*
      INTEGER ACCTM, ACCTW, COUNTM, COUNTW
      CHARACTER*10 INFOM, INFOW
*
      OPEN(UNIT=11, FILE='IN1GM', ACCESS='SEQUENTIAL',
     +     STATUS='OLD', FORM='FORMATTED')
      OPEN(UNIT=12, FILE='IN1GW', ACCESS='SEQUENTIAL',
     +     STATUS='OLD', FORM='FORMATTED')
      OPEN(UNIT=13, FILE='OUT1GA', ACCESS='SEQUENTIAL',
     +     STATUS='NEW', FORM='FORMATTED')
*
      COUNTM = 0
      COUNTW = 0
      READ(11,5)ACCTM, INFOM
      READ(12,5)ACCTW, INFOW
    5 FORMAT(I3,A10)
*
   10 IF(ACCTM.NE.999.OR.ACCTW.NE.999)THEN
*
         IF(ACCTM.LT.ACCTW)THEN
            WRITE(13,5)ACCTM, INFOM
            COUNTM = COUNTM + 1
            READ(11,5)ACCTM, INFOM
         ELSE
            WRITE(13,5)ACCTW, INFOW
            COUNTW = COUNTW + 1
            READ(12,5)ACCTW, INFOW
         ENDIF
*
         GO TO 10
*
      ENDIF
*
      WRITE(13,5)ACCTM
      ENDFILE(UNIT=13)
      PRINT*, 'NUMBER OF RECORDS IN IN1GM =', COUNTM
      PRINT*, 'NUMBER OF RECORDS IN IN1GW =', COUNTW
      PRINT*, 'NUMBER OF RECORDS IN OUT1GA =',
     +        COUNTM, COUNTW
      PRINT*, '(DOES NOT INCLUDE TRAILER RECORDS)'
*
      END
```

7

```
      SUBROUTINE REPORT(NUM)
*
*  THIS SUBROUTINE PRINTS THE
*  INVENTORY FILE IN STOCK ORDER
*
      INTEGER STOCK, QUANT
      CHARACTER*10 DESC
*
      CLOSE(UNIT=NUM)
      OPEN(UNIT=NUM, FILE='IN17I', ACCESS='DIRECT',
     +     STATUS='OLD', FORM='FORMATTED', RECL=23)
*
      DO 10 I=1,999
         READ(NUM,5,REC=I,ERR=10,END=10)STOCK,
     +              DESC, QUANT, PRICE
 5       FORMAT(I3,A10,I4,F6.2)
         PRINT*, STOCK, DESC, QUANT, PRICE
   10 CONTINUE
*
      RETURN
      END
```

9

```
      PROGRAM ADD
*
*  THIS PROGRAM ADDS RECORDS
*  TO THE INVENTORY FILE
*
      INTEGER STOCK, QUANT
      CHARACTER*10 DESC
*
      OPEN(UNIT=11, FILE='IN17I', ACCESS='DIRECT',
     +     STATUS='OLD', FORM='FORMATTED', RECL=23)
*
      PRINT*, 'ENTER NEW STOCK NUMBER(9999 TO QUIT)'
      READ*, STOCK
*
   10 IF(STOCK.NE.9999)THEN
         PRINT*, 'ENTER DESCRIPTION, QUANTITY, PRICE'
         READ*, DESC, QUANT, PRICE
         WRITE(9,5,REC=STOCK)STOCK, DESC, QUANT, PRICE
 5       FORMAT(I3,A10,I4,F6.2)
         PRINT*, 'ENTER NEW STOCK NUMBER(9999 TO QUIT)'
         READ*, STOCK
         GO TO 10
      ENDIF
*
      END
```

11

```
      PROGRAM NWDESC
*
*   THIS PROGRAM UPDATES THE DESCRIPTION
*   FOR SELECTED STOCK ITEMS
*
      INTEGER STOCK, QUANT
      CHARACTER*10 DESC, NEW
*
      OPEN(UNIT=11, FILE='IN17I', ACCESS='DIRECT',
     +     STATUS='OLD', FORM='FORMATTED', RECL=23)
*
      PRINT*, 'ENTER STOCK NUMBER FOR UPDATE'
      PRINT*, '9999 TO QUIT'
      READ*, NUM
*
   10 IF(NUM.NE.9999)THEN
         READ(11,15,REC=NUM,ERR=20,END=20)STOCK,
     +   DESC, QUANT, PRICE
   15    FORMAT(I3,A10,I4,F6.2)
         PRINT*, 'ENTER NEW DESCRIPTION'
         READ*, NEW
         WRITE(11,15,REC=NUM)STOCK, NEW, QUANT, PRICE
   20    IF(NUM.NE.STOCK)THEN
            PRINT*, 'RECORD NOT FOUND'
         ENDIF
         PRINT*, 'ENTER STOCK NUMBER FOR UPDATE'
         READ*, NUM
         GO TO 10
      ENDIF
*
      END
```

13

```
      PROGRAM UPDATE
*
*  THIS PROGRAM UPDATES A DIRECT FILE USING A
*  STOCK NUMBER AS THE KEY
*
      INTEGER STOCK, CHANGE, QUANT
      CHARACTER*10 DESC
      LOGICAL MORE
      DATA MORE /.TRUE./
*
      OPEN(UNIT=10, FILE='IN17T', ACCESS='SEQUENTIAL',
     +     STATUS='OLD', FORM='FORMATTED')
      OPEN(UNIT=11, FILE='IN17I', ACCESS='DIRECT',
     +     STATUS='OLD', FORM='FORMATTED', RECL=23)
*
      READ(10,5)KEY, CHANGE
    5 FORMAT(I3,2X,I4)
      IF(KEY.EQ.999)MORE = .FALSE.
*
   10 IF(MORE)THEN
         READ(11,15,REC=KEY,ERR=20,END=20)STOCK,
     +           DESC, QUANT, PRICE
   15    FORMAT(I3,A10,I4,F6.2)
         QUANT = QUANT + CHANGE
         IF(QUANT.LT.0.0)PRINT*, 'ITEM', STOCK,
     +                   'HAS NEGATIVE QUANTITY'
         WRITE(11,5,REC=KEY)STOCK, DESC, QUANT, PRICE
   20    IF(KEY.EQ.STOCK)THEN
            PRINT*, 'NO MATCH FOR TRANSACTION',
     +              'WITH STOCK NUMBER', KEY
         ENDIF
         READ(10,5)KEY, CHANGE
         IF(KEY.EQ.999)MORE=.FALSE.
         GO TO 10
      ENDIF
*
      END
```

Chapter 8

1 0.25D+00

3 1.0D+00/3.0D+00

5 108.3D+00

7 CX | 1.5 + i2.0 |

9 CX | 0.5 + i1.0 |

11 CX | 5.0 + i0.2 |

13

```
      SUBROUTINE PRDATA(NAME, DIST, N)
*
*  THIS SUBROUTINE PRINTS DATA ARRAYS
*
      DOUBLE PRECISION DIST(N)
      CHARACTER*20 NAME(N)
*
      DO 10 I=1,N
         PRINT*, NAME(I), DIST(I)
   10 CONTINUE
*
      RETURN
      END
```

15

```
      SUBROUTINE SOLAR(NAME, DIST, N)
*
*  THIS SUBROUTINE DETERMINES THE OBJECTS THAT
*  ARE NEAREST THE SUN AND FARTHEST FROM THE SUN
*
      DOUBLE PRECISION DIST(N), DMIN, DMAX
      CHARACTER*20 NAME(N)
*
      DMIN = DIST(1)
      DMAX = DIST(1)
      DO 10 I=2,N
         IF(DIST(I).LT.DMIN)DMIN = DIST(I)
         IF(DIST(I).GT.DMAX)DMAX = DIST(I)
   10 CONTINUE
*
      PRINT*, 'CLOSEST TO SUN'
      DO 20 I=1,N
         IF(DIST(I).EQ.DMIN)PRINT*, NAME(I), DIST(I)
   20 CONTINUE
*
      PRINT*, 'FARTHEST FROM SUN'
      DO 30 I=1,N
         IF(DIST(I).EQ.DMAX)PRINT*, NAME(I), DIST(I)
   30 CONTINUE
*
      RETURN
      END
```

17

```
      SUBROUTINE SORTN(NAME, DIST, N)
*
*  THIS SUBROUTINE SORTS THE NAME AND DIST ARRAYS
*  INTO ALPHABETICAL NAME ORDER
*
      DOUBLE PRECISION DIST(N), TEMPD
      CHARACTER*20 NAME(N), TEMPN
      LOGICAL SORTED
*
      SORTED = .FALSE.
    5 IF(.NOT.SORTED)THEN
         SORTED = .TRUE.
         DO 10 I=1,N-1
            IF(NAME(I).GT.NAME(I+1))THEN
               TEMPD = DIST(I)
               TEMPN = NAME(I)
               DIST(I) = DIST(I+1)
               NAME(I) = NAME(I+1)
               DIST(I+1) = TEMPD
               NAME(I+1) = TEMPN
               SORTED = .FALSE.
            ENDIF
   10    CONTINUE
         GO TO 5
      ENDIF
*
      RETURN
      END
```

Appendix B

1 $_{b}$0.40E−03

3 **

5 ****

7 single space from previous line

TIME$_{b}$=$_{bb}$4.55$_{bb}$RESPONSE$_{b}$1$_{b}$=$_{bb}$0.00074

TIME$_{b}$=$_{bb}$4.55$_{bb}$RESPONSE$_{b}$2$_{b}$=$_{b}$56.83000

9

ID	1456
HT	14.6
WIDTH	0.7

11 line or card 1:

col 1–6	TIME	F6.3
col 7–12	DIST	F6.3
col 13–18	VEL	F6.3
col 19–24	ACCEL	F6.3

13

line or card 1:	col 1–3	TIME	F3.2
line or card 2:	col 1–4	DIST	F4.1
line or card 3:	col 1–3	VEL	F3.2
line or card 4:	col 1–4	ACCEL	F4.1

15 TITLE | ENERGY ALTERNATIVE A |

17 TITLE | ENERG$_{bbbbbbbbbbbbbbb}$ |

19 Single spacing
`METERSbbbb`

21 Single spacing
`bbbbbMETERSbbbb`

23 Single spacing
`bb0.141786D+02`

25 Single spacing
`F`

27 Single spacing
`b2.3b0.2`

INDEX

G

H

I

J

K

O

P

R

S

W

X